AMERICAN
KLEPTOCRACY

AMERICAN KLEPTOCRACY

HOW *the* U.S. CREATED *the* WORLD'S
GREATEST MONEY LAUNDERING
SCHEME *in* HISTORY

CASEY MICHEL

ST. MARTIN'S PRESS
NEW YORK

First published in the United States by St. Martin's Press, an imprint of St. Martin's Publishing Group

www.stmartins.com

Library of Congress Cataloging-in-Publication Data

Names: Michel, Casey, author.
Title: American kleptocracy: how the U.S. created the world's greatest money laundering
    scheme in history / Casey Michel.
Description: First edition. | New York, NY: St. Martin's Press, 2021. | Includes bibliographical
    references and index.
Identifiers: LCCN 2021026596 | ISBN 9781250274526 (hardcover) | ISBN 9781250274533 (ebook)
Subjects: LCSH: Money laundering—United States. | Banks and banking, International—
    United States. | Financial institutions—Moral and ethical aspects—United States. | Commercial
    crimes—United States.
Classification: LCC HV6769 .M53 2021 | DDC 364.16/80973—dc23
LC record available at https://lccn.loc.gov/2021026596

Our books may be purchased in bulk for promotional, educational, or business use. Please contact your local bookseller or the Macmillan Corporate and Premium Sales Department at 1-800-221-7945, extension 5442, or by email at MacmillanSpecialMarkets@macmillan.com.

First Edition: 2021

10 9 8 7 6 5 4 3 2 1

To my parents, of course

And to my Sha

Criminals, by nature, are a cowardly and superstitious lot.

—Jeph Loeb

The Cold War is over. The gangsters won.

—Paul Massaro

CONTENTS

PART IV: UNITED STATES OF ANONYMITY

KLEPTOCRACY BY THE NUMBERS

Estimated amount of private wealth located in global financial secrecy jurisdictions: $24–32 trillion

Total percentage of global wealth held in offshore financial assets: 10 percent

Amount developing countries have lost in unrecorded capital flight since 1980: $16.3 trillion

Annual global foreign aid: $135 billion

Total number of companies formed in Delaware: 1.5 million

Topline estimate of assets held in anonymous South Dakota trusts: $900 billion

Percentage of U.S. in which anonymous real estate purchases are still legal: 98 percent

Total amount Donald Trump properties made from clients matching money laundering profiles before 2016: $1.5 billion

The country most complicit in helping individuals hide their finances, according to the Tax Justice Network: the United States of America

AMERICAN
KLEPTOCRACY

TOO BIG TO SEE

"The rich were just the tracer dye in the water, the clearest evidence of cultural drift."[1]

—Michael Lewis

When Teodoro "Teodorin" Nguema Obiang Mangue was growing up in the small central African country of Equatorial Guinea, he appeared to have it all. He was born with power: since the late 1970s, his father had run the country as a despot overseeing a murderous regime buoyed and financed by unending flows of crude oil. As a result, Teodorin enjoyed flaunting his wealth however he could. He had diamond-studded Rolexes and hilltop megamansions. He owned fleets of high-end cars—Lamborghinis, Maseratis, you name it—which he steered around the nation's capital, Malabo, attracting the interest of struggling street peddlers, impoverished shop owners, and the emaciated schoolchildren who populated the streets. He had women on his arm, from places as far away as Spain, Brazil, France, or even the United States. He poured money into private jets and bespoke suits and parties that would last for days on end, and told confidants about plans to build 200-foot yachts fitted with shark tanks. He even dreamed of one day creating an international entertainment empire, setting himself up as the Jay-Z of Africa. Frankly, he had more wealth than he knew what to do with—less a big fish in a small pond and more a giant whale in an impossibly small puddle.

But there was, behind it all, an insecurity impossible for Teodorin to escape: A trembling lack of self-worth, which everyone around him could pick up on. A feeling that he could never quite measure up, either to his father or to the billionaires he met with, traveled with, or consorted with. Much of that insecurity came from the fact that Teodorin's father, now the longest-serving dictator in the world, never thought much of his son. Ignoring him, talking down to him, the dictator treated his son as he did many of his other underlings: dismissively, as nothing more than an imbecile, with as little talent as he had acumen. While his father tortured political opponents and jailed journalists, eliminating opposition and laying the groundwork for his heir apparent, Teodorin lacked the discipline and focus of a leader-in-training. He was always more interested in playing with his luxury cars, or indulging in yet another weeklong drug binge with his friends and hangers-on, than in perfecting the skill set required to oversee a modern dictatorship. When his father tried to teach him the details of foreign policy, or how to manage the country's economics, Teodorin would try to pay attention, but, still groggy from the night or week or month before, he couldn't get it to stick. Constantly hungover or strung out, he showed little promise, and constantly left his father embarrassed and angered at his son's incompetence. "Teodorin is so stupid, so self-indulgent, so selfish that discretion is the last thing that he has," said one investigator who has followed Teodorin's exploits over the last two decades. "I think Teodorin"—a man now pushing into his fifties—"reached his potential maturity when he was about ten."[2]

That rampant insecurity also had to do with the reality that so much of Teodorin's wealth, which may now stretch into the billions, was so obviously, so transparently, ill-gotten. That it was so clearly tied to his father's bloody, savage rule, which allowed only his family and a handful of others in their small, nub-shaped country to profit. That it came about only because his father controlled the levers of power in Equatorial Guinea, a country whose state-run media referred to the dictator as a "god," a man "in permanent contact with the Almighty."[3] Despite being the country with the highest per capita GDP on the continent, Teodorin's Equatorial Guinea now has one of the lowest life expectancies

(58 years) and highest infant mortality rates (6 deaths per 100 live births) in the world.

The money in Teodorin's pockets wasn't illegal, per se; given the nature of his father's dictatorship, everything he and his family did was technically legal according to Equatoguinean law. But this money was illegitimate: pilfered from his country's treasury, stolen from the people it should have served most, available only because he was the son of a dictator. And everyone—both domestically and internationally—knew it. No matter how much money Teodorin threw around, no matter how much he was worth, his money would always be tainted.

Which points directly to the final reason for Teodorin's insecurity. With his dark skin and charcoal eyes, Teodorin, born in 1968, came of age when the only members of the billionaire class were Europeans or North Americans—when wealth was, in essence, white. Sure, there were members of the monied class who were non-white. But they tended to be either fellow tyrants, like Haitian dictator Jean-Claude "Baby Doc" Duvalier (estimated to be worth nearly $1 billion), or neighboring megalomaniacs, such as the Democratic Republic of Congo's Mobutu Sese Seko (worth upward of $5 billion, and whose name translates to "the all-powerful warrior who, because of his endurance and inflexible will to win, goes from conquest to conquest, leaving fire in his wake").[4]

There was one figure, though, who by the mid-1980s proved that the world of stratospheric wealth wasn't reserved only for the lily-white: Michael Jackson. The pop singer may have been American, but he—his reach and his status, his music and his model—was global. He was an icon in corners of the world that Americans had never heard of. That was especially true for the rising postcolonial *nouveau riche* generation emerging in sub–Saharan Africa. "From an early age, Teodorin wanted to give this air of being cool, being a big star," Tutu Alicante, an Equatoguinean activist who's arguably done more than anyone to highlight Teodorin's crimes, told me. "And Michael Jackson was a global sensation for young kids in Africa to see—to see this Black kid become so successful."[5]

Which is why, when Jackson died in the summer of 2009, Teodorin spied an opportunity. He came up with an idea that would help with multiple aims simultaneously: how to transform his suspect money into perfectly clean, perfectly legitimate assets; how to honor the man who showed that being Black and wealthy was perfectly acceptable; how to take a significant step toward becoming the celebrity mogul he'd long dreamed of being; and how to try to convince his father that, actually, he knew what he was doing with his money, and that he could be trusted whenever the time came for transition in Equatorial Guinea. It may not have been a wise plan—it's unclear exactly why Teodorin thought his father would look at Michael Jackson memorabilia as a sign of his son's abilities—but it was his plan, and he was determined to succeed.

At the time, Teodorin already had a massive Southern California mansion, a private jet and fleets of million-dollar automobiles, and many of the other trappings that came with modern celebrity. Now he would take the next step: he would become the world's largest collector of Michael Jackson memorabilia. And in doing so, he would help convert some of his family's dirty lucre into legitimate assets, and take another step toward transforming himself from African despot to international celebrity—and prove to his father that he possessed some of the acumen that everyone else assumed he lacked. He would look to the country that had already welcomed some of his dirty millions with open arms, with little to no scrutiny. A country that had perfected the biggest system of transforming dirty, suspect money into perfectly legitimate finances and assets, obscuring its illicit origins in the process. A country that was so good at it, in fact, that Teodorin was far from alone—many other wealthy and corrupt individuals had been cashing in for decades.

He turned to the United States of America.

* * *

AROUND THE SAME time, in June 2010, a whiskered, fleshy-faced 23-year-old named Chaim Schochet touched down a world away, in Cleveland, Ohio. As Schochet walked past the baggage claim and through the airport's sliding doors, the summer sky yawned over him. A low breeze off Lake Erie curdled around the city, cutting a bit of the humidity already forming. He hopped in a waiting car, closed the door, and began his ride downtown.

At first blush, there was no real reason for Schochet to be traveling to a place like Cleveland. He had no real connections to the city, or to the Midwest, that anyone knew about. He lived in Miami, where he'd graduated from the Rabbinical College of America with a degree in Judaic Studies. But there he was, nonetheless, arriving in Cleveland—on an investment trip, he claimed, funded by his parents' money. According to those familiar with his operations, he had one aim: to become the biggest real estate holder Cleveland had seen since the days of the great American oil magnate John D. Rockefeller.

At the time, the real estate market in Cleveland—considered a "second-tier" market, behind the metropoles of New York or San Francisco or Dallas—was reeling. The 2008 financial crash had wiped out investment interest in the city. Already declining by the turn of the century, Cleveland saw any potential for a turnaround obliterated by the Great Recession. "During those years, you could shoot a cannon off at 5:00 p.m. in downtown Cleveland and not hit anybody," one local real estate agent said of the city's decline.[6] Which is why city officials and real estate brokers lit up when they heard that the kid from Miami was coming to town.

Schochet's excitement was palpable. He spun stories of falling in love with the city's architecture, with the "historic nature of the buildings." Cleveland, he claimed, would be the perfect place to put his parents' money to work, and to build a real estate empire of his own. He could be the savior the city needed. And unsuspecting locals lapped it up; he was the "most important guy you've never heard of," as the *Cleveland Plain Dealer* described him.[7]

Schochet's first stop was 925 Euclid Avenue, the address of Cleveland's famed Huntington Building. Constructed during the Coolidge administration, it was once the nation's second-largest office tower, with the largest banking room America had ever seen. Its pediments featured murals by American painter Jules Guérin, capturing the spirit of the age. The building stood, in many ways, as a reminder of Cleveland's zenith—and as a monument of unfulfilled promise.[8]

By 2010, the building was beaten down, with crumbled cornices, chipped corners, and old cabinets that were impossible to open. Nesting house sparrows found refuge inside, cohabitating in spaces abandoned by former tenants. The entire construct, just like downtown Cleveland, looked to most people like a cavernous husk of its former self. But not to Schochet.

When he first arrived out front, he took in the building's mountainous scope. There was nothing like it in the Midwest, at least outside Chicago: a 1.3-million-square-foot colossus, a time capsule of what Cleveland once represented, and what those in the city hoped to recapture.

Inside, Schochet shuffled along the white-marble floor, running his hands across the ribbed columns. He looked up at the century-old skylight. One of the locals accompanying him asked if he wanted to explore any of the other floors. This was basic due diligence, to make sure Schochet knew all that the building could be, and what work would be required to rejuvenate it. Schochet scratched his ink-black beard, and shook his head. He'd seen all he needed to see. This building, this heirloom of Cleveland's boom-time past, would do just fine. He would buy it, but he did have a separate question: Instead of going through a lender, could he pay cash?[9]

In most cases, commercial real estate purchases go through a rigorous vetting process, with financing structures that involve corporate mortgages and third parties. But Schochet said he wanted the building as soon as possible, and said he wouldn't need any other parties involved for the purchase.

Well, that would be just fine, one of the local representatives said, shaking Schochet's hand.

To be fair to all the parties involved, there was no legal compunction for either the realtors or local officials to say otherwise. (Who wants to deal with all of that extra paperwork when third parties are involved, anyway?) Nor was this move a surprise to anyone who knew Schochet. This was his preferred tactic: cutting out the financing middleman, streamlining the purchase, paying out of pocket. According to those who worked closely with Schochet, he'd done this before, all across the city, all across the Midwest writ large, in places like Cleveland and small towns in Ohio and Kentucky and Illinois. He'd show up, walk around the lobby or the front lawn, look around for a few minutes, and then pledge to pay millions of dollars. Easy, efficient, done.

He was good for his money, too; none of his previous multimillion-dollar checks had bounced. Besides, Schochet was charming and persuasive. He pledged that these purchases were just the first step toward a revitalization that would transform Cleveland once more into a global hub, a glorious return for a much-admired piece of America's Rust Belt. "His fondness for this city is really apparent," one local developer named Deb Janik claimed.[10] And those on the receiving end hardly wanted to ask too many questions about Schochet's money or why he didn't appear to know (or care) much about the details of his new purchases. It's not as if Cleveland had many other suitors, anyway. "It's really a coup for the city to have someone like [him] investing," another developer swooned.[11]

But if they'd looked beyond Schochet's checkbook, they would have uncovered two things. First, as later court records and investigations showed, Schochet's claims of being smitten with the city appeared to be a complete falsehood—a story he spun to punt any questions into his financing. In speaking with those familiar with his operations, little evidence suggests that Schochet cared about Cleveland at all. Second, and perhaps more important, his sellers would have been surprised to learn that this was no rich kid playing and investing with his parents' money. In reality, his finances were linked directly to a post-Soviet oligarch named Ihor Kolomoisky, who posed as a Ukrainian steel and banking magnate—and who at the time was allegedly helping to run one of the largest Ponzi schemes the world had ever seen, conning depositors who used his Ukrainian bank. Kolomoisky was hardly a well-known name in the U.S. Yet this Ukrainian businessman was not only the secret money behind Schochet's network—he was also a key oligarch rising in power and wealth alike, threatening Ukraine's democratic trajectory while allegedly pilfering billions of dollars from unsuspecting Ukrainians along the way.

On paper, Kolomoisky appeared as the head of Ukraine's largest private bank, dubbed PrivatBank. But as Ukrainian and American investigators would later discover, Kolomoisky and his partner, Gennadiy Bogolyubov, had transformed PrivatBank into their own private piggy bank. Cowing and threatening employees at the bank into doing their bidding, Kolomoisky and his partner allegedly swindled over $5 billion from unsuspecting depositors, disguising their thievery as loans and investments.[12]

However, Kolomoisky couldn't simply keep the looted money in bank accounts, which could be seized by authorities. He needed to hide it so effectively that no investigators, tax authorities, or international monitors would come after it. So, like Teodorin, he turned to the United States—where, as Kolomoisky knew, there was no finer place to hide and transform pilfered loot.

While he was rarely directly involved in the U.S. operations, Kolomoisky had a network—fronted by Schochet and his team in Miami—that was more than happy, according to American authorities, to help the oligarch launder billions. With the young American as his loyal foot soldier, connected to the oligarch via a family network we'll detail in chapter 4, Kolomoisky viewed the U.S. the same way Teodorin did: as a jurisdiction wide open for as much dirty money as he could provide. "As far as I could tell . . . it was dirty money all the way," one American involved in Schochet and Kolomoisky's network told me. "And it was all a washing machine scheme. They were all cleaning money."[13] And Cleveland provided the perfect opening. Schochet could claim the money was for revitalization, which would persuade his unsuspecting local interlocutors. But the entire operation, as American officials later alleged, was a farce.[14] Long and detailed investigations would later show that this was simply the tip of the iceberg. Using Delaware companies and Ohio steel mills, using investments in Texas and Kentucky and Illinois, and using a series of skyscrapers and office buildings in Cleveland, Kolomoisky could take full advantage of America's money laundering services—all to help clean the proceeds of his massive Ukrainian Ponzi scheme.

But that wasn't all. It would take years, as the following chapters will reveal, for us to learn that this Ukrainian oligarch, who had become the kingpin of Cleveland, had also become the embodiment of something else entirely. For it wasn't just American money laundering that Kolomoisky was interested in. Rather, he was also interested in learning how to use all these American networks, all these American operations, for his own ends. How to exploit America's transformation into a massive dirty money haven in order to bend U.S. foreign policy to his own will. How to manipulate the most corrupt American administration in generations into doing his own bidding. And how to use American kleptocracy to threaten the future of both the U.S. and Ukraine in the process.

* * *

THESE TWO STORIES—OF Teodorin as despot-cum-dilettante pouring his ill-gotten money into American assets, and of Kolomoisky using a network of Americans to park his money across the U.S. in places he never thought anyone would look—act as a pair of case studies for the larger story of what this book is really about: how America became the largest provider of money laundering and financial secrecy services in the world, and who took advantage, and what it means for the rest of us.

For years, the U.S. has largely turned a blind eye to the billions of dollars—and potentially more—in dirty and suspect money flooding into the country every year, stolen from national treasuries or made via bribes or smuggling or trafficking of humans and drugs alike. Much of this money has, for the better part of the last few decades, come to the U.S. in order to be washed clean, to be transformed into legitimate assets, and to obscure any links to its previous criminal owners. All of which can be done in the U.S. perfectly legally.

But in order to actually discern how America's transformation took place—and how Teodorin and Kolomoisky and all the other crooks and criminals detailed in this book took full advantage of America's implosion—it's worth defining a range of terms at the outset.

The first is the classic of the financial secrecy lexicon: "offshore." For many, the notion of a jurisdiction being "offshore" conjures up all kinds of images: swaying palm trees, white-sand beaches, maybe a bit of Don Ho playing in the background. For the most part, these offshore havens of our imagination are small and secluded, dotting places like the South Pacific or the Caribbean.

In a way, that imagined offshore isn't far from the truth. Nevis and the Bahamas, the British Virgin Islands and the Caymans, Mauritius and the Seychelles: these island chains and their sand-splattered neighbors have all built their own miniature offshore empires. They've all capitalized on the trillions of dollars in illicit capital sloshing around from tax evaders and drug cartels, wildlife poachers and human-trafficking networks, corrupt officials and crooked regimes around the world. They've all gotten their pieces of the dirty money pie. And they all exist, quite literally, offshore.

But that definition of "offshore" has been a misnomer since the late twentieth century. It fails to account for a turning point toward the end of the Cold War, during a transition that just so happened to coincide with the fall of the Berlin Wall in 1989. All of a sudden, the postcommunist states opened to the West—and the communist apparatchiks were replaced by rapacious oligarchs, all of whom watched their net worth explode, mirroring the elite wealth gathering in other postcolonial regions. And it didn't take long for officials and industrial leaders in the U.S. to suddenly realize how they could profit from that transition. The marriage of American private property rights and American financial secrecy provisions presented an advantage that the tropical, sand-strewn islands couldn't compete with. "It is not Panama or the British Virgin Islands or Switzerland that is now the best place in the world to [launder] assets," one Swiss lawyer enmeshed in the offshore world recently said. "It is the United States."[15]

Those offshore havens still exist, but because of the U.S., whatever rhetorical lines that once existed between "offshore" and "onshore" have been effectively obliterated. Put another way: the world of the "offshore" has, in a very real sense, been brought back onshore. And with the U.S. at the middle, that "offshore-onshore" world has, over the past few decades, acted as a giant magnet for the kinds of dirty, illicit, and off-the-books money stolen from people and countries around the world, made via criminal regimes and criminal networks and criminal predations.

The amount of money involved in this process has been staggering. To take just one data point, the pro-transparency organization Global Financial Integrity tabulated that developing countries had lost some *$16.3 trillion* in unrecorded capital flight since 1980[16]—slightly larger than the entire GDP of modern China, making the "offshore-onshore" world something of a superpower in its own right.[17] (Compare that to the $135 billion—entire magnitudes smaller—in annual global foreign aid, and you can see why these aid programs don't seem to make much of a dent.[18]) Part of that capital flight is a significant chunk of the *tens of trillions of dollars* of private financial wealth located in global financial secrecy havens.[19] According to the best estimates, nearly 10 percent of all global wealth now exists in offshore havens abroad.[20] And much of it is now hidden in the U.S.—sucked into an "offshore-onshore" world that is, in many ways, simply too big to see.

If this is all a surprise to you, you're not alone: the U.S.'s position as the world's leading "offshore-onshore" center hasn't gotten nearly the attention it deserves (and is one of the main reasons this book exists). It is often obscured by convoluted schemes that don't translate well into mainstream media coverage or by jargon and technical terms meant to confuse outsiders. However, as the following chapters will reveal, it's a role and a reality that's been decades in the making.

The second term to define up front is "dirty money," which, for the purposes of this book, we can lump together with similar phrases like "illegitimate assets" or "ill-gotten gains." "Dirty money" remains a slippery topic to define. But it is, at its core, money gained via illicit or immoral means. It's not necessarily illegal; Teodorin procured millions (and potentially more) via perfectly legal means in Equatorial Guinea. But as we'll see in the first chapter, all of his wealth can and should be considered "dirty"—due purely to his proximity to his father's dictatorship, which is brutal by any definition. The same can be said for Kolomoisky; as we'll see in the third section of this book, all of his looted wealth was allegedly swiped via a Ponzi scheme of historic proportions. For the purposes of this book, "dirty money" is shorthand for any wealth gained by underhanded means. All wealth attached to dictatorial regimes, as well as their families and inside circles, should be considered "dirty." So, too, should the wealth gathered by oligarchs acting as robber barons, and also the proceeds of trafficking or poaching or illicit drug dealing. To swipe a phrase, you know "dirty money" when you see it. If it smells dirty, if it looks dirty, then it's dirty and illegitimate and ill-gotten.

But it doesn't always stay that way. Indeed, there's a kind of built-in inertia: money emerges dirty and inevitably heads straight to the cleaners. It needs to get washed clean. It needs to become legitimate. Which leads us to the third term worth defining: "money laundering." The term is somewhat self-explanatory. It is, at its simplest, a process of transformation: "dirty" money goes in, and legitimate money and assets come out. The transformation provides two benefits: legitimate money can go much further (actually, it can go anywhere), and investigators and journalists like myself are usually unable to trace the source, even after a diligent hunt for the moment it went from bad to good. In effect, you get new, sparkling, legitimate money or assets, while simultaneously snuffing out any evidence your money was ever tainted.

There are a thousand different ways to launder money, often involving cash businesses or purchases, as shows like *Ozark* (which involves a casino) and *Breaking Bad* (which involves a car wash) have illustrated. While plenty of these money laundering mechanisms will be detailed throughout this book, the key ingredients are usually all the same (though you'll be surprised to know that your favorite shows depict operations that pale in size to the real thing).

Once "dirty money" is cleaned, it can be used for a wide range of activities. These can be as simple as enjoying the assets purchased—the mansions, the cars, the yachts—while turning the oligarch or despot into a self-styled celebrity. The money can also go toward setting up a nest egg for loved ones and future generations that investigators and authorities can't touch. With money comes protection, which is why it also goes into funding lobbyists and legislators who will prevent reforms or unsavory investigations. Likewise, with money comes status, which is why it also shows up as donations to Western universities and Western think tanks who will whitewash the reputations of the regimes and oligarchs in question—effectively using the laundered money to then launder reputations. It can, as we'll see in the book's final section, even go to funding lawyers and bagmen to whisper in an American president's ear about how to upend U.S. foreign policy—with none of us any the wiser.

Those terms—"offshore," "dirty money," "money laundering"—bring us to our fourth, and perhaps most misunderstood, term: "kleptocracy." It has enjoyed something of a renaissance over the past few years, thanks in no small part to the rise of Donald Trump and the kinds of practices and proclivities he perfected, which will be explored in the fourth section of this book. Emerging first in the early nineteenth century—and initially used to describe Spanish organized crime—kleptocracy means, quite literally, "rule of thieves," describing a regime dedicated entirely to predation and pillaging of the population. During Trump's presidency, it was fashionable to refer to his administration as a "kleptocracy." A quick scan through some headlines of the Trump era highlights that fusion: "How Donald Trump's Kleptocracy Is Undermining American Democracy"[21] (*Vox*); "No to the Trump Kleptocracy"[22] (*Washington Post*); "Russian-Style Kleptocracy Is Infiltrating America"[23] (*The Atlantic*). All of these articles highlighted the Trump administration's range of unprecedented crimes, historic corruption, and penchant for authoritarian methods. But all of them misunderstand what kleptocracy truly is. Modern kleptocracy isn't something that can be attributed to one man, or one administration, or even one regime. It's not something that can be created or crafted by an illiberal strongman or a blood-spattered dictator.

Rather, it's a *system*, involving multiple parties, across multiple jurisdictions. It begins with individuals building empires of illicit and ill-gotten wealth abroad, and ends with those who—often in the U.S.—welcome the dirty money with open arms, laundering the loot through perfectly legal tools like anonymous shell companies or sprawling real estate holdings or unregulated hedge funds. (Or Michael Jackson memorabilia.) "Kleptocracy is inherently multi-jurisdictional," journalist Oliver Bullough once wrote. "To hide stolen loot, kleptocrats must move it across borders, and obscure it behind corporate structures that make it look legitimate."[24] And in the U.S., industries have sprung up to make sure that those trillions of dollars tied directly to noxious regimes or their oligarchic minions or the criminal networks tracing the globe can quickly become—*poof!*—clean, legitimate, and available. In so doing, they have helped the U.S. become the greatest kleptocratic haven in the world, and the biggest money laundromat known to man.

And it's not just that all this staggering wealth can be masked using America's offshore-onshore services. Kleptocracy isn't simply the act of cleaning money. It also includes exploiting those funds to boost the reach and the reputations of regimes, oligarchs, crooks, and criminals of all stripes, *ad infinitum*. Massive, sprawling networks now exist in the U.S. to make sure that the figures at the heart of this book are viewed and treated as "philanthropists" and "financiers," as "benefactors" and "allies," rather than the morally repugnant and criminal figures they actually are. The irony is glaring: the system transforms them into "democratizers" and "pro-Western" and "reformist" figures. As a result, investigations are blocked and reforms are stalled, all while these kleptocrats continue to expand and entrench their financial foothold and power.

This can only occur *systematically*, rather than in a geopolitical vacuum or within national borders. It cannot exist in isolation. Which is also why it cannot exist without culpable American lawyers, real estate agents, financial specialists, or PR professionals—aiding and abetting this sinister iteration of the American Dream. And it's all legal.

It's a phenomenon that should reframe our understanding of both domestic and international politics. Because in this kleptocratic environment, the West isn't the Cold War victor as understood in the popular imagination. Instead, another group appears to have won: the gangsters, the oligarchs, and the criminal networks masquerading as governments around the globe. The U.S., which helped make this world a reality, simply profited along the way.

American Kleptocracy, anchored by the stories of Teodorin and Kolomoisky, reveals how we got here. Broadly, it is a story of how the U.S. transformed into the global leader in pro-kleptocratic industries, and all that that entails. It's also a book about key players in the fight to reform the U.S. systems—people like Carl Levin, a senator out of Michigan, who carved a career out of pushing anticorruption and counterkleptocracy policies—and how those reform efforts fell apart, assaulted by forces both within and outside the U.S. It's about how the Trump era was, in so many ways, the logical outcome of this trajectory—and how it always was, and always has been, bigger than a single administration, however corrupt. It's about a range of topics I've been researching and writing on for years, both as a journalist and member of the advisory board for the Hudson Institute's Kleptocracy Initiative, trying to catalogue all of modern kleptocracy's myriad threads, its range of impacts, its players and patterns, and all that it says about capitalism in the twenty-first century.

As this book lays out, dirty money doesn't infect only the places we may assume, like luxury real estate in Manhattan or beachfront condos in Malibu. It isn't limited to any specific geographic space, or any specific financial institutions. Modern kleptocracy oozes into the nooks and crannies and unsuspecting corners of everyday life. It reaches into the public pensions and private endowments steered by private investors, who are under no compunction to check the source of the money they're accepting. It smothers factories and mills across industrial America, those beating iron hearts of small towns whose best days are behind them, gutting any prospects of recovery. It captures entire state governments in places like Nevada and Wyoming and South Dakota, transforming those states into international offshore havens and outposts of financial secrecy of their own, which then block any and all efforts at reform. And it reaches into our own political system, upending elections and threatening America's democratic experiment in the process.

All of this began before Trump ever arrived on the political scene. But he was the first global leader to emerge from one of the key pro-kleptocracy industries—American luxury real estate—and was a clear, obvious symptom of America's descent into the center of the offshoring world. While the end of Trump's term saw unprecedented, historic antikleptocracy reforms, those capitalizing on America's kleptocratic, offshore-onshore services are now beginning to steer American policy to their own ends, without any say from the public, and to strip the U.S. for parts, just as they've done elsewhere.

This is a story and a trajectory that's been decades in the making. And it's a complicated story, full of interweaving parts and players, shadowboxing across industries and jurisdictions, involving those looking to launder their loot in the U.S. and those dedicated to stopping them. What follows is my attempt to untangle a broader phenomenon through a series of stories and characters that illustrate how we got here, and what's at stake if we keep going down this path. It may be too big to see, but once you do, it will become impossible to ignore.

PART I

STATIONARY BANDITS

———

"I'm out in Cali / Why the f*** my company in Delaware?"

—Lil Dicky[1]

THE SOLE MIRACLE

"We will go through the motions, we will push democracy, but we'll live with what's put together there because we do not have any good options. We need their oil."

—American official on Equatorial Guinea[1]

When Teodorin was born in 1968, Equatorial Guinea—a small hangnail of a nation on the central African Atlantic coast, sandwiched between the much larger Cameroon and Gabon—was still a vestigial remnant of Spain's onetime empire. While much of Spain's power concentrated in Latin America, bookended by Christopher Columbus's voyages and Simón Bolívar's eventual wars of independence, Spain had also grabbed this small, Massachusetts-size chunk of central Africa, which it would eventually call Guinea Ecuatorial.

By the late 1960s, as the wave of decolonization crested across Africa, calls grew for Madrid to join the march of European nations out of the African continent. And in late 1968, with Teodorin only a few months old, the Spanish government finally acceded. Equatorial Guinea gained its independence, and was almost immediately subsumed by a newly established dictatorship under the rule of Francisco Macias Nguema. After Macias won the country's initial presidential election, he set the tone for the kind of governance the country would experience for decades thereafter—and the kinds of governmental predations, and human rights violations, that would condemn Equatorial Guinea to a pariah status for the rest of the twentieth century.

"Macias destroyed the whole country," Ken Hurwitz, an American lawyer with the Open Society Justice Initiative, told me.[2] Macias's alleged crimes ranged from the brutal (reportedly offing his main electoral opponent, with the death formally listed as a "suicide") to the fantastical (including burying the entire Equatoguinean treasury underneath his house, and dubbing himself "The Sole Miracle of Equatorial Guinea"[3]). Tens of thousands of Equatoguineans died or disappeared under Macias's decade-long rule. By the late 1970s, he changed his nickname to the "Implacable Apostle of Freedom," and became "a genuine psychopath," added Hurwitz, who's tracked Teodorin's exploits for years. "He would have been as famous as [Ugandan despot] Idi Amin if Equatorial Guinea had been bigger."[4]

Throughout his reign, Macias compiled a roster of domestic enemies. One of those—unbeknownst to Macias, until it was too late—included his nephew who oversaw the National Guard and Equatorial Guinea's Black Beach prison, dubbed "Africa's most notorious jail," where he was specifically tasked with torturing those who would dare to speak up against the Sole Miracle. That nephew was Teodorin's father, named Teodoro.

Teodoro Obiang Nguema Mbasogo, born in 1942, exudes an air of refined scholarship, with wire-rimmed glasses and prim suits. If you passed him on the street, you might mistake him for an accountant. Even when he was charged with torturing Macias's political enemies, real or imagined, he never gave off an especially intimidating air—even when, in 1979, he turned on his uncle, leading to Macias's overthrow and execution, and announced the formation of the longest-running dictatorship in the world.

*   *   *

It didn't take long for Equatoguineans to realize that Obiang's regime would offer much of the same as Macias's. Under Obiang, dissidents have disappeared, and independent media remains an oxymoron. He even tried to one-up his deposed uncle when it came to his outlandish claims, with state media proclaiming that Obiang is "in permanent contact with the Almighty"[5]—and that he could "kill without anyone calling him to account," which Obiang and his regime have done for decades without much consequence.[6]

In nearly half a century, Obiang has become a dictator who makes the other regional despots—those in Rwanda and Gabon and Cameroon, even the likes of Mobutu Sese Seko and Idi Amin—look restrained by comparison. At last check, Freedom House pegged his rule as the sixth most repressive regime in the world, between those in Saudi Arabia and North Korea. Reporters Without Borders scores the country's media freedoms worse than Somalia and Kazakhstan.

In his four decades of rule, Obiang has managed to create a police state that rivals those of North Korea's Kim Jong-un and Syria's Bashar al-Assad in terms of rank brutality—but, surprisingly, even exceeds them in terms of elite predation. "The unification of the state with the ruler, and the chutzpah of the corruption—the brazenness of the corruption," Hurwitz said, positions Obiang's regime as "off the rails in terms of pure state capture."[7] The dictator rarely pretends to have his population's best interests at heart. Not that many would necessarily believe him. Nearly 80 percent of the country lives in abject poverty, slogging by on subsistence farming and little else, with most Equatoguineans living almost completely outside the monetary economy. Over half the country has no access to clean water. Some 15 percent of the country's children die before reaching the age of five, while a staggering two-thirds of those who survive don't stay in school past middle school. One out of every three Equatoguineans never sees the age of 40. None of this is different from the precedent Macias set. As one American official drearily summed up, "The political leadership is illiterate and brutal in its crude way, but they know how to stay in power."[8]

And Obiang's regime has one key tool that allowed it to stay in power: oil. In the 1990s, after Equatorial Guinea spent years existing as what journalist Ken Silverstein—one of the leading reporters to catalogue the family's malfeasance—described as a "pariah state with few international allies," oil began gushing forth off its coastline. It was a gift of geography, and the key to the kleptocracy that soon followed.[9] The discovery lubricated everything, including relations with cloying Western governments in search of oil who, in return, hoped to transform Equatorial Guinea into the Dubai of central Africa—a glitzy, dictatorial regime and an indispensable energy hub. With riches comes protection, and Obiang benefited in two ways. First, the oil accelerated access to international resources in ways previously unavailable to a burgeoning despot, and second, any international criticism of his suffocating rule—and human rights abuses—was drowned out by an army of paid-off lackeys, lawyers, and lobbyists who operated on the regime's behalf.

"Before oil money came in there was not a lot of money to steal, and when the oil money did start coming in there were no safeguards in place," one local consultant admitted, watching Obiang's government siphon billions into his family's personal coffers that should have been spent on public works. "There was no culture of government oversight, no media, let alone an independent media, no independent judiciary, and no outside scrutiny, because the country had been largely forgotten by the outside world. That all allowed corruption to flourish in ways it did in very few other countries."[10]

Nor was Obiang alone in such dreams about the doors the oil could open. His son, Teodorin, was in his early twenties when the oil burst forth, and suddenly enjoyed pride of place in a regime watching its annual oil revenues climb into the hundreds of millions of dollars—figures that would only continue climbing as oil prices grew through the turn of the century. The specific numbers, though, were almost so gargantuan that they became immaterial; when the oil started flowing, Teodorin suddenly had, in effect, unlimited wealth. Unlike his father, though, Teodorin wanted that money spent. And he wanted it seen. Unlimited wealth offered unlimited potential for him to upend entire industries—and, as we'll see, to exploit the mile-wide loopholes the U.S. provided to launder as much money as he could.

* * *

TEODORIN FIRST ARRIVED in the U.S. in the early 1990s to study at Pepperdine University in Malibu, California. That, at least, is what he claimed on his visa application. Instead of hitting the books, though, he began exploring and enjoying the kind of celebrity lifestyle he'd always wanted—the kind that Hollywood created, produced, and projected around the world. Almost immediately, he dropped any pretense of being a normal student. Rather than staying in dorms, Teodorin rented rooms at the luxe Beverly Wilshire Hotel. One former professor said that he loved to arrive on campus in a range of sports cars and limousines. "He rarely came to class," the professor added.[11]

Late nights and bottle service, lavish meals and expensive rides: Teodorin loved it all, and all of it added up. His bills soon climbed to tens of thousands of dollars per month. However, he had a patron who would pick up the tab: Waller International, an oil firm out of Houston that had begun exploring Equatorial Guinea's oil reserves. As part of their explorations, executives at Waller International were willing to take steps to remain in the Obiangs' good graces. Not that things were necessarily easy for the firm; one rep, according to *Harper's*, was reportedly "pulling out her hair" trying to manage Teodorin's finances.[12]

Teodorin enjoyed all the Southern California trappings—the parties at his hotel, the late-night joyrides in his luxury cars, the benders that bled into the mornings—during his time at Pepperdine. But he eventually tired of the pretense of being a student and announced he would be dropping out of the university. His father, by all appearances, was unsurprised by his son's academic failure. But he wouldn't let him remain in the U.S. Instead, he flew him back to Equatorial Guinea, where the dictator had an assignment for his son.

The fact that Obiang wanted Teodorin by his side wasn't necessarily a surprise—though, according to those who know them both, the two are hardly close, and have never really been. "The typical Equatorial Guinea kid does not tend to have a very strong relationship with their father," said Tutu Alicante.[13] Teodorin was no different, instead spending much more time with his mother, Constancia. He also spent much of his youth apart from his father, living with extended family in neighboring Gabon, away from his great-uncle's and, later, his father's dictatorship.

But as Teodorin grew and his father aged, both of them realized that there was a significant problem to address: succession, and whom Obiang would appoint as his heir. As the eldest son, Teodorin was the natural heir. To be sure, even then, the dictator never thought much of his son's skill set, political or otherwise. ("The only reason Teodorin will be president is because he's going to kill everyone else around him," one former Equatoguinean official told me.[14]) But with Teodorin dropping out of Pepperdine, Obiang had an offer for his son, one that would allow his son to dip his toes into political waters—to get a feel for what dictatorship really required. He wanted him to become Equatorial Guinea's newest Minister of Forestry.

Teodorin knew nothing about forestry management, or timber harvesting, and was far more familiar with different hard liquors than different hardwoods. But timber was, and remains, the country's second largest export commodity, outpaced only by the flood of oil that continues to pour out. And Teodorin's father wanted someone he could trust overseeing such a lucrative industry. He also wanted his son to try to at least learn something, anything, when it came to overseeing others—a skill set he'd need when he eventually succeeded his father. And Teodorin was only too happy to oblige, and to prove he could run the portfolio as effectively as his father expected.

* * *

WHEN OIL WAS first discovered in Equatorial Guinea, American oil firms were quick to woo the family in order to access the country's fields. Feting Obiang and his family, they threw lavish junkets, paid for lavish entertainment, and hosted lavish parties, praising Obiang and his rule at every step. American oil companies couldn't outright bribe officials like Obiang—such bribery was made illegal by the U.S.'s Foreign Corrupt Practices Act (FCPA), which we'll revisit in chapter 15—but there were workarounds available, such as overpaying the Obiang family's security firm for protection, or offering to pay for the tuition of younger family members attending American schools (as Waller International was doing for Teodorin).

On its face, the oil wealth should have belonged to the broader nation. It could have gone to buoy education budgets, health budgets, and infrastructure budgets, as it has in other oil-rich places like Norway or

Alaska. But instead, the flush of new money went primarily to those at the top—to a predatory regime creating a patronage network to solidify and fund the country's dictatorship. It may not have been illegal—Obiang could simply rewrite the laws to make sure everything was technically legal—but it was clearly corrupt. Obiang directed the millions of dollars coming in every month in a series of different directions. Some of it went to security services dedicated to tracking and muffling (or worse) opposition figures. Some of it went to funding the military, keeping the country's army brass happy and preventing any coup similar to the one that had initially launched Obiang to power. And much of it went directly into Obiang's pockets, or into the pockets of his family and cronies, who continued to pledge fealty to the dictator making all of them obscenely rich.

Indeed, Equatorial Guinea may be the purest example of the "resource curse" described by political scientists, which sees economies built largely around a single commodity like oil tending toward autocracy and dictatorship.[15] Much of the country remains mired in poverty, stripped of any democratic rights, while those at the top watch their bank accounts continue to swell.

Teodorin saw how his father dominated the country's oil industry, and he was well aware of the millions pocketed every month from the proceeds. He realized he could bring the same playbook to the country's timber sector. Shortly after assuming his new position, Teodorin immediately demanded the foreign timber export companies operating in the country pay a personal fee just to work, equal to 10 percent of the total export value of the wood they shipped. Malaysian companies, Filipino companies, European companies, African companies—all of whom, unlike American firms, had no restrictions on bribing local officials—agreed to Teodorin's terms. All of them would have to effectively bribe Teodorin just for the right to harvest the country's wide-open forests. Equatorial Guinea's beleaguered national forests were also available, for the right price. (Teodorin would soon become known as the "minister of chopping down trees."[16])

Yet those personal fees weren't enough. In 1996, he took things further, implementing a retroactive "tax" on these foreign companies, calculated at an extra $10 per cubic meter of timber that they had ever harvested from Equatorial Guinea. When a handful of companies refused to pay the new "tax," he promptly confiscated their machinery, claiming the legion of bulldozers and backhoes as his own.[17]

Teodorin's interactions with one company, the Spain-based ABM lumber firm, encapsulated his corrupt management style. According to Antonio Cabanellas, who oversaw ABM's operations in the country, dealing with him was like dealing with a combination of Jimmy Buffett and Jimmy Hoffa. "He would call us to come to his office, which meant wearing a suit and tie," Cabanellas remembered. "He would keep you waiting for five hours and then appear wearing shorts. He would then tell you how much he wanted you to pay him, and that you had a week to do so."[18] If they didn't hand over the money, they would lose everything—even a company like ABM, which had been logging in Equatorial Guinea since the 1970s.[19]

That May, after Teodorin gave ABM four days to pay a retroactive "tax" of $1.5 million, the company balked. They refused the payment. But whatever political capital they thought they'd built up in the country— whatever reputation they thought they'd built in their decades-long efforts to ingratiate themselves with the regime—meant little in the face of the spurned son.[20]

Following ABM's refusal, Teodorin sent police to the company's local offices. They barreled through the firm's front doors, and immediately evicted ABM's employees from the grounds. He then announced that they would all be banished from the country entirely, just for having the temerity to turn him down. "We had to flee the country," Cabanellas recalled. "He was demanding millions."[21] But that wasn't all. Teodorin forced ABM's leadership, already in the process of packing to leave, to hand over control of its local forestry operations in their entirety— effectively nationalizing the firm, with all proceeds now heading to himself. Gracious as ever, the dictator's son paid a nominal fee for the transfer of ownership, magnitudes below the company's actual worth. He then followed this "sale" by arresting ABM's now-former lead operator, who was only released after a $3 million payment.[22]

Teodorin, though, had little interest in actually managing the firm he'd just picked up. He forced a separate Malaysian logging company, Shimmer—which had already bribed Teodorin in order to harvest Equatorial Guinea's protected national forests—to purchase ABM's abandoned equipment. The cost to Shimmer, according to later court documents, came at "significantly inflated prices."[23] And all of it went directly into Teodorin's pocket.

* * *

CONSIDERING THAT THE annual worth of all of Equatorial Guinea's clear-cut timber ran into the hundreds of millions of dollars, all of these kickbacks provided Teodorin with a steady stream of seven-figure payments. None of this, of course, trickled down to the people, who remained among the world's poorest. But he continued to implement new "taxes," and he continued to watch his swelling nest egg grow and grow.

So he began asking around about how to transform all of that stolen wealth into something more substantial.

He began to focus on the Persian Gulf, especially Dubai, where some of the world's wealthiest people spent their wealth. At the time, Dubai was already transforming from a sleepy desert enclave into a megalopolis, rising on the tide of the region's gas reserves. But after arriving in Dubai, Teodorin looked around and realized that plenty of others had the same ideas. He was hardly the only one with bottomless pockets popping up in the region. Rather than being a whale in a small puddle in Equatorial Guinea, Teodorin was suddenly one fish among many. "Dubai is not his thing," one former Equatoguinean official told me. "Everybody there has money like him, everybody has a car like him—so he doesn't feel like a prince."[24]

Teodorin then tried Paris briefly, which made sense: he'd learned French during his younger days spent in Gabon, and it was better than his Spanish. But Teodorin soon wore out his welcome, not least because he was filmed speeding down the Champs-Elysees in a Bentley, and later totaled another luxury car on the Paris streets, all between the days-long benders.[25]

But there was another option. One that other kleptocrats like him had begun looking to in greater and greater droves—one that was more than happy to help vacuum up billions. It was perfect: Teodorin could begin transforming his wealth into whatever he liked. And it was all perfectly legal, without any questions asked.

WHY NOT DO AS THE AMERICANS DO?

"In the mafia, there's a special name for the people who discreetly remove all the traces after the act: cleaners."

—The Panama Papers[1]

The greatest financial secrecy tool the world has ever invented isn't something you can hold. It's not something you can see, or touch, or peer into, trying to ascertain what exactly it contains. It is, in a very real sense, something of a fiction: it exists solely on paper, and solely to conceal the names of the people, and the sources of their money, for whom it was created.

It's called an "anonymous shell company."[2] Like regular companies, these anonymous shell companies can be registered quickly: a few phone calls, a bit of paperwork, and a new company can be had in a short period of time. On paper, it's often difficult to tell the difference between the founding of a legitimate company and the founding of an anonymous shell company. But where a regular company will soon begin building out its enterprise—hiring employees, creating its brand, selling its products and services—these anonymous shell companies almost never serve any legitimate purpose. Instead, they've done arguably more damage, caused more bloodshed, and obscured more dirty money than anything the world has ever known, all while cloaking more illicit and ill-gotten assets than we'll ever know about. And they're something the U.S. has been creating, and selling, for decades.

For instance, in 1986, the *Wall Street Journal* featured a full-page advertisement aimed at readers in East Asia. The splash page featured a smiling photo of S. B. Woo, a lieutenant governor of Delaware—a small American state tucked between New York and Washington, D.C., on the country's Eastern Seaboard, a jurisdiction smaller than places like Kuwait or Israel. Woo had a simple question for the readers: "Are you thinking of investing in the USA?" One suggestion, in all caps for emphasis, declared: "WHY NOT DO AS THE AMERICANS DO!"[3]

The advertisement served as an effective launching pad for the lieutenant governor's tour through much of Asia. Alongside Michael Harkins, Delaware's secretary of state, Woo visited businessmen, potential investors, and high-ranking officials alike. Touring Taiwan and China, Indonesia and the Philippines, Woo and Harkins had one goal in mind: to draw as much attention, and as much money, as they could to Delaware—a state few outside the U.S. had ever heard of, or had much reason to.

In the meetings they'd set up, Woo highlighted why those deep-pocketed officials and businessmen they met with should consider Delaware for all of their anonymous financial needs. The meetings raised few eyebrows; at the time, there were hardly any concerns about these kinds of companies. Instead, they were part of a far broader campaign of American outreach, searching out new markets to help spread the gospel of American capitalism—markets that Delaware wanted a piece of. Woo's travels took him farther than any Delaware official had ever been in an official capacity. He struck up a relationship with the Chinese ambassador and built up ties with regional exporters, as well as the wealthy Hong Kongers who would later funnel their wealth out of the island territory following its 1997 reunification with China.

During all of these talks, one of Woo's favorite props was, according to *New York Times* coverage of the trip, a "bilingual pamphlet." Despite the fact that it "resembled something dreamed up by the *National Lampoon* back in the days when it was funny," it carried a simple promise to those in the turbulent region: "We Protect You From Politics."[4]

The pamphlet pointed specifically to something that few of the businessmen and politicos they met with likely knew about. Woo and others had dubbed it an anonymous shell company—and it would allow all those they met with, and all of the millions of dollars those people controlled, to effectively disappear, if the need should ever arise. On their face, there was nothing corrupt, and certainly not illegal, about these anonymous shell companies. The state of Delaware—known for being one of America's original 13 colonies and not much else—had made them perfectly legal. And plenty of officials from American states similarly visited foreign environs on investment trips, especially toward the end of the 1980s and early 1990s. In that sense, the visit from the Delaware officials was no different.

But this anonymous shell company product perked more than a few ears. A month after the *Wall Street Journal* ad ran, Filipino protesters ousted the gluttonously corrupt Ferdinand and Imelda Marcos, revealing to the world the details of Ferdinand's financial crimes. (They also helped reveal things like Imelda's sprawling shoe collection, which ran into thousands of pairs.) New Filipino authorities and long-suffering Filipino investigators began the process of tracking down the Marcoses' looted wealth in order to reclaim what rightfully belonged to the Filipino people. Doing so would also ensure that the couple couldn't enjoy any of their illegitimate assets after they were ousted from power.

As such, Woo's audience in these nondemocratic countries, skittish about potentially being overthrown or watching their financial lifelines dry up, was receptive. They were eager to hear more about these magical get-away-free tools—these anonymous shell companies—that this small, distant state was selling. As they read the pamphlet, Woo's interlocutors learned just what these anonymous shell companies could do. By purchasing one of these anonymous shell companies in Delaware, they could enjoy all of the legal protections those in Delaware already enjoyed. "[I]n the event of an emergency in your home country, such as insurrection or invasion by a hostile power," the pamphlet read, "your company can temporarily or permanently move its domicile and be protected by the laws of The State of Delaware."[5] Of course, as Woo pointed out, the officials and businessmen he met with didn't need to wait for an insurrection or invasion; they could start purchasing and setting up these anonymous shell companies as soon as they liked.

The campaign worked: Woo and Harkins ended up signing rafts of new clients excited by American financial protections. Delaware made some $1 million from their trip—a remarkable sum, considering that setting up one of these anonymous shell companies in the state can run as little as about $100. But $1 million was just the beginning, and a sign of things to come. It was clear, as the *New York Times* reported that year, that thanks to these anonymous shell companies, Woo and Harkins had hit on "a way of making everybody rich" in the state—and that more would soon be flocking to "happy Delaware."[6]

* * *

THESE ANONYMOUS SHELL companies are subsets of what we know as "companies": entities registered with government officials for purposes of commerce, contracts, taxation, and all of the capitalist wonders that come alongside. You've probably even heard of the variant called a "corporation," a broad subset of "companies," which provides many of the same services. There are some technical discrepancies between "companies" and "corporations," but when it comes to the kind of money laundering services America provides, the two are effectively interchangeable. And in the eyes of the criminal and the corrupt, both serve the exact same ends: obscuring the origins of their wealth, and transforming that suspect money into seemingly legitimate assets.

For many, "companies" and "corporations" include familiar brands— Nike, Microsoft, Taco Bell—providing goods, services, and employment. They are relatively transparent, at least when it comes to their reasons for being. Their leadership is easy to identify. Their revenue numbers are easy to find. Their output—their new lines of sneakers, their new operating systems, their roster of burrito-related offerings—is often just a quick Google search away.

But this subset that Woo and Harkins were peddling exists as something altogether different. On the face of it, there's little difference when it comes to setting up a viable, legitimate company and an anonymous shell company. Both can be set up quickly, and both are registered with state officials. For the company service providers—those filing the paperwork and making sure all the payments and registration information are up to date—there's little way to tell at the outset whether they're helping a new, promising company register with the government, or if they're helping set up the perfect financial getaway vehicle for a corrupt oligarch abroad.

Still, there are some key differences. These anonymous shell companies don't provide any information on who's actually behind them. (Who, to drop in a technical term, their "beneficial owners" actually are.[7]) They have no shareholders or employees. They have no offices where actual business is conducted. They have no apparent purpose. If you manage to locate their records in corporate databases, you might find where and when they were formed, or even who filed their paperwork with the government to formalize their formation. But you won't find anything else.

Instead, the only benefit is exactly what Woo and Harkins were selling: anonymity. And it's that anonymity that holds the key to the kingdom of kleptocracy—the necessary ingredient for transforming dirty money into legitimate financing, and for removing all traces of the dirty money from its origins. Perhaps you're a cartel head, with tens of millions of dollars from the opiate or fentanyl trade, looking to hide your assets from authorities and investigators.[8] Perhaps you're a human trafficker, looking to hide the ownership of a series of illicit massage parlors.[9] Perhaps you're an oligarch worried about crossing your country's dictator, and want to secretly funnel your assets out of the country.[10] Or perhaps you're a family member of those running a despotic regime, and you realize that there's a revolution brewing, and you want to make sure that all of the lucre you've pilfered can't be reclaimed by the pro-democracy forces who will soon be coming to power.[11] Anyone searching for anonymity— anyone searching to protect their assets, especially those of illegitimate origins—has reason to look to anonymous shell companies for succor.

As one World Bank analysis of 150 major corruption cases found, the "main type of corporate vehicle used to conceal beneficial ownership" was the anonymous shell company.[12] This comes despite a raft of major international agreements—from the G20, from the Organisation for Economic Co-operation and Development (OECD), and others— that have demanded their elimination. "There are few if any legitimate business purposes employing anonymous shell companies," one financial crimes researcher summed up in 2014.[13] Proponents disagree with the assessment, pointing to cases where that anonymity was necessary to avoid tipping off potential competitors—such as when Disney purchased the land for Disney World in Florida, doing so in secret in order to avoid landholders demanding higher prices.[14]

But those examples of legitimate applications of anonymous shells are sparse and buried by all of the other illicit uses to which these companies have been applied. "If organized crime depends on financial secrecy, untraceable shell companies are the most important means of providing it," one group of researchers summed. "Shell companies are the most common and important enablers of large-scale corruption."[15]

* * *

THE PROCESS OF using an anonymous shell company for laundering money is disarmingly simple. With an anonymous shell company, you can move your money almost anywhere—into almost any industry, into almost any sector—without detection. Since your name isn't attached anywhere to the anonymous shell company, pesky journalists can't follow your money, nor can any of the human rights activists tracking connections to brutal regimes, nor can investigators in democratic countries trying to figure out who's funding antidemocratic operations. Yet anonymous shell companies can do anything you need them to do: purchase buildings, skirt sanctions, bankroll political campaigns, or build financial empires, without any of the rest of us having a clue. Anonymous shell companies have become the perfect financial get-out-of-jail-free cards—and have helped move billions, and potentially trillions, of dollars clean out of sight.

Say, for instance, you're a member of the ruling inner circle in a post-Soviet dictatorship like Kazakhstan. The country's brutal dictator names you the head of Kazakhstan Railways. It's a reward, he says, for years of loyalty. And it's a way of making sure the job goes to someone he can trust.

You don't know the first thing about railway management, and you can hardly tell the difference between track gauges and Thomas the Tank

Engine. But that doesn't matter. It turns out that running a nationwide monopoly on railways in a dictatorship like Kazakhstan is a great way to wring your populace dry and drain companies relying on the rails of any extra savings they may have been building up. As such, you start jacking up transit fees and demanding bribes from those requiring rail usage. You also keep landing massive no-bid contracts from the state, often for railways that lead nowhere. (It's not like there's much the people can do, given that you control all the rails—and that your buddy, Kazakhstan's thug-in-chief, has already disemboweled the country's independent media and political opposition.)

Your personal financial intake keeps growing and growing. But there's one hitch. Even as your net worth continues to explode, it's clear to all involved—to Western governments, to international anticorruption investigators, even to a restive domestic population increasingly chafing under the decades-long corruption rotting their entire nation—that your money's no good. That it's ill-gotten. That it's dirty.

Yet you still want to spend your money, or park it in assets abroad. You want to live among the caste of the world's wealthiest, with whom you feel you belong—but whose governments, at least nominally, look down on dirty money. And, anyway, you never know when the long-beleaguered population in Kazakhstan will erupt in revolution, with new authorities coming in, looking through corporate records, and seizing all your assets (as has already happened in neighboring Kyrgyzstan multiple times in the past twenty years).

Enter the anonymous shell company, which services all of your laundering and anonymity needs. It will remove all trace of any suspicious origin from the money suddenly spilling out of your pockets. It will sever the link between the obviously dirty *source* of the funds and the funds themselves—and make it impossible for authorities and investigators to ever figure out who's actually behind the shell company in question.

You know that when using an anonymous shell company, dirty money goes in and (*poof!*) clean money or assets come out, unable to be traced to the initial bribe or embezzlement or cronyism that allowed you to grow so wealthy. Still, an anonymous shell company *from Kazakhstan*—a country overseen by a decades-long dictator, saturated in corruption—would raise too many questions. But one from America? That's a different story.

Thankfully, you've already met with someone like Woo. You've already listened to them describe how an anonymous shell company is a bit like a black box, a magical device that transforms dirty money into something that neither investigators nor authorities can unravel. And you're already aware that they're happy to sell anonymous *American* shell companies to any and all. So you give the Americans a call, and ask them to set up an anonymous shell company for you, one that won't contain your name anywhere. You tell your contact you want to call it, say, "Hiding Money LLC." The American on the other end of the line says they'd be happy to set you up. It's in their best interest, after all, as they'll be taking fees along the way for their services. And there are no laws to deter them from setting up an anonymous shell for anyone they want.

In as little as 15 minutes, you suddenly have one: this basic building block of modern kleptocracy. All it took was a phone call, a bit of your time, and an American who didn't care one whit about the source of your money—and suddenly, this magical black box is yours to use however you want, laundering and obscuring whatever funds you need it to. For many looking to launder their ill-gotten gains, this is the first step in constructing a modern kleptocratic network. These shells are the foundation upon which to build an offshoring empire.

In order to use the anonymous shell company, though, you'll need a bank account. No problem. You call up your local banker, the one at the Kazakhstani bank overseen by the dictator's oleaginous son-in-law, and tell him that you'd like to open a new account in the name of your brand-new anonymous shell company. Absolutely, the banker responds. With a few keystrokes, a new bank account appears—now attached to your new anonymous American shell company. You then tell the banker to transfer, say, $100 million into this new account (plus an additional $10 million for the Kazakhstani dictator's son-in-law, as a gesture of appreciation for him and his family).[16]

A few minutes, a few phone calls, and it's done. Your name isn't attached anywhere, and international investigators or the few remaining independent journalists in the country will never be able to trace it to you. But your money is there: waiting to be transformed into mansions and megayachts, Picassos and private jets, skyscrapers and stadiums and sprawling tracts of land. Waiting to be bounced around into other new accounts elsewhere, or into anonymous trusts abroad, or anywhere else you'd like it to go—especially in a country like the U.S., which has let these shell companies effectively do whatever they've wanted to for years.

All of it, done completely anonymously.

If this example seems a bit outlandish, just look at any dictator over the past few decades—those who've spent the better part of their time in power looting their nations, immiserating entire countries, and threatening American national security in the process. Peek below the hood of any dictatorship around the world and you'll find a mountain of shell companies operating to help entrench the regime.

Muammar Gaddafi? The deceased Libyan leader reportedly squirreled his and his country's fortune away inside a series of anonymous shell companies abroad. Slobodan Milosevic, the genocidal Serbian autocrat? He used anonymous shell companies to skirt sanctions and to continue his carnage against prone populations in Bosnia and Kosovo. Vladimir Putin, Xi Jinping, and Kim Jong-un?[17] All of them[18]—including their family members and inner circles[19]—have funneled untold billions through anonymous shell companies, far away from the eyes of their people and Western investigators alike.[20]

And more often than not, these dictators and their cronies and their oligarchs have turned to the U.S. to do it.

* * *

IF THERE'S ONE central piece, one underlying rot, at the heart of America's mutation into the center of modern kleptocracy, it's exactly that: the U.S.-born and -bred anonymous shell company. The ease of setting up an anonymous shell company in the U.S. is impossible to overstate. It's unclear where the first anonymous shell was formed, or exactly when. But it's clear that the U.S. has refined the product into an art, making it more efficient and more accessible than anywhere else. And that efficiency is one of the major reasons that the U.S. churns out millions of companies annually, more than any other country in the world—and more than the next 40 global tax havens, places like Malta and Cyprus and the British Virgin Islands, *combined*.[21]

A few years ago, a trio of academics tried to uncover just which jurisdictions around the world had the easiest processes for setting up these anonymous shells. The experiment was straightforward. The researchers sent thousands of emails to company service providers—the people who, for a nominal fee, file the paperwork registering these companies, so you don't have to bother yourself with the details. Sometimes the academics posed as Danish consultants, simply looking to help a client, while other times they posed as government officials from notoriously corrupt countries like Pakistan, trying to whisk their gobs of stolen wealth out of the country.[22]

But the three always asked, in effect, the same question: If they wanted to set up an anonymous shell company, how easy would it be? The results were striking. Nearly half of the company service providers didn't bother to require identifying documents certified by any government body, and more than a fifth didn't even require any photo identity documents at all. As one of the researchers pithily wrote, "Disturbingly, the results presented here suggest that those selling shell companies are almost completely insensitive to the danger of corruption."[23] And one country stood out more than all others: the U.S, where setting up an anonymous shell company was obscenely easy.[24]

Given the capitalistic, deregulatory ethos of the country, it makes sense that the most efficient means of setting up these anonymous shells would come in the U.S. Plus, there's an entire industry already built up to service legitimate, perfectly aboveboard companies in the U.S.—an industry whose tools just so happen to work perfectly for corrupt officials or narcotraffickers or foreign oligarchs trying to set up anonymous shells as well.

But the ease with which American company service providers set up these shells still shocked the researchers. As they found, all it required was as little as a hundred dollars, and as few as 15 minutes on the phone with a company service provider to walk you through the paperwork. All you need is a name for the company and a check made out to the company service provider (or, better yet, direct payment from a foreign bank account, preferably one that U.S. authorities couldn't trace even if they wanted to).[25] If you want, you can even select what's known as a "nominee," a front-person who will act as the anonymous shell company's director, shareholder, or partner: someone who could, if authorities come knocking, claim to be the only person involved with the company. But don't worry: in the U.S., these "nominee" figures never need to know your real identity, either.[26] And if that's not enough anonymity for you, you can even layer your anonymous shell company operations, with shells owning shells owning shells, bouncing across states, across oceans, across the world, burying your identity under a matryoshka doll of shells, each one nested inside another, each one as anonymous as the last.[27]

The researchers found that less than 10 percent of American company service providers requested basic identifying information. And only a minuscule 1.5 percent of the company service providers in the U.S. complied with international best practices. "A person searching for a provider willing to violate international standards . . . could start searching at the beginning of the day and probably be finished by lunch," the researchers summed.[28] Or as one of the other researchers put it, "There is strong reason to think that the United States, given its central place in the global financial system and the number of companies involved, is the worst in the world when it comes to regulating shell companies."[29] On the flip side, they found that countries and jurisdictions that required the most information from those trying to set up an anonymous shell company included either traditional "offshore" havens (the Cayman Islands or the Isle of Man) or outright dictatorships (like Belarus or Gaddafi's Libya). "What came through pretty clearly," Brigham Young University's Daniel Nielsen, one of the researchers behind the project, told me, "is that among all of the venues in the world, the easiest place to get an anonymous shell company is the United States."[30]

And it's worth highlighting some of the responses the researchers got from these American company service providers, which were laced with the sort of American condescension familiar elsewhere. In response to one email from the researchers, which saw them posing as a Danish consultant, one American company service provider said, "Regarding what information is required. None! Hard for Europeans to understand we have a word in our constitution which is privacy!"[31] ("Privacy" is, in fact, not found anywhere in the U.S. Constitution.[32])

Nor did those responses change when the researchers approached American company service providers as corrupt officials. With the researchers posing as an official in Pakistan, a notoriously corrupt country, one American company service provider hurled epithets at them for their approach, and for their clear signs of corruption. But then, in the very next breath, he revealed that he'd be happy to help them—if the researchers ponied up enough money. As the company service provider wrote:

> Your stated purpose could well be a front for funding terrorism, and who the f*** would get involved in that? Seriously, if you wanted a functioning and useful [anonymous American shell] corporation you'd need someone here to put their name on it, set up bank accounts, etc. I wouldn't even consider doing that for less than [$5,000] a month, and I doubt you are going to find any suckers that will do it for less, if at all. If you are working with less than serious money, don't waste anybody's time here. Using a f***ing [internet email] account also shows you are just a f***ing poser and loser. If you have a serious proposal, write it up and we will consider it. Your previous message and this one are meaningless crap. Get a clue. Just how stupid do you think we are.[33]

In other words, for the right sum, all can be forgotten.

Maybe that's unsurprising. The U.S. has seen decades of deregulation across its economy, often pushed in the name of easing burdens on businesses. This "pro-business" ethos, ascendant since the 1980s, conquered much of the American body politic, on both sides of the political aisle. And as we'll see time and again throughout this book, that ethos infected all of the industries that have transformed into the linchpins of American kleptocracy. In many ways, those attempts to ease business operations—and to attract as much capital to the U.S as possible—are the core reasons that the U.S. transformed into the world's greatest off-shore haven.

After all, deregulation didn't just open the U.S. to a new world of clean, legitimate capital flows. It also opened America's arms to as much dirty money as the world could provide.

*   *   *

IN FEBRUARY 2020, the Treasury Department specifically singled out anonymous shell companies for their role in gouging holes in America's efforts to counter money laundering—those processes that allow dirty money to transform into legitimate assets. Anonymous shell companies, the Treasury wrote, give "both U.S. and foreign criminals a method of obfuscation that they can and have repeatedly used, here and abroad, to carry out financial crimes."[34]

Nor were they just a means for oligarchs and dictatorships. The U.S. Government Accountability Office in 2019 listed specific examples of such criminal usage, revealing that the Department of Defense had been scammed time and again by these schemes.[35] One group the report highlighted utilized American shell companies to reroute millions of dollars that had been intended for the upkeep of post-Soviet nuclear plants, while another used anonymous shell companies to pose as disabled veterans. Some even swiped entire Pentagon contracts—effectively building American military products without Washington having any idea who they were.[36] All of this was possible for one simple reason: anybody could get an anonymous American shell company, whenever they wanted. There was no law, and no regulation, that said otherwise.

But then, these governmental reports have been saying the same thing for years. In its 2015 National Money Laundering Risk Assessment, the Treasury highlighted the threats of these companies, and specifically highlighted the role they play for "[post-Soviet] organized crime groups," who were of "particular concern because of their systemic use of sophisticated schemes to move and conceal their criminal proceeds using U.S. banking institutions and U.S. incorporated shell companies."[37] (This came amidst efforts of the same members of these post-Soviet organized crime groups who were using anonymous shell companies to help propel Trump to the presidency, as we'll see in the book's final section.)

Yet for years, efforts to do anything about these companies—to prevent their creation, or to at least pull back the curtains of anonymity—went nowhere. That's because, when it comes to the U.S. and anonymous shell companies, there's one catch. Where most countries across the world see their national government charged with regulating the creation of companies, the U.S.'s federal structure means that company creation isn't overseen by Washington. Instead, it's overseen by *state* governments, in places like Austin or Juneau or Sacramento or Indianapolis. Thus, states are in *competition* with one another to try to attract corporate business. The U.S.'s federal approach means that states can tinker and evolve and adapt, and introduce new tools and tactics to try to attract corporate clients, without having to worry about regulations from the federal government. And it means that it's the states that are making millions from corporate registration fees, which they can use to buoy their budgets.

With this competition—with states offering increasing efficiency and protections for corporate clients, including those who wanted anonymity—American states engaged in a so-called race to the bottom. And where that bottom lies remains anyone's guess.

CONTROL EVERYTHING, OWN NOTHING

"Imagine the possibilities!"

—Wyoming Corporate Services[1]

Most of the audiences S. D. Woo encountered when traveling had never heard of Delaware, or knew anything about the state. Even most Americans would be hard-pressed to rattle off more than a few facts, if any, about the state. One of the smallest and, in terms of national coverage, least consequential of the American states, Delaware hardly has any cultural imprint or any real legacy in the broader American story, beyond being the first state to ratify the U.S. Constitution. Aside from President Joe Biden, Delaware's rarely produced a figure of any renown—a remarkable achievement, considering it was one of the original 13 colonies. Where most states have clear associations—Texas and cowboys, Oregon and timber, Louisiana and jazz—Delaware is known for, in effect, nothing. Which, for those searching for anonymity, makes it the perfect place to help hide their ill-gotten gains. What better place to stash your funds than a state few ever think about?

The story of Delaware's transformation into one of the world's leading kleptocratic havens is one that's decades, even centuries, old. But in order to trace how Delaware transformed into the heart of the U.S.'s role in the offshore-onshore world—how the state became, as one former SEC chair described, a "pygmy state interested only in revenue"[2]—you have to cycle back to the early days of the American republic. And you have to focus less on the role Delaware played in propelling the U.S. Constitution to ratification and more on how the earliest days of American capitalism operated.

In the lead-up to the American Revolution, companies created in the American colonies—still under the thumb of authorities in London— were overseen by the colonies themselves. Soon thereafter, once the Americans successfully declared independence, those new American states opted to retain the same oversight structures. Dealing with plenty else—national security, foreign policy, the structures of American government itself—early American legislators simply opted to keep this company oversight system in place, with the states. "The best historical evidence," one academic study found, "indicates that after the American Revolution the state legislatures simply followed the precedent of the colonial assemblies."[3]

Companies formed in those early days of the American republic were, likewise, far closer to their British precedents than anything we see in twenty-first-century America. And they were far more restricted in what they could do than their modern counterparts. Early corporate structures in the U.S. remained largely limited to things like educational institutions and charitable organizations (and, oddly, cemeteries). Indeed, corporations themselves were far rarer than they would eventually become; as one corporate historian wrote, they were "very uncommon."[4]

Looking at the kinds of early regulation involved in setting them up helps explain some of this scarcity. Each early American corporation required its own separate bill to pass through state legislatures before it could operate, a remarkably onerous procedure just to create a corporation. (If states still employed this setup, their state legislatures would never get anything else done.) Legislatures eventually looked for a way to streamline the process. By the 1830s, proposals arose for transferring company oversight from the state governments to the federal government, unburdening state legislatures from overseeing the process. But by that time, Jacksonian populists, the kind suspicious of federal power—except when it came to things like the ethnic cleansing campaigns targeting Native American populations, at least—ruled the federal government. And they wanted to keep Washington's hands off corporate formation.

So those supporting reform efforts tried a different approach. If they couldn't get Washington to oversee corporate formation, why not just decrease the regulatory burdens on the states?

And that's exactly what began happening—and, in a very real sense, only continued happening in the century and a half following. Through the remainder of the nineteenth century, those onerous requirements for setting up an American corporation slowly waned. Gone were the requirements to pass a bill for every single corporation. Gone were the hearings and the debates over each and every new company. While Congress occasionally agitated for more control over the process—including in the aftermath of the Civil War, amidst massive civil rights reforms—populist voices still didn't want the federal government to consolidate oversight. Better, they thought, for states to retain control. Much of that stemmed from the developing American ethos of restricting the federal government's hand in the country's economics. As one researcher summarized, many of those who "understood how business and corporations operated [still] trusted the state and local free market to provide the proper level of regulations and therefore, never would have considered pushing for increased federal oversight and control over corporations."[5]

*   *   *

DURING THE LATE nineteenth century, amidst broader economic transitions and trajectories that would end in the Gilded Age and the ensuing Progressive Era, corporate formation entered a new epoch. While monopolies grew to dominate industries like steel and oil, one state began dominating the company formation industry. But it wasn't Delaware.

New Jersey, just north of Delaware, had long been economically dominated by New York. But by the 1870s, New Jersey realized that rolling back corporate formation regulations could be just the financial solution needed to help boost its own economy. In order to entice this new corporate business—new corporations that New Jersey could tax and require fees from, helping boost the state budget—the state passed a slate of reforms. Previously, corporate charters had been limited to a few decades, but in New Jersey, state legislators removed chronological caps on new corporations, allowing them to remain in perpetuity. Legislators also moved to allow companies to hold stock in other companies, a move that allowed the creation of so-called holding companies—companies within companies, in effect. (As America would soon learn, these holding companies turned out to be a key step in the development of the great monopolies of the end of the nineteenth century.[6])

More importantly for our story, New Jersey also repealed regulations that required companies to even operate in the state. With the state taking a chunk of revenue from every company registered there, New Jersey regulators had spied another means of making money—even if the companies themselves never did business in New Jersey. All of a sudden, anyone from Hartford to Houston to Honolulu could create a New Jersey company, enjoying the state's new benefits without actually setting foot there. Geographic restraints that had previously limited company formation became a thing of the past. And the reaction was swift. As the *New York Times* reported, "Needless to say, companies raced to New Jersey; by 1902, its income from [taxes and fees on the new corporations] was so great that it abolished the property tax."[7] New Jersey watched its state coffers explode. One writer at the time said it was "as though a Klondike gold mine had been discovered in New Jersey."[8] The state was soon making enough revenue from those rushing to set up companies that it even began remitting taxes back to local cities. Everyone in the state, it appeared, benefited from New Jersey's corporate reforms.

But other states took notice. So many companies uprooted for New Jersey that officials in other states began referring to the Garden State as the "Traitor State," sucking up taxes and fees the other states suddenly lost out on. And the resultant effect could have—and probably should have—been predicted. The corporate sprint to New Jersey sparked a response from other state governments looking to get their share of this new Klondike gold mine. A renaissance in "business friendly" regulations quickly followed, with regulatory rollbacks racing from state to state. Thanks to these turn-of-the-century innovations, as one researcher related, U.S. states found themselves in that "race to the bottom,"[9] with new laws imposing fewer and fewer "restraints on potential corporate abuses."[10] Basic corporate regulations—things like requiring shareholder input, or assuming liability for any malfeasance or accidents—suddenly began disappearing across states. And along the way, requirements for publicly identifying those behind the corporations also disappeared. Anonymity, as Delaware would later discover, was a perk that sold well— especially when paired with all of the other corporate regulatory rollbacks.

But not everyone in New Jersey appreciated the state's new role as the epicenter of company formation. Woodrow Wilson, serving as the state's governor from 1911 to 1913, was one of those who had second thoughts about New Jersey's transformation. Propelled by a reformist bent, and concerned about who might be taking advantage of New Jersey's loose regulations, Wilson clamped down, undoing some of the recent rollbacks. Corporate lobbyists decried Wilson's moves. But their calls fell on deaf ears. While Wilson wasn't able to return New Jersey to a corporate *status quo ante*, he effectively halted New Jersey's deregulatory momentum.

Suddenly, those looking for lax corporate regulation had to turn elsewhere. But they didn't have to look far. Just a few miles south stood Delaware, poised, ready to capitalize on Wilson's decision, and ready to swipe the pro-corporate crown from New Jersey. "Delaware," read one article in the *American Law Review* from the era, was "gangrened with envy at the spectacle of the truck-patchers, sand-duners, clam-diggers and mosquito-wafters of New Jersey getting all the money in the country into her coffers." And the state was "determined to get her little, tiny, sweet, round, baby hand into the grab-bag of sweet things before it is too late."[11]

⊀ ⊀ ⊀

MUCH LIKE TODAY, the Delaware of the early twentieth century wasn't known for much. The state maintained a small service sector, and an even smaller industrial base. Without any real natural resources or tourist attractions, the state scraped by trying to leech business from those traveling between New York and Washington, D.C. Indeed, there were plenty of similarities between Delaware and New Jersey—at least before the latter's corporate reforms.

As such, when Wilson's new policies began to take effect in New

Jersey, Delaware saw an opportunity. To be sure, other states also spied the same opportunities, watching New Jersey suddenly turning its back on the corporate gold mine. But Delaware was perfectly placed to profit off New Jersey's decision. The state enjoyed many of the same geographic advantages New Jersey offered, situated as it is between America's financial (New York) and political (Washington, D.C.) capitals. ("Who wants to fly to Alaska [for corporate litigation]?" one journalist wrote, highlighting Delaware's prime location.[12]) And while Wilson spooked corporate clients and pro-corporate interests with his pro-regulation reforms, Delaware never followed suit. As Delaware governor Pete du Pont would later say, "You can't trust the [Delaware] legislature to do a lot of things, but you can rely on it to keep the corporation law up to date."[13]

While New Jersey's deregulatory reforms stalled under Wilson, Delaware's state government picked up the baton. It was, in a sense, a move straight out of the story of American capitalism: the state saw an opportunity to attract business, and enacted the necessary reforms to make it so. The pro-business ethos that has propelled American capitalism translated into, quite literally, "pro-business"—pro-corporation, pro-company formation—moves in Delaware. None of it was illegal. None of it was even necessarily unexpected. After all, if it hadn't been Delaware, another state would have grasped at the corporate revenue Wilson had pushed out of New Jersey and redirected those corporate fees into their own state budgets (and maybe even reduced tax burdens on happy citizens). Maybe it would have been another small state, like New Hampshire. Maybe it would have been another overlooked state, like Rhode Island. Some state, somewhere else, would have taken similar steps, redirecting that firehose of corporate fees to their own coffers. But Delaware happened to be the first.

The steps Delaware took effectively opened the doors for companies to relocate as easily as possible into the state, enticing them with new pro-corporate laws. In addition to the reforms already implemented in New Jersey, Delaware soon began allowing corporations to reimburse directors for damages incurred if and when upset shareholders filed suit (invaluable protection as America grew more and more litigious).

The state also soon began exempting corporations from state taxes—meaning that the new Delaware company's only real connection to, or interaction with, the state ended the moment the paperwork was filed.

But there was one advantage that Delaware held that no other state could provide, which has allowed Delaware to entrench its leading status as a global offshore center well into the twenty-first century: Delaware's Chancery Court. Birthed in 1792, the Chancery Court has been producing a steady stream of corporate law for nearly as long as the nation itself has existed.[14] Uniquely dedicated to determining the minutiae of Delaware corporate law, the Chancery Court proved a key weapon in Delaware's pro-corporate arsenal—a tool no other state could match. As a pair of American academics found, this state-level court has provided "expert judiciary and [an] ability to resolve quickly complex business disputes," effectively providing Delaware with a far deeper well of corporate case law than any other state in the country—a godsend for lawyers ever vigilant for any threats their corporate clients may face.[15]

By the 1920s, Delaware's position as a leader in the corporate race to the bottom was all but assured. The state, to steal a political science term, had been effectively "captured": beholden to its corporate regime and to the revenue brought to the state from the company-formation industry.[16] There was also one other advantage Delaware maintained. In a nod to the U.S.'s schizophrenic offshore-onshore status, Delaware managed for years to avoid the reputational taint that more traditional offshore havens suffer from. "Delaware doesn't carry the same stigma as the Caymans or Bermuda," North Carolina State University's Bradley Lindsey, who has researched Delaware's status as an offshore haven, said. "Why not attract business to my little state and get something at the expense of the other states?"[17]

And why not? By the 1930s, revenue from the companies housed in Delaware amounted to 42 percent of the state's total revenue. By the dawn of the 2020s, that ratio was largely similar—but the numbers were now stupefying. Every year, Delaware makes nearly $1.5 billion from all those seeking out its corporate-friendly regime.[18] That number's not only far more than any other state, but it's a massive financial crutch for a state that doesn't maintain a sales or property tax.

Or look at another number: 1.5 million. That's the approximate number of corporations that are now registered in the state,[19] with over 225,000 now created annually.[20] A century ago, Delaware's reforms were meant to help fund services for its citizens. But given that Delaware doesn't even have a million residents, we're now facing a situation in which, as BYU's Daniel Nielsen said, Delaware legislators' "constituents, in a very real sense, are companies."[21]

* * *

AT THE TURN of the twenty-first century, Delaware's company-formation industry was still working overtime to make sure anyone could set up anonymous shell companies as easily as possible. The state had whittled down wait times for an anonymous shell company to less than an hour, and some places in Delaware even offered "expedited services," getting you an anonymous shell company in as little as ten minutes.[22] Delaware's office of the secretary of state, which oversees company formation, even stays open until 10:30 p.m. on Friday nights.[23] Along the way, Delaware became the only state to hire lobbyists to argue against transparency reforms in Washington.[24]

And then there's the anonymity. Since, as described above, Washington never managed to grab control of corporate registration from states—and since neither Congress nor state legislatures ever bothered to demand information about the "beneficial owners" of these companies—Delaware felt free to offer anonymity as one of its pro-corporate services, no matter who wanted it. As one of Delaware's company service providers advertises on its website, those selling anonymous shell companies in Delaware are "not required to keep any information on the beneficial owner, and the state of Delaware does not require that the beneficial owner's identity be disclosed."[25] Or as David Finzer, the chief executive of one of Delaware's major company service providers, said about information on those behind the anonymous shell companies, "Basically, [Delaware] requires none. Delaware has the most secret companies in the world and the easiest to form."[26]

All of which is to say: Delaware may not itself be a hive of scum and villainy—but it's where the entire hive goes whenever it needs to conceal its finances, cover up its financial tracks, and transform all of its blood money into untraceable assets. Rather than the "laboratories of democracy" American states purported to be, Delaware's transformation meant that American states had started to become, as scholar Bryce Tuttle noted, "laboratories of secrecy."[27]

*   *   *

VIKTOR BOUT WAS one of the leading members of the long list of international crime lords who raced to Delaware, building out his operations with the anonymity the state could provide. A scrawny, Tajik-born Russian national with a bushy mustache the size of a clipped cigar, Bout had built an arms-trafficking empire amidst the collapse of the Soviet Union. (For a taste of Bout's murderous exploits, check out Nicolas Cage's title character in the 2005 film *Lord of War*, which was based on Bout.[28])

Tracing clients and partners from Central America to Central Asia, from warlords in sub–Saharan Africa to proxies working closely with the Taliban, Bout shadowed almost all of the major illicit arms transfers through the 1990s and early 2000s. Fighter jets and antiaircraft weapons, machine guns and machetes: the products didn't matter. All that mattered was moving merchandise to waiting clients—and making sure that those investigating him, including American officials, never uncovered the financial networks that facilitated Bout's arms-trafficking work.

Bout, nicknamed the "Merchant of Death," was eventually picked up in Thailand in 2008, and remains housed in a supermax prison in Illinois—but not before splattering nation after nation with bullets and blood.[29] And as later court documents made clear, much of the butchery left in Bout's wake tracked directly back to anonymous shell companies, including two based in Delaware, right under the noses of American officials who spent years trying to track him down.[30]

But Bout was hardly the only globe-trotting criminal to turn to Delaware. Jack Abramoff, maybe the most notorious lobbyist this side of Paul Manafort, oversaw a sham Delaware company to manage millions in illicit, off-the-books payments between congressional officials and criminal networks elsewhere.[31] Timothy Durham, nicknamed the "Midwest Madoff"[32] for conning thousands of elderly investors out of hundreds of millions of dollars, centered his operations in Delaware, as did Stanko Subotic, a Serbian national sentenced to years in prison for his role overseeing international smuggling rings.[33] A Romanian accountant named Laszlo Kiss—who once wrote a book (accurately) describing the U.S. as a tax haven—apparently got a bit too familiar with his research and allegedly used a series of Delaware shell companies to help hide millions and millions of dollars.[34]

The examples are too numerous to count. International criminals and crooked foreign officials, gun smugglers and rhino poachers, human traffickers and inside traders—all of them look to Delaware. And these are just the examples we know about. As one lawyer said in 2017, "It's not entirely beyond the realms of possibility that ISIS could be operating companies . . . domiciled in Delaware."[35]

All of which points to one clear, inescapable conclusion: Delaware's role as the most corporate-friendly state in the union—and the greatest font of anonymous shell companies the world has ever seen—has extracted blood from corporate stones. Much of this has been, as we saw above, a direct outgrowth of reforms a century prior—and in that sense, was never predicated on necessarily transforming Delaware into an offshore haven, or in creating the tools that kleptocrats and others would eventually need. But by the time postcolonial and post-Soviet regimes started opening up, the state's offshoring infrastructure—its corporate regulatory regime, the Chancery Court, and the like—were already in place. Figures like S. B. Woo didn't transform Delaware into this offshoring mecca on their own. Instead, officials in the state were perfectly happy to share a range of offshoring and anonymous services that were already in place, regardless of who ended up taking advantage.

And there's little evidence that Delaware ever cared much about who was taking advantage, anyway. As one of its official websites states, "Delaware is not a secrecy haven, any more than any other state or the United States itself"—which is telling, given that, as the thrust of this book argues, the United States itself *is* a secrecy haven.[36] And the claim would be laughable if the state's anonymous shell corporations hadn't been linked directly to the deaths of hundreds of thousands, the swindling of billions of dollars, and the looting of entire nations. Nor does it change the fact that, as the Tax Justice Network recently wrote, Delaware "is the biggest single source of anonymous corporations in the world."[37]

But just as Delaware once knocked New Jersey from its perch, other states watching Delaware rake in billions in corporate fees in recent years have begun putting forth their own financial secrecy reforms. These other states want to attract some of the capital—clean, dirty, it doesn't matter—that Delaware had sponged up. And while they haven't stolen Delaware's crown, they've begun carving out empires of financial anonymity of their own.

* * *

FERNLEY, NEVADA, LIES an hour east of Reno along a stretch of barren desert. The town, a planned community with a population of 20,000, is decades past its prime, with one publication recently describing it as little more than a "truck stop town."[38]

It does, though, have one claim to international notoriety. Fernley is the home of a company service provider called Nevada Business Incorporated (NBI). Run by Robert Harris—who oversees the business from his beige bungalow, complete with a "No-Spin Zone" Fox News doormat greeting visitors—NBI is one of the few companies in this space that has opened its doors to journalists and researchers, offering a peek into why foreign despots and human traffickers look to the U.S. And why, specifically, they would come to a state like Nevada.

Sitting in his living-room-turned-office, Harris, slightly balding and with the kind of wan skin you get from sitting at a computer all day, unspools a tale of why he now sells anonymous shell companies. He used to work as a bartender, he says, helping lubricate all those prospecting for gambling gold. As the years went on and he started getting a bit older, he noticed that club and casino owners kept replacing his coworkers with younger, female employees. He got the message, he says.

In 2001, at the age of 50, he left the hospitality business. A friend suggested he explore the nascent world of company service providers—becoming someone who helps set up anonymous shell companies for whoever comes calling.

Nearly 20 years later, Harris estimates that he's set up thousands of companies. It's not like it's a lavish living, he says, revealing that he only makes mid-five figures annually. He supplements his income by selling books on what he describes as "Bible Prophecy," with one of his books featuring a cover image of Jesus—wearing a Zorro mask, for some reason—juggling a half-dozen glowing balls.

When asked what his day consists of, Harris talks about rote tasks. He answers the phone or responds to his emails, and he explains to potential clients the details of what an anonymous shell company entails, and what it will require of those on the other end of the phone or the email chain. If they're game, Harris tells me, he can set up an anonymous shell company for them in as little as an hour—theirs to do with what they wish.

When it comes to the identities of his clients, Harris doesn't pry. If they tell him their names and sources of income, that's fine. But if they don't, well, there's no reason for him to ask. He doesn't need to know—and the less they tell him, the less information he'll have to hide if anyone comes looking. "There's no pressure to identify any beneficial owners" behind the anonymous shell companies he sets up, Harris tells me. "There are no worries. There's no pressure."[39]

When I ask about what would happen if, say, someone steering an organized crime syndicate called him up and asked him to set up an anonymous shell company on their behalf, Harris coughs and leans back in his chair. "Not everybody in Nevada is a crook, or is looking to hide money," he says.[40]

That is true; there's no allegation that any work Harris has done has been illegal, or that Harris has done anything that will land him or any of his clients in prison. Everything that Harris has done has been permissible, in the eyes of both the state of Nevada and the federal government. And it's that rhetoric—that the majority of the clients are perfectly fine, perfectly legitimate—that has been a staple of those opposed to counter-kleptocracy reforms for years. These small-time company services providers, or the bankers and realtors and hedge fund providers we'll meet throughout this book, claim time and again that their industry, or their clients, are all aboveboard, legitimate customers, looking simply to take advantage of America's capitalistic services. Maybe there are a few bad apples that slip through, but should we upset the entire cart trying to track them down? Should we upend entire American industries—hell, the entire edifice of American capitalism—trying to make sure there's no dirty money slipping through the cracks of the American economy?

Harris, then, is hardly an outlier. If anything, Harris's NBI is a microcosm of a trend a few decades in the making—a transformation that hasn't gained as many headlines as Delaware, but one that's been just as disastrous for the rest of us.

*   *   *

NEVADA HAS LONG been associated with all kinds of experiments in modern capitalism, from gambling to prostitution to the bizarre electric amoeba that is Las Vegas.[41] As such, Nevada's transformation into a massive offshore haven in its own right fits, like Delaware's, firmly within the state's historical trajectory.

Still, Nevada's transformation had to start somewhere. For that, you have to go back a few decades. In the early 1990s, Nevada faced a budget shortfall. Legislators in Carson City got a whiff of what Delaware was shopping around, and wanted a slice of the action. Because company formation remained firmly in state hands, Nevada's state government began rolling back related regulations. It was, as we've seen, a move that U.S. states had tried, time and again.

But for Nevada, that budget shortfall kept expanding. By the turn of the century, even with those earlier regulatory rollbacks, the state was still staring at a $130 million hole.[42] And in a state that already lacked personal or corporate income taxes—and that required a two-thirds supermajority to approve any future tax increases—there were only so many roads to revenue generation. As such, officials hit on an idea. Delaware had been an unchallenged capital of financial secrecy for decades. But why couldn't Nevada try to steal the crown? Why not transform Nevada, as the legislators began saying, into the "Delaware of the West"?[43]

"The impetus [in 1991] was income," the University of Nevada, Las Vegas's Eric Franklin, who's studied Nevada's descent into a global financial secrecy haven, told me. "There's a lot of literature on the 'race to the bottom' in terms of corporate laws, and by saying 'Delaware of the

West,' the code is 'business friendly'—as business friendly as possible."[44] Repealing the few remaining regulations on corporate formation— including any requirements that might force those behind the anonymous shell companies to reveal themselves—Nevada legislators aimed to open the state to a raft of new money and clients looking for financial anonymity. State legislators, including future Nevada senator Dean Heller, proposed a motion to allow complete anonymity in shell company formation as part of an "educational enhancement package," directing proposed revenue from new anonymous shell company formation to pay for Nevada teachers' salaries.[45] "There was really no other option," one person familiar with the motion—who, ironically enough, asked to remain anonymous—told me.[46]

The motion passed nearly unanimously. All restrictions on who could form a company in the state, and what kind of identifying information they needed to provide, were eliminated. It was suddenly easier to get an anonymous shell company in Nevada than it was to get a library card. On the budgetary side, the move was a godsend. Two decades later, the revenue from the anonymity has turned into a flood, generating over $100 million for the state annually. "It's one of the top revenue generators we have in our state," Franklin told me.[47] (It was a genius move, really, with the revenue now going toward funding Nevada's teachers. Who could be against that?) Soon, Nevada was raking in millions of dollars in untraceable money, registering tens of thousands of brand-new companies, without any requirements to identify who was behind them. "My Labrador Jack, if he were a natural person, could be a [company service provider]," one Nevada official said, "because he has a Nevada address and is capable of fetching the paper."[48]

There was never any explicit chatter in Nevada about how the reforms would attract all kinds of suspect and dirty money looking to be laundered. But it wasn't hard to imagine who would soon be taking advantage. "What a terrible message we are now sending to the business world," said Dina Titus, now a member of Congress. "We might as well hang out a shingle: 'Sleazeballs and rip-off artists welcome here.'"[49] Thanks to Nevada's self-propelled transformation into an offshore haven, one academic said, "Nevada has all but hung up a 'no law' for-sale sign." Or as Titus added, "Nevada has sold its soul."[50]

* * *

THE WEBSITE FOR Robert Harris's company, NBI, is a case study in how those regulatory rollbacks have taken root. For as low as $249, Harris offers an anonymous shell company to any and all: to Colombian drug smugglers, to Vietnamese human-trafficking rings, to post-Soviet oligarchs trying to interfere in American politics. For a bit more money, you can splurge on Harris's "Presidential Package," which adds an official company seal, and even a new bank account. Harris also sells what he describes as "Nominee or Privacy Services to eliminate your name completely from [the] public record." (As Harris's website adds, NBI's "business principles are derived from faith in Christ."[51])

One of Harris's main competitors in Nevada is a company service provider called Incorporate123. "We began in 2000 by offering traditional Nevada incorporation services," Incorporate123's website reads, noting that they "quickly realized that our clients would benefit from services and procedures that were traditionally offered only by 'offshore' service providers." Incorporate123's specialty is peddling "shelf companies": shell companies created years ago sitting unused on a digital "shelf," offering a patina of legitimacy simply because they're not brand-new.[52]

Even more than Harris, Incorporate123 trumpets anonymity at every turn. As the splash quote on Incorporate123's main page reads, "Control everything, own nothing."[53] Scrolling down a bit, the site, broken English and all, details its ethos of anonymity:

Since 9/11 and the introduction of the U.S.A. Patriot Act, and under the guise of Anti-Money laundering, Governments and Big Corporations have continually demonstrated an ever increasing disregard for your personal and business PRIVACY. Most Nevada [company] service providers have simply "rolled over" and "shared" their clients' private information upon receiving a simple (and often times not even legal) "request" from any Government Agency or powerful Corporation. Our conscience would not allow us to "roll over", so we "internationalized" our services in order to give you the privacy that you still deserve.[54]

It's unclear what Incorporate123 means when it claims it "internationalized" its services. But a 2016 piece in *USA Today* offers a hint. The paper identified David Batrick as Incorporate123's head—but quickly discovered that Batrick wasn't even based in Nevada. When contacted, Batrick "declined to disclose his country of residence or citizenship, but said it was not . . . the United States."[55]

That is to say, one of Nevada's major company service providers doesn't even appear to be a citizen of Nevada, or of the United States. Or put another way: a non-American appears to be running a massive, sprawling operation setting up anonymous American shell companies for anonymous clients, without any idea who the clients actually are, or where they're from, or whether any of their financing is tied to human rights violations or the most brutal regimes the world has ever known.

* * *

IN EARLY 2016, thousands of leaked internal documents from the Panamanian law firm Mossack Fonseca spilled into the open. Known as the Panama Papers, the leak revealed the details—names, dates, amounts of money—tied to myriad figures around the world who'd turned to the Panamanian firm for help hiding, and in some cases laundering, their money. The names revealed in the leak included prominent politicians from all regions of the world, including British prime minister David Cameron, Azerbaijan's despotic leader Ilham Aliyev, and even those hiding money on behalf of Russian dictator Vladimir Putin.[56] The fallout from the revelations was swift. Not only did it prompt Panama to begin cleaning up its own offshoring services industry—the country, like many of its Caribbean neighbors, had served as an offshore jurisdiction for years—but it also helped topple governments from Iceland to Pakistan.[57]

The Panama Papers were, and still are, an unprecedented peek behind the offshore curtain. And while much of it centered on Panama's offshoring services, the Panama Papers also provided some insight into who has been taking full advantage of Nevada's sprint toward financial anonymity. One of the things authorities and researchers learned from the reams of documents: those behind Mossack Fonseca, a firm specializing in the secrecy and sorcery of the offshore world, couldn't get enough of Nevada.[58]

According to the leaked documents, accountants at Mossack Fonseca had personally helped set up over a thousand anonymous shell companies in Nevada for their clients. And it wasn't difficult to see why they sent their clients to the state; as one of the leaked documents, pitching Nevada as a potential anonymous home, read, "non-U.S. Persons remain confidential and do not, simply by virtue of owning an interest in a U.S. entity, have to file or disclose [their identity]."[59]

More simply: Mossack Fonseca specifically pitched Nevada to its global clientele because of the state's anonymity—for the fact that no one would ever know who secretly steered the anonymous Nevada shell companies in question. As Mossack Fonseca added, anonymous incorporation in Nevada, "where virtually no Due Diligence is required," was "thriving."[60]

As the secrets of those Nevada companies tumbled out for all to see, it was clear that Nevada had transformed into that den of "sleazeballs and rip-off artists" legislators had feared. "The corporate records of 1,000-plus Nevada business entities linked to [Mossack Fonseca] reveal layers of secretive ownership, with few having humans' names behind them, and most tracing back to a tiny number of overseas addresses from Bangkok high rises to post offices on tiny island nations," one examination found.[61]

The clients Mossack Fonseca funneled to Nevada spanned the globe. One company listed in the leak, Cross Trading LLC, was allegedly at the center of a bribery scheme involving FIFA, the soccer world's major governing body. Another dozen of the companies tracked back to a family of Thai oligarchs, the Chirathivat clan, billionaire investors in Thai real estate and developments.[62] Some of the companies were even embroiled in the unfurling oil-and-bribes embezzlement scandal then rocking Brazilian politics—a scandal that would eventually discredit Brazil's entire ruling class and give rise to the far-right presidency of Jair Bolsonaro.[63]

* * *

THE DOCUMENTS ALSO pulled the curtain back on the lengths to which Mossack Fonseca went to keep its Nevada-based business open—and just how important Nevada was to these global money laundering operations, as one case in particular illustrated.

In the early 2010s, billionaire hedge fund manager Paul Singer tried to recoup some $1.7 billion in Argentinean bonds his fund had purchased. Turning down Buenos Aires' offers at restructuring the debt, Singer instead began tracking down Argentinean assets elsewhere, hoping to seize them and use them as leverage in negotiations. Shortly after Singer's efforts got underway, an Argentinean prosecutor revealed that Lazaro Baez, a millionaire businessman close to former Argentine president Nestor Kirchner, was one of the beneficiaries of a multimillion-dollar embezzlement scheme that used hundreds of anonymous shell companies based in Nevada.[64] They all happened to share the same Nevada address as M.F. Corporate Services—a none-too-subtle nod to Mossack Fonseca, which was then setting up hundreds of similar anonymous shell companies throughout the state. Maybe, Singer thought, there was a way to pry into these companies to identify some of the assets secretly held by Argentinian officials.

As journalist Jake Bernstein detailed, Singer's lawyer sat for a seven-hour deposition in 2014 with Patricia Amunategui, the woman helping run M.F. Corporate Services. Amunategui spent the entire interview denying that she worked for Mossack Fonseca. Instead, she claimed Mossack Fonseca had nothing to do with M.F. Corporate Services, or with any of the hundred-plus companies suddenly tied to the embezzling scheme swirling around Argentina's former president. Remarkably, Jürgen Mossack—the company's namesake—backed her up, saying that Mossack Fonseca and M.F. Corporate Services were entirely separate entities.[65] For Singer, it was a dead end; that cloak of anonymity had stalled his efforts, forcing him to move on. But not long after, the Panama Papers revealed that the two companies were, as Singer suspected, one and the same—and that they had helped Argentina's corrupt elite use Nevada to stash and launder their embezzled loot.[66]

The leak also revealed the lengths to which Mossack Fonseca went just to keep its Nevada pipeline open. Mossack Fonseca's IT manager wrote in one of the leaked documents that he'd called Amunategui shortly after her deposition, "discussing ways to build more distance between the two offices," Bernstein recounted. Mossack Fonseca promptly began separating Amunategui's computer system from Mossack Fonseca's overall operations, and proceeded to scrape logs from Amunategui's computer wholesale—all to make sure the links between Mossack Fonseca and Nevada were "obscure to the investigators," as the IT manager wrote. It even flew another of its employees to Nevada directly, where he "cleaned up everything and brought all documents to Panama."[67]

For a while, those efforts worked. Mossack Fonseca's Nevada pipeline lived on, with no one, from officials in Washington to individuals like Singer, any the wiser. But then, in early 2016, the Panama Papers exploded into the world, and revealed all the sordid details of Mossack Fonseca's anonymous shell company operations. They offered granular details of the symbiotic relationship between Nevada and Mossack Fonseca and all of the autocrats and criminals they serviced.

And they also revealed a link to another state: one of the other main cogs in America's descent into an offshore mecca—and one that helped introduce the world to the most popular means of money laundering in the first place.

* * *

FRANK BURKE NEVER imagined that his primary legacy would lie in the art of offshoring. As a wildcat oil driller working across the Western Hemisphere in the 1970s, the last thing Burke was interested in, as those familiar with the man told me, was helping provide the world's crooked and corrupt with the perfect means of anonymity. He just wanted to drill, and to support his family, and to make sure he and his business were protected from potential suits and damages along the way—especially from the deep-pocketed oil and gas competitors driving Burke and his wildcatters into extinction.

Harried by the major energy companies trying to dominate as many markets as they could, Burke and his teams of drillers had an idea. They'd discovered a company structure in Panama called a *limitada*. It was deceptively simple: not only did it shield owners from corporate liability— limiting damages in potential lawsuits from any and all—but it qualified under Panamanian law for preferential tax benefits, which wildcatters like Burke were always on the lookout for to cut rising costs.[68]

At the time, there wasn't anything comparable in the U.S. To Burke, that didn't make sense. Why couldn't the U.S set up something that would limit liability like this? Why couldn't U.S. states let him set up some kind of "limited liability company"? With that thought, the modern LLC was born—the same LLC structure we see everywhere, across too many industries to name, often used for perfectly legitimate means. It's a structure that offers protections to proprietors, saving them from debilitating lawsuits, limiting their liability if their company goes sideways. But those protections don't extend just to legitimate entrepreneurs. As we'll see, they also protect the kinds of oligarchs and corrupt figures sniffing around for anonymity, and for even further protections for their dirty money.

But first, Burke had to convince legislators that the LLC was an idea that could work. In the mid-1970s, Burke returned to the U.S. to pitch his idea, looking for a state legislature he could easily lobby. Alaska, with the lowest population of any state, seemed promising. "Think about it: in Alaska and Wyoming, it's a whole lot easier to get to the legislators and go have coffee, or go hunt or whatever, than getting to New York or California and penetrating their legislature," Susan Hamill, a law professor at the University of Alabama who interviewed Burke before he died in 2010, told me.[69] But his idea eventually died in the Alaskan legislature, weighed down by partisan squabbles. Still, Burke didn't give up. Instead, he uprooted for Wyoming. And as Hamill said, "the Wyoming folks welcomed them with open arms."[70]

Burke took legislators out for coffee, took them hunting, and pitched them his plan for what he called a "limited liability company," or LLC for short. And the Wyoming legislators, in 1977, bit. It wasn't difficult for them to see the benefits. In a nod to the decades of corporate innovation U.S. states like Delaware had already seen, Wyoming legislators realized they could use these LLCs to entice new corporate clients to the state, potentially reaping millions in fees from the new companies that bloomed. And if they could bundle these LLC structures with the kind of anonymity more and more voices were demanding, all the better.[71]

To be sure, an LLC is an incredibly common corporate structure, and often used for perfectly legitimate means. Most small companies rely on LLC structures to facilitate their business, given not only how easy they are to set up but also, as Burke and others realized, because they help shield them from debilitating lawsuits that could have previously ruined those small operators. (Hence the "limited liability" in the name.) Just because you come across an LLC does not mean that that company is operating as an offshore vehicle, or is part of a broader money laundering enterprise.

But even while Burke and his wildcatters were happy, others soon realized that Burke's innovation could be used for something else entirely. All Burke had wanted was a means of protecting his business, and his few clients, and the few remaining wildcatters he worked with. Instead, he—with the help of the Wyoming legislature—gifted the world the perfect variant of the anonymous shell company.

"They weren't looking to facilitate the hiding of the true identity of real estate [owners], of moving wealth offshore to make it harder to tax," Hamill said.[72] But that's exactly what happened. These LLC company structures offer increased protections against things like lawsuits by distancing the owner from the company, one of the primary reasons LLCs tend to dominate the market when it comes to anonymous shell companies. (There's a reason our "Hiding Money LLC" anonymous American shell company from the previous chapter was an LLC.) If you're a kleptocrat interested in anonymous U.S. shell companies, you want the one that will offer the most protections from prying eyes, or from potential fallout. Enter the LLC.

In just a few years, as the following sections will detail, Burke's LLCs had taken on offshoring lives of their own. As Hamill said, if Burke saw what his LLC had since become, "Frank would roll over in his grave."[73]

*   *   *

WYOMING'S STORY IS, in many ways, the exact same one that played out in Delaware and Nevada. States looking for ways to increase revenue realized they could start offering offshore and financial anonymity services—and that there was a clear market available for such services. Wyoming state legislators and company service providers began pitching Wyoming as the state that "invented the LLC," and thousands of anonymous shell companies and millions of dollars in revenue soon followed. Wyoming, like Delaware and Nevada, realized it had struck corporate gold.[74] And Wyoming, also like Delaware and Nevada, only became more and more enraptured with this new revenue stream, and more and more reliant on the fees raked in from setting up these anonymous shell companies—no matter who was behind them.

To be sure, there are a few quirks in Wyoming that set it apart. The state doesn't have a corporate income tax—yet another corporate draw—and it allows all company records to be kept outside the state, and even out of the country. (What better way to assure anonymity than by keeping your Wyoming corporate records in, say, Turkmenistan?) These were all part of the state's "secrecy perks," one investigator said.[75]

And those "secrecy perks" clearly worked. (As one company service provider in Wyoming said, "Anybody can say they are anybody."[76]) In the four decades since Burke's idea took root, there are now tens of thousands of LLCs swamping the state—which means there's now about one business entity for every household in Wyoming, which remains America's smallest state in terms of population size.

Wyoming also boasts some of the cheapest anonymous shell company fees in the country, driving prices as low as $100 just to set one up. "I think the biggest reason we've been doing so well is because [setting up an anonymous shell company is] so cheap," Dan Zwonitzer, a state representative from Cheyenne, told me. "We make it a little more difficult than other states to search shareholders, so you can only search by the company's name. If you're just trying to find individuals, you can't search by an individual's name. You have to know the name of their company. And if they have a weird company name, you're never going to find them."

"We call it," Zwonitzer adds, "'business-friendly.'"[77]

* * *

AND ALL OF those developments began attracting serious flows of dirty money to the state in the mid-1990s.

Many of those funds came, unsurprisingly, from the shattered Soviet Union, which had fractured only a few years prior. One of those attracted to the state was Pavlo Lazarenko, whose corruption placed Wyoming on the global kleptocratic map—and kick-started a flow of dirty post-Soviet money that people like Ihor Kolomoisky, whom we met in the prologue, would soon take full advantage of.

Lazarenko—jowly, often seen wearing ill-fitting suits—served as Ukraine's prime minister for a few years in the mid-1990s. Like many of that initial post-Soviet generation, he was more interested in dipping into state coffers, extending his links of corrupt networks, and entrenching his own power bases through whatever crooked means he could.

During his time as prime minister, Lazarenko skimmed significant proceeds from Ukraine's gas transit, capitalizing on Ukraine's role as a middleman between Russia and the European Union. (It's an easy scheme to pull off, as we'll see later on.) By all appearances, Lazarenko was wildly successful when it came to swindling money that should have gone to Ukrainian citizens; according to Transparency International, Lazarenko pilfered and laundered hundreds of millions of dollars during his tenure—enough to place him among the twentieth century's greatest kleptocrats, sharing space with Indonesia's Suharto and the Democratic Republic of Congo's Mobutu Sese Seko.[78]

Lazarenko's graft, though, eventually caught up with him. Ousted in 1997 and facing corruption charges at home, Lazarenko attempted to hide out in the U.S., waiting for the furor over his fraud to die down. But American authorities didn't go along, and soon filed money laundering charges of their own against Lazarenko. Held in California, Lazarenko was sentenced by an American court in 2009 to eight years in prison, alongside a forfeiture order totaling $30 million.[79]

According to the U.S. Attorney's Office, Lazarenko's sentence "should send a strong message to corrupt foreign public officials: They will be held accountable if they misuse their office and try to make safe harbor in the United States."[80] (It turns out that message fell on deaf ears, as Obiang and Kolomoisky and the entire past decade have illustrated.)

Lazarenko's conviction was welcome news in Washington and in Kyiv, but it revealed a parallel reality that those "corrupt foreign public officials" had long known. As court documents revealed, Lazarenko had funneled and laundered tens of millions of dollars in the heart of the U.S.—right in a small brick home in residential Cheyenne, Wyoming.[81]

This nondescript house, nestled in a sleepy part of a sleepy town, was actually home to thousands of anonymous shell companies. "[The] walls of the main room are covered floor to ceiling with numbered mailboxes labeled as corporate 'suites,'" Reuters found in 2011. It was, they added, "a little Cayman Island on the Great Plains."[82] The house—set between a church and a barber shop, as I found when I later visited—held Wyoming Corporate Services, one of Wyoming's leading company service providers.[83] As with others in Nevada and Delaware, Wyoming Corporate Services pledged to protect the anonymity of all. "A corporation is a legal person created by state statute that can be used as a fall guy, a servant, a good friend or a decoy. A person you control . . . yet cannot be held accountable for its actions," Wyoming Corporate Services wrote on its website.[84]

(The language wasn't as jarring as another Wyoming company service provider, whose website screamed that "YOUR NAME IS ON NOTHING!"[85] and that they could provide "complete companies by TOMORROW MORNING!"[86] It's unclear why they felt the need to shout at readers and potential customers.)

The man behind Wyoming Corporate Services was a local named Gerald Pitts. Pitts later told reporters that he fully recognized that the LLCs his company set up "may be used for both good and ill," which was at least more than most company service providers would admit.[87] But Pitts apparently didn't care, revealing that he would go so far as to set up bank accounts for his anonymous clients, and would sometimes even add lawyers as company directors for his clients in order to provide a layer of attorney-client privilege that no investigator could ever crack.

All of these schemes, Pitts insisted, were perfectly legal. And in that sense, he was perfectly right: everything Pitts did for Lazarenko was legally aboveboard and, in the eyes of both Wyoming and the U.S., completely permissible. But that's little comfort to the millions of Ukrainians who watched Lazarenko bleed their state dry, swiping hundreds of millions of dollars that could have gone toward things like schools or first responders or, as Ukraine would learn in 2014, a desiccated military that Russian forces steamrolled on their way to the annexation of Crimea—and to everything that has come since.

*   *   *

THAT, THOUGH, WAS all in the future. While Lazarenko stood in court, and the details of his Wyoming exploits spilled out, Mossack Fonseca—just as it did with Nevada—was simultaneously directing clients to the state, telling them that Wyoming provided "robust protections for the assets" with "no state taxes levied on offshore and banking transactions."[88]

Wyoming wasn't quite as popular with Mossack Fonseca's clientele as Nevada, with only a few hundred of the state's shells linked to the Panamanian firm. But when the 2016 Panama Papers leaked, the revelations appeared to rattle Wyoming officials even more than their counterparts in Nevada. Shortly after the Panama Papers first flooded out, officials in Cheyenne announced a formal audit of Mossack Fonseca's official Wyoming subsidiary, M.F. Corporate Services Wyoming.[89] That company was itself managed by another company service provider, named AAA Corporate Services, whose office sits in the heart of Cheyenne's spare downtown—one of a dozen different offices for corporate service providers, which continue to spread like a fungus throughout the entire city.[90]

The state's audit found that M.F. Corporate Services Wyoming had "failed to maintain the required statutory information" for a company service provider.[91] As such, the state announced it was shuttering M.F. Corporate Services Wyoming. The move appeared to be the start of

Wyoming finally—finally—cracking down on the anonymity coursing through the state.

But then, nothing else happened. In fact, state officials promptly went back to writing legislation to help shore up all the anonymous protections.

In a stunning statement, Ed Murray, Wyoming's secretary of state, claimed that Wyoming "will not compromise the privacy of our customers."[92] Astoundingly, Murray didn't offer to consider changes to Wyoming's corporate oversight structures, or even to study the issue. Rather, Murray announced that any calls to increase transparency in Wyoming would be completely ignored. Where other American officials paid lip service to transparency and reform, Murray didn't even bother with those niceties—and instead fell back on the deregulatory, "pro-business" ethos that had propelled so many of these kleptocratic developments.

"The release of the 'Panama Papers' has led to some renewed calls for transparency and the revealing of beneficial ownership information for entities registered not just in Wyoming, but across the United States," Murray said. "Such a move would increase red tape and limit business formation and innovation in Wyoming." Murray concluded, in a statement entirely at odds with reality, that "Wyoming, alongside Delaware and Nevada, has been the most proactive in directly confronting those same concerns related to improper use of shell companies."[93] No mention of the oligarchs racing to the state, or findings from researchers about how wide open the state remained to anyone with even a modicum of dirty money.

Even after the biggest offshore bombshell the world had ever seen, officials in these states had flipped the findings on their head. Rather than reform, they lied as baldly and broadly as they could, and pledged to change absolutely nothing. Anonymous American shell companies, those building blocks of modern kleptocracy, would continue on, as ever. They could continue providing anonymity to any oligarch or regime insider or cartel head or human slaver who wanted it, allowing them to open bank accounts and purchase billions in assets or bankroll political campaigns with funds that could never be traced back to them, let alone returned to the victims they continued to immiserate.

And it wouldn't take long for others out of Ukraine to imitate Laza-renko's model—and to show just how easy it would be to trace the rot of America's kleptocratic transformation directly to the implosion of small towns across the American Midwest, directly to the gutting of major American metropolises, and directly into the White House itself.

NECK-DEEP

"The collapse of the Communist superpower, the Soviet Union, is the single most important event prompting the exponential growth of organized crime round the world. . . . This [post-Soviet] process of enrichment was quite simply the grandest larceny in history."

—Misha Glenny[1]

Ihor Kolomoisky, the Ukrainian billionaire we met in the introduction, doesn't initially strike those who see him as a rapacious oligarch at the center of a transnational money laundering scheme. With shaggy hair and a swelling belly, a cherubic face and a cheery smile, Kolomoisky often looks like a friendly uncle just having a laugh. It's an image that Kolomoisky has no problem cultivating in public. As he tells people, his nickname, "Benya," comes directly from a cuddly Soviet-era cartoon lion, one whose mane happened to resemble Kolomoisky's own.[2] He "tries to create an image that he's a kind grandpa, this kind, funny old man," Daria Kalenyuk, one of Ukraine's leading anticorruption advocates, tells me.[3]

But Kolomoisky is hardly a genial uncle spinning jokes for friends and family. In reality, Kalenyuk continues, "he's a mobster," an "evil person" tied to alleged contract killings and armed militias and jaw-dropping larceny.[4] Anyone familiar with his operations will attest to as much. So will investigators in both Ukraine and the U.S., who revealed that he laundered hundreds of millions of pilfered dollars throughout the U.S., allegedly leading one of the largest money laundering schemes the world had ever seen.[5]

Indeed, for those in his inner circle, Kolomoisky cultivates an image not of a happy-go-lucky raconteur but of something far darker, as those who've visited his office in the central Ukrainian city of Dnipro will reveal. While much of the office is itself typical of any other—with tables, chairs, and such—there's one unique addition: a five-meter-long shark tank. Most of the time, while entertaining guests, Kolomoisky ignores the tank. Sometimes, though, the guests ask for a bit too much, or come begging forgiveness for some slight. Maybe they'd shirked a recent bribe, forgetting to pay off the right official. Maybe they'd accidentally bad-mouthed a local official who looks to Kolomoisky for protection. Or maybe they'd just overstepped some invisible boundary, without even realizing it.

In those cases, according to those who've visited, Kolomoisky hears his visitors out. And then he stands, and walks over to the shark tank. With the push of a button, the oligarch releases crabmeat into the mammoth tank, or sometimes takes a bucketful of waiting shrimp and dumps it directly into the water. The sharks will swarm the food, shredding it in front of the perturbed visitors. It is, to be sure, all slightly ridiculous, a parody of something you'd see in a cheesy action flick. "He is a fantastic and picaresque character who by comparison puts about half the villains in James Bond films to shame with his antics," as one Ukrainian political analyst described him.[6]

But it's Kolomoisky's preferred method of getting a point across. And it's not only a method that allowed Kolomoisky to allegedly launch the greatest money laundering operation in American history—but one that led him directly to the ears of those close to an American president who didn't seem to mind that corruption one bit.

*　*　*

KOLOMOISKY WAS BORN in Soviet Ukraine in 1963, the child of engineer parents. Raised in the industrial town of Dnipropetrovsk (since renamed to Dnipro), Kolomoisky enjoyed a fairly typical Soviet childhood, reared with an emphasis on math and hard sciences. In time, he enrolled in the local metallurgical institute, learning the science of making and molding metals and alloys, and earning a degree in metallurgical engineering.[7]

By the time he graduated, though, the Soviet Union of his youth was barreling toward a crack-up. Economic stagnation and a flailing war in Afghanistan melted into restive nationalism that the Soviet Union had never quite been able to quell. In the late 1980s, instead of launching a career as a Soviet metal-man, Kolomoisky watched a world he thought he knew begin to shift and collapse under his feet. As economic restrictions relaxed by the turn of the 1990s, part of Mikhail Gorbachev's doomed attempts at Soviet restructuring, Kolomoisky took full advantage of the new capitalistic opportunities. Alongside a pair of friends, Gennadiy Bogolyubov and Oleksiy Martynov, he launched an office equipment firm, shuttling between Moscow and Dnipropetrovsk and searching out new customers across the country.[8]

But that country hardly lasted much longer. Thanks in large part to nationalist agitation out of Ukraine, the Soviet Union soon splintered into fifteen separate republics, relegated, to steal a Bolshevik phrase from decades previous, to the ash heap of history.

Kolomoisky, by all appearances, navigated the new tides rushing through the post-Soviet space as nimbly as anyone. Living in central Ukraine, he avoided the post-Soviet bloodshed that rocked parts of neighboring Moldova and Russia. He soon spied economic opportunities that would have been unthinkable just a few years earlier. With the new government in Kyiv effectively broke, independent Ukrainians were starved for sources of cash. Filling the void, Kolomoisky and his partners launched something that Soviet authorities never would have allowed: a private bank, which they called (straightforwardly enough) PrivatBank. There was nothing special about the bank, per se; it's not as if Kolomoisky had hit on a new means of small-scale lending. But timing was everything. Kolomoisky and the bank immediately found a niche, propping up local enterprises and quickly swelling its consumer base through Dnipropetrovsk.[9]

The government, though, continued to flail, its finances faltering further. So it did what other new, floundering post-Soviet states did: it launched a large-scale privatization scheme to try to stanch some of the fiscal bleeding. The program was relatively straightforward. The new Ukrainian government provided vouchers to all Ukrainian citizens, with each voucher representing small-scale ownership of previously state-owned enterprises like steel mills and gas fields. (Imagine if the U.S. government gave every American a slip of paper representing a small bit of ownership over, say, the national park system, and you'd get something similar.) The government then allowed those holding these vouchers—shares, effectively, in assets the government had previously controlled—to trade, to swap, to sell them as they saw fit. If every citizen had a stake in the economic success of what had up to that point been state-owned factories, pipelines, mines, and oil fields, what could go wrong?[10]

This was the exact tactic Russia tried around the same time, but to disastrous results. Russia's voucher program, launched in the 1990s, allowed all Russian citizens the same opportunity to trade or sell their vouchers. Given that many Russians remained effectively destitute in the 1990s, many of the voucher sales or trades went for basic necessities, such as food or water (or alcohol). A handful of individuals spied an opportunity. Vacuuming up as many vouchers as they could, these figures grabbed significant shares of what had previously been Soviet-controlled assets: industrial crown jewels that could, with the right management, turn into significant profit-generating enterprises. These men came to be known as "oligarchs"—those industrial magnates, former KGB officials, and new businessmen who grew ludicrously wealthy by consolidating ownership over all of these assets.[11] Toward the end of the 1990s, these rising Russian oligarchs helped install Russian president Vladimir Putin in power—assuming, incorrectly, that they could control the new president and continue to grow insanely wealthy in the process.[12]

While Ukraine never saw its own Putin rise to power, Kyiv's voucher scheme had the exact same result when it came to the creation of an oligarchic class that would soon dominate the country's economic and political space. Some of these new Ukrainian oligarchs cornered the country's coal market, steering exports from the country's fertile coal basins. Some of them gained control of the country's gas exports, capitalizing on Ukraine's position as a transit country between Russian hydrocarbon producers and European customers. And some looked enviously at Ukraine's swath of state-owned factories, and how someone with a metallurgic background—like Kolomoisky, for instance—could turn them into massively profitable enterprises.[13]

Buoyed by his profits from PrivatBank, Kolomoisky soon collected as many vouchers as he could, and quickly gained control of many of Ukraine's most prominent mills. The oligarch would later say that he leaned on his own industrial background in picking out which plants to add to his portfolio, which is almost certainly true. But Kolomoisky also gained a reputation as a key practitioner of *reiderstvo*, or "raiding," which saw him resort to gangsterish tactics to swipe those factories he couldn't land with his vouchers—often through force.[14]

Indeed, his penchant for theatrics made him stand apart from other Ukrainian oligarchs. For instance, he once lined the lobby of a Russian oil company he wanted to push out with a series of coffins. (Coffins being easier to transport and install than shark tanks, apparently.) In another instance, as *Forbes* reported, "hundreds of hired rowdies armed with baseball bats, iron bars, gas and rubber bullet pistols and chainsaws forcibly took over" a steel plant that Kolomoisky reportedly eyed.[15] As Kolomoisky later admitted to a *Forbes* reporter, "Give me a 1 percent stake and I will take over the entire company."[16] Along the way, as Ukrainian journalists would report, Kolomoisky and his network made a habit of paying off local judges and magistrates, who would provide legal cover for such rapacious tactics. Given the clear malfeasance associated with his actions, such tactics were the major reason that Kolomoisky's wealth, as with so many other post-Soviet oligarchs, is widely viewed as dirty, ill-gotten, and entirely tainted.

By the turn of the century, Kolomoisky was firmly ensconced as one of Ukraine's leading steel magnates. But he and his partners had begun extending their financial empire beyond just their metallurgical holdings. Privat Group, a conglomerate Kolomoisky and his partners founded, soon bought ownership stakes in oil fields and natural gas wells across the country. Given Ukraine's central location in European gas transit, entering the hydrocarbon markets made clear sense. But that wasn't Kolomoisky's only expansion. Shortly thereafter, the oligarch also entered Ukraine's punchy media landscape, which eventually transformed into his outright ownership and control of Ukraine's leading 1+1 television outlet.[17]

While Kolomoisky consolidated energy and media holdings, Privat-Bank kept expanding. In time, PrivatBank gained nearly 40 percent of the country's retail deposits, and some 20 percent of the country's total banking assets—thanks in large part to to Kolomoisky's leadership.[18] Banking, energy, metals, media: buoyed by his myriad holdings, Kolomoisky was, on paper, a clear Ukrainian success story. But by the mid-2000s, Kolomoisky had much bigger ambitions. As the *Kyiv Post* wrote, he wanted to "corner the global ferroalloy market"—to become not just the metals king of Ukraine, but the leading steel provider across multiple countries and multiple continents.[19] In other words, a global steel baron. In 2008, Kolomoisky steered Privat Group's purchase of one of the world's largest manganese operations, subsequently gaining control of the extraction of manganese ore in places like Australia and Ghana.[20] (Manganese is a mineral that, as the U.S. Geological Survey says, "turns iron into steel [and does so much more].")[21] Around the same time, Kolomoisky grabbed a controlling stake in manganese production in the post-Soviet state of Georgia. With these and a few other moves, Kolomoisky had in just a few short years come to control nearly half of the global manganese trade.

But there was one market Kolomoisky still eyed: America. However, to take full advantage of America's anonymity—to take full advantage of America's rapid transformation into the offshore nirvana he'd begun hearing so much about—he'd need help. He'd need partners who could assist him in navigating the best places and tools to use in the U.S. And he already had some potential candidates in mind.

*   *   *

IN THE 1990s, Kolomoisky had crossed paths with an American named Mordechai Korf, known by his friends as "Motti." The circumstances of their initial meeting in Ukraine remain unclear—and in many ways their paths couldn't have been more different.

The balding, bespectacled Korf enjoyed something of a traditional American upbringing.[22] Raised in a deeply pious Jewish household, Korf grew up alongside his parents and eight siblings in Miami in the 1970s. His parents had previously moved from Brooklyn to South Florida at the behest of Orthodox rabbi Menachem Mendel Schneerson, one of the most renowned Jewish voices in the world at the time and the leader of Chabad, an international Hasidic movement. The shift from the brick and brownstones of Brooklyn to the sultry sprawl of Miami was, for the young family, a culture shock—and not just because of the warm winter weather. At the time, few Jewish families lived in South Florida, with kosher food so difficult to come by that Korf's father, who was also a rabbi, "slaughtered chickens himself and [his mother] salted and soaked them," wrote *Forward*.[23] Nor was there much to fall back on, either. As Korf's sister Leah Jacobson later said, the family "lived on a shoestring budget," with their father consistently emphasizing service over salary. "If those were my calculations, the money, I would never have gone [to Florida]," their father, Abraham, once said. "I didn't raise my children to make those calculations."[24]

Initially, Korf stood eager to follow in his father's footsteps. Rather than going into business after finishing rabbinical school, he announced that he'd enrolled in a humanitarian mission to a part of the world he'd never before visited: Ukraine. The mission combined the two things his father had instilled, bringing both service and sacrifice, all of it embedded with a Jewish faith and Jewish identity. And he apparently took to it: Korf stayed in Ukraine for three years, spending his time learning Russian, immersing himself in all things Ukrainian, and dabbling in small-scale commercial activity. (He traded everything, "ranging from light bulbs to hammers," he later recollected.)

At some point during those early 1990s travels in Ukraine, though, Korf's priorities appeared to shift. Business, in a short time, supplanted sacrifice. It's unclear what exactly prompted this shift, as Korf never responded to my questions or requests for an interview. But one figure crossed his path that, by all appearances, helped steer this new direction: Kolomoisky.

The two, in many ways, couldn't have been more disparate: one a young American, flitting between New York and Florida, exploring a transitioning Ukraine on a humanitarian mission; the other a Ukrainian oligarch-in-the-making, imperiling rivals and gobbling as much of Ukraine's nascent industry as he could. While the source of their first meeting remains a mystery, there was one clear area of overlap between the two, which Korf's father would likely have approved of. Like Korf, Kolomoisky was Jewish—and he happened to be deeply involved in Chabad, the organization Korf's entire family was closely associated with. Ukraine has boasted a substantial Jewish population for centuries, producing everyone from famous writer Ilya Ehrenburg to infamous Bolshevik Leon Trotsky. (In 2019, Ukraine elected only the second Jewish head of government in the world when it voted Volodymyr Zelensky—whom we'll revisit in the final section of the book—into office.)

In an ethnically heterogeneous state like Ukraine, Kolomoisky's Jewish background mattered little when it came to affairs of both business and state. But it opened new connections for him abroad—and allowed him to add to his sheen of public respectability, positioning himself as a pious observer of the faith. "Kolomoisky is deeply engaged in the Jewish communities," Daria Kalenyuk told me. "He portrays himself as a religious person who cares about his soul."[25] At one point in 2014, *Haaretz* wondered aloud if Kolomoisky was "the most powerful" Jewish person in the world.[26]

And he was also willing to back up those claims with financial investments, becoming the largest funder of Chabad operations in Dnipro, where Korf also worked—funding that hasn't gone unnoticed within the Chabad community in the U.S. "There are very close personal ties between Kolomoisky, Chabad, and certain *Chabadniks* in the U.S.," Zvi Gitelman, a professor emeritus at the University of Michigan, who's focused much of his work on the Jewish diaspora in the U.S., told me. "What the nature of those relations is I don't know."[27] And Korf couldn't have been more closely tied to the Chabad network; in addition to his father's leading role in the organization, at least three of Korf's siblings still work directly for the Chabad community.[28]

Whatever the terms of their first meeting, Korf and Kolomoisky quickly found common ground. After his three-year stint bouncing around Ukraine, Korf returned to South Florida. There, according to corporate records, Korf and a friend named Uri Laber, who also worked in Ukraine, founded an American company called Optima International in 1994—an umbrella entity that would, over the next twenty years or so, allegedly act as a springboard for Kolomoisky to open the spigot for his dirty money to spray directly into the U.S.[29]

* * *

It DIDN'T TAKE long for Korf to help Kolomoisky scout potential investments in the U.S. Given Kolomoisky's metallurgical background, America's steel belt was an obvious place to look. One steel mill in particular caught Kolomoisky's eye. Located in a slice of northeast Ohio known as "Steel Valley," the Warren Steel Mill sat only a fifteen-minute drive from Youngstown, squat between Pittsburgh and Cleveland. Built in the township of Warren, and sprawling hundreds of acres, the mill spent years churning out the steel bones of America's booming midcentury growth. The mill's success placed Warren on the American manufacturing map. "Warren had the first municipal streetlights, had a General Electric light bulb plant, had a Packard plant. . . . This was the Silicon Valley of its day," Ken MacPherson, a member of Warren's city council, told me.[30]

And the mill—just as those throughout the rest of the Steel Valley—provided economic lifelines to anyone who worked there. When the mill's blast furnace, which fired the mill's operations, would run early in the morning, it "would make plenty of noise, and the earth would shake a bit, and I'd wake up and smile, and then go back to sleep," MacPherson, who followed his father into the metallurgy business, remembered.[31]

By the mid-1970s, though, the mill had started to show its wear. Its blast furnace was no longer state of the art, and rust had started creeping in. With prices stagnating across the board—and with foreign operators, like those in China or Brazil, willing to resort to steel dumping, reducing the market for Warren's output even more—the mill changed hands multiple times. The final company charged with steering the mill, CSC Industries, tried to turn things around, reinvesting in repairs. But little changed. And soon thereafter, CSC filed for bankruptcy.[32]

As the bankruptcy proceedings rolled on, CSC began casting around for potential buyers. One company, Warren Steel Holdings LLC, expressed interest. Registered in Delaware in 2001, representatives from the new LLC broached a potential purchase from CSC.[33] The two sides agreed on a final number: $13.5 million for a complete transfer of ownership of the mill to the new LLC.[34] It's unclear how much CSC, or the city elders, knew at the time about this Delaware-registered company. But as court records would later make clear, Warren Steel Holdings LLC wasn't just another American outfit looking to pick up a competitor, trying to revitalize an aging, sagging construct whose best days were clearly behind it. Rather, Warren Steel Holdings LLC was part of the Optima International portfolio—which was connected to none other than Kolomoisky.[35]

Obtaining the Warren plant launched a spending spree: in a time when American steel manufacturing was in clear decline, Optima International began gobbling up as many American plants on offer as it could. There was a plant in the small town of New Haven, West Virginia, constructed in 1952, that Optima snapped up in early 2006 for $20 million.[36] There was a seamless steel tube factory in South Lyon, Michigan, founded in 1927, that Optima grabbed just a couple months later.[37] Not long thereafter, in the crease where Kentucky, West Virginia, and Ohio meet, Kolomoisky's network found a 450,000-square-foot steel mill in the town of Ashland, Kentucky, on the block, and shelled out a substantial $112.5 million for the plant.[38] And soon after that, it used one of their Delaware LLCs to purchase another major plant on the opposite side of the state, in a tiny place called Calvert City (population 2,566).[39] Final sale price for this 400,000-square-foot plant: $188.1 million.[40]

In the span of just a few years, Kolomoisky's network had collected a half-dozen major mills across the American heartland, each of them the beating economic hearts of the surrounding regions. All of them had fallen casualty to America's yearslong manufacturing slump, part of America's broader deindustrialization that began in the 1970s. All of them were eager for any injection of financing they could get, and for any promise of a brighter future—no matter the source of the income. And all of them were now connected directly to Kolomoisky's network, to this corporate lattice of shell companies, including some in Delaware. When the nine-figure purchasing spree was through, Kolomoisky had cemented his role as a global kingmaker—so much so that he at one point controlled over half of the U.S.'s production of silicomanganese, one of the key ingredients in producing high-grade structural steel.[41]

It remains unclear how Kolomoisky and Korf identified the specific plants to purchase. But it's clear that Korf played a key role in directing operations. "Motti just cares about data and money," one American broker who worked with Korf, who requested anonymity because of litigation connected to Korf and Kolomoisky, told me. "He can be in a basement for a week, get a little sunlight, and then go back out. He's the brains behind it all."[42]

But for the Ukrainian oligarch, seizing chunks of American metal manufacturing was never the end goal of his American operations. Which is why he needed one more American to help him navigate a new American market that was suddenly opening itself to the pools of wealth spilling out of the former Soviet Union. He needed Chaim Schochet.

* * *

ACCORDING TO THOSE who've met him, Schochet is, by nature, a man prone to fidgeting. He fidgets when you sit with him, glancing constantly at his iPhone. He fidgets when you speak with him, deflecting questions with jokes and sarcasm, giving an impression that he's simultaneously aloof and awash in nerves. Confidence is, on the whole, not a characteristic most ascribe to Schochet. He has always been more of a follower than a leader. As one American real estate agent who knew him told me, Schochet always seemed like a "whipping boy."[43] Or as another person told me, "I don't know how savvy Chaim ultimately is."[44]

Emerging from much the same world that Korf and his family helped create in South Florida, Schochet, the sixth of eight children, never exhibited much drive in his younger days. He waffled through the Rabbinical College of America, bouncing between Miami and New York and Toronto, graduating with a Judaic studies degree in 2006. Unsure of his next steps, Schochet traveled to Singapore for a year of volunteer work. When he returned to South Florida, as the U.S. tipped headlong into the Great Recession, Schochet began pulling on family connections to try to land work. He'd met a young woman, Rachel, and begun a courtship that would soon result in marriage, and a pair of twin boys soon after. Along the way, Schochet got to know one of Rachel's dour, workaholic brothers, who always seemed to be juggling new projects, new trips, and new instructions from partners in Ukraine. It was Motti Korf.[45]

Schochet had previously dabbled in real estate and architecture, with a hobby of sketching potential projects on the side. "I've always had a thing for architecture," he told a journalist in 2012. "I always was fascinated when they put up big buildings, little buildings, monumental buildings. And then, I guess, from that it evolved into wanting to work with them."[46] ("I doubt any of [the sketches] would pass code approvals," Schochet sheepishly added.[47]) But he saw an opportunity with his new brother-in-law, and pitched his services. Why not let him try to turn some of that interest in architecture and real estate into something worthwhile? Why not use him as a footman, as a bagman, as someone willing to slog across the country to help scout new places to invest Optima's—and Kolomoisky's—money? "Chaim wanted to get into the business, and Motti said 'No, no, no, no,'" one American who worked with them both said. "Chaim finally broke him down."[48]

By the time Schochet joined, Optima was already well established in the American steel market. But Kolomoisky wanted a foothold elsewhere. He wanted another market to dominate—and another place to park his money, safe from any Ukrainian authorities or investigators who may begin snooping around. A market that wouldn't attract any attention. He'd already saturated the steel market with his money. What about real estate?

Kolomoisky's American helpers scouted parts of Kentucky and Texas. But one market in particular kept catching their eye: Cleveland. Like nearby Warren, Cleveland's best days were clearly in the rearview mirror, especially when it came to a dying downtown buffeted by both population declines and a rampaging recession. And it turned out that Schochet, according to at least one person who worked with him, happened to have friends who were studying there already. Why not have Schochet see if he could prove his worth to Kolomoisky, and to Korf, in Cleveland?

In the midst of the recession, Schochet "came into our market, and [he and Korf] basically portrayed themselves as Miami-based money managers involved in manufacturing businesses, who had some sources of foreign money they were interested in investing in U.S. real estate," David Browning, a local broker, remembered. It was clear that Schochet wasn't like other potential buyers. "He was twenty-two," another broker recalled, "and was trying to have these professional meetings in designer jeans. . . . It was just odd."[49]

But Cleveland couldn't turn him away. He was, as one real estate agent said, "the first out-of-town money for Cleveland," at least in any substantial measure. And for a city reeling from the Great Recession, Schochet was a godsend. He claimed he was fronting family money, made off profits from distant Soviet gas wells. Those in Cleveland, though, didn't care what his story was. They were more than happy to help him spend that family money however he saw fit, as we'll revisit in the book's third section.

Soon he was "neck-deep" in the Cleveland market, dominating not just downtown but the city as a whole, fronting as a family man just looking to get a city back up on its feet. "I can tell you that he's a person who cares about the city of Cleveland and wants it to do well," one local real estate agent, Mark Vogel, would later say.[50]

But for those who worked with him, though, there was a clearly different, and far darker, side to Schochet's public claims. In time, his fidgety habits soon turned into something else completely: fear.

"Chaim would come in," one real estate agent told me, "and he would say, 'You have no idea the people I have to deal with. If I can't come through, I could be in big trouble. Basically, they said they could kill me.'"[51]

SLAP IN THE FACE

"I understand the Interior Department is just about to close a contract to lease Teapot Dome, and all through the industry it smells. . . . I do feel that you should tell the president that it smells."

—Walter Teagle[1]

For years, the U.S. has looked the other way when it comes to the flood of dirty money racing into the country to be washed clean. It ignored how anonymous American shell companies could move money into any asset they wanted—into, as we'll see, real estate and investment funds and luxury goods and priceless art—while stripping the names and identities of those who actually controlled the shells. It ignored how the kinds of American "business-friendly" reforms Dan Zwonitzer mentioned were, in reality, attracting billions of dollars in untraceable funds to the U.S., barreling through any safeguards that may have been in place. It ignored how America's financial sectors began seeing tidal waves of dirty money joining the tidal waves of legitimate funds flooding the country, part of an ocean of international capital looking for a home.

But the U.S. has known about the issue for *decades*—as the saga of the Bank of Credit and Commerce International (BCCI) can attest.

Founded in the mid-1970s by a Pakistani banker named Agha Hasan Abedi and bankrolled by a United Arab Emirates leader named Sheikh Zayed bin Sultan Al Nahyan, BCCI was always supposed to be different. It pitched itself to international clients from South Asia to South

America as the go-to bank for the postcolonial Third World. No Westerners would be connected to the bank. Instead, the bank would be the first of its kind: a major financial player dedicated solely to the stability and growth of forgotten markets, specifically for small-scale depositors in pockets of the world Western bankers had long overlooked.

For over a decade, that pitch worked. Starting from a few locations in Pakistan and the United Arab Emirates, BCCI swelled into a behemoth of the postcolonial banking world, eventually operating by the late 1980s in over 70 countries and holding some $20 billion (about $50 billion in 2020 dollars) in total assets. BCCI, by all appearances, looked well on its way to Abedi's goal of becoming the world's largest bank by the year 2000.[2] Most impressively, the bank swelled to such size by apparently bucking the practices of its Western peers. Instead of targeting profit margins and attracting deep-pocketed patrons, the bank claimed a different model entirely—one infused with morality above all else. "No material end can be achieved without a moral aspect behind it," Abedi once said, adding another time that the "spirit of BCCI is permeated by a moral dimension, and this eases the burden of management." In that vein, BCCI founded something called the "Third World Foundation," which it said would help "relieve poverty and sickness" in the developing world, and even created an award to mirror the Nobel Peace Prize. It eventually opened branches in places like the U.S. and the U.K., whose domestic banking industries looked askance at BCCI's model.[3]

Thus, when BCCI collapsed in early 1991 under the weight of unprecedented money laundering and embezzlement allegations totaling nearly $10 billion, the waves of surprise circled the globe, bouncing between hemispheres and governments who'd never second-guessed Abedi and his bank. Morality, it seemed, couldn't quite stop Abedi and his buddies from pocketing billions of dollars they'd stolen from depositors. Issuing doctored statements, lying widely to the public, Abedi and his cronies had effectively turned the bank into a Ponzi scheme, claiming the bank held the assets that insiders had secretly stolen. "Abedi and his associates had cynically turned a Third World institution into a mechanism for robbing depositors from developing countries," journalists Peter Truell and Larry Gurwin wrote in 1992. "And the beneficiaries were rich sheikhs from the Persian Gulf, BCCI's associates around the world, and the bank's own management."[4] Billions of dollars had simply disappeared, pocketed by the Saudi officials and Emirati sheikhs—as well as by clients like Saddam Hussein, Ferdinand Marcos, and Panamanian-president-turned-drug-kingpin Manuel Noriega—who had steered BCCI into the ether, and then into the ground. BCCI's collapse was, as U.S. attorney Robert Morgenthau said, "the largest bank fraud in history."[5]

Later investigations unspooled exactly how BCCI operated, setting up sham shell companies to hide its executives' financial tracks—even setting up dummy corporations to purchase other legitimate banks elsewhere, turning them into unsuspecting prongs of Abedi's Ponzi scheme and laundering the proceeds across the West. These investigations also revealed just how close BCCI higher-ups got to people like U.S. president Jimmy Carter; how BCCI affiliates helped bankroll things like Senator Gary Hart's 1988 presidential campaign; and how journalists investigating BCCI ended up beaten and bloodied on the streets of London, their findings stolen, forever unpublished.[6]

In scope and scale, there was nothing like BCCI's collapse. But beyond the final numbers, one thing was clear: BCCI had created a blueprint that numerous kleptocrats and international criminals would soon follow. It was one of the earliest case studies in what would grow into the modern kleptocracy playbook, which targeted the West for all of its money laundering and offshoring needs. It was also a clear, blinking red light indicating that the kinds of deregulatory reforms sweeping the West—which were still ascendant at the end of the Cold War, as entire new regions began getting their first whiffs of capitalism—wouldn't attract only clean, legitimate capital to the U.S., but would act like a beacon for all the dirty money starting to slosh around the globe.

* * *

FOR DECADES, INTERNATIONAL money laundering—the transformation of dirty money into clean—was largely an afterthought in Washington. There was some acknowledgment that, say, Colombian cartels or central-African smugglers needed to wash their profits clean, and that they sometimes splurged on things like private jets or Miami condos with those profits. But looking over some of the late–Cold War legislation, which rarely targeted high-level financial malfeasance, shows just how indifferent Washington was to the threat of transnational money laundering.

For instance, it wasn't until 1970 that the U.S. passed the Bank Secrecy Act (BSA), which presented the first real reforms aimed at addressing some of the dirty money flowing into American banks.[7] At the time, the banking sector roared with righteous indignation: Who was Washington to try to regulate the banks? Who were these bureaucrats to tell American banks who they could or couldn't deal with? "The whole idea of banking was, 'We're bankers, we're not responsible for the actions of our customers,'" Jack Blum, a former Senate investigator who worked closely in drafting later anti–money laundering legislation, told me. And those bankers, at the time, had a point. Blum added, "There WAS 200 years of common law and statutory law in places like New York that literally absolved bankers from responsibility for anything their customers did."[8]

But in hindsight, it's almost laughable just how small those BSA regulations were. American banks were simply required to file "currency transaction reports" for anything exceeding $10,000 per day. Even then, those regulations didn't prevent American banks from working with any customer they wanted, no matter the size (or source) of their till—nor were those regulations even enforced for the decade or so after the BSA's inception. By the 1980s, transnational money laundering had gained a few more eyeballs in Washington, leading to the 1986 passage of the Money Laundering Control Act.[9] On its face, the law was a significant moment for combating money laundering; as one later Senate hearing noted, it was "the first [law] in the world to make money laundering an independent crime."[10] Or put another way: before 1986, there was no law *in the entire world* that specifically criminalized money laundering.

The new law explicitly prohibited any financial transaction involving the proceeds from crimes like drug trafficking, fraud, and terrorism. It also opened up every type of asset—planes, cars, Jet Skis, Elvis Presley's used guitars, autographed Portland Trail Blazers jerseys, and the like—to "civil forfeiture," allowing the government to seize the assets even if no one was charged with a crime. A few years later, the U.S.'s anti–money laundering regime tightened further. Follow-up legislation increased penalties on banks that knowingly aided money launderers, creating new reporting requirements that compelled banks to file Suspicious Activity Reports (SARs) with the federal government whenever they suspected clients of using their services for money laundering.[11]

But as with the BSA, the legislation was meaningless without enforcement. Even the new SAR requirements only opened up more holes. The new law required American banks to fill out a SAR—disclosing who the customer was, what they deposited, what type of wrongdoing bank employees suspected, whether they'd tried to bribe the teller, etc.—and file it with the Treasury Department. Beyond that, the banks had no other legal obligations; once they filed the SAR about a certain client, they could continue to work with that client—even if that client had, say, just identified themselves as Pablo Escobar's sister or Slobodan Milosevic's nephew, or dragged in a dozen duffle bags full of shrink-wrapped bills. Bankers should be on the lookout for suspicious financial flows, the government said—but they don't need to actually *stop* working with those suspicious figures. "U.S. banks can file the SAR, and get on with the business," the anticorruption watchdog Global Witness once wrote. "It is up to law enforcement to act on the SAR, and to follow the trail after the money has gone. But if the authorities are overworked or asleep and do not follow up the information in the SAR, the bank can effectively do business with a corrupt dictator's son with impunity as long as it continues to file a SAR for each suspect transaction."[12]

For years throughout the late Cold War period, this was how American banking operated. A banker might lose a few minutes filling out SAR paperwork, and then they could get back to tending to whichever customers they wanted. It was more of a formality than anything else— and that was only when a banker thought anything was suspicious.

* * *

BUT THEN, WITH the implosion of BCCI in the early 1990s came all manner of revelations, from the fact that BCCI's affiliates had covertly paid off prominent Democratic politicos to the fact that BCCI secretly managed a number of American banks while simultaneously clearing checks for dictators like Pakistani leader Zia ul-Haq.[13]

Perhaps the most staggering revelations, though, centered less on BCCI and more on how little things like the BSA or the Money Laundering Control Act had done to stem the flow of suspicious and dirty money directly into American banks, American territory, and American hands. "Before the BCCI affair, foreign banks were allowed to operate in the U.S. in a way that was unregulated, period," Blum, who as an investigator with Senator John Kerry's staff had helped drive the questions and pressure that finally broke BCCI's back, told me. "In theory, foreign banks were regulated by their home governments. But at the time, the U.S. said, 'Look, as long as you don't take on American customers, we won't bother you.' And that's how BCCI operated."[14] (Blum's never been one to mince words; he once described a sweetheart deal American authorities offered to BCCI as a "fucking outrage."[15])

It was as if a billion-dollar light bulb had suddenly gone off over the heads of policymakers in Washington. The BCCI scandal wrenched Washington's attention toward a burgeoning field: kleptocracy, and America's role therein. "Suddenly, U.S. federal authorities had to confront the proposition that banks theoretically within their purview were running criminal enterprises," Blum added. "Once that was on the table, suddenly the question of the regulation of foreign bank operations in the U.S. became a serious matter of concern."[16]

And powerful voices in Washington took note. Around the same time, the George H. W. Bush administration, spearheaded by the president himself, led efforts to establish the Financial Action Task Force (FATF).[17] Creating international standards against money laundering, the FATF represented a groundbreaking multilateral effort to coordinate governments against illicit networks. Over three decades later, the FATF remains, by all measures, the foremost international body dedicated to organizing such anti–money laundering regulations and principles—and to convincing recalcitrant governments to sign on to basic transparency protocols.[18] With prominent voices like Kerry publicly highlighting the growing threat of international money laundering—and how it helped dictators like Panama's Manuel Noriega or Iraq's Saddam Hussein hide and fund their operations—the U.S. seemed poised to clamp down on these illicit financial networks.

But not everyone was on board. Blum recalled one moment toward the end of the first Bush administration, even after Bush had helped launch the FATF. "There was an assistant secretary of the Treasury who, while Kerry was pushing [an anti–money laundering] bill on the floor, was standing outside and yelling at me and other members of Kerry's staff that we were going to destroy American finance for all time," Blum said. "The assistant secretary was hysterical . . . [saying,] 'Oh my God, you can't do this—you'll destroy the American economy!' We kind of just laughed at the guy. It was pathetic."[19]

Still, concerns about cratering American finance—about cutting off the inflow of international money into American banks—were enough to stall those initial efforts at reform. Not that there wasn't a logic to opponents' arguments. With so much international capital flowing into the U.S., they argued, any potential new oversight and regulations could have cascading effects on both legitimate and illicit flows alike. And given that the dirty money followed the same paths as legitimate financial flows, any effort to cut off the tap of illicit monies would invariably slow down the legitimate flows. And in a country whose "pro-business" ethos still reigned, that was a nonstarter.

At least, that's what "pro-business" voices opposed to anti–money laundering regulations claimed. But the incoming Clinton administration was interested, both as a matter of national security and a means of claiming anticorruption leadership. As journalist Misha Glenny observed, "The Clinton administration elevated its [anti–money laundering] strategy to a list of its most solemn commandments."[20] The White House launched a campaign to get international allies to criminalize things like foreign bribery, which had previously been, incredibly, tax-deductible for officials and businessmen from allies like France and Germany.[21] The

Cold War was over, and suddenly transnational money laundering—the underpinning of what we'd eventually describe as kleptocracy—loomed as an ever-increasing threat.

* * *

NOR WAS THE new administration the only branch in Washington suddenly grasping just how wide open America appeared to foreign dirty money. In the Senate, one subcommittee in particular took interest. The Permanent Subcommittee on Investigations (PSI) enjoyed a lengthy, if checkered, history. Launched during the Truman administration, the PSI was composed of a bipartisan slate of senators dedicated to (as the name implied) congressional investigations.[22] It initially examined everything from World War II profiteering to Nazi war criminals. That promising start was quickly derailed, however, when Wisconsin senator Joe McCarthy corralled the PSI in his embarrassing pursuit of supposedly covert communists. Thankfully, the PSI shook off the taint of McCarthyism and eventually launched investigations into a wide range of topics, including the Italian-American Mafia, pension and credit card fraud, corruption in the U.S. military, and even abuses in federal student aid programs. The PSI's successes ran wide. ("PSI stands for pretty scary investigations," an opponent once quipped.[23]) Things like the Money Laundering Control Act were direct outgrowths of the PSI's investigations and public hearings—as was the Racketeer Influenced and Corrupt Organizations (RICO) legislation, which effectively buried the Italian-American Mafia as an organized crime force in the U.S.[24]

By the mid-1990s, the PSI was scouring for new investigative territory. And there stood the BCCI revelations: about modern offshoring, about transnational money laundering, and about all of their handmaidens along the way. The PSI started looking into some of the money laundering and offshore banking schemes gaining interest in Washington. Toward the end of the decade, the PSI's interest in this new world of foreign dirty money received a significant boost when a new voice joined its ranks—a man who would eventually become the face of America's anti–money laundering efforts.

Michigan senator Carl Levin, broad-faced and bespectacled, first joined the Senate as a Democrat in 1979. By the time he rose to become Michigan's senior senator in the mid-1990s, he'd gained a reputation as a fan of plain talk and due diligence. "Facts have always been Levin's stock-in-trade," one observer noted.[25] When looking for committee assignments, there was one logical slot for him to put that talent to work: the Permanent Subcommittee on Investigations. Joining the PSI as the ranking minority member, Levin's investigative antennae quickly pointed in one direction: money laundering, and who was profiting from it, and how to stop it before it all ended in disaster. "Senator Levin got hooked on the anti–money laundering aspect of the work we could do," one of his staff told me.[26]

It didn't take long for him to make his mark. In just a few years, Levin "revolutionized" America's entire anti–money laundering regime.[27] And the timing was propitious. Just as he was joining the PSI, an entirely different affair, just beyond America's southern border, confirmed suspicions that transnational money laundering was more important than many had previously assumed.

In 1995, Mexican police arrested Raul Salinas, the elder brother of the recently ousted Mexican president, on murder allegations. According to Mexican authorities, Salinas had offed his brother-in-law, who was himself a prominent Mexican politico. The case already generated enough drama. But shortly thereafter, Salinas's spooked wife fled for Switzerland, where she was arrested amidst her efforts to withdraw some $84 million from the Swiss bank Banque Pictet.[28] Not long thereafter, Swiss authorities revealed that Salinas's in-country assets totaled some $114 million.[29]

Needless to say, Salinas couldn't account for the vast bulk of his wealth, and much of it was safely assumed to be dirty due to high-level corruption in Mexico. (Mexican first families are paid well, but not that well.) More interestingly, documents pertaining to these Swiss holdings revealed that some of Salinas's ill-gotten money had taken a circuitous route to Zurich—and that much of it had traveled directly via a major American bank, Citibank. Citibank had helped move the funds from Mexico to New York before they landed in accounts at Citibank's Swiss branch, ready to be used by Salinas and his wife.[30]

For Levin and his staff, Salinas's case was the perfect mixture of in-
trigue and proximity. American authorities could hardly ignore such
staggering corruption—and its political implications—out of Mexico
City. Plus, there was Citibank, one of America's flagship financial entities, suddenly twisting in the wind, trying to disclaim any connection to
Salinas. Levin's money laundering moth had suddenly found its flame,
and his staff immediately began requesting and poring through as many
documents as they could find. It didn't take long to outline just how
Citibank had actively aided and abetted Salinas's sprawling money laundering network.[31]

As Levin and his team uncovered, Salinas had relied heavily on one
Citibank banker in particular, named Amy Elliott. Elliott helped steer
Citibank's "private banking" arm—a department that specifically ca-
tered to high-net-worth individuals, no matter the source of their income. Elliott opened up myriad Citibank bank accounts for Salinas's
operations, in New York and Switzerland alike. Whenever Salinas or his
wife presented cashier's checks from other Mexican banks to Citibank's
Mexico City branch, the local branch manager would promptly wire
the funds to New York—where Elliott would then take the reins, funneling the funds on to Switzerland or London for Salinas's use. Elliott,
in effect, acted directly as Salinas's money manager. But it wasn't just
transferring ludicrously large sums of money. Elliott and her Citibank
colleagues, looking to protect their client's requests for secrecy, made
sure that Salinas's name was never attached to any of the accounts. Instead, Citibank assigned Salinas an anonymous shell company to act as
the account holder.[32] (Elliott dubbed Salinas "Confidential Client #2" in
internal communications, and even opened an account for him under
the fictitious name of "Bonaparte."[33])

After Levin and his staff began probing the payments, Citibank's
defense waffled. The bank initially claimed ineptitude, stating that they
had no idea about any of the corruption allegations swirling Salinas.
They then moved to outright obstinance, with bank officials stating time
and again that they'd done nothing wrong. And in a strictly legal sense,
they weren't necessarily wrong. Even if they'd known the funds stemmed
directly from the Salinas family's rank corruption, there was nothing

on the American books making it illegal to handle the funds, including setting up anonymous shell companies for their owners. In shepherding Salinas along, Elliott had technically followed the law. As long as they filed their SARs—the only legal requirement at the time when it came to American banks handling the proceeds of foreign corruption—they could effectively help Salinas launder as much money as he could get his hands on.

"Even if its private banker had known that some deposits were the product of foreign corruption, U.S. anti–money laundering laws did not prohibit Citibank from accepting those funds," Elise Bean, one of Levin's lead staff investigators, later wrote. "At the time, it wasn't against the law for U.S. banks to knowingly accept corruption proceeds as bank deposits, so long as the corrupt acts took place outside U.S. borders."[34]

But the PSI investigations found that Salinas was hardly Citibank's only corrupt client. There was Citibank's private bank in New York setting up shell companies for the decades-long dictator of the African country of Gabon, with internal documents describing his staggering wealth as "self-made." The bank was doing the same for the family of Nigeria's military dictator, helping him and his cronies move and conceal tens of millions of dollars looted from Nigeria's national treasury. So many examples emerged that one of the PSI investigators, according to Bean, "suggested a new investigative theory which he called 'the unitary theory of evil'—it postulated that, if you looked hard enough during those years, you might find Citibank as the financier behind many of the big-time corrupt dictators around the globe."[35] As Levin told me, "Carrying on these kinds of activities is just a slap in the face of every American taxpayer."[36]

But as Levin and his staff came to realize, Citibank was hardly the lone American bank playing this role. Thanks to the whopping loopholes in things like the BSA and the Money Laundering Control Act, American banks could freely work with whomever they chose, or with whichever anonymous shell company they wanted, no matter whom those shell companies concealed. And they had every incentive to. After all, the demand was clearly there: kleptocrats around the world were increasingly looking to move their money, hide their money, offshore their money. The demand only continued rising. And American banks, which took a cut of the proceeds they were moving, had every reason to welcome as much dirty money as they could find. There was no regulatory apparatus, no series of laws or oversight bodies, to stop them. For those in the corporate suites, for those in middle management, for those interacting with the customers, the incentive pointed in one direction: increasing revenue streams. And anything that didn't explicitly break American law was fair game.

It wasn't malicious, per se. And in many instances, aside from bank officials interacting directly with the corrupt officials, those on the American side of things didn't know—couldn't know—whose money they were helping move. It was a dynamic that we'll see play out time and again throughout this book, and through this story of kleptocracy. As the demand side rose, and as the tides of dirty money continued to swell, incentives to provide laundering and financial secrecy tools, those supply side instruments of modern kleptocracy, rose as well.

And anyway, if giants like Citibank were already catering to the world's worst—and, until Levin's inquiry, doing it perfectly freely—why shouldn't the rest of the American banks? Why should Citibank be the only one to get a piece of this growing dirty money pie?

* * *

FROM THERE, LEVIN and his staff's findings only continued to pile up. They discovered that American banks, for instance, routinely set up "correspondent accounts" in the names of foreign banks *within* American banks. These effectively allowed foreign banks to operate from within their American partners. But because they were still *foreign* banks in control of those accounts, they weren't subject to even minimal U.S. anti-money laundering regulations. As an added bonus, American authorities didn't have legal authority to seize the funds held in these "correspondent accounts," even when they were housed at American banks in New York or Miami or Los Angeles. Even when investigators or democratic reformers knew these accounts contained money looted by dictators, there was nothing Washington could do. It was as if U.S. authorities knew about the millions in dirty money an American bank held in its right hand, but could only freeze what the bank held in its left.[37]

One group of foreign banks that took advantage of these correspondent accounts were known as "shell banks." These foreign shell banks didn't even bother with brick-and-mortar buildings, but existed as a "bank" on paper only. Despite existing only on documents, they could still open as many correspondent accounts as they liked in American banks, enjoying all of the opportunities and protections and help of American bankers like Amy Elliott, without having to worry about any pesky regulations or American authorities freezing their accounts. (BCCI, for instance, set up a shell bank for just these purposes on the Caribbean island of Anguilla—a British territory that made a fortune selling shell bank licenses to anyone who came knocking.)[38] By the turn of the century, there were thousands of these shell banks scattered around the world, seeming to exist for no reason other than hiding money.[39]

"U.S. banks hardly thought twice before opening an account for another bank, even if it was an offshore bank with no physical presence anywhere, operated in a secrecy jurisdiction known for sleaze, and used its U.S. account to engage in dubious transactions," Bean said."[40] As Levin later wrote, "The lackadaisical treatment was based on an assumption that a bank was a bank and could be trusted, instead of considering that some banks might be a center of corruption."[41]

The information uncovered by Levin and his staff put to rest any remaining claims that the U.S.'s anti–money laundering laws were effective. American banks had, clearly, become giant magnets for much of the world's dirty money—and existing laws made American officials impotent to do anything about it. As such, in 1999 Levin joined Republican senator Arlen Specter to draft a bill with a range of proposed legislative fixes, including banning shell bank operations, pushing for greater oversight of "correspondent accounts," and instituting basic due diligence requirements on billions of foreign dollars barreling into American banks. But the bill ended up in the Senate Banking Committee—whose chair was Texas GOP senator Phil Gramm, some of whose key constituents were

Texas-based banks that were popular destinations for the deluge of dirty money flowing north from places like Mexico and Central America. None of the members of the Texas Bankers Association, with Gramm as their effective mouthpiece, saw any reason to change business as usual. "Gramm responded to our bill with a deafening silence," one of Levin's staff said.[42]

From there, Levin's anti–money laundering window only seemed to shrink. The election of George W. Bush revived an antiregulatory ethos in Washington, decreasing the appetite for banking restrictions and oversight, even those advancing the anti–money laundering campaign his father's administration helped propel. "For Bush and his team, the only good anti–money laundering strategy was no anti–money laundering strategy," Glenny summed.[43] Regulations, to opponents, would only get in the way of American business. And for an economy still centered on the kind of deregulatory ethos ascendant since the 1980s—and for American industries watching billions flowing in—those regulations were a nonstarter.

Still, Levin didn't give up. In the summer of 2001, the senator corralled a half-dozen cosponsors, including a number of Republicans, to launch a second, even stronger anti–money laundering bill. But just as before, Gramm, at the behest of the Texas Bankers Association, welcomed the bill into his Senate Banking Committee and strangled it in the crib.

And then, a few weeks later, September 11 changed everything.

* * *

WHILE THE GROUND still smoldered in New York, Washington, D.C., and the fields of Pennsylvania, legislators and investigators in Congress suddenly scrambled. They had to figure out how transnational financial flows had helped bankroll transnational terrorism: how militant extremists deep in the caves of Afghanistan could fund the most devastating terror attack the U.S. had ever seen. How did they pay for their activities in America? How did they pay for training? How did they pay for everything that led to the worst terrorist attack in the country's history? And who had helped them do so?

It didn't take long to find the answers. The attackers, as Levin testified just two weeks after the attack, had "used cash, checks, credit cards, and wire transfers involving U.S. banks in states such as Florida, New York, and Pennsylvania," with security footage showing them freely "using a U.S. bank's ATM machine." It wasn't that they were just the same tactics, the same tools, that Salinas and BCCI and despots in regimes around the world had used. It was also that they were mixing their terror-tainted funds with all of the other legitimate flows in the financial system. And there would have been little way for anyone to tell the difference—to tell which monies were going to finance the attacks on that Tuesday morning. "The evidence is clear that terrorists are using our own financial institutions against us," Levin concluded.[44]

None of this should have come as a surprise. But all of a sudden, in the aftermath of 9/11, the threats of unchecked dirty money financial flows finally sank in. "9/11 provided a window to push legislation," Blum remembered. "Until then, every time legislation had been proposed, it didn't get anywhere. And suddenly we had a chance to really make a difference here."[45] As Levin told me, "It was 9/11 which then gave a whole, big impetus to the issue."[46]

It was clear: the wind was at the reformers' backs. "There was a 180-degree flip," one senior economist in the Bush administration said. "After 9/11 no anti–money laundering regime [was] too strong for the U.S. Any kind of concerns about secondary effects go out the window. The brief is, everybody has to have this regime, and the stronger, the more onerous, the better—no cost is too high."[47]

Thankfully, Levin and his colleagues' previous reform packages were still viable. When a package of national security reforms began hurtling through Congress, bundled into what would be called the Patriot Act, Levin spied an opportunity. The senator convinced his counterparts that any national security reforms would "have no teeth" without his proposed anti–money laundering reforms. Levin, as anticorruption crusader Raymond Baker remembered, thundered that "money laundering had helped and would otherwise continue to help fund terrorist groups intent on the mass murder of Americans."[48] Levin's anti–money laundering proposals—boosted by the support of Senator Paul Sarbanes, a

Democrat who'd taken the helm of the Senate Banking Committee from Gramm—joined the effort.

But there was one hiccup. An old friend came to call on Levin and his allies: Citibank. Backed by the American Bankers Association, Citibank's lobbyists cornered legislators and intimidated staffers, crowing that the connections between terrorism and anti–money laundering reform—despite the documents, despite the hearings, despite the footage—were negligible. "How could anyone think that money had anything to do with 9/11?" they asked. The lobbyists "mounted a campaign bitterly opposing inclusion of strengthened anti–money laundering provisions," Baker said, and "desperately wanted to continue [their] lucrative business." Any hope of comity disintegrated: "Civility collapsed; shouting matches between Citibank officers and congressional staffers erupted in the halls of Congress."[49] Added Baker, who later founded the Global Financial Integrity think tank, "How the biggest banks in New York, following the city's most tragic event, a shattering experience for the whole of America, could go to Washington and argue against tougher anti–money laundering provisions directed in good part at terrorists is for me unfathomable."[50]

Levin, though, wasn't cowed. Insisting that he'd hold up the passage of the entire Patriot Act if his provisions weren't included, he and his colleagues never buckled under the pressure from the banks. The Senate Banking Committee waved his reform proposals through unanimously. The moment those reforms finally latched on to the Patriot Act, Elise Bean remembered, was "magical."[51] And understandably so. When Bush signed the Patriot Act into law in late October, American banks' halcyon days of serving dictators and despots and drug runners were, with a single pen stroke, over. No longer could American banks freely open accounts for "shell banks," nor could they simply shuffle funds into a "correspondent account" to prevent seizure by U.S. authorities. No longer could they welcome whomever they wanted into their private banking divisions. Due to a provision authored by Sarbanes, American banks would have to set up their own internal anti–money laundering programs. And, at long last, handling all those proceeds of foreign corruption became a criminal offense.[52]

"It addressed virtually every one of the problems identified in our three-year money laundering investigation," Bean, who now helps run the Levin Center at Wayne State University law school in Detroit, later wrote. "It was an oversight triumph."[53] Added Baker, the entire slate was "a stellar example of transparency-based reform."[54]

*   *   *

IN MANY WAYS, the Patriot Act—somewhat ironically, given how roundly the rest of the bill has been condemned since—is, to date, the greatest single piece of anti–money laundering legislation the U.S., and arguably the world, has ever seen.

But dirty money still seeps through the cracks, oozes through the loopholes, finds a way through the openings and the exemptions. Dirty money is always—*always*—looking to be washed clean. And the Patriot Act was, despite the deserved praise on the anti–money laundering front, no different. Despite all it accomplished, it was still subject to one small, trifling loophole, which helped open a new chapter in America's grand transformation into the world's greatest offshore haven.

The loophole arose from the fact that the Treasury secretary is allowed to issue exemptions from financial regulations for financial institutions. It was like a fail-safe switch, allowing the Treasury secretary to shield any part of the American financial sector from these new anti–money laundering checks. And it wasn't long before that switch was flipped and new exemptions suddenly came into play—and before America's anti–money laundering policies took five steps forward and five steps quickly back.

In statements that few paid much attention to—lost in the din of the continued war in Afghanistan and the lead-up to the invasion of Iraq—the Bush Treasury Department announced in early 2002 that it was exempting a number of industries from these historic anti–money laundering reforms. It was a wide range. Real estate agents and those overseeing escrow accounts, managing millions and millions of dollars. Private equity and hedge fund managers, managing *billions* of dollars. Luxury goods vendors, those selling things like private jets and million-dollar automobiles. All of these would receive "temporary" exemptions from basic anti–money laundering checks, according to the Treasury Department, in order to "study" the effect these new requirements might have. They wouldn't have to set up any internal anti–money laundering programs—they wouldn't even have to do any due diligence on the sources of the money, or even who the money was necessarily connected to. For good measure, Treasury made clear that it also wouldn't extend the new anti–money laundering program requirements to things like American lawyers or American art dealers and auction houses, either (which we'll learn plenty about in coming chapters). The Treasury Department also batted away any questions about requiring American shell companies—all those anonymous vehicles popping up in the thousands in Delaware and Nevada and Wyoming—to identify who was behind them.[55]

There's no evidence that any of these moves were malign, or done with the express intent of expanding American money laundering services. The new legislation, after all, was a qualitatively new approach: forcing banks, a major pillar of America's economy, to enact significant reforms, redirecting resources toward new anti–money laundering policies, compelling them to finally comb through all of the legitimate and illicit assets coming in. And it wouldn't be an easy task, because the money and assets, both legitimate and illegitimate, followed the same financial pathways—which meant that, suddenly, everything would get a closer look.

Because no one was quite sure what effect that would have on the U.S. financial industry, Treasury wanted to make certain they weren't inadvertently tripping up entire sectors of the American economy. As such, they gave real estate and private equity and luxury goods dealers a pass until the U.S. could sort out the best approach. Until the U.S. could figure out how to keep the baby—the clean, legitimate money of international capital—while throwing out the bathwater—the dirty money increasingly wending its way into the U.S.

Banks, then, were the only major American institutions that would actually have to comply with these new anti–money laundering regulations. They weren't the only ones—security firms, money service businesses, mutual funds, and insurance companies also had to follow suit.

But those were small-fry organizations, at least compared to banks and those industries enjoying these new exemptions.

Yet these "temporary" exemptions were a gut punch to reformers. When pressed about the surprise exemptions, Treasury said it just wanted more information about how the new regulations would affect the assorted industries. Shortly thereafter, in early 2003, Treasury announced that it was requesting public comment and public input about these exemptions—part of its "study" of the issue, Treasury claimed. Before these regulations could be expanded, Treasury would have to make sure these regulations didn't cut American industry off at the knees.

But nobody knows what the results of those public comments were; Treasury has never revealed the outcomes of its "study."[56]

And two decades later, almost all of those "temporary" exemptions still remain in effect.[57]

PART II

LIFESTYLES OF THE RICH AND FAMOUS

"Go get honest work. . . . To me, they're not a whole lot better than pimps or drug dealers in suits."

—Senator Sheldon Whitehouse,
on the Americans aiding the kleptocrats[1]

SCOOPING CAVIAR WITH A SHOVEL

"When I was in Equatorial Guinea the first few weeks, I asked, 'Why are there no newspapers?' And they said that the people weren't interested, that the people don't read a lot. Which is also why there were no libraries."

—Former senior U.S. State Department official[1]

For those in Washington, Riggs Bank—a small American bank founded in 1836, the same year Texas seceded from Mexico and Martin Van Buren was elected president—had always had a different air, a different aura, about it. A small, boutique outfit, Riggs pitched itself to clients in Washington as the "bank of presidents,"[2] catering to diplomats, politicians, and their assorted retinues. And it had the legacy to back it up: Riggs could track its clientele back to Abraham Lincoln, having helped finance everything from the invention of the telegraph to the purchase of Alaska. It was one of the oldest banks in America's capital, and was, as one write-up described it, "venerable."[3]

At the turn of the twenty-first century, that reputation remained intact. While other banking giants spun off in new directions, Riggs's clientele appeared localized to the power players in Washington and the foreign officials passing through. Riggs was "seen as a small but powerful bank, cornering a niche market," one Senate investigator told me. "They serviced embassies, heads of state and family members, other officials from other countries who were living in Washington."[4] By one estimate, Riggs at its height worked with over 95 percent of the foreign missions and embassies in and around Washington. "Embassy Banking," they called it.[5] (As Riggs later said, they were happy to open an account for anyone holding diplomatic credentials from the U.S. State Department.) Overseen by Joseph Allbritton, who'd served as the bank's director since 1981, Riggs's client list grew at a steady rate toward the end of the millennium, with its total assets reaching about $6 billion, enough to make it the largest bank based in Washington (though still far more boutique than, say, globe-spanning behemoths like Citibank).[6] In comparison to other competitors, Riggs always remained small—and always pitched itself as the cultured, elegant bank for its cultured, elegant clientele.

Then, in early 2003, the mask slipped. While investigators in Washington continued tracking the roots of the 9/11 terrorists' financing, rumors began trickling out that they'd found links between Riggs and the suspicious Saudi money tied to the 9/11 attacks. Tens of millions of dollars connected to Saudi ambassador Prince Bandar bin Sultan and his wife intersected with dozens of accounts they maintained at Riggs—as did numerous questions about Bandar's connections to key contacts for the 9/11 terrorists.[7] But that wasn't all. Reports surfaced that Riggs had also gotten a taste for some of the dirty money that had spent years pouring into the U.S., probing for weak spots—and that some of that money was linked to a small, despotic government in central Africa suddenly enjoying gushes of oil wealth, without any idea what to do with it. According to the whispers, the Obiang family had found a welcome embrace from Riggs. Most importantly, they had found a way to get their money into the U.S., without any questions asked.[8]

Not far from Riggs's Washington headquarters, Senator Levin and his staff got wind of the rumors and reports about a relationship between Riggs and the Obiangs. Still at the PSI, Levin was unsatisfied with the recent Patriot Act anti–money laundering legislation he'd spent so much time pushing. Not the language, per se—the prohibitions and proscriptions were as tight as any in the world—but with compliance. A law, after all, is only as effective as its enforcement. And Levin wanted to know: Were American banks actually complying with these new regulations?

And were the bodies tasked with oversight—the Treasury Department, most especially—actually following through?[9]

"We saw that a journalist had done a piece about Equatorial Guinea and Riggs," one of Levin's investigators remembered. With the alleged connections between Riggs and the Obiangs, Levin's "radar just went off."[10] This was it, Levin said: Riggs would be their test case to examine just how effectively those new post-9/11 regulations were working, or if American banks were still the laundromats processing dirty money tied to these putrid regimes. By March 2003, Levin and his staff began issuing subpoenas, collecting documents, and organizing interviews.[11] In time, they would amass over 100 boxes of packed folders and electronic material—all with thousands of pages of bank statements, wire transfers, and emails—amidst their piling evidence from Riggs. And what they would find in just a year would rock activist communities and political bases from Chile to the United Kingdom—and, by 2005, topple Riggs entirely, killing off Washington's most venerable bank for good.

* * *

WHEN SENATE INVESTIGATORS began questioning the bank, Riggs initially attempted to play down its links with Equatorial Guinea. The bank revealed that it maintained a few dozen accounts on behalf of clients from the small nation, but that they were no different than any of the other accounts maintained on behalf of foreign clientele. The first account had been opened in January 1996, shortly after Equatorial Guinea's offshore oil wealth began flowing. But none of the deposits had ever raised any red flags, either then or now, Riggs said. All of the money appeared perfectly aboveboard, the bank claimed.[12]

Levin and his staff were hardly convinced. Part of that was due to the nature of the Obiang regime in particular, buttressed as it was by torture, human rights atrocities, and corruption almost without compare. But much of that suspicion also stemmed from a middle-aged Riggs employee named Simon Kareri. In a role similar to Amy Elliott's at Citibank, Kareri had served as the private banker for a number of Riggs clients, rising to become the bank's senior vice president. When Senate investigators scanned Riggs accounts, Kareri's name kept popping up, time and again, for account after account after account.[13]

When Levin and his staff initially sat down with him, Kareri dodged questions about his role, or about how the relationship between Riggs and Equatorial Guinea began, and even about how the bank had handled the new Patriot Act requirements Levin had forced through. After all, American banks were now prohibited from working with the proceeds of foreign corruption. Given the mountains of evidence against the Obiang family already, how could Kareri and Riggs explain their continued work with them? Riggs, like Kareri, initially defended its ties with the Obiangs. "Riggs initially said [Kareri] was a good guy," one Senate investigator remembered, saying that Riggs claimed they'd never had reason to doubt him and his work.[14] But there was something—something in the way Kareri had feigned concern, something in the way he slow-walked answers back to the PSI investigators—that only provoked Levin and his staff. The entire staff's "shady-dealings radar had immediately begun pinging" when it came to Kareri, one of Levin's investigators recalled.[15]

And it soon became apparent why. Levin's investigators discovered that while Riggs and Kareri had turned over certain information about the Obiang accounts, they had failed to turn over information about dozens more accounts linked to the dictator and his family. Riggs claimed, bizarrely, that their accounting system was still run manually, which was why they'd initially missed the accounts. (If true, Riggs would have been the only bank in America without a fully electronic accounting system.) As a result, Levin subpoenaed even more documents, this time pertaining specifically to Riggs's anti–money laundering program, which the bank was required to enact following the Patriot Act in order to make sure it wasn't processing foreign corruption proceeds. But as the new documents were coming in, Levin and his staff heard something they didn't expect: rather than continue to appear for questions with investigators, Kareri had fled the country—and had found refuge in Equatorial Guinea.[16]

At that point, Riggs immediately flipped on Kareri, pegging him as the fall guy for every misstep that the bank had taken with the Obiangs since the mid-1990s. "Riggs at first said Kareri is a good guy, but all of a sudden he fled to Equatorial Guinea, and they did a 180-degree turn," one investigator told me. "Kareri turned out to be a bum."[17] The bank's tactics changed almost overnight. Kareri wasn't the reputable, upstanding guy the bank had previously claimed: he was the bad apple, suddenly turned exile. After that, the bank's attorneys "rolled over," one investigator remembered. "They basically said, 'Whatever you want, you've got.'"[18]

New documents came cascading in. Some revealed Kareri's habit of showing up at Riggs with suitcases of shrink-wrapped bills, personally depositing millions of dollars in straight cash on behalf of the Obiangs. (Quipped Levin, "If that kind of cash deposit does not make a bank sit up and ask questions, I am not so sure anything will."[19]) Other documents detailed meetings set up by Kareri between senior Riggs officials and Obiang's aides—as well as President Obiang himself—with Allbritton, the bank's longtime chief, personally overseeing a committee dedicated to expanding its relationship with the Obiang family.[20]

Indeed, the meetings between the Obiangs and the Riggs officials, and Kareri's role therein, were some of the glaringly obvious signs that Riggs knew exactly what it was doing with one of the most corrupt families Africa had ever produced. Once Senate investigators scratched the surface at Riggs, the bank's higher-ups' willingness to do whatever they could to move the Obiangs' money was almost impossible to miss. Much of that has to do with the fact that when it comes to the Obiangs, subtlety is in short supply. Everything about the family's corruption is blindingly obvious. Riggs couldn't simply plead ignorance.

But for most American bankers dealing with kleptocrats—for most middle managers, for most tellers, even for most executives—things would never be quite so obvious. Other kleptocratic figures simply blended in with the rest of the high-net-worth clients they were servicing. They could slip their dirty money in with the tides of legitimate finance continually flowing into the country. Differentiating the two was all too often above the pay grade of a banker dealing with dozens of clients per week—difficult to parse, even on the best of days.

All of which is to say: if the Obiangs could get away with their dirty money flows at a bank like Riggs for years and years, stopped only by a high-profile Senate investigation, what did other, less conspicuous kleptocrats have to worry about?

* * *

BUT IT WASN'T just Kareri's efforts to funnel as much of Obiang's money as he could to Riggs. As other documents revealed—and as we saw with Citibank and its dirty clients—Riggs employees had helped Obiang set up several shell companies to further obscure their money on the off chance anyone came looking. The main shell company, called Otong Ltd., was registered in the Bahamas in 1999. Time and again, Riggs accepted million-dollar cash deposits, meant for the Obiang family, on the shell company's behalf—including in 2002, well after the new Patriot Act provisions went into force. Riggs claimed that Otong was an "exporter of timber," despite knowing full well that the shell company had no employees and was little more than a front for President Obiang. (Riggs documents also claimed that the Obiang family made their money from "cocoa farming and businesses," and didn't say anything about the fact that the family oversaw a horrific dictatorship.[21])

Nor was that all. Levin and his staff found that Riggs had additionally opened accounts for payments from American oil companies owed to Obiang and his regime. That is, rather than depositing payments for oil extraction with, say, Equatorial Guinea's treasury, the Obiangs directed the companies to route those millions into their U.S. accounts at Riggs for their personal use—a setup that Riggs facilitated. And that money could then be withdrawn perfectly easily, with a simple signature from either President Obiang, who would stop by on his trips to Washington, or from his wayward son.[22]

When the tabulations finally stopped and the documents finally ran out, the findings were staggering. From 1995 through 2003, Riggs hosted a mountainous $700 million for the Obiang regime in dozens of different accounts—all of it presumably dirty, made from embezzlement, corruption, and the perks of being a dictator.[23] Riggs allowed the Obiang family to cycle their dirty funds through the bank and withdraw it on the other side as perfectly clean money, complete with the imprimatur of the "bank of the presidents," to be spent on anything they liked. The bank was, in essence, a bottomless ATM for the family. More astonishingly, that total amount made the Obiang regime the *largest single client* of Riggs Bank.[24]

By the early 2000s, Riggs had gone from relying on American presidents and their entourages to leaning heavily on one of the most corrupt regimes on the planet. Perhaps most remarkable, the bank hadn't flagged a single one of the dozens and dozens of accounts as high-risk, or subjected them to any additional scrutiny, as regulations required. Given the fees the bank charged the Obiangs to host their money, it was best, Riggs decided, not to look a kleptocratic gift horse in the mouth. "We have a dictator here who is, according to the reports that you can read and I can read . . . someone who is a human rights violator and who runs a country as though it is his own private fiefdom," Levin would say in a 2004 hearing on his staff's findings. "But I have to tell you, I do not see any fundamental difference between dealing with an Obiang and dealing with a Saddam Hussein."[25]

*　*　*

ON THEIR FACE, the stories Levin and his staff unearthed regarding Riggs and Citibank were little different. Both involved private bankers who ran wild with their ludicrously corrupt customers, helping them set up shell companies to cover their tracks, obscuring their ties in public, and making millions while freely processing gobsmacking amounts of dirty foreign money. Like Citibank, Riggs had actively assisted some of the most corrupt customers on earth; also like Citibank, Riggs tried to keep the pipeline open as long as it could, no matter the source of the income.

There was one difference, though, between Citibank's ties with noxious regimes and foreign crooks and Riggs's transformation into the Obiangs' preferred money laundering vehicle: the law. Citibank had gone about its malfeasance before those Patriot Act provisions had placed new restrictions on America's banking sector. Riggs, however, simply pretended that those new restrictions never took place. As Levin later said, Riggs "ignored its anti–money laundering obligations before the Patriot Act, and continued to ignore them afterward."[26]

As Riggs and the Obiangs so clearly illustrated, when an onrush of dirty foreign money floods Washington, it can overcome even the kinds of anti–money laundering laws that have both momentum and public support behind them. As Levin and the PSI learned in their inquiry, Riggs had not only continued processing the Obiangs' dirty money through the entire saga of the passage of the Patriot Act, but it hadn't even bothered to flag any of the Obiang-related accounts as high-risk until late 2003, well after the first suspicions about the bank's foreign ties began trickling out and after Senate investigators had already begun asking questions.[27]

And it soon became clear why. Part of the banking regulations required officials at the Treasury Department to oversee compliance with anti–money laundering procedures. In the case of a client like the Obiangs, those regulations centered on making sure that the bank wasn't servicing the proceeds of foreign corruption—that the accounts the bank held on behalf of foreign officials appeared to match what could be expected of those foreign officials' incomes and assets. And if those at the bank are clearly turning a blind eye, as those at Riggs did time and again with the Obiangs, American regulators tasked with making sure banks complied with these anti–money laundering procedures were supposed to clamp down and make sure the new measures were followed.

But the American officials in charge of monitoring Riggs weren't simply asleep on the job—they actively swept Riggs's practices under the rug. They, in effect, colluded with Riggs's transformation into a laundromat for the Obiangs. As the Senate investigators uncovered, the U.S. official charged with overseeing Riggs's compliance—known as the examiner-in-charge (EIC), working out of the Treasury Department's Office of the Comptroller of the Currency (OCC)—"appeared to have become more of an advocate for the bank than an arms-length regulator." The official, R. Ashley Lee, worked as Riggs's EIC for several years, including through the post-9/11 debates just a few halls away on the U.S.'s new anti–money laundering regulations. For Lee, though, those regulations were apparently little more than suggestions—ones he could freely ignore as he saw fit. Lee apparently thought that because no one had necessarily taken banking regulations seriously before, at least when it came to handling foreign corrupt monies, there was little reason to think they would start now.[28]

On multiple instances, Lee recommended against taking any action against Riggs. Even with numerous internal complaints from anti–money laundering bank examiners, watching the Obiangs move their money through Riggs, Lee did nothing. As one of Lee's employees wrote him, Riggs's clear breach of anti–money laundering provisions "compels me to formally express my fear of what we have yet to uncover at this bank." Yet Lee kept approving the bank's operations and stalling any disciplinary action every time he had a chance. Lee claimed that the bank had "promised to correct identified [anti–money laundering] deficiencies," and that Riggs "was planning to remedy the identified deficiencies." Year after year went by, though, with nothing changing.[29]

If that had been all, Lee would have come out of the PSI investigation looking like a dupe, his ineptitude matched only by Riggs's greed. But there was another angle to the relationship, as Levin and his staff uncovered. When Lee announced he was retiring as EIC in 2002, Riggs immediately swooped in and offered Lee a new—and lucrative—management position. Lee was technically free to take the position, however unseemly it looked from the outside. After all, he'd hardly be the first bureaucrat to capitalize on a cozy relationship with the entity he was supposed to be overseeing.[30]

But federal post-employment regulations barred any sit-down meetings between former officials and the bank regulators for at least two years—a restriction Lee apparently ignored, appearing almost immediately after he left the government as an official representative of Riggs. Lee, remarkably, didn't deny his presence at these meetings, but his defense bordered on the absurd. As a later Senate report noted, "When the [PSI] asked him about these meetings, Mr. Lee acknowledged attending them, but claimed that he made a deliberate decision not to speak at them so that he would not violate the post-employment ban."[31] In other words, after remaining silent on Riggs's laundering for years, Lee remained silent when he was officially in Riggs's employ.

It was a clear case of what's known as "regulatory capture," when industry and officials become so cozy with one another that any dividing lines effectively disappear. The relationship between Riggs and Lee was hardly the first example of this happening—but, given the hundreds of millions of dollars making up the Obiangs' relationship with Riggs, it was perhaps the most expensive instance of "regulatory capture" in American history.

* * *

THERE WAS ONE other key discovery in the PSI's deep dive into Riggs, which neither Levin nor any of the members of his staff ever expected to find. With hundreds of boxes, thousands of documents, and even more potential leads to sift through, Levin needed as many hands as he could find for the examination of Riggs. One of those tapped for help was Laura Stuber, known as a dogged PSI forensic investigator. During the inquiry, Stuber spent time combing through some of the account ledgers Riggs had delivered, looking for names that might lead somewhere. There was one that caught her eye.

"There were some ledgers that said 'O. Pinochet'—and I said, 'Oh, that's interesting,'" Stuber, now working for the California Attorney General's Office, told me.[32] Pinochet: the last name of Augusto Pinochet, the grisly, decades-long military dictator in the South American country of Chile, responsible for the country's 1973 coup and for a regime that killed thousands. (Another of Pinochet's claims to fame: launching a successful assassination campaign against political opponents exiled in Washington.) But his name didn't begin with an "O." Maybe it was a relative, or a family member?

So Stuber pulled on the thread—and immediately discovered that this was no family member. This was the man himself: yet another dictator, who'd plowed millions upon millions of dollars into Riggs, with no questions asked. Tracing the names and numbers in ledger after ledger, Stuber untangled how Pinochet had bounced his money to and through Riggs, laundering it for his own use since the mid-1990s. As she followed the money he shuffled through different banks, there were scans of different passports the Chilean strongman used, with photos of him in various disguises—some where he was balding, some where he had a new mustache, some where he was wearing glasses. She also uncovered the different names he'd used to set up the accounts, some with variants of his own name ("Augusto Pinochet Ugarte") and some in the names of Chilean military officials who'd helped buttress his brutality. There were, in total, nearly 30 accounts linked directly to the Chilean kleptocrat—all of them allowing him to continue bankrolling his lavish lifestyle after stepping down from the presidency in 1990 (and promptly taking office as senator-for-life in the Chilean legislature).[33]

And there, in all their actuarial glory, the bank documents recorded all the ways Riggs had not only sought out Pinochet's ill-gotten money but had helped him conceal and launder the funds—even while thousands of Pinochet's victims were demanding justice in Chile. As the documents revealed, Riggs specifically recruited Pinochet to the bank, describing his wealth in internal documents as stemming from "family and salary." (Just a dictator trying to make an honest living, apparently.) Carol Thompson, the private banker assigned to Pinochet's accounts, met with the former dictator multiple times a year, with Riggs even providing Pinochet with offshore corporations that helped conceal his financial transfers.[34]

Even after Pinochet was finally placed under house arrest in London in 1998, with a British court ordering a freeze of all his assets, Riggs helped Pinochet work around the freeze by transferring his money through shell company accounts to keep it hidden yet accessible. In other words, Riggs helped Pinochet—again, one of the late twentieth century's most notorious butchers, known for tossing political opponents out of helicopters—specifically evade a court-ordered asset freeze.[35]

And there, over and over, was R. Ashley Lee. Yet again, Lee didn't bother to raise any concerns when he learned that Riggs was catering to Pinochet's financial needs. In one remarkable incident, Lee also excluded all paperwork related to the Pinochet accounts from the OCC's own electronic database—relegating them instead to a single hard copy, effectively making the accounts all but invisible to anyone else in Treasury who may have wanted to take a look.[36] (This was about a month before Lee accepted his sparkling new job at Riggs.)

Remarkably, up until the PSI's findings, Pinochet had somehow escaped developing a reputation for high-level corruption. Chileans viewed him as an authoritarian figure, a bloody impediment to Chile's democratic path—but he was never seen as someone who profited from his position. And then Levin and his staff's findings came out, and that reputation completely crumbled. "We thought he was this modest guy, and it created this huge uproar in Chile," Stuber told me. "We didn't know it was going to have that big an impact. We thought it was a big deal, but didn't know it was that big."[37]

But it was. Suddenly, Pinochet's remaining reputation in Chile collapsed in on itself. The façade he'd maintained for decades—that he was interested only in order, not in lining his pockets—crumbled. His corruption was suddenly there for all to see, no longer bundled behind the benefits of American secrecy. As the story dominated Chilean headlines, whatever soft spot Pinochet may have retained among nostalgic Chileans imploded. "He had a reputation of being a patriot, or of at least being an honest ruthless dictator," Levin told me. "And we destroyed that."[38]

* * *

AFTER LEVIN AND his staff finished sorting through the hundreds of boxes and thousands of documents and millions of financial details, the conclusions were stark. Riggs, by the mid-2000s, had transformed into a substantial engine for kleptocracy. Riggs made a mockery of claims that the Patriot Act's new anti–money laundering regulations were sufficient. Without enforcement—and with Treasury banking regulators allowed to jump ship to the banks they were supposed to be monitoring—the new legal restrictions were hardly worth the congressional paper on which they were written.

"Osama bin Laden boasted that his modern new recruits knew the 'cracks' in the 'Western financial systems' like they knew the 'lines in their hands,'" Levin said during a charged 2004 Senate hearing announcing the PSI findings on Riggs and the Obiangs' corruption. "That chilling statement helped fuel a new effort to strengthen our defenses against terrorists, corrupt dictators and others who would use our financial systems against us. . . . [But] the Riggs case history shows we still have a long way to go."[39]

Riggs, as it was, wouldn't get a chance to finally implement the reforms Lee had long allowed them to skirt. After coughing up over $40 million in penalties—the largest then in American history, including nearly $10 million to a fund dedicated to the thousands of victims of Pinochet's brutality—Riggs finally shuttered the Obiang-related accounts, divesting itself of its largest client.[40] Shortly thereafter, limping along, Riggs effectively folded, selling out to another American bank. Lincoln's bank, mortally wounded by the revelations about its money laundering machinery, was finally no more.

And yet, almost none of Riggs's higher-ups spent any time in prison. Kareri, who'd christened Riggs's relationship with the Obiangs, pleaded guilty on multiple counts, including bank fraud and money laundering. But even then he received only a two-year sentence—not much for a banker responsible for propelling one of the most blatant money laundering schemes ever seen in the nation's capital. Yet that sentence was still more than Lee or Carol Thompson, Pinochet's private banker, received, with both of them getting off scot-free. Allbritton, Riggs's longtime head, had already resigned his position in 2002, handing over the bank's stewardship to his playboy son, Robert Allbritton, who claimed ignorance of the entire affair.[41] (The younger Allbritton, now the publisher of *Politico*, blamed his lack of awareness on the fact that he spent much of the time cavorting and skiing across Europe.[42])

In the end, the Riggs story was a bit of American kleptocracy in miniature. Even with the new laws, a member of the American financial sector (Riggs) nonetheless kept working with a series of foreign officials (the Obiangs). On its face, such a relationship mirrored its work for the bank's other clients, many of whom also sought banking security and secrecy. But there was one glaring exception: the Obiangs oversee one of the most brutal regimes on the planet.

Yet the bank didn't need to worry, since the American bureaucrats supposedly overseeing the operation were in on the action. And if the American officials didn't care, then who would? The only thing Riggs didn't count on was Levin and his staff finally poking around and making an example of Riggs to the rest of the world.

The Obiangs, meanwhile, simply moved on. Their Riggs accounts were no more. But their grip on Equatorial Guinea's surging oil wealth—and on the levers of the country's political system—never wavered. Instead, they simply sniffed out new outlets for their money laundering enterprises. The hundreds of millions in dirty money they'd piled into Riggs was suddenly in search of a new home. And a continent away, Teodorin thought he'd found a solution. Where one avenue closed, a dozen others opened—loopholes, there to exploit.

So when Levin and his staff finally closed the Riggs investigation, Teodorin returned to an old haunt: Southern California. No longer was he simply a student a million miles from home, skipping his lessons and drinking until the early morning hours. Now, he was bringing with him an entire fleet of helpers: drivers and housekeepers, estate managers and professional cooks, security teams chock-full of retired police officers.

And it was there, in California, that Teodorin would plot his next moves for his transnational money laundering enterprise—there, as one contact said, to take full advantage of the loopholes in the Patriot Act, to splurge on as much bling and as many baubles as he could find, and on so much caviar that, as one source told *Harper's* in 2009, "you could have scooped it with a shovel."[43]

MENSA-CERTIFIED GENIUS

"We pride ourselves on being a country of asylum for those who have been persecuted or prosecuted, but we've never been a dumping ground for despots or dictators or people who have plundered a nation."

—Ted Kennedy[1]

While senators held hearings on Riggs, Teodorin pulled up outside a 12 foot-high wooden gate in Southern California. Flanking him were a pair of turrets: perfect spots for guards to perch as lookouts. Palm trees leaned overhead, stretching out beyond, swaying slightly. Under a warm sun, Teodorin looked to his right, just past the palm trees, knowing that if he followed the road he'd find homes that belonged to celebrities like Britney Spears, Mel Gibson, and Kelsey Grammer.[2]

But Teodorin wasn't interested in visiting those homes. He wanted the one that was right in front of him. Just behind the gate, a driveway wound on. On the right side, a tennis court sat unused next to a sand-colored guesthouse. As the driveway continued, the horizon opened up just to the left, and the Pacific Ocean came into view, stretching into the distance. Those who visited the property actually compared the view to an infinity pool: the sixteen-acre yard's giant grassy sprawl ended at the edge of a sheer cliff, immediately dropping off, leaving nothing but the view.[3]

At the end of the driveway, spread out like an inverted horseshoe, was a building that was less a house than, as visitors said, a palace. Part Spanish mission, part sprawling mansion, the bluff-top building had 15,000 square feet of space: six bedrooms, eight bathrooms, a foyer larger than most homes, a hot tub and (actual) infinity pool nestled alongside. The closets alone stretched into thousands of square feet.[4] ("The closet was bigger than my house," one visitor later told me.[5])

The home, built in 1991, was fit for a prince.[6] Which is why, when he stopped by for the first time in 2004, Teodorin realized that he had to have this property. Little matter that legislators in Washington were publicly debating his family's corruption. They may as well have been on Mars for all he cared. They couldn't touch him, or his money, or his plans.

There was one issue, though. All that money Teodorin had been tapping into at Riggs—all that money his family swindled, money that should have gone to schools and hospitals and roads and libraries—was suddenly marked. Everybody following the news knew his money was dirty. Thanks to Senator Levin's hearings and the fact that Riggs had suddenly become the poster child for housing and laundering dirty money, Teodorin could no longer simply open an account in his own name, wire as much money as he wanted to an American bank, or hand it off in shrink-wrapped millions to an American banker for in-person deposits. He would need help sniffing out new destinations for his money. And for that, he knew just what he needed: an American lawyer.

* * *

THE PATRIOT ACT's anti–money laundering provisions, as we saw earlier, imposed a number of new restrictions on U.S. banks and other financial institutions, and created new money laundering crimes regarding funds gained via foreign corruption. Along with banks, real estate agents, luxury goods vendors, and investment advisers—those running things like hedge funds and private equity firms—had all been targeted by American legislators for strict new anti–money laundering regulations, even though they'd since received "temporary" exemptions from Patriot Act requirements. But there was one glaring omission from the new requirements: lawyers. Despite playing key roles in scandals like the

BCCI implosion, American lawyers never got a mention in the Patriot Act's anti–money laundering provisions. There was no legal requirement for American lawyers to ask clients where they got their money from, or run basic due diligence checks on their clients' dirty money.[7] All that mattered was that their clients—American or otherwise—needed legal services. And the deeper the pockets, the better.

In reality, anti–money laundering checks for American lawyers are something of an oxymoron. American lawyers can work with whichever clients they want, providing their services to oligarchs or dictators or anyone with a bit of dirty money waiting to be put to use. The American Bar Association (ABA), the primary professional association representing America's legal industry, has issued multiple "guidances" for attorneys, instructing them how to avoid handling dirty money, or how to avoid getting caught in kleptocratic money laundering networks writ large. How to avoid becoming, as experts describe them, "enablers," or those "enabling" the flow of dirty funds into the U.S.[8]

And yet, these "best practices" remain mere suggestions. They're completely voluntary. There's nothing legally binding about them. U.S. lawyers can choose to comply, or not, as they wish.[9] It makes no difference in the eyes of American law, or even in their standing within the ABA or other legal associations.[10] Even with other jurisdictions having moved forward to prevent lawyers from handling dirty money—the European Union issued its first directive requiring member countries to impose anti–money laundering policies way back in 1991—America's legal sector remains unchanged, free of any legal anti–money laundering requirements.[11]

A 2016 video sting from the anticorruption organization Global Witness illustrated just how willingly segments of America's legal sector would roll around in the filthy money pouring in. Posing as an adviser to an African minister looking to move millions in suspect, dirty money—someone like Teodorin, for instance—Global Witness sat down with a dozen different American lawyers to ask their advice on how best to hide the funds in the U.S., and to see how willing they'd be to do so. "We said we needed to get the money into the U.S. without detection," Global Witness wrote. The results, Global Witness found, were "shocking." All but one of the lawyers immediately dove into the details of how best to launder the funds in the U.S., and how to obscure any links to the African minister in question.[12]

Setting up anonymous shell companies was, of course, a popular theme. Not only would the links between the shell company and the kleptocrat remain concealed, but if the lawyer was involved in the shell company's creation, there would be the added benefit of attorney-client privilege—another layer of secrecy protecting the kleptocrat in question if anyone asked. But some went even further. A number of the lawyers caught on tape suggested funneling the dirty money directly into the law firms' own bank accounts, effectively mixing the dirty money in with the firms' own funds, and offering cover of the law firm as assurance that the money in question was perfectly aboveboard.

One unwitting interviewee, James Silkenat, detailed how the African minister could work around the new anti–money laundering checks American banks were supposed to enforce. The key: having the lawyers identify which banks were still less than enthusiastic about enforcing the anti–money laundering requirements. "[Silkenat] explained that some banks carry out less rigorous checks on their customers and he said that he had experience at identifying such banks," Global Witness wrote. As Silkenat told them, "We would have to look into how far specific banks look into the know-your-customer laws and how far they would dig."[13] (The kicker? Silkenat was the head of the American Bar Association.) Nor were these small-scale firms. Around the same time, the law firms Shearman & Sterling LLP and DLA Piper were intimately involved in a massive, billion-dollar Malaysian corruption scheme,[14] and the powerhouse firm Skadden Arps was raking in millions while helping direct shady lobbying efforts out of Ukraine.[15] Small firms, large firms, it didn't seem to matter—all proved more than willing to help their dirty-money clients, time and again.

But again: none of this was illegal. American lawyers remain free to work with whatever clients they want. They can set up shell companies, trusts, or significant purchases for any client—and then, if any investigators come knocking, they can claim attorney-client privilege and refuse to reveal any details. It's yet another layer of anonymity and protection to enjoy. In many ways, U.S. lawyers are the perfect friend to have if you're a kleptocrat.

The BCCI collapse and the Salinas hearings, the Patriot Act and the resulting Riggs scandal: all of them had upended anti–money laundering realities for American financial institutions. But for American lawyers, almost nothing has changed. Which is why, when Teodorin started searching out new American uses for his money—and for the best way to snap up his Malibu mansion—he sought out lawyers who knew exactly how wide the loopholes for American attorneys remained. And one in particular, a California lawyer named Michael Berger, proved the perfect guide to the remaining—and legal—loopholes any kleptocrat would need.[16]

* * *

FOR THOSE INVESTIGATORS who got to know him, Berger wasn't someone you'd want to spend much time with. He was, at least according to one Senate investigator, "a slimeball," someone who, another investigator said, was clearly not a "top lawyer."[17] The kind of work Berger seemed to prefer, as one DOJ prosecutor told me, was as unethical as it comes: "That's not why I went to law school," the prosecutor said, reflecting on Berger's work. Berger, though, doesn't seem to mind. With a bulbous forehead and stretched smile, the attorney clearly thinks highly of himself. As the site for his law firm reads, "Mr. Berger is a Mensa, certified genius, with the intellectual ability to craft creative solutions to even the most difficult legal problems."[18]

For Teodorin, as later congressional and court documents revealed, there was one other reason Berger was ideal. Berger's willingness to barrel through legal loopholes, to set up all the anonymous shell companies Teodorin would need, and to scour bank after bank for the most lax anti–money laundering enforcement extant—and then uproot for a new bank whenever they caught on—was a perfect fit for an African kleptocrat with dreams of becoming a California superstar. Based in Los Angeles, Berger initially connected with Teodorin in 2004, just as Levin and his colleagues in Washington began blasting Riggs and broadcasting the rank corruption rotting the Obiang family's wealth. Yet none of those details or revelations ever seemed to perturb Berger. (It's unclear how the two of them first met; Berger declined to comment for this book, citing "the privilege between myself and my client."[19]) Teodorin told him that there was a property just north of them—perched along the Malibu coastline, fit for a prince—that he wanted. And he wanted Berger to help him get it. So Berger got to work—pocketing hundreds of thousands of dollars, as well as numerous other perks, along the way.

First, Berger called a neighbor, a real estate agent he'd known since the early 1990s. Neil Baddin was a Minnesota native who had worked as a real estate agent in the greater Los Angeles area since 1981. Baddin later said he'd never heard of Teodorin before Berger's call, and hadn't been closely following the hearings in Washington into the Obiang family's wealth. So when he got a call from Berger, and when Berger told him a wealthy client was looking for someone to help with a "delicate and intricate sales transaction," he didn't think twice.[20]

Not that there was any reason for him to do so. As we already saw, the Treasury Department had specifically exempted real estate agents like Baddin, who at the time worked for the Coldwell Banker realty firm, from anti-money laundering requirements. As with Berger, there was no legal reason for Baddin to check the source of Teodorin's cash flow, to do a due diligence review of him or his family, or to even bother with a cursory Google check. He didn't even need to know Teodorin's identity as his client. Baddin would later claim there were "no red flags" obvious to him.[21] As Baddin would tell Senate investigators years later, the real estate agent "had no legal obligation to [inquire about Teodorin's finances,] and such questions made most clients uncomfortable."[22]

And he was right. As with the banks before them, for real estate firms, kleptocrats and other high-net-worth clients could appear little different on paper. Dirty money entered the slipstream of capital flowing into American real estate, often looking indistinguishable from other finances tied to celebrities, to media moguls, to billionaires achieving their American dreams. Real estate agents, thanks to the Patriot Act exemption, were under no compunction to check under the hood of the finances—to see if they could track down where it came from, and whether their client was actually a kleptocrat searching out their own American dream. Even if they did prod about a client's wealth, they ran the risk that the client would simply look for a different, less curious real estate agent. Plus, what if the client simply used an anonymous shell company? How was the real estate agent supposed to pierce that veil? How was anyone—a real estate agent in California, a banker in Washington, a lawyer filing all the necessary paperwork—supposed to tell if that Delaware shell company behind the purchase was secretly run by a man sitting on billions in ill-gotten gains?

And given the amounts of money involved, why would they ever bother to check if there wasn't even a law against it?

* * *

THAT OCTOBER, SITTING in a suite at the Beverly Wilshire Hotel, Baddin met Teodorin for the first time. Sweeping in with his tailored suit, wide-rim glasses, and a model-thin woman on his arm, Teodorin struck him, Baddin remembered, as "bigger than life." Baddin successfully pitched his services to the kleptocrat sitting across from him. A month later, Berger phoned to let Baddin know Teodorin wanted to hire him. They drew up a retainer agreement, with one goal in mind: obtain the Malibu property—"one of the most extraordinary pieces of property I've ever seen in my life," Baddin said. The cost was irrelevant.[23]

While Baddin got to work carving out an agreement with the Malibu property sellers, Berger had other duties in Teodorin's employ. Teodorin, after all, still needed a way to hide all the dirty money he could no longer keep in Riggs. And as with so many others, Berger knew precisely where to turn: anonymous American shell companies. In October 2004, the lawyer filed paperwork to create an anonymous American shell company called Beautiful Vision, Inc. Not long later, he formed a second anonymous shell company for Teodorin dubbed Unlimited Horizon, Inc. As Berger and Teodorin both intended, the filings for Beautiful Vision and Unlimited Horizon never once mentioned Teodorin by name.[24]

Shortly after Berger helped Teodorin create Beautiful Vision, the lawyer swung by a local branch of Bank of America to open a pair of checking accounts in the shell company's name. According to bank records, Berger identified himself as the shell company's owner and president—and then proceeded to navigate the legal loopholes available to him as Teodorin's lawyer. Teodorin had already transferred significant funds into Berger's own attorney-client account at the bank. Berger then transferred some of those funds from the accounts for his law office—which, again, had no legal obligation to look into Teodorin's blindingly obvious links to foreign corruption—to the shell company accounts. On paper, it looked like the accounts for Berger's law firm had simply started bankrolling shell company accounts—leaving the bank, and those inside the bank on the lookout for potential money laundering, none the wiser about the funds' true origins. In just a few months, Berger helped supply the new accounts with the nearly $10 million needed to pay Teodorin's bills and expenses.[25]

Still, with the stench of Riggs wafting out of Washington, Bank of America grew skittish, and started taking a closer look at the shell company accounts' activities, which had included a series of substantial cash transfers. Internal auditors scoured the accounts' transactions and discovered a series of suspicious payments, including stays at hotels in Las Vegas and Hawaii and transfers from Equatorial Guinea. It didn't take long for the bank to realize who was really behind the shell company accounts—Teodorin. Less than a year after their opening, both accounts were shuttered by Bank of America. While the bank later admitted it could have moved more quickly to close the accounts, its anti–money laundering protocols had, on the whole, worked—a testament to the Patriot Act provisions, and Carl Levin's efforts in Washington.[26]

Except, there was one catch. Bank of America allowed Berger to keep his firm's long-standing attorney-client accounts—the ones that had helped funnel millions into the shell company accounts in the first place—open and operating. And even while Bank of America shuttered the shell company accounts, the bank allowed the attorney-client accounts to keep receiving funds, time and again, from Teodorin's accounts in Equatorial Guinea. After all, there was no legislation or regulation requiring the bank to close the attorney-client account. As far as the bank was concerned, they'd followed the letter of the law. The bank closed the shell company accounts—but effectively allowed the rest of the operation to continue as before.[27]

And that decision, as investigators later discovered, proved the key to keeping Teodorin's entire money laundering operation going. A state-based bank, Union Bank of California, proved just as open. Using the same methods—opening accounts in the names of new shell companies and using the separate law firm accounts at Bank of America as the go-between—Teodorin managed to transfer millions more into his Union Bank of California accounts. And Berger decided to open an account at the new bank for his law firm, initiating yet another stream through which to move the money. (Ironically, even though some of the bank's internal auditors flagged a number of the account transactions for review, the bank couldn't act on the questions for months—mainly because the bank was simultaneously negotiating with the Department of Justice over the bank's faulty anti–money laundering systems.[28])

Eventually, eyeing the seven-figure sums that kept rolling in and out of the shell company accounts, the bank took a closer look at where the money was coming from and what it was being used for. Sure enough, they concluded that the funds were suspicious. But unlike Bank of America, Union Bank of California specifically singled out Berger for his role. As the bank's own report detailed, "The investigation found the use of multiple corporate vehicles by Michael Berger . . . to disguise the identity of [Teodorin] as well as layer and integrate funds derived via international wire transactions from a high risk jurisdiction [Equatorial Guinea], which had the appearance of money laundering activity."[29] The findings couldn't have been starker: Berger had apparently acted as the facilitator of a transnational money laundering scheme. The bank's response was swift, closing all the accounts—including the attorney client fund—in question.[30]

Yet Berger and Teodorin were not deterred. There were banks aplenty, all throughout California, to turn to. The two even eyed Citibank—the centerpiece of the Salinas investigations just a few years prior—and opened several new accounts there before the bank realized the accounts were "inconsistent with the account profile," closing them before they could do more damage.[31] As court documents later detailed, Berger obfuscated in order to keep the accounts open; as a later complaint filed by the government alleged, "When the bank inquired about [an account affiliated with] Unlimited Horizon, Berger lied that it was to help one of his clients pay a female employee without the client's wife knowing about it."[32]

Berger, who kept a file of articles highlighting all the facets of Teodorin's rank corruption, didn't seem to mind his role in helping the kleptocrat move his money. In addition to the six-figure payments Berger earned, documents later revealed that Teodorin had introduced Berger to a lifestyle the lawyer had never known, taking Berger to party after party around Southern California, including one called the "Kandy Halloween Bash" at the Playboy Mansion. In response, Berger couldn't help but gush. "I appreciate the super VIP treatment that you gave me," Berger wrote in one email. "I appreciate you telling your friends that I am your attorney. I am proud to work for you. . . . The food was great, the drinks were better than great, the house, the view, the DJ, the white tiger were all SO COOL!" After the Playboy bash, Berger blushed, "I had an awesome time. I met many beautiful women, and I have the photos, e-mail addresses and phone numbers to prove it. If the word gets out that you are looking for a bride, women all over the world will go even more crazy for you. . . . Your loyal friend and attorney, Michael Berger."[33] As a journalist at *Forbes* later quipped, "Berger seemed to enjoy the perks of being a kleptocrat's henchman."[34]

Along the way, Teodorin also enlisted the help of a second California lawyer. George Nagler had more pedigree than Berger, having graduated from Harvard, and appeared at least a little more scrupulous than Berger. ("Nagler wasn't so personally despicable [as Berger]," one Senate investigator told me.[35]) Nagler even freely admitted to suspicions about the origins of Teodorin's money; as he later told congressional investigators, he was "well aware of the suspect origins of [Teodorin's] funds." But, again, there was nothing on the books—no law, no regulation—forcing Nagler, as an American lawyer, to do anything about those suspicions.[36]

It was the same story, time and again. There was Nagler forming a number of American shell companies on Teodorin's behalf, with names like Sweet Pink, Inc., and Sweetwater Malibu LLC. There was Nagler opening accounts for the companies at banks both familiar (Union Bank of California) and new (Cal National Bank, City National Bank, Pacific

Mercantile Bank). There were the new accounts sucking up millions directly from Equatorial Guinea, or via transfers from Nagler's own law firm account, free for Teodorin to use in the U.S. before the banks ever caught on.[37] (One of the accounts actually featured rap megastar Eve as the account-holder—which makes sense given that, as we'll see in the next chapter, she'd begun dating Teodorin.)

On and on the process continued. By the time any bank caught on, it was already too late—and there were numerous other banks to run the same scheme through. It was, said one Senate investigator, a "cat and mouse game"—one made infinitely easier by the fact that Berger and Nagler could freely work with whichever clients they wanted, even those embedded in the most barbaric regimes on the planet.[38] "How do they look themselves in the mirror?" Rick Messick, an anticorruption consultant who spent years trying to track Teodorin's crimes, told me. "How much money does it take?"[39]

* * *

WHILE BERGER AND Nagler ran Teodorin's money through a carousel of unsuspecting banks, Baddin, Teodorin's real estate agent, was still negotiating with the selling agents at the Malibu megamansion. Given the magnitude of the purchase, Baddin wanted to make sure to hew as closely as possible to Teodorin's instructions. But even that was an uphill battle: not only would Teodorin regularly ignore Baddin's phone calls but there were numerous times when Teodorin would blow off a scheduled meeting with him, forcing Baddin to wait for hours to no avail—even when the two were only a single floor apart.[40]

Still, Baddin pushed on. After bandying millions back and forth, in early January 2006 Baddin and the selling agent finally settled on a number all parties could agree to: $30 million for the house, plus an additional $750,000 for some of the furnishings, in one of the most spectacular home sales in the U.S. that year. And as with the bankers, as with the lawyers, as with the shell companies, Teodorin got more than just the house. Thanks to American loopholes, he also got to enjoy the anonymity that came with it. As documents later revealed, Teodorin opted to pay for the house with an account attached to one of his anonymous shells: Sweetwater Malibu LLC. Baddin later said that Nagler specifically made sure Teodorin's name never appeared on the deed or title for the house.[41]

The selling agent set up an escrow account with First American Title Company, which would then transfer the funds to Wachovia Bank in order to pay the sellers. (Escrow is an arrangement in which a third party temporarily houses significant sums of money or assets, typically between buyer and seller.) But there again, another loophole: thanks to the Treasury Department's "temporary" exemptions, escrow agents, overseeing the escrow accounts, were excepted from any anti-money laundering provisions. Banks still had to run basic anti-money laundering checks on the escrow agents themselves—but after that, with an escrow agent in charge of the account, the oversight ended. Escrow agents could effectively use the Treasury Department's "temporary" exemption as a magic wand, removing themselves from any obligation whatsoever. The banks, meanwhile, were legally allowed to look the other way and not peek under the hood of the money coming into the escrow account. As later Senate documents revealed, banks' anti-money laundering checks "depended upon the escrow agents policing their own clients"—but there wasn't a single law forcing those running the escrow accounts to do so. As Wachovia later told investigators, the money came in "with no questions asked."[42]

It was American kleptocracy, in real time. You had an anonymous shell company, a lawyer who didn't need to know anything about his client's finances, and industries and tools—in this case, real estate and escrow accounts—that could skirt basic anti-money laundering protocols. Anonymity, legal protections, industries that didn't need to do anything besides cash your checks—what more did a kleptocrat need?

Nor was that all. As Baddin later revealed, Teodorin forced the real estate agent, and all those involved in the purchase, to ink a separate confidentiality agreement. Baddin was now legally barred from disclosing Teodorin's role in the purchase to anyone. But even then, the agent claimed that the confidentiality agreement was hardly a red flag; he'd signed others in the past, "usually for a celebrity type of person." Teodorin, though, appeared to be the first rapacious kleptocrat he'd ever signed one for.[43]

In April 2006, the deal closed. Teodorin, who was the subject of high-profile congressional investigations into his corruption, had secured a beautiful house through his American conduits, and he managed to do so legally and anonymously throughout the entire process.

Teodorin's marriage of American shell companies and American lawyers and American real estate was, in a sense, as clear a model of American kleptocracy as you could find. And it was a model replicated across the country, all for the benefit of regimes buoyed by corrupt cash. It was the same method that Iranian government officials used to anonymously purchase Manhattan skyscrapers in order to skirt sanctions.[44] It was the same method kleptocratic Venezuelan oligarchs used to anonymously purchase South Florida luxury properties,[45] and crooked Nigerian politicos used to inject dirty money into Houston's housing market.[46] It was the same method the spawn of dictators in Uzbekistan[47] and Gambia[48] and the Republic of Congo[49] used to launder their corrupt wealth up and down America's coastlines (and a method that included, as we'll see in the final section, Trump properties). It was the same method that saw billions and billions of dollars race into America's housing market over the past two decades, inflating prices for the rest of us, allowing these human rights abusers to freely enjoy the fruits of their brutality.

At last, with his Malibu mansion in his pocket, the road to celebrity was wide open for Teodorin. He immediately began plotting out his next steps on his parade to stardom. And he promptly began staffing up, creating a hive of activity around the Malibu property, bringing in dozens of waiters and cleaners and employees who could fill out the place and who, on Teodorin's instructions, would form a standing line to applaud him every time he left the house and every time he returned. It was almost as if the Riggs hearing, which had revealed his family's gross corruption just 18 months prior, had never happened.[50]

But while Teodorin started leading the life of American royalty he'd long sought, a federal investigator, thousands of miles away in South Florida, was sitting at his breakfast table, flipping through a newspaper. There, on one of the lifestyle pages, something caught his eye. Something curious, about an African prince snatching up as many Rolexes as he could find. It was a moment that sparked a pursuit that would, a decade later, result in the Malibu mansion changing hands once again—and finally snuffing out Teodorin's American kleptocracy dreams for good.

FISH PHYSICIAN

"You've been hit by—you've been struck by—a smooth criminal."

—Michael Jackson[1]

In 2003, the Bush administration offered full-throated support for the passage of the United Nations Convention Against Corruption, a groundbreaking multilateral agreement providing guidance on everything needed to combat corruption and dirty money.[2] Shortly thereafter, Bush issued Presidential Proclamation 7750, which allowed the U.S. to specifically bar foreign officials accused of profiting from corruption (plus their families) from visiting the U.S. ever again.[3] "High-level corruption by senior government officials, or kleptocracy, is a grave and corrosive abuse of power," Bush would later say.[4]

Elsewhere in Washington, bureaucratic decisions followed suit. In March 2003, Congress birthed the Department of Homeland Security, which would thereafter house the U.S.'s Immigration and Customs Enforcement (ICE).[5] ICE would later gain notoriety as the most prominent face of Donald Trump's domestic crackdowns.[6] At the time, however, ICE fell into something of a crack within America's antikleptocracy regime. The FBI traditionally manned domestic anticorruption outfits, while the CIA tracked and trailed foreign operations—the kinds increasingly looking to the U.S. for all of their laundering needs. But ICE straddled both worlds, monitoring foreign funds racing into the U.S. and tracing their routes through the states thereafter. Following the White House's example, ICE leadership in 2003 announced the formation of the Foreign Corruption Investigations Group, an organization specifically tasked with tackling the kleptocrats running their networks throughout the U.S. in order to "identify, trace, freeze, and recover assets within the United States illicitly acquired through kleptocracy."[7]

As with plenty of other governmental initiatives, though, the difference between theory and practice couldn't have been wider. These kinds of kleptocratic networks suddenly bubbling up—an autocratic Cambodian prime minister dumping dirty money into New York real estate;[8] a crooked Malaysian financier living the high life in Las Vegas;[9] corrupt Central Asian figures traveling up and down the West Coast[10]—involved legal questions that the new ICE anticorruption agents had never fielded, and jurisdictions with which they had no experience. The group identified potential candidates for investigation in the first few years, but ran into bureaucratic roadblocks and the difficulties that come with trying to pry open things like anonymous shell companies.

By 2006, without much to show for its efforts, the ICE anticorruption group appeared at risk of wasting away. Then, in a personnel shuffle, new leadership stepped in. The group's new supervisor, Bobby Rutherford, came with a rocky Southern accent, an openness to new ideas, and the experience that comes with 16 years of monitoring how Latin American drug dealers saturated South Florida with illicit drugs—as well as how they moved their money. Rutherford was initially told that the ICE group would primarily focus on Latin America and the Caribbean, especially the cartels growing in prominence. But Rutherford had a different idea. "I had done the 'taco circuit' for so long with drug cases—the Caribbean, all that—I just didn't want to mess with it anymore," Rutherford told me. He was tired of chasing the same networks, the same bagmen, the same drug runners infesting Bogotá and Caracas and Mexico City, island-hopping through the Caribbean to reach their final destinations in the U.S. It was time to think a bit bigger.[11]

The ICE group's headquarters would remain in Miami, but with Rutherford as the new supervisor, they were going to expand their writ. They were going to think the same way their prey did: globally. The organization "was in existence as a money laundering group to target Central American, South American officials that were stealing and bringing the stolen merchandise—money—into the U.S.," Rutherford told me. "When I took over the group, [I said,] 'Why are we just doing South America? We should be doing the whole world—no one else is doing it.' No one was doing it. And I told everyone that we were the group: 'We're starting to cover the whole world.'" With all eyes at the time focused on Iraq and transnational terrorism, there wasn't much pushback in Washington: "Everyone at headquarters had just changed positions and didn't know any different, and so they went along with it, too."[12]

Rutherford's staff wasn't big, just a few dozen agents at the maximum, tasked with hunting the whales of the offshore world. They initially began digging into some potential kleptocrats to corral, including crooked Taiwanese figures and a Nigerian state governor burying his dirty oil money deep in the heart of Texas. But those cases had languished, with the group either unable to find cooperative officials in the home countries or getting stuck in all of the anonymity that buried the trails.

One morning, before arriving at his Miami office, Rutherford opened the newspaper, just to scan the headlines. There was a name he'd never seen before. "There was an article about [Teodorin] Obiang purchasing a Rolex and some other luxury items," Rutherford remembered. "It was like a society-page-type article on this big guy from Africa, who came over here with his government position and bought this and this and this, and he's partying here. And that was pretty much it.

"And I go, 'Oh, who is this guy?'"[13]

* * *

THAT GUY, ACCORDING to later documents, was someone suddenly inhabiting a life of luxury that few could have dreamed of, let alone enjoyed. Ensconced in his new Malibu palace, overlooking the most immaculate coastline California had to offer, Teodorin began plotting out his next steps. He already had the American lawyers in his pocket, helping oversee his financial networks, even with American banks on the lookout. He had his American shells, and he had a seemingly bottomless pot of dirty money to draw from, courtesy of his father's regime and his own behavior back home.

His California mansion was already humming with staff. Alongside the gardeners and the assistants, Teodorin began flying in a number of former police officers from Equatorial Guinea to provide security—including a "chase team" that followed Teodorin when he ranged around Malibu on his daylong benders.[14] (Teodorin would reportedly sometimes sleep as late as 9:00 p.m., waking only to keep the party going.)

All of these staffers, of course, needed to be paid. Shouldn't be a problem, Berger said. Thanks to their shell company and law firm accounts, Teodorin could pass his ill-gotten gains through an unwitting American bank, masked by attorney-client and shell company accounts, funneling tens of thousands of dollars and more to his security details and top-flight chefs and drivers whisking him around town. Later bills even showed one shell company account that directed some $7,500 for something called a "Fish Physician," for help maintaining Teodorin's new koi pond.[15]

Not that the money wasn't earned. Teodorin's security team later complained that he would "drive like a maniac," routinely blasting through red lights. One chauffeur complained that he had to clean out "bottles of urine" that were left in the car. Another assistant accused Teodorin of sauntering up in nothing but an open robe while at home, saying menacingly, "When someone comes through these gates, they're in Equatorial Guinea." The same assistant later revealed that he carried shrink-wrapped bills in a Nike shoebox for girlfriends and escorts alike to go purchase whatever dresses they'd like.[16]

One of the dozens, possibly hundreds, of girlfriends Teodorin cycled through during his Malibu stint reportedly fell in love with the kleptocrat. "She was smitten by [him]—smitten," one investigator told me. He "just showered her with gifts, $50,000 Rodeo Drive shopping sprees. She was literally in love with the guy. She told her mom, 'Mom, I met the prince, and my life is going to forever be changed.'" One problem: Teodorin promptly forgot about her, including an agreement to meet on her birthday. "When [he] finally figured out, 'Oh shit, I forgot that she's sitting there,' he sent over a couple of his goons who took her out on a shopping spree on Rodeo Drive. And we asked her, 'Well, did you go shopping?' And she said, 'Of course I did.'"[17]

After negotiating a $4 million deal with an interior decorator, Berger bragged about dropping the designer's commission a few percentage points. "I feel good about saving you money," Berger wrote to Teodorin. "I enjoy working for you." On one occasion, one of Teodorin's assistants told Berger that the kleptocrat wanted to buy something called "jumping stilts." "The boss saw a guy running down the street in these contraptions and wanted them," the assistant wrote, to which Berger replied that the best method of payment would be via their Unlimited Horizon shell company. (It's unclear if Teodorin ever ended up bouncing around his house in these jumping stilts.[18])

And there were the toys. In the span of just a few years, Teodorin fleshed out his Malibu pad with an incredible *thirty two* luxury, high-end cars and motorcycles. Enough to start his own dealership, and leave plenty of inventory to open new locations. Teodorin raced up and down the coast, pocketing anything that caught his eye. All he had to do, according to later investigations, was write personal checks attached to his shell company accounts, with the checks listing things like "Ferrari" or "Pay off 2005 Lamborghini Roadster" in their memo lines.[19]

The fleet was remarkable. There was a $2 million Maserati, and a $1.3 million Bugatti. There were seven Ferraris, four Rolls-Royces, and four Bentleys, in addition to a pair of Maybachs and a pair of Mercedes, and a Porsche and a Lamborghini and an Aston Martin. There were days he would spend hundreds of thousands of dollars at a single Beverly Hills Ferrari dealership—and then, a few weeks later, hundreds of thousands more at a separate Beverly Hills Lamborghini vendor. There were so many cars that Teodorin couldn't even keep all of them; he had to house a number of the purchases at the Los Angeles Petersen Automotive Museum.[20]

Still, Teodorin never missed a chance to show off his collection. As journalist Ken Silverstein wrote, "One night, Teodorin parked his Bugatti Veyron near the entrance of L'Ermitage, a favorite hangout where he'd gone for drinks. When he saw gawkers stop to admire it, he sent [his driver] back to Malibu by cab so [he] could drive back his second Bugatti to park next to it." (As he would say to his staff, "I'm wearing blue shoes, so get me the blue Rolls today."[21])

He was, according to one source, at one point considered one of the top luxury car customers not just in Malibu, but in the entire U.S.[22] All of it, funneled via his American shell company accounts. Yet again, the luxury auto dealers didn't have to concern themselves with the source of Teodorin's income. To them, he appeared no different than any of the other high-net-worth clients they worked with. They were happy to cash his checks, and keep the cars flowing off their lots and directly into his stead.

Teodorin also developed a taste for things that float. For Christmas 2006, he spent some $700,000 to rent out Paul Allen's 300-foot yacht, named *Tatoosh*, to fete his most well-known girlfriend, Grammy-winning rapper Eve.[23] Taken with the boat, Teodorin promptly announced that he was going to build one of the world's largest superyachts himself. He immediately commissioned Kusch Yachts, a German boat-builder, to draw up plans for a 200-foot custom yacht—one that would have, à la Kolomoisky, a shark tank aboard, in addition to a movie theater, restaurant, and fingerprint-operated doors. Total price tag: $380 million.[24]

While the designs for Teodorin's new megayacht (code-named "Project Zen") were finalized, he also sought out smaller options.[25] He picked up multiple performance racing boats from a dealer in Fort Myers, Florida, going for about $1 million apiece—and coming without any requirements from the sellers to inquire about the source of the money. These so-called go-fast boats topped out at almost 200 miles per hour—and could go even faster when tricked out with helicopter engines, which he reportedly demanded.[26]

But it wasn't always smooth. In 2009, Teodorin tried to ship one of his go-fast boats to Maui, but the boat slipped off the trailer, requiring substantial repairs. The kleptocrat apparently didn't even realize that Maui marinas didn't sell the leaded fuel the boat required, so he was forced to ship the gas at hundreds of dollars per barrel. With the craft fixed and fueled, the local boat pilot took him and a few of his arm-candy women out on the water. But immediately after dropping them off after the day trip, the pilot frantically called his assistant: the earlier repairs had faltered, and a hole in the boat's hull immediately started guzzling water. The boat, in short order, capsized. Fuming, Teodorin was forced to fly in a "special team" from Honolulu to salvage the thing, bringing with them a separate helicopter and a number of trucks to accomplish the feat.[27]

*   *   *

AND THEN THERE was the jet. A Gulfstream GV—a "gee-five," in modern parlance—which soars over 50,000 feet, ranges over 10,000 kilometers, and uses a pair of high-end Rolls-Royce engines to fly so fast it can nearly break the sound barrier. Mark Cuban, owner of the Dallas Mavericks, has one, as does former Google CEO Eric Schmidt, as did Apple savant Steve Jobs. And in early 2006, Teodorin decided that he needed to join their club.[28]

With the help of his lawyers, Teodorin found a $38.5 million GV for sale, held by a wealthy family out of Indonesia. Registered in Oklahoma City, the jet was technically subject to U.S. jurisdiction and U.S. law. Thankfully for Teodorin, though, there were no anti–money laundering or antikleptocracy laws regarding the sales of multimillion-dollar planes, since sellers of private jets—like luxury yachts, like luxury cars—were exempted from the requirements American banks shouldered.[29] It was high-flight kleptocracy, out of reach of authorities and regulators alike.

There was a small hitch, though. With high-end purchases like this, both sellers and buyers often use the aforementioned escrow accounts to hold funds, especially after an agreement has been finalized but inspections are still ongoing. Teodorin's jet purchase was no different. Using accounts linked to yet another shell company to hide his identity—this one called "Ebony Shine International"—Teodorin bundled millions of dollars in payment into a Bank of America escrow account controlled by McAfee & Taft, an Oklahoma-based law firm that often doubled as an escrow agent for private plane purchases.[30]

But the law firm, which initially appeared gung-ho on the new deal, balked. To be sure, like the American real estate agents and American luxury vendors elsewhere, McAfee & Taft was exempt from those pesky Patriot Act restrictions that targeted American banks. But the firm had adopted a voluntary anti–money laundering program, going above and beyond the legal requirements to try to sniff out dirty money where it could. And after receiving an initial payment from the Ebony Shine shell company in March, a representative from McAfee & Taft did something few other law firms, and few other Americans in Teodorin's orbit, had done: they requested more information. As the firm wrote Teodorin's lawyer, "We need some more information" regarding the shell company, as well as the "identity of the source of funds."[31]

The firm didn't hear anything back. And the money kept coming, in million-dollar tranches. On April 4, the escrow account received the first payment of $2.6 million from an Equatorial Guinea bank. Two days later, another $2.6 million, also from Equatorial Guinea. One day after that, over $5 million in a single transfer. All while Teodorin's lawyers ignored McAfee's questions about who was behind Ebony Shine, or about why the millions were coming in from a notoriously corrupt jurisdiction.[32] And why would they answer? Few other American companies or figures had ever turned down Teodorin's money previously, especially when they didn't have to.

Nonetheless, McAfee & Taft wouldn't bite. Spooked by Ebony Shine's silence, and the fact that the millions were coming from Equatorial Guinea, the firm announced just a few days after receiving the final payment that it was canceling the transaction and returning the funds. One McAfee rep later said that he "expected an angry phone call" from Ebony Shine, but none ever came.[33] It's unclear what ultimately caused the firm to pull out of the deal. Perhaps it didn't want the bad press of being associated with Equatorial Guinea? Perhaps it actually had firmer corporate morals than its competitors, willing to forgo clearly dirty money if it could? For a fleeting moment, it seemed like a sign that the idea that those industries exempted from anti–money laundering laws could self-regulate—that they didn't need any additional regulation from the government—may have been right.

That feeling didn't last long. A few days later, Teodorin's team located another escrow agent, Insured Aircraft Title Services (IATS), which announced that it would be happy to help the buyer join the likes of Cuban and Schmidt and Jobs in owning a Gulfstream. Just a week after McAfee & Taft proved that some firms could take a higher road, IATS illustrated that there was really no need to, as long as they were getting paid. A few weeks later, the sale was finalized without IATS ever learning who the buyer was, or who the millions in question actually belonged to. IATS's in-house lawyer happily—and correctly—assured all parties that no laws had been broken. As investigators later wrote, "U.S. escrow agents selling multi-million-dollar aircraft have no legal obligation to know their customers, evaluate the source of the funds used in aircraft purchases, or take special precautions when dealing with" anonymous shell companies like Ebony Shine.[34]

It didn't take long for Teodorin to put his new investment to use. Flight records over the next few years showed Teodorin zooming around the world, from Bermuda to Dubai to Brazil to France. From March 2007 to November 2009, the plane arrived and departed from the U.S. an incredible 35 times.[35] (One of those stopovers saw him swing by Las Vegas yet again, where the bill for his $5,000-per-night stay in the Four Seasons' presidential suite referred to him directly as "Prince" Teodorin.[36]) Girlfriends and models and escorts—more women convinced they'd finally found their prince—usually rode along, to destinations extraordinaire.

*　*　*

FEW WOMEN, THOUGH, could compare to Teodorin's favorite female flying guest: Janet Jackson. It's unclear how exactly Teodorin and Janet first met. By the late 2000s, though, the two were clear friends, with Janet a "frequent visitor" to Teodorin's Malibu palazzo.[37] Other friends, according to one of the federal investigators I spoke with, were Tito and Jermaine, two lesser-known Jackson brothers. "The Michael Jackson family," the investigator told me, were "frequent fliers" alongside Teodorin.[38] But there's no record of Teodorin ever meeting his idol—the man he, and so many of his generation, worshipped. After Michael Jackson died unexpectedly in the summer of 2009, Teodorin's opportunity to befriend his hero disappeared.[39] As journalist Ken Silverstein wrote, Teodorin reportedly drove a Rolls-Royce Phantom to Jackson's memorial, but he'd never have the chance to meet the man he'd idolized growing up.[40]

Yet that didn't mean he couldn't remember the King of Pop, and continue his legacy, in other ways. As such, Teodorin had an idea: he would buy up as much of Michael Jackson's estate as he could—as many baubles and trophies, as many gold-plated records and Neverland trinkets, as many moments of icon and legacy tied directly to the pop singer—no matter the cost.

Thankfully, there was an easy way to do so, courtesy of the loopholes provided by the U.S. government. In the U.S., art and collectibles vendors, including big-name auction houses like Sotheby's and Christie's, have never been subject to any kind of due diligence or anti–money laundering regulations. Despite the fact that the U.S. has the world's largest art market—clocking in at nearly $30 billion, some 44 percent of global sales[41]—the entire industry has long escaped any kind of regulatory oversight. For the auction houses that sell this kind of material, as a 2020 Senate report later found, there is no "mandate [for] detailed procedures to prevent money laundering and verify a customer's identity." To be sure, the art dealers and auction houses can adopt voluntary anti–money laundering policies. But "there is no legal requirement for the [auction houses] to confirm the identity of the buyer or that the buyer is not laundering money through the purchase."[42]

Or more simply: anyone can buy anything, for any amount, with any money, at any American auction house.

* * *

THROUGH A TANGLE of contacts in the music industry, the Los Angeles–based Julien's Auctions landed the rights to distribute the lion's share of Jackson's estate. Selling off Jackson's estate was a natural fit for the auction house, which had already helped drive demand for everything from Marilyn Monroe merch to Muhammad Ali swag to Barbra Streisand tchotchkes. Founded by the genial Darren Julien in 2001, the auction house had ridden the wave of the growing memorabilia industry—a wave that had already attracted the interest of malign figures elsewhere. "I go back to the auction business in the late 1990s with classic cars, which were laundered for drug money. . . . The car auction company I worked for in the late 1990s, we got raided because the consignors were drug dealers," Julien told me. Even with that history, though, Julien didn't seem perturbed by kleptocrats eyeing his auction house as a potential means of transforming their dirty money into valuable memorabilia. Dirty money is worth just as much as the clean—and all that matters is that these auction houses attract clients. "At the end of the day it's really, what someone does with the money, how they obtain it, that's not our [business]," the affable Julien told me.[43]

It didn't take long for Teodorin to make his presence felt at the auctions offering Jackson memorabilia. These auctions, which began in mid-2010, fit the traditional mold of auctions elsewhere. Rows of potential bidders sit in front of a dais. An auctioneer, standing in front, introduces the item in question, offering a few descriptive tidbits about the item and its provenance—and then opens the bidding. The buyers compete to match the bid, setting off a race to the finish, with the auctioneer spitting out higher and higher numbers until only one buyer is left standing. For the Julien auctions, Teodorin assigned one of his assistants, a young, slender Los Angeles resident named Wanda Kelley, to outcompete anyone interested in Jackson merchandise.[44] According to investigators and later receipts alike, Kelley was only too happy to oblige. In a number of separate auctions throughout the year—some in Beverly Hills, some in Las Vegas, even one held in Macau, where Teodorin's team phoned in their bids—Teodorin funneled millions of dollars to secure as much Jackson memorabilia as he could.[45]

There was a signed basketball from Jackson and basketball superstar Michael Jordan, each an MJ, which Teodorin grabbed for $245,000.[46] There was the silver-sheen MTV Video Music Awards "Moonman" trophy, snapped up for $60,000. There was Jackson's gold record for "Beat It," one of Jackson's autographed jackets from the seminal "Thriller" music video, a "life mask" of Jackson's face when he was still alive—all bought for hundreds of thousands of dollars. There were even life-size statues of Jackson that the pop star had sprinkled across his Neverland ranch, life-size imprints of himself, which Teodorin shelled out thousands more for.[47] (If he couldn't hang out with the pop star himself, why not a half-dozen life-size replicas?)

One video survives of these auctions, which took place in Las Vegas in the summer of 2010.[48] A middle-aged woman, the auctioneer, stands at the dais in a powder-blue blazer in front of a black banner emblazoned with "Julien's AUCTIONS," flanked by photos of celebrities like Paul McCartney and Ringo Starr. She looks down over the dozens of buzzing attendees, all of them carrying paddles to raise to place their bids. "Listen to me—I'm going to do something," she starts. "I'm going to open this at a buck, so that everyone who has a paddle will be able to bid on it at least once." Her voice starts to get louder, the crowd's noise rising in turn. "And then you can tell your children," she proclaims, "that you came to this auction"—she starts to point at the crowd, practically yelling at this point—"and you—bid—on—that—GLOVE!"

A flash on the television screen to her right reveals what she's talking about. It's an item anyone familiar with Michael Jackson lore will recognize: a white cotton glove, with a snap closure at its wrist, swathed in hundreds of hand-sewn Swarovski lochrosen crystals. It's Jackson's fabled "Bad" glove, the pinnacle of Jackson's cultural imprint, the most garish, most inescapable legacy of Jackson's celebrity.

The auction starts—"one dollar!"—and all the paddles immediately jump. The numbers immediately spiral upward, the auctioneer peppering the crowd with figures, the paddles pumping up and down. The amounts quickly reach six figures. Electricity is running through the crowd, shrieks and screams and murmurs and gasps suddenly bouncing around. The auctioneer reaches $140,000, and pauses: "That's all you got?" Another paddle goes up: $150,000. And another: $160,000. The auctioneer pauses, looks across a waiting audience. "At $160,000, fair warning," she says. She looks around once more, and raises her hand. "Going once, going twice, at $160,000 . . . SOLD!"[49]

The crowd immediately bursts into applause. The auctioneer smiles down at the winner. "I think they want you to stand, take a bow!" she says. There, in the front row, the young woman in the gray dress slowly stands, turns around, and curtsies for the crowd. Few in the crowd, if anyone, would recognize her. But as investigators later identified, the woman was Wanda Kelley, Teodorin's assistant, who'd just won the prize piece. As she said after the auction, "Let's just say I wasn't walking out of here without that glove."[50]

Payment for the glove, and the rest of the memorabilia, was straightforward. Since the auction house didn't have to concern itself with the source of a buyer's income, the auction house could simply accept a wire transfer directly from Teodorin's accounts in Equatorial Guinea. But that didn't mean that Teodorin necessarily wanted it getting around that he was the one behind Kelley's bids. After one auction in which he shelled out $80,000 for Michael Jackson's crystal socks and another $140,000 for a jacket and shirt—an entire outfit, nearly—one of Teodorin's assistants wrote the auction house: "Please make sure that [Teodorin's] name does not appear anywhere. . . . Please make sure that where a name needs to be, my name is there. This is very important." He should be, the assistant added, "invisible." The auction house was only too happy to comply. "I assume I need to rewrite the invoices in the same fashion as I've done in prior sales? (putting all lots on one page, adding catalog page numbers and changing [Teodorin's] name)," one employee wrote after another raft of Jackson sales.[51]

In the span of just a few months, the bulk of Jackson's mementos transferred directly from the pop star's estate, via the auction house, into Teodorin's possession for what amounted to, a year or so since the singer's death, the most spectacular Michael Jackson collection in the world.

"Our interaction with [Teodorin] was always pleasant," Julien would later tell me. "He was definitely an enthusiastic Michael Jackson collector. . . . He was always a decent guy." And all those allegations about how Teodorin made his money? "It's hard to—he's a client—hard to take that hat off and look objectively," Julien added. "Because he did help our business—and was a good client."[52]

* * *

BACK IN MIAMI, around the same time, Rutherford had hit a wall. Each agent he assigned to look into Teodorin's case ended up distracted, dejected, or both. Some ran into frustrations from trying to glean any-thing from counterparts overseas; ICE didn't exactly have the insti-tutional or bureaucratic heft that someone from the FBI could throw around. Others ran into confusion about the shell company networks Teodorin employed, tripped up by the anonymous structures. One by one the agents fell off or were reassigned elsewhere.

Shortly thereafter, though, Rutherford met an agent named Robert Manzanares. Brusque, with close-cropped hair and known for freely cussing—"fuckhead," "motherfucker," and variations therein are frequent conversation companions—Manzanares joined Rutherford's team in 2008 with prior money laundering and corruption experience, though that was only in the domestic context. But there was an open slot to look into Teodorin—and Rutherford thought Manzanares might just be the man he was looking for. "They threw me into this fire," Manzanares told me. "I couldn't even pronounce 'Teodorin Obiang,' or 'Equatorial Guinea,' the pronunciation of 'kleptocracy.'" Manzanares knew about laundering. But things like "kleptocracy," with oligarchs and regimes pillaging entire countries and stashing their looted assets in places like the U.S., was magnitudes larger than anything he'd seen before. "I didn't know all these buzzwords," he added. "This was brand new for me. I did corruption work in the past, but foreign corruption—no, no. This was a different animal."

But at a certain level, dirty money is dirty money, and money laun-dering remains the same, no matter the source. And when Rutherford asked him to take over the Teodorin inquiry, Manzanares didn't hesitate: "What am I gonna say, no?"[53] (Rutherford would later call Manzanares a "gold mine."[54])

Manzanares immediately threw himself into the nascent investi-gation, digging through the previous reports and notes. He thought back to something one of his former supervisors had said. "One of my mentors always taught me to look through the canceled checks, look through the canceled checks, look through the canceled checks," he recalled. And there, amidst the reams of documents the other agents had compiled, was just what Manzanares was looking for. Listed as payment for a boat trailer, the check was a stroke of good luck—not least because the check was made out to a trailer company not far from the ICE foreign corruption office. "It was finding the needle in the haystack," Manzanares later remembered.[55]

Manzanares immediately hopped in his car and drove directly to the boat trailer company. He found the manager, introduced himself, and asked if he may have remembered the buyer linked to the check in his hand. "Oh yeah," the manager responded. "That's the boat for the prince."

"The prince?" Manzanares responded.

"Yeah, the guy from Africa, the prince," said the manager. "He came here with all of his bodyguards." Could this be Teodorin? The manager unspooled a tale of this "prince" building boats in Florida, and told Manzanares which boat company he should contact.

The investigator promptly reached out to the company. He told them what he was looking for, and said that he was trying to trace any financial documentation about how Teodorin paid for the boat he'd apparently purchased from them. The company rep told him they knew exactly who he was talking about. "And that's when they told me, 'Well, Robert, it's not one boat—it's three boats,'" Manzanares said. The company said they'd be happy to help.

When Manzanares arrived to pick up the documents, he struck up a conversation with one of the female employees sitting nearby. They talked about this "prince," and why anyone would need a boat that travels 200 miles per hour. In the middle of their back-and-forth, the employee said, "You know, he got the glove." Manzanares looked at her. He had no idea what she was talking about—he was there to talk about boats, not clothes. "I'm like, 'Lady, what are you talking about?'"

"The glove—the Michael Jackson glove."

"The sequined glove?"

No one—not Manzanares, not any of his colleagues, not anyone outside Teodorin's immediate network—knew about the glove. Except, apparently, for this woman at this South Florida boat company. Manzanares asked her how she could possibly know that Teodorin got the glove. Her response: "His assistant told me. She was bragging about it."

He already knew who Teodorin's assistant was, but he needed more information on this "Michael Jackson glove." Sitting at his computer, he began searching, and soon came across the video of the auction—and of Kelley landing the bid to win the glove. There was the auctioneer. There were the bids racing upward. There was Kelley winning, and getting up to curtsy. As soon as the clip ended, Manzanares picked up the phone and called the prosecutors ICE had been working with to try to get a case going against Teodorin.

"I said, 'I'm going to be forwarding you this auction where [Teodorin] buys Michael Jackson's glove,'" Manzanares recalled. The other line was quiet for a moment.

"And they're like, 'What?'"[56]

UNITED STATES V. THRILLER JACKET

"Once the question was, 'To be or not to be.' Now it's, 'To have or not to have.'"

—Øistein Akselberg[1]

Immediately after Manzanares discovered that Teodorin was secretly behind the purchase of Michael Jackson's crystal-studded glove, he reached out to the man who had made the entire purchase possible: Julien, whose auction house had enabled Teodorin's memorabilia spree for years. When the investigator and Julien first spoke, the auctioneer blanched: Had he done something wrong? Had he committed any crimes? Was he under suspicion? The investigator soothed him, telling Julien that he was interested only in tracking Teodorin's assets. After all, auction houses like Julien's still remain exempt from basic anti–money laundering and antikleptocracy requirements. There was no reason for Julien to worry. He'd done nothing wrong, Manzanares told me. "Absolutely nothing. They had nothing to report. They had no duty to report. Zero. Zero."[2]

Still, Manzanares told him, there would be a subpoena coming in order to track the details of how Teodorin was moving his money on the back end, and how he'd managed to fund the purchase of the glove. Julien said he'd be happy to help. But he wanted Manzanares to know one thing about Teodorin: "This is a good-paying client," Julien claimed, according to Manzanares. The investigator thought for a moment. This was a conversation about a glove—a single, five-fingered Swarovski set.

Just the one item. But Manzanares now had a new question: Are there other items he should be looking into? Are there other Michael Jackson trinkets and trophies he should be asking about?

"Then there was that pregnant pause," Manzanares remembered, recounting Julien's sudden, conspicuous silence. It was a silence he'd encountered in cases before. A silence that confirmed a new trail. "And I knew right then and there I hit a gold mine." Before Julien could respond, Manzanares continued on, letting the auctioneer know that he would be expanding the scope of the subpoena to include other items Teodorin, or any in his network, had purchased. "And boom: we hit the mother lode there," Manzanares recounted years later, laughing as he did.

Suddenly, the glove was no longer the single thread for Manzanares and American officials to pull on. Julien complied with the subpoenas, and the documents began flooding in: dates, names, records, transactions. All of it, including emails from Wanda Kelley, the woman wielding Teodorin's paddle, trying to cover Teodorin's tracks. "In one of the emails Wanda says, 'Listen guys, remember, [Teodorin] has to remain a ghost. He needs to be a ghost. No one can ever know that it's him,'" Manzanares said. "She wasn't smart enough to understand that a subpoena is gonna get me that information."

And there were the details of Teodorin's obsession—his "fetish," Manzanares called it—with Michael Jackson. The statues and awards, the gold-plated records and gilded socks, the fedoras and photos and sheet music—all the details of Teodorin's new, sprawling collection were there, all bought with the dirty money he'd brought directly into the U.S. An entire world of Michael Jackson memorabilia beckoned. The biggest single collection in the entire world. "When we got that info back . . . you can start seeing the momentum carrying on and pushing the case a little bit further," Manzanares said. "And I knew then and there that if it went to trial, that just made the case so much sexier. The sex appeal was all over that case."[3]

* * *

BACK IN WASHINGTON, a new administration was taking note. A decade after Levin's hearings in the late 1990s began lifting the lid on the aquifer of dirty money seeping through the American banking system, policymakers in Washington continued to look for an opening for long-overdue fixes. But where the Bush administration focused largely on the role these dirty money operators played in terrorist financing, a new crop of American politicians took a more holistic view.

The Obama administration, after all, had ridden to power on the back of a bruised, bleeding financial system, which exposed all the rot under-pinning America's supposed financial security. And stories of the illicit wealth tied to foreign oligarchs and megalomaniacal dictators—stories like those of the Obiangs and Riggs Bank, which in many ways set the precedent for the stories of negligence and deceit emanating from other "too big to fail" American banks—continued circling Washington. For an administration wedded to patching up a broken financial system, tar-geting the funds of the powerful and the corrupt still zooming into the country seemed like a natural fit.

It didn't take long for the Obama administration to redirect Ameri-can anticorruption efforts from combating the likes of the Taliban and its terrorist allies to something far bigger: kleptocracy. In the summer of 2010, during a visit to the African Union summit in Uganda, Attorney General Eric Holder announced the formation of a new shop in Wash-ington dedicated to just that topic. "As my nation's Attorney General, I have made combating corruption, generally and in the United States, a top priority," Holder told the attendees. "And, today, I'm pleased to announce that the U.S. Department of Justice is launching a new Klep-tocracy Asset Recovery Initiative aimed at combating large-scale foreign official corruption and recovering public funds for their intended—and proper—use: for the people of our nations."[4]

The Kleptocracy Asset Recovery Initiative was just as it sounded: a new group dedicated to identifying, seizing, and recovering assets purchased with dirty money linked directly to brutal regimes. Holder announced that the U.S. would be forming a team of specialists, a ros-ter of dedicated prosecutors, who would target the kleptocrats blasting through the holes in the U.S.'s anticorruption framework. "We're assem-bling a team of prosecutors who will focus exclusively on this work and build upon efforts already underway to deter corruption, hold offenders accountable, and protect public resources," Holder said.[5] Roping in personnel from the DOJ's Criminal Division, including from the Money Laundering and Asset Recovery Section, the initiative would "ensure that corrupt leaders cannot seek safe haven in the United States for their stolen wealth," another DOJ figure said.[6]

The U.S. could, technically, just bar these corrupt officials from visiting the country. But that wouldn't change the actual ownership structures of those megamansions or private jets or luxury goods; they would still be owned by those crooked officials elsewhere. And there was nothing preventing a future administration from rescinding the visa ban and allowing those corrupt oligarchs and officials from diving right back in.

Instead, the new Kleptocracy Asset Recovery Initiative would do exactly what its name indicated: recover those assets. This process, known as civil asset forfeiture, had a lengthy history in the domestic context of the U.S., allowing authorities to seize ownership of assets purchased with corrupt or embezzled funds. But with the Kleptocracy Asset Recovery Initiative, there was a new step: returning the seized funds themselves to the populations pillaged and brutalized back home. "If we uncover such wealth, the Justice Department will forfeit and return this stolen money to its rightful owners—the people and governments from whom it was taken," Assistant Attorney General Lanny Breuer said shortly after Holder's announcement.[7]

This freeze-seize-return plan, according to one of the DOJ prosecutors involved in the initiative's early days, solved one of the major issues that had bedeviled other antikleptocracy efforts. If the crooked officials in question got wind of an investigation targeting them and their assets, or if they suddenly found themselves under criminal investigation, they could—thanks to everything from their deep pockets to their diplomatic immunity, available to officials both crooked and clean—simply board a flight out of the country and head back home, where they wouldn't need to worry about extradition or prosecution. "One of the things that'll sometimes happen when you realize you're under federal investigation is that you just won't come to the U.S. anymore," the prosecutor said.[8]

But those assets they'd plowed their dirty money into often can't hop on a plane with them—leaving things like real estate and other assets open to seizure by American authorities. Furthermore, civil forfeiture cases have a far lower threshold for success than criminal prosecutions. "You can't do a criminal trial in the U.S. in absentia," the DOJ prosecutor continued. "And then there's the evidentiary burden. For criminal cases it has to be beyond a reasonable doubt, but for civil cases it's just a preponderance of evidence. And there's also the statute of limitations: for criminal cases it has to be five years from the event, but civil forfeiture has a much more forgiving statute of limitations."[9]

A new DOJ task force, specifically targeting kleptocrats and charged with specifically using civil forfeiture against their U.S. assets: it was one of the most forward-thinking moves the U.S. had ever taken in its escalating fight to beat back the kleptocrats swarming the country. And there was one candidate above all others whom the new initiative wanted to target: Teodorin.

* * *

SOON AFTER THE initiative's launch, the DOJ's new team connected with Manzanares and Rutherford, who were still overseeing the ICE investigation into Teodorin. The two agents would remain leads on the investigative side, but the DOJ prosecutors would begin patching together the actual asset seizure filings—all in order to convince a judge that the money Teodorin plowed into his American assets was, indeed, the proceeds of one of the most corrupt regimes in the world.

To that end, the two investigators began delving into the inner workings of the regime that spawned Teodorin. Which meant one thing: interviews, and lots of them. The Americans already knew they wouldn't get much from the Equatorial Guinea officials they contacted, all of whom either cowered or profited from the Obiang family's operations. Instead, they decided to seek out some of those who helped build out Equatorial Guinea's infrastructure: its pipelines, its roads, its palaces. They decided to search out the European firms that helped propel the Obiang regime—and that, as we saw earlier in this book, often lost everything, caught in the maw of the Obiang family's ever-widening greed.

The two agents flew to London and Rome and Madrid, but the glamor of these visits quickly wore off. ("The first time you go it's fantastic, but after going to London seven times in a year it gets old," Rutherford remembered.) On every trip, there were sit-down meetings in hotel lobbies and restaurants and U.S. embassies with those who'd seen the interior workings of the Obiang family's monstrosities—and who'd escaped with little more than their lives. "A lot of the interviews were with former contractors that thought that they would be able to do business in Equatorial Guinea," Manzanares said. "Then after several months of doing work you would have either [Teodorin] or his father—normally it was [Teodorin]—who'd levy a tax on their work, on products coming in, on any type of machinery coming in. And then all of a sudden the relationship that these contractors had with the president, [which had been] an open door—those doors were closed."[10]

Overnight, the interlocutors told the American investigators, those business arrangements collapsed. Whenever Teodorin or his father saw fit, the machinery—the entire business operations, and all the profits that came with them—of these foreign companies who'd run afoul of the regime was simply seized. And all the contractors could do was leave as quickly as possible. "They were being threatened to the extent that they ended up having to leave the country in the middle of the night, and leave all their equipment, which was all misappropriated by the regime there," Manzanares continued. "Unfortunately, we spoke to many people that way." They also heard stories of those who couldn't make it out in time, or who refused the regime's dictates—and who lost out on more than just construction equipment or drilling rigs. "[Obiang's thugs would] strap them down on a gurney, or some type of flat piece of wood," Manzanares remembered learning. "They'd strap their legs down, their arms down, and they took an iron pipe and would hit the bottom of their feet until it was just blood oozing out. When you saw the people walking and limping, you knew then that that person had been tortured."[11]

But even after exile, not every contractor the agents spoke with had given up the idea that, maybe, it was all just a big misunderstanding. That the Obiang family had simply misjudged the businessmen's intentions. That maybe, if they returned, all would be fine. "There was an Italian national that was working in Equatorial Guinea in the construction [sector]. And obviously . . . they welcomed him in with open arms, with all of his equipment. And then months later they kicked him out of the country," Manzanares recounted. Yet the Italian contractor, the one just booted from the country wholesale, couldn't move on. "We met with him in Italy, and I remember telling him 'Sir'—through a translator—'Sir, let it go. Do not go back there. You do not know what they're capable of doing. And they're capable of doing some vicious things.'"[12]

Not long after, Manzanares received a phone call. The Italian he'd spoken with—the one who just wanted the money he was owed for all the equipment appropriated—had ignored the American's advice and returned to the country. "He went back to Equatorial Guinea," Manzanares remembered hearing. "He got into his car, turned the car on. And the car exploded." It didn't take much to guess who was responsible. "There were people that subsequently told us, especially [the DOJ prosecutors] and me, that we should never step foot in that country because they would poison us," the investigator continued. "They were a savage, savage family."[13]

*   *   *

DURING THE INVESTIGATION, the two agents picked up hints of where Teodorin stashed his other assets across the U.S. After all, despite the anonymity when it came to how his money cycled through the U.S., Teodorin couldn't help but place himself in the limelight whenever possible. Just ask the boat vendors who heard the gossip of Teodorin's Michael Jackson stash, or the California luxury car dealers only too happy to service Teodorin's ever-swelling armada of automobiles, or the locals who didn't take long to realize who the new owner of the palace overlooking the Pacific—who this new fresh prince of Malibu—was. "I come from the drug world, where you try to keep what you're doing secret, undercover," Rutherford said. "You can start immediately dealing in the drug world with destruction of evidence, covering your tracks. With [Teodorin] it didn't make a bit of difference. He didn't try to cover his tracks. He didn't start destroying evidence. He kept going. That's just who he is—to our benefit."[14]

Nor were Manzanares and Rutherford working alone. The DOJ prosecutors continued to help, building the case one piece of evidence at a time. And simultaneously, an old nemesis of Teodorin's revisited the scene: Senator Levin, with his talented staff in tow. Levin and his colleagues at the PSI had spent the post-Riggs years turning over rocks in the broader world of corruption: on embezzlement in the United Nations, on tax haven abuses, on fraud around the world. But by early 2010, Levin and his staff wanted to revisit the topic they'd focused on in those post-9/11, post–Patriot Act days. They wanted to see what loopholes remained and what new loopholes had emerged to upend the U.S.'s anti–money laundering efforts. And whom better to revisit than the Obiangs?

In February 2010, the PSI dropped its hammer. In a 328-page report titled *Keeping Foreign Corruption out of the United States*, Levin and his colleagues detailed how corrupt foreign figures lean on American lawyers, American real estate agents, American escrow agents, and American shell companies to steer their dirty money on a path to cleanliness.[15] Surveying the landscape of corrupt regimes laundering funds in the U.S., Levin's staff uncovered how the ruling regime in the African country of Gabon used an American lobbyist named Jeffrey Birrell to purchase armored cars, without breaking any laws.[16] They found that a corrupt Nigerian politician named Atiku Abubakar leaned on his wife, a U.S. citizen named Jennifer Douglass, to secretly funnel some $40 million into the U.S.[17] They also discovered how a number of crooked figures out of Angola had utilized American shell companies to hide millions linked to an arms dealer named Pierre Falcone.[18]

And, in the most detailed section of the new report, they found that an old friend was up to his same tricks. Over nearly 90 pages of details, minutiae, and an incredible 538 footnotes, the report illustrated exactly how Teodorin had relied on real estate agents like Neil Baddin and lawyers like Michael Berger and escrow agents like IATS to move, hide, and spend his dirty money—and how they could claim to do so perfectly legally. There were the details of Teodorin's mansion purchase, and how he had compiled his armada of luxury automobiles. There were the details of sycophantic lawyers who'd helped Teodorin move and hide his money. There were the shell companies, still whirring along in order to help hide the true ownership of all Teodorin's assets. There it all was:

how Teodorin, even after Riggs Bank was wiped from the face of the financial map, had kept his money laundering operations going.[19]

Even with such detail, though, there were still questions about Teodorin's operations in the U.S. Teodorin and his American helpers "did some very weird things," one of Levin's staffers told me. "We looked at where [Teodorin's] jet had landed, and we found that he went to this weirdo airport [just across] the Mexican border. We talked to the people at the airport, and they said that Teodorin lands his plane here . . . and has armored cars come to the airport, and offloads all these boxes to the armored cars." Levin's staff could never quite square what Teodorin was doing in this dusty Mexican airport, or what was in the boxes. But the report clearly revealed that the private plane Teodorin and his cronies had gone to such lengths to purchase was for more than just his faux mogul lifestyle. "These planes are not just playboy things—they are cargo planes that engage in who knows what," Levin's investigator continued. "It could have been drug-running, it could have been stacks of cash, or something else that they were taking over the Mexican border. . . . Their planes are much more than simply playboy stuff."[20]

Because of a range of factors—not least the economic struggles that were still dominating headlines—the 2010 report didn't cause the same splash as the PSI's previous dive into the Obiangs. But it laid out Teodorin's post-Riggs operations, and all the Americans who greased the wheels of his activities, and the loopholes his American enablers abused to help their corrupt client continue to launder all of his ill-gotten gains across the United States.

* * *

WHILE LEVIN AND his staff were dropping their latest report on Teodorin, Manzanares, Rutherford, and their DOJ allies had already come to the same conclusions about the African "prince." In their conversations, in their subpoenas, in the dozens of flights and thousands of documents obtained, they began forming a case: one that would allow an American judge to green-light a seizure of all of Teodorin's American assets. Thanks to the civil forfeiture proceedings mentioned above, all they would have to do is prove the material was purchased with dirty money, which would then allow them to seize the assets outright from Teodorin—and eventually funnel the proceeds back to the Equatoguinean populations suffering under the Obiangs' dictatorship.

Their initial play to freeze-and-seize Teodorin's American holdings relied primarily on his Michael Jackson memorabilia. While the judge was sympathetic to the case, she felt, as Manzanares recounted, that there wasn't a "lot of meat on the bone"[21]—that a case built solely around targeting Michael Jackson memorabilia was hardly enough for the Kleptocracy Asset Recovery Initiative to tackle as a first case. As the judge told them, they might as well go for broke. So the team dug more, putting out public press releases regarding their search for Teodorin's loot. And they uncovered an entirely new slate of assets tied to the man whose dreams of celebrity were slowly falling apart. There was the private jet, and the escrow agent workarounds. There was the flotilla of Ferraris and Bugattis and Maseratis. There were, as they learned in conversations with foreign counterparts, homes tied to Teodorin in places like Brazil and South Africa and France, themselves also purchased with the proceeds of foreign corruption.[22] The U.S. had no jurisdiction to issue seizure warrants for those properties. But there was, as Levin and his staff had likewise discovered, that estate in Malibu, those acres upon acres of sprawling space and infinity pools and a mansion that was larger than all of the American investigators' houses combined. That American palace, investigators realized, was something they could try to seize, if the judge signed off.

At some point—no one's quite sure when—Teodorin realized what was happening. He'd escaped the Riggs implosion, shifting his financial flows through the tides of American anti–money laundering loopholes. And for a while, in the eyes of the law, those assets appeared on paper as perfectly legitimate. But his luck had finally run out.

Through the work of Levin and his staff, who had focused extensively on Teodorin's crooked family, and through the chance of Rutherford stumbling across the newspaper story, his American assets were suddenly a millstone around his neck. His dirty money had transformed into something tangible: into cars and a private jet, into a mansion and more Michael Jackson swag than anyone else in the world owned. And those assets could, as the DOJ laid out in its announcement of the Kleptocracy Asset Recovery Initiative, be seized, and be taken from the man who'd taken everything he'd wanted prior.

It was something of a catch-22 for Teodorin. If he'd kept his money circulating in the banks, it likely never would have been seized, and could have flowed anywhere he wanted. (There's a reason those banking funds are called *liquid* assets, after all.) But as soon as it became something *tangible*—something outside of the bank, there for all to see—it was suddenly there for the taking. Or put another way: the dirty money in the banks could be shifted at a moment's notice, but the supposedly "clean" assets in the real world were the ones at risk. It was a tension that the Kleptocracy Asset Recovery Initiative focused on—and that eventually deprived Teodorin of his favorite American assets.

By the time Teodorin realized that there would be (maybe for the first time in his life) consequences for his actions, it was too late. Manzanares and Rutherford organized all of their findings, and the DOJ prosecutors, those tasked by the Obama administration as the spearheads of a new antikleptocracy effort, then bundled those details into a formal case against him. In October 2011, the DOJ filed two forfeiture actions, one in California and one in Washington, D.C., targeting the jet, mansion, cars, and Michael Jackson memorabilia.[23]

But Teodorin didn't back down. After the DOJ made its first moves, his lawyer pledged that his client "would not remove any of his assets from the United States," so long as the original forfeiture complaint remained under seal. But promises meant nothing to Teodorin—they could be, as the contractors he'd targeted back in Equatorial Guinea knew only too well, easily broken. Shortly after the pledge, and unbeknownst to investigators at the time, an employee of his named Emmanuel Asamoah traveled to Malibu. He had one job: to smuggle as much of the Michael Jackson memorabilia out of the country as he could. Two days later, he flew to Equatorial Guinea by way of France—taking with him, among other things, the most famous glove in the world. (After returning to Equatorial Guinea, Teodorin stuffed the cultural center in the country's capital with some of his Michael Jackson merchandise. It's unclear where the rest of the smuggled Michael Jackson mementos currently are, or if they keep him company in one of his other mansions somewhere else.)

That wasn't all. While Teodorin's lawyer convinced American authorities that all the assets would remain in the U.S., his entourage managed to ship most of the cars to France, sending his luxury automobiles halfway around the world, just to escape U.S. law. The kleptocrat also flew his Gulfstream out of American airspace, free to enjoy it anywhere the U.S. couldn't seize it.[24]

But there were some items he couldn't flee with. There was a $500,000 Ferrari, which, for reasons unexplained, Teodorin left parked in his Malibu garage. There was the series of life-size Michael Jackson statues that his employee couldn't carry with him, scattered around his Malibu grounds like confused onlookers. And there was the mansion itself—Teodorin's pride, Teodorin's palace, Teodorin's claim to American celebrity and American royalty. A megamansion that would remain tucked along the Pacific coastline. A testament to his greed, and all the loopholes and enablers that had led him there.[25] ("The house was just gaudy," Rutherford remembered of entering the place for the first time. "It was just gaudy, it was a huge house. The rooms were huge. You had to have huge furniture, but it was not anything you or I would have picked."[26])

While Teodorin and his lawyers managed to stretch out negotiations with the American investigators, they could hardly play down Teodorin's clear corruption. When the DOJ announced the settlement of the case—which began as United States of America v. One Michael Jackson Signed Thriller Jacket and Other Michael Jackson Memorabilia, and ran on from there—their press release was stark.[27] "Through relentless embezzlement and extortion, [Teodorin] shamelessly looted his government and shook down businesses in his country to support his lavish lifestyle, while many of his fellow citizens lived in extreme poverty," said Assistant Attorney General Leslie Caldwell. "After raking in millions in bribes and kickbacks, [he] embarked on a corruption-fueled spending spree in the United States. This settlement forces [him] to relinquish assets worth an estimated $30 million, and prevents [him] from hiding other stolen money in the United States, fulfilling the goals of our Kleptocracy Asset Recovery Initiative: to deny safe haven to the proceeds of large-scale foreign official corruption and recover those funds for the people harmed by the abuse of office."[28] And all that seized wealth would be sent to the original source: the people of Equatorial Guinea, whom Teodorin and his family had spent decades looting. (Given that the Obiangs still run the country as their personal fiefdom, it remains unclear how exactly the money is supposed to be returned.[29])

"This was the first case filed after the Kleptocracy Asset Recovery Initiative was announced, so a lot of people saw it as a test case," one of the DOJ prosecutors involved told me. "And one of the things that the case did show is that these cases are doable."[30]

As the seizure documents laid out, Teodorin had acted like a virus, constantly on the move, infecting the openings and industries American kleptocracy had provided. He and his enablers had taken full advantage of the years of deregulatory developments across the American economy—those "pro-business" moves and loopholes carved out, attracting as much capital and revenue as possible, regardless of the source. Teodorin was, in many ways, the logical end point of those deregulatory decisions: of allowing quick, anonymous access to American companies; of allowing U.S. lawyers to work with whomever they wanted, and helping clients hide their money along the way; of allowing access to American real estate and American luxury goods and American art dealers and auction houses to the world of clean and dirty money alike. The U.S. had thrown its arms open to anyone who wanted a piece of the American economy, provided they could pay. Of course a kleptocrat like Teodorin would show up on America's doorstep.

And even though he was eventually found out, the result of Teodorin's prosecution and settlement revealed the limits of asset recovery. "For the average Equatoguinean, used to seeing Teodorin flaunt his ill-gotten assets and act with absolute impunity, the case in the U.S. represented an opportunity for some sort of real, tangible justice, so . . . many of us still feel that the proceedings [and] the ensuing results thus far have been incomplete," said Tutu Alicante, the Equatoguinean activist who'd dedicated so many of his years toward upending Teodorin and his father's regime. "But at the same time, it gives us hope that Teodorin's and other kleptocrats' assets, thanks to the Kleptocracy Asset Recovery Initiative . . . are not going to be welcome [in the U.S.]. So we're learning to celebrate the small victories and continue fighting for greater accountability mechanisms against kleptocrats."[31]

Manzanares, meanwhile, knew there were threads left dangling. "Would I have liked to have seized the aircraft? Yes," he said. "Would I have loved to seize all the Michael Jackson memorabilia? Yes. Would I have liked to have arrested everyone associated with taking the Michael Jackson memorabilia out of the country? Yes." And those Americans who'd gleefully helped Teodorin cycle his dirty money through the American laundromat, profiting along the way, who never had to face any jail time as a result? "Would I have loved to have gone and put handcuffs on Michael Berger?" he asked. "Oh, yeah."[32]

* * *

STILL, TAKING STOCK of the world of antikleptocracy efforts in the early 2010s, the victories far outweighed any losses or missed opportunities. Teodorin had, finally, been stopped. "We did something that, quite frankly, nobody ever thought could ever be done," Manzanares said.[33] And other countries took note. Shortly after the Americans came down on Teodorin, law enforcement colleagues from Brazil to France followed suit, unearthing details of his purchases in their own countries—and seizing and freezing them along the way.

In many ways, the disintegration of Teodorin's American empire was a high-water mark for anti–money laundering efforts in the U.S., and for efforts to root out the corrupt networks worming their way through the country. It was a test case, sure, but one that succeeded more than any had initially thought. It showed how joint squads from Washington, comprising both prosecutors and investigators under the nascent Kleptocracy Asset Recovery Initiative, could work to target the licit networks propping up illicit funds and make an example of the most corrupt actors relying on the U.S. for their money laundering needs. And more broadly, it revealed that a new administration in the White House was more than willing to actually put its forces behind the antikleptocracy rhetoric just beginning to pick up steam, both in the U.S. and elsewhere. American leadership, resources, and ingenuity: all of it had been marshaled to stop, as Manzanares dubbed him, the "poster child of kleptocracy"— and to make sure all those following in Teodorin's footsteps thought twice.[34]

PART III

AMERICAN WARLORDS

"We were not going to accomplish anything by getting money to the Russians that was going to get lost in some Swiss bank account or funneled into some oligarch's business."

—Larry Summers on why the U.S. didn't issue a Marshall Plan for Russia in the aftermath of the Soviet Union's implosion[1]

NOT A GAMBINO

"Real estate was so perfect, it might have been built to launder."

—Tom Burgis[1]

In the late 2000s, in the years before social media exploded around the world, a user on a website called YouTube uploaded a video that introduced the world to a city few had actually visited: Cleveland, located along the northern rim of Ohio. This "Hastily Made Cleveland Tourism Video" stood as one of the first of what would be known as "viral videos," racking up millions of views and introducing untold users to the phenomenon. And it's not hard to see why. The video—crafted by a local comedian who claimed he'd received $14 million from the Cleveland Tourism Board for his efforts—features fifty seconds of shaky, handheld camera footage. The video's color palette ranges from a musty gray to a dirty brown, with all the footage captured under overcast skies. "Fun times in Cleveland today!" the narrator sings, flipping between shots of empty public squares, decaying stadiums, and startled pigeons.[2]

One shot in the video centers on an open bridge, with a half-dozen unused silos behind. ("Here's the place where there used to be industry!" the narrator warbles.) Another clip follows a train past an empty concrete plain. ("This train is carrying jobs out of Cleveland!") Another traces a pair of scruffy men, wandering aimlessly. ("Cleveland leads the nation in drifters!") As the video racked up millions of views, a sequel popped up, claiming to be another Cleveland tourism video. This second video featured shots of seagulls and pay phones, broken windows and sagging signs, dead fish and slate-gray clouds. Clips of stalled building projects ("under construction since 1868!") near the gooped-up Cuyahoga River ("see our river that catches on fire!"), and more aimless bodies and empty storefronts and treeless concrete ("our main export is crippling depression!"). A place where you could, as the narrator shares excitedly, "buy a house for the price of a VCR!"[3]

This, then, was Cleveland in the late 2000s. While American cities elsewhere transformed themselves into new magnets for new migrants, Cleveland watched its residents uproot for other, more promising places. Once a boomtown of American industry, the city's population decline began a few decades prior, when the country's industrial heartland began emptying out in earnest. But the death spiral didn't begin until the 2000s. Capped by a Great Recession, Cleveland—its dying downtown, its abandoned industry—saw a population that by 2010 was less than half of the city's peak nearly a century earlier, and continuing to decline.[4]

And then, as we saw in chapter 4, a man from Miami arrived. A man with a jet-black beard, and money to burn. A man who couldn't have been more than 25, and didn't quite seem to know what he was doing, but who said something about family money (or was it connected to gas wells?), and who said that he wanted to help get Cleveland back up on its feet. A man named Chaim Schochet, who said he saw something that few, if any, in Cleveland did: promise. Or, to steal a term from a certain new president in the White House: hope. As one city councilman would later say of Schochet's arrival, "It was like bringing water to a very thirsty person."[5]

* * *

WHEN SCHOCHET ARRIVED in Cleveland in 2008, Optima—the American arm of Ihor Kolomoisky's sprawling international portfolio, fueled by the Ukrainian oligarch's swelling banking and ferroalloy holdings in Ukraine—was still a lean operation. Led by Mordechai Korf, Kolomoisky's American branch had picked up a number of metal mills across forgotten pockets of the Rust Belt, in Michigan and Ohio and West Virginia. As one press release read, they "saw the potential of the region."[6]

But Korf, connected directly to the Ukrainian oligarch, dreamed bigger. If Kolomoisky really wanted to work his way into the American market—if he really wanted to exploit that rampant American anonymity we've already seen, and conceal nine-figure purchases behind webs of Delaware shell companies and purchases that no city officials would question—Optima would have to adjust its strategies. American real estate still worked for massive money laundering operations. But Teodorin-style mansions, playboy pads, and beachfront sprawls in places like Miami or Malibu would never work for someone like Kolomoisky, busy as he was looking for ways to hide his assets from nosy Ukrainian investigators and tax authorities. They'd catch too much attention. What about something else? What about, say, commercial real estate—nondescript office buildings and the like? And what if, instead of flashy cities like New York or Miami, these buildings were located in a city or an area that no one would associate with the global uber-rich?

Enter Cleveland, Ohio.

Schochet immediately jumped at the idea. He could visit Cleveland. He could make the contacts. He could scout the locations. He could make those purchases he could bundle, conceal, and inject that tainted Ukrainian money directly into the heart of the city. Schochet, as we saw in chapter 4, made an immediate impression. And not just because of the money he said he could move. The 22-year-old was skittish, fidgety, prone to colorful outbursts—a far cry from the dour, reserved world of real estate management. "He's one of these people who just love to make a statement," said David Browning, managing director of one of Cleveland's main brokerage offices. "Maybe it's an outrageous statement. And he throws it out in a conversation in order to get a reaction. That's part of his style."[7]

But still, Schochet said the right things. "I asked him: 'Why Cleveland? Why now?'" said Deb Janik, who helmed the real estate section of the Greater Cleveland Partnership, a private-sector development group. "His perspective was that it's a market where acquisition was possible. But, also, it was really his description of the city. He loves the historic nature of the buildings, the density of the city." Where others saw de-crepit office space and empty windows, where others saw trains that took jobs out of the city and "crippling depression" as the main export, Schochet claimed to see something different. "He has an eye for taking things that people don't necessarily see as desirable and doing some-thing with them," said Mark Vogel, a local investment banker. It was something "more art than business." Vogel was so taken with Schochet's promise that he later attended the latter's wedding in Brooklyn. "It's re-freshing to have someone be so active in Cleveland," Vogel continued. "I can tell you that he's a person who cares about the city of Cleveland and wants it to do well." When he arrived in Cleveland, Schochet also put on a bit of an air, playing up his New York connections. "I laughed when I saw [Cleveland's downtown] was three blocks," he told one reporter. "Your entire downtown would be like Midtown in New York."[8]

According to those who dealt with Schochet, the stories about the sources of the money he suddenly flushed into Cleveland consistently rotated. To some people, he tied the money to his parents. To others, he claimed some vague connection to post-Soviet gas extraction. "A fam-ily connection helped to get me initial consideration [in the real estate industry]," he said at one point. "But I'm on my own here, and I—and I alone—am accountable to our investors for my decisions and my work."[9] On at least one occasion, he let slip that the funds linked back to Privat-Bank—a clear clue for anyone interested that the money was tied directly to a Ukrainian oligarch growing in notoriety. But no one, it seemed, paid much attention. No one wanted to look too far into Schochet's financ-ing, descending on Cleveland like manna from heaven. "He loves to get out into the market, walk through other buildings, meet people," said Brian Hurtuk, another Cleveland broker. "You wouldn't necessarily see Chaim at a huge real estate event, but if you talk to him and you rattle off names of other owners in town, other developers, key attorneys, he's pretty much made the rounds."[10]

Still, it's worth noting that not everyone in Cleveland was immedi-ately taken with Schochet's talk, with Schochet's claims of adoring the city, or with Schochet's supposed dreams of what Cleveland could be. Something about him remained off. Something odd. "It became pretty obvious that something was not completely right," one Cleveland broker familiar with Schochet and his network told me. "I'm not a Gambino, but this [wasn't] Real Estate 101. Something doesn't add up here." Something in the numbers, and the plans, and the promise that Schochet claimed to see. As the broker said, "To be frank, it looked like money laundering."[11]

But Schochet claimed he would help shower hundreds of millions of dollars on Cleveland, and invest in a place few others thought worth their time—a place that no one would suspect could be a new center of transnational money laundering operations. And, for the city, that was enough. As the local journalist who asked to speak on background said, Schochet simply "showed up in Cleveland and started buying when no one else was buying"—beginning what would become, according to analysts and authorities alike, the greatest money laundering scheme the U.S. had ever seen.[12]

* * *

IN ORDER TO begin plowing Kolomoisky's money into Cleveland, Schochet and the Optima team had to identify potential candidates for purchase. The first building that caught Schochet's eye was a chisel-shaped behemoth called One Cleveland Center, built in 1983. Standing smack in the middle of downtown, flanked by a Dunkin' Donuts and a takeout pub, the office space soars over 30 stories high and houses over a half-million square feet. As one of the downtown's most architecturally distinct buildings—if you squint just right, the construct resembles a large, aluminum-sided razor—the building was the perfect way for Schochet to announce his arrival.[13]

At the time, the building still retained a high tenancy rate, according to one of the brokers who eventually worked with Schochet. The office space within One Cleveland Center was nearly 90 percent full when the Optima team swooped in. But given the broader economic trajectories and the steady outflow of tenants from other office buildings, the building's prospects weren't especially bright. Which is why Schochet's offer stunned locals: $86.3 million—nearly a third more than the building had sold for just a few years prior.[14] "All you had to do was wait a little to get a bargain," said one local familiar with the operations. "But he didn't wait."[15] The locals involved in the sale would have been fools to decline.

All of a sudden, with this single purchase, Optima had arrived in Cleveland. And Schochet now had a reputation, one that would eventually see the *Cleveland Plain Dealer* describe him as "confident," as an "aggressive, quick-thinking deal-maker" who had built a "downtown Cleveland empire."[16] It's unclear how Korf reacted when he heard the news in Miami—that this scruffy, wayward twenty-something his sister had married for some reason could, despite the doubts, actually pull this deal together. That it actually worked. If Schochet and Korf and Kolomoisky could snatch a building like One Cleveland Center—a staple of the Cleveland skyline, slicing the air off Lake Erie—why not see what else they could grab?

Four blocks east, another office building beckoned. Known as 55 Public Square and squatting over downtown's eponymous plaza for a half-century, the building housed 420,000 square feet.[17] At one point Cleveland's tallest building, 55 Public Square hosted a number of white-shoe law firms, given the building's proximity to local courthouses. And it was now on the market. As the deal on One Cleveland Center closed, Schochet began conversations with the brokerage firm selling 55 Public Square. The building stood smaller than the One Cleveland Center colossus, and was significantly older, which is why it was valued at only $26 or $27 million. But just to be safe, Schochet had a different number in mind: Would, say, $34 million be enough?[18] And would it be okay if—instead of roping in a mortgage, or setting up some kind of third-party financing arrangement—he paid cash?

"The building goes on the market to sell, and the next thing I know, Chaim shows up—and he doesn't do any due diligence," one of the brokers, who asked to speak on background to discuss the deal, told me. The broker, working for a New York–based firm, called his Manhattan headquarters to run the offer past them. "I call New York, and they ask, 'Can you do some background on this guy?'" After all, who shows up and offers eight-figure payments—in a spiraling recession, in a decaying city—for an office building, let alone millions more than the amount for which it's appraised? But Schochet appeared clean. "I couldn't find anything," the broker continued, sheepish a dozen years after the deal closed. "But he wanted to buy the building cash, seven or eight million dollars over [the appraisal]." There was no reason for anyone to think twice. "I say sure—I'll *walk* to New York to make this deal happen," the broker laughed.[19]

Eyes opened after Schochet's first purchase. Heads now turned with news of the second one. The chattering classes in Cleveland suddenly had a single name on their lips: Schochet. But the twentysomething wasn't done yet. He'd pocketed two of Cleveland's downtown staples, but more stood there, ready to be plucked, ready to be placed in his—and Kolomoisky's—portfolio.

There was the Huntington Building, which we met in the prologue, running some 1.3 million square feet, described by the *Cleveland Plain Dealer* as "one of downtown Cleveland's largest and most prominent office buildings." Schochet's price: $18.5 million.[20]

There was the Penton Media Building, another half million square-foot heavyweight, kitty-corner from One Cleveland Center. "It's a way to cover the whole [downtown] market," one of Schochet's colleagues said, giving Optima "another arrow in our quiver." Schochet's price: $46.5 million.[21]

And there was the Crowne Plaza Building, a 472-room hotel-conference center, the second-largest hotel in the entire city, with another 20,000 feet of meeting space (some of which had previously housed the moribund Lehman Brothers). "I don't believe there will be another downtown hotel that will mirror our hotel in terms of . . . its luxury," Schochet said at the time. His price: $9 million.[22]

That final investment, finalized in October 2011, was a bit different and is worth pausing on momentarily for a brief detour into another tendril of American kleptocracy. To finalize the deal, Schochet broached a joint venture loan with a local investment outfit called the Cleveland International Fund, overseen by an Iranian immigrant named Eddy Zai.[23]

It's unclear why he set up this joint venture. But Zai raised his end of the funds by shopping so-called "golden visa" schemes to foreign nationals from places like China and Brazil—a type of scheme that has, with few paying attention, transformed into one of the key overlooked

elements of modern kleptocracy. These golden visas, marketed in the
U.S. as the EB-5 visa program, allow deep-pocketed figures abroad to
shell out a nominal fee—usually around $1 million—to the U.S. govern-
ment, alongside a pledge to initiate a jobs-creation program in the U.S.,
all in return for American residency and an eventual path to American
citizenship. The program allows oligarchs and kleptocrats to effectively
buy American citizenship, regardless of the source of their income.
These American golden visas are little different than so-called "golden
passport" programs in places like Cyprus and Malta, which have proven
magnets for a world of dirty money, most especially out of corrupt hives
like Beijing and Moscow.[24]

Yet the American version has received little attention, and little criticism. This despite the fact that the program, which has been dominated
by wealthy Chinese oligarchs, has been linked multiple times to schemes
of large-scale money laundering and bank fraud.[25] "[A]lmost nothing is
known about the backgrounds of applicants for the EB-5 program," analyst Belinda Li wrote. "The only information made available to [Amer-
ican immigration officials] is provided by applicants themselves on their
application forms."[26] Embarrassingly, many of the forms remain hand-
written, with no digital copies existing. Trying to find a criminal hand
behind the EB-5 applications, or to sniff out the dirty money behind
the applicants, is like trying to find a needle in a haystack—but without
knowing which haystack to even look in.

All of which is to say: while the reasons for Schochet's partnership
with Zai remain unclear, getting to know a man like Zai—who could
help foreign oligarchs scheme their way to American citizenship—
would be a wise move for a kleptocrat looking to slide into the U.S.

* * *

THROUGH SCHOCHET, KOLOMOISKY's total portfolio in Cleveland
stretched over millions of square feet, and into hundreds of millions of
dollars—making the oligarch and his crew the largest commercial owners and landlords in this major American city.[27] "I've not seen anything
like this before," one local agent involved in the sales said at the time.
"They really, really believe in Cleveland." Nor was Kolomoisky's net-

work done. Schochet had, as he said, "big-picture plans" for the city. Just a few years removed from life as a nobody, Schochet had transformed Optima into the "largest holder of real estate in Downtown Cleveland," as Schochet's Wikipedia page reads.[28] As the *Cleveland Plain Dealer* wrote, Schochet was now the "most important guy you've never heard of."[29]

At least, that's how it appeared on the outside. For those inside, there was a different story. A select few got to step behind the fun-house mirror to see what was actually happening. "They were the first, call it 'out of town,' money for Cleveland that came in," one American familiar with their operations said. "But from the start of it, it was questionable. . . . There was a lot of shady stuff." Much of that, of course, had to do with the fact that Schochet appeared to have no idea what he was doing: not bothering to run any inspections, overpaying time and again for buildings that held little promise. But much of that had to do with the method of payment. According to both American officials and those familiar with their operations, one of Schochet's and Optima's preferred payment methods was straightforward: cash, made out via personal check. No banks, no mortgage lenders, no third-party financiers. Just a checkbook and a pen, and a final number that, in most cases, stood millions of dollars more than the building's estimated value. With a bank as a lender, you have multiple options down the line—about payment structures, about refinancing, about handling a potential recession—if your financial circumstances change. Then again, with a bank's involvement, the lenders are going to spend weeks, and potentially longer, negotiating the sale, poking through all the financing and figures. But when it came to Schochet and Optima, they just wanted the buildings—that was all that mattered, according to those who saw the operations from the inside.

Still, if Schochet wanted to overpay for the buildings he didn't even bother to inspect, no one would force him to do otherwise. After all, his checks cleared. So Schochet began touring the entire region, pocketing entire cities and towns on behalf of a Ukrainian oligarch no one in America had ever heard of.

* * *

IT WASN'T ONLY Cleveland. Kolomoisky's Optima group also picked up steel mills and related plants—lifebloods of entire towns, and entire regions—in places like Warren, Ohio; Buffalo, New York; Griffith, Indiana; Ashland and Calvert City, Kentucky; Cicero, Illinois; Gibraltar, Michigan; and Letart, West Virginia, with the combined sales prices stretching into the hundreds of millions of dollars.[30] They'd started dropping their money in new metro markets as well, picking up an office park in Dallas and an office tower in Louisville. The combined price tag for those two properties alone: $124 million.[31]

Everywhere they went, Schochet and Optima reportedly said the same things. They were bringing jobs and dreams, renovations and revitalization. The world may have forgotten the American Rust Belt, may have overlooked these towns and these mills and these beating iron valleys. But not Schochet. Not Optima.

It was the same spiel Schochet unfurled when he drove to a place called Harvard, Illinois, a speck of a town equidistant from Chicago and Milwaukee in the American Midwest. Like the other towns in the region, Harvard's best days were decades behind it. But in the late 1990s, thanks to a couple of well-placed connections, the chairman of the massive Motorola telecom company made a surprise announcement. The telecom giant would be placing a new manufacturing plant in Harvard. Construction soon began on what would become the largest building not just in Harvard but the entire region: a 1.5-million-square-foot facility, sprawling over 320 acres, part office and part plant, shaped like a giant wishbone. "It's a huge, huge building," one local, Ed Soliz, said. "It looks like a small university."[32] With a $100 million price tag, Motorola announced it would require a staggering five thousand employees to operate—to help craft the next generation of Motorola phones, and lead the global telecom market into the twenty-first century. "Physically, it's overwhelming to the town," Charlie Eldredge, head of the local Harvard Economic Development Corporation, told me, adding that Motorola and local construction groups immediately began building a half-dozen new subdivisions to house all the projected workers.[33]

It might be tough to remember now, but at the time, no one surpassed Motorola in the world of mobile phones. The original mobile operator,

Motorola set the precedent that behemoths like Apple and Samsung would eventually follow. And there was no reason to think Motorola couldn't retain that leading position at the turn of the twenty-first century—especially given that it was confident enough to make a $100 million investment in an American farming town few could find on a map.

But then, as the construction finished in Harvard, Motorola looked up and realized all of its competitors had passed it by. Motorola thought it could remain analog in an increasingly digital world. Customers, though, thought otherwise. In a matter of just a few years, the bottom fell out of Motorola's business model. And suddenly, the building in Harvard had no purpose. It would never be the cell phone plant originally envisioned. Rather than a testament to Harvard's future, it was a testament to corporate blinders. And for years it sat, like a beached whale, waiting.

Then Schochet showed up. Pulling the same move he'd perfected in Cleveland, Schochet offered $16.75 million for the empty building.[34] A far cry from the Motorola investment, but given the lack of any other real offers, the price tag was more than locals could have hoped for. They happily accepted. Glimmers of potential sprang once more. "Hope burns eternal," Roger Lehmann, another member of the Harvard Economic Development Corporation, said at the time.[35]

That optimism immediately washed over Harvard—all centered on a building that had long been vacant, a lifeblood that had long sat empty.

"It's been sitting there for so long," Soliz added. "It's like the building is cursed."[36]

THE WILD WEST

"The Greeks knew that democracy is not likely to fall to the charms of totalitarianism, authoritarianism, or oligarchy; it's much more likely to fall to a corrupted version of itself."

—Tony Judt[1]

While Kolomoisky was building his empire in the U.S., Ukraine began falling to pieces. In the mid-2000s, a roster of pro-Western figures had come to power in Kyiv, promising an end to the elite-level corruption that cannibalized the country's wealth, whisking it out of the country in the process. By the end of the decade, though, the reformers were exhausted, frustrated, fractured. As a result, in the 2010 presidential election, Ukrainians backed an opposition figure named Viktor Yanukovych—a man whom they'd ousted via revolution just a few years prior, but who now promised a different path forward.

To those who knew him, Yanukovych was little more than a brute, an imbecile, an unreconstructed Soviet who viewed Russia's neighboring dictatorship with envy. But in those post–Great Recession days, Yanukovych had an ace up his sleeve: an American named Paul Manafort, a man with the gift of turning any would-be autocrat into someone who could actually win an election. Hired by Yanukovych and his team to improve the strongman's image, Manafort crafted a campaign to spin Yanukovych as warm and welcoming, as a font of competence in these incompetent times. Thanks in no small part to Manafort's efforts, Yanukovych won the 2010 presidential election.[2]

But it didn't take long for Yanukovych's façade to fall apart. In November 2013, after months of pressure from Moscow, Yanukovych, with his cronies busy looting state coffers, abruptly pulled Ukraine back from negotiations with the European Union. Perturbed by the decision, protesters waving the blue-and-yellow flags of Ukraine and the EU alike gathered in Kyiv's downtown square, known as the Maidan. Slowly, the protesters gathered steam, even in the face of Yanukovych's thuggish security services. Tensions soon spiraled—and in February 2014, Yanukovych's forces opened fire, with snipers raining bullets over the unarmed protesters, resulting in dozens of deaths. Realizing the murders had only galvanized the protesters, the autocrat tucked tail and fled to Russia.[3]

In hindsight, it was likely the right move for Yanukovych. Shortly after his ouster, journalists flocked to his megamansion outside Kyiv. In addition to finding everything from ostriches to a golden loaf of bread (as well as nude portraits of Yanukovych himself) at the estate, journalists elsewhere discovered a range of documents pointing directly to Yanukovych's financial malfeasance.[4] Documents about offshore payments. Documents about secret ledgers. Documents about certain Americans, like Manafort, with whom the public would soon become intimately familiar.[5]

* * *

BUT WE'LL COME back to those documents later, because it's in those heady postrevolution days that we rejoin our story of Kolomoisky and American kleptocracy. As Ukraine teetered in the days following Yanukovych's ouster, the Kremlin began barreling into southern Ukraine, claiming Crimea as an area that had "always" been Russian (and repressing the indigenous Tatar populations who highlighted that falsehood). From there, Russia began flooding swaths of eastern Ukraine, beginning the process of wresting provinces known as Luhansk and Donetsk. Ukraine's army quickly disintegrated; Yanukovych, it turned out, had spent the past three years selling Kyiv's military for parts, mothballing tanks, and stripping entire regiments.[6] Crimea was already gone—and just a few weeks later, it appeared that the entirety of eastern Ukraine would follow suit and soon rejoin a revanchist Russia.[7]

Which is the point where Kolomoisky reenters the Ukrainian story, and where he becomes something more than simply a banking-and-metals oligarch with a strange fetish for sharks. Watching Russian proxies chewing through chunks of eastern Ukraine, Kolomoisky had an idea. What if he bankrolled forces of his own to face down the Russians? What if he funded, organized, and armed thousands of Ukrainian patriots, eager to beat back the rising Russian nationalism rumbling through Dnipro and its neighboring regions?

The new government in Kyiv immediately agreed. Appointing Kolomoisky as the interim governor of the entire Dnipro province, they offered him broad writ to organize his own militia. According to one of his aides, Kolomoisky immediately got to work, ponying up tens of millions of dollars to help arm some 15,000 Ukrainian militiamen, siccing his new brigades on the pro-Russian separatists. "We are doing all this in agreement with the central government," one of those aides said. "We coordinate and cooperate with Kyiv, [and] they accept that we are influential as a consolidating factor in the east."[8]

Not that everything centered only on national interests, necessarily. As Borys Filatov, Kolomoisky's deputy, added, "The idea was to save the country and save [his] assets at the same time."[9] (Nor did the oligarch ditch the shark tank; when meeting with new pro-Western officials from Kyiv, he would routinely press a button on his desk to release crayfish meat to his pets, unnerving guests as the water behind him turned bloody.[10]) But he played the patriotism card as best he could. Calling Putin a "schizophrenic of short stature,"[11] the Ukrainian oligarch pledged a $10,000 bounty for pro-Russian militants captured with guns.[12] As one of the battalion commanders said, Russians "should come to [Dnipro], because here we will kill them."[13]

The Russians, though, never made it that far—largely because they and the pro-Russian locals soon bogged down, stopped by a regrouping Ukrainian military and by the thousands of militia forces flocking to Kolomoisky's banner. "He took charge, and is still seen as this oligarch who was patriotic, who was pro-Ukrainian—who basically saved the [Dnipro region] from what happened in Donetsk," one Ukrainian journalist told me.[14] By the end of 2014, a stalemate emerged across a swath of eastern Ukraine, covering far less territory than Putin and his proxies initially wanted. It turned out that Kolomoisky, as the *Wall Street Journal* dubbed him, had been Ukraine's "secret weapon" all along.[15] As the oligarch later said in the third person, "A large number of people think Kolomoisky's great—and the only patriot in the country."[16]

* * *

BY EARLY 2015, the oligarch looked to consolidate his gains. He already controlled Ukraine's largest bank, and sat at the center of Ukraine's tangled web of gas extraction enterprises. And now he stood as governor of one of the key regions in one of the key countries for Europe's, and the West's, broader future. But new Ukrainian president Petro Poroshenko, an oligarch himself, looked to clip Kolomoisky's wings. In March, new reforms out of Kyiv undercut Kolomoisky's control of the country's largest oil and gas conglomerate, called UkrTransNafta, whose chair had been a close Kolomoisky ally.[17]

In response, Kolomoisky threw a fit. In a video later posted to YouTube, dozens of men clad in camouflage and balaclavas, lugging boxes and bags and weaponry, are seen hustling into the company's headquarters under cover of night. They block the entryways, affixing metal grills to the doors, turning back inquiring journalists. One man lets slip the group's affiliation: they were Kolomoisky's militia, come to help their patron.[18]

Shortly thereafter, Kolomoisky himself appears. Walking to reporters waiting outside, wearing a striped blazer and black t-shirt, the oligarch initially appears calm. But one question about why he was there sends the oligarch spiraling. "Why don't you ask how the corporate raid on UkrTransNafta happened? And how Russians infiltrated the place? Or you just want to fucking see Kolomoisky?" the oligarch spits, referring to himself in the third person. "We liberated the UkrTransNafta building from Russian saboteurs. And you and your [colleagues] sit here and fucking guard it, like some bimbo with her cheating husband."

The journalist who asked the question stood in stunned silence, while Kolomoisky continued taunting him. "Why aren't you saying anything? Do you have any questions? Or did your tongue get lost in your ass?"[19]

It was a bizarre, addled sight: Ukraine's revolution just a year prior was supposed to have made these moments a thing of the past. Yet here Kolomoisky was, an oligarch resurgent, steering the country's banking and metal and gas sectors, spitting venom at reporters, siccing his masked marauders on those who opposed him. One Ukrainian journalist told me Kolomoisky has a "psychopathic personality."[20] "I think Kolomoisky is super-dangerous," an American official then working in the embassy in Kyiv said. "He is probably one of the most dangerous oligarchs because he's one of the ones who's willing to get his hands dirty . . .

"He was one of the first oligarchs who began to act like a warlord."[21]

* * *

BACK IN THE U.S., while Kolomoisky continued building his empire across the Midwest and Rust Belt, folks in Washington continued building on their momentum after toppling Teodorin. Levin and his staff found a new rapport with the new administration in the White House. Buoyed by the Kleptocracy Asset Recovery Initiative, the U.S. under Obama showed signs of reorienting resources toward fighting and regulating the kinds of kleptocratic tools that helped the crooked regimes hollow out and destabilize countries like Ukraine. A decade after Levin arm-twisted the U.S. banking sector into complying with basic anti–money laundering checks, the wind was suddenly in anticorruption activists' sails. Yet as we'll see through the rest of this chapter, for each step forward in the fight against dirty money and the offshoring world, there was another clear, and unexpected, step back.

First, the victories. In late 2007, a middle-aged, ginger-haired American named Bradley Birkenfeld approached Levin's staff with a bombshell revelation. He disclosed that he had worked for a number of years at the flagship Swiss bank UBS. And what he saw shocked him. According to Birkenfeld, the Swiss reputation for banking secrecy was well earned—and wasn't viewed as being nearly as nefarious, or disgusting, as it should be. Birkenfeld unspooled a raft regarding details of UBS's operations that made Levin's staff furious.[22]

The former banker told them that UBS specifically targeted high-net-worth American individuals looking to limit their tax payments—keen to take full advantage of Swiss secrecy laws—in order to starve Washington of revenue. A "formidable force"[23] of Swiss employees traveled to the U.S. multiple times per year to "target U.S. clients and convince them to hide money abroad."[24] They would go to Miami art shows, or to yachting events, or to golf and tennis tournaments and whisper about all the services the Swiss could provide for them. Birkenfeld, part of UBS's U.S. operations, participated in these schemes, actively advising American clients about a range of tactics to hide their money from the government: "destroy all offshore banking records existing in the United States; [use] Swiss bank credit cards that they claimed could not be discovered by U.S. authorities; and file false U.S. individual income tax returns."[25] One UBS banker even memorably helped a client move money by smuggling diamonds in a tube of toothpaste.[26]

The revelations made Levin's team blanch—but UBS was hardly the lone Swiss bank advising wealthy Americans on how to shortchange the U.S. government. Later investigations revealed that Credit Suisse, another Swiss banking behemoth, went to even greater lengths in its subterfuge, with bankers there actively promising to shred any compromising documents, and even slipping clients confidential banking information hidden between the pages of *Sports Illustrated*.[27] And wealthy Americans were only too happy to participate. Later filings revealed that Swiss banks maintained over 50,000 secret American accounts, part of the $20 billion in Swiss accounts linked to U.S. clients—billions of dollars untaxed, hidden by Americans exploiting Swiss secrecy.[28]

The reaction to Birkenfeld's revelations was swift. One month into the new Obama administration, Washington slapped a $780 million penalty against UBS, forcing the formidable Swiss bank to admit that it conspired to defraud the U.S.[29] The move was "an earthquake in the offshore world," Elise Bean later wrote. "Expressions of shock reverberated around the globe at the first cracks in Swiss secrecy. . . . It was a huge U.S. victory over the world's biggest tax haven bank."[30] Not long after, the

administration one-upped itself, forcing Credit Suisse to pay a staggering $2.6 billion in penalties.[31]

In short order, the U.S. had cracked open Switzerland's decades-old
secret banking sector, upending Switzerland's offshoring industries,
sending its suspect money and all of its enablers scrambling. "This was
the first real nail in the coffin for Swiss banking secrecy in particular,
and offshore secrecy in general," Peter Cotorceanu, an expert in Swiss financing, wrote afterward. "In light of the UBS scandal, the United States
became the flag-bearer for greater transparency."[32]

Nor was that all. In 2010, just a year after pummeling UBS and
the entire façade of Swiss secrecy, Congress passed a piece of legislation to follow the administration's lead. Dubbed the Foreign Accounts
Tax Compliance Act (FATCA), the new legislation required all foreign
banks to report American holdings to the IRS. In order to coax them to
obey, the U.S. threatened a 30 percent withholding tax on noncompliant
banks—as well as a pledge to share information with foreign governments about any foreign nationals who may be using American banks
to skirt taxes back home.[33] It was a simple enough model, and one other
countries were eager to follow. The most prominent FATCA-inspired
program was called the Common Reporting Standard (CRS), a blueprint that required signatory countries to share account information
with one another.[34] Launched in 2014, the CRS quickly roped in 100 different countries, becoming, in effect, one giant pool of account-sharing
information.[35] All of it thanks to Washington—thanks to a program
that, as *The Economist* wrote, "ushered in a global revolution in financial
transparency."[36]

* * *

BUT EVEN WHILE the administration was applauding itself for the blows
to global offshoring and tax-dodging, a parallel force gurgled to the
fore, threatening to undo much of the progress Washington had already
made.

South Dakota, a state in the Upper Midwest, is a bit like Delaware.
Resource-poor, often overlooked, the state is something of an afterthought in the U.S. And it's been that way for decades. From the outside,

aside from Mount Rushmore, there's little reason to think about South Dakota.

But in the 1980s, the state produced a figure who would upend the world of financial secrecy—and who would help transform South Dakota into the newest American bastion of kleptocracy.

William Janklow—"Wild Bill," as others dubbed him—was as much a *bon vivant* as he was a visionary. The wide-set Janklow was, as *The Guardian* described him, a "bottomless store of anecdotes: about how he once brought a rifle to the scene of a hostage crisis; how his car got blown off the road when he was rushing to the scene of a tornado." As a sixteen-year governor in the state, Janklow swaggered as a titan of prairie politics, perfecting the art of arm-twisting in the tiny state capital, Pierre. Which is why, when South Dakota saw its economy crater in the early 1980s, the entire state turned its eyes to him. The state didn't have the infrastructure to attract new manufacturing plants. Tourism could only bring so many jobs. And given South Dakota's landlocked status, it's not like the state could transform into a new trade hub or become an import-export bastion.[37]

Janklow, though, had a plan—a plan that those politicians decades prior in Delaware, a state similarly cursed with few economic opportunities, would have recognized. In 1978, the U.S. Supreme Court had ruled in a little-noticed decision that American banks would no longer have to be limited by low caps on interest rates, which had been kept to a minimum by "anti-usury" laws stretching back decades, preventing banks and credit companies from charging inordinately high interest rates. The ruling happened to coincide with banks increasingly dipping their toes into something called "credit cards," which allowed consumers to borrow on credit—so long as they were willing to pay the interest rate charged. With those two developments, Janklow stumbled across an idea. Putting out feelers to the banks in New York, Janklow had a question: What would happen if he got South Dakota to abolish all of these nuisance "anti-usury" regulations? What if he got the state to allow these banks to issue whatever interest rates they'd like?[38]

The banks were all ears. Citibank in particular told Janklow that it could provide hundreds of jobs if the governor repealed the interest limits. "They weren't sure that any state would let them come in, because no state ever had let any bank come in from the time they passed those laws fifty years earlier," Janklow later said. "To me, this wasn't a credit card deal; it was a jobs deal. It was an economic opportunity for the state." Janklow and Citibank swiftly came to an arrangement.[39] In 1981, Janklow oversaw the repeal of South Dakota's previous interest rate limit. And the repeal was an immediate hit with banks and consumers alike. Interest rates suddenly exploded—as did the concomitant consumer debt that resulted from the higher interest rates.[40] ("It's unbelievable, the lack of sophistication that we have as a society to deal with what I'll call consumer credit," Janklow later said. "It really is unbelievable. Do I think I helped foster some of that? The answer is yes, I do."[41]) Not that South Dakota minded. "To some, South Dakota is a 'fly-over' state," one of the state's supreme court justices would later say. "While many people may find a way to 'fly over' South Dakota, somehow their dollars find a way to land here."[42]

But Janklow wasn't done. If it was easy enough to repeal those interest rate ceilings, were there other limits worth repealing? The governor had something in mind: trusts.[43]

* * *

TRUSTS HAD A far longer legacy than credit cards, or South Dakota, or even the U.S. itself. First developed in the Middle Ages, trusts were simple constructs: a person (the "settlor") would hand over legal control of finances and assets to another person (the "trustee"), who was then charged with managing and distributing the finances and assets for future recipients (the "beneficiaries"). For instance, a father—the settlor—would sign over the legal ownership of his estate to a friend—the trustee—who would at an undefined future date relinquish that legal ownership to the father's grandchildren—the beneficiaries. That's it. Simple. Deceptively so—especially since trusts generally remain secretive, unavailable for public scrutiny.[44] "Trusts are powerful mechanisms," journalist Nicholas Shaxson once wrote, "usually with no evidence of their existence on public record anywhere."[45]

That's how trusts operated for centuries, through the Enlightenment, through the great wars, through the ascent of America on the global stage. By the early 1980s, trusts stood broadly similar to their medieval precedents. And then Janklow showed up, and trusts turned into something else entirely.

Shortly after Janklow torpedoed interest rate caps, he hit on a new idea: What if South Dakota removed the cap on the chronology of trusts? Trusts generally expired after a century, or a few decades after the death of the settlor, forcing the distribution of any remaining assets. Anything else would have been ludicrous. And yet, that's precisely what Janklow wanted. In 1983, the South Dakota legislature repealed the "rule against perpetuities"—the regulation that limited the duration of these secretive trusts. In their wake, South Dakota introduced a new tool to the world: "perpetual trusts," sometimes called "dynasty trusts."[46] These new perpetual trusts, according to the South Dakota legislature, have no end. They can last as long as you want. They can last until South Dakota slips into the sea, or until the sun burns from the sky. They can outlast us all— and do so in perfect secrecy.

Those dynasty trusts, of course, needed lawyers. They needed accountants. They needed managers. They needed white-collar South Dakotans to oversee them and their operations. As with the interest rate repeal, this new perpetual trust industry created thousands more jobs in South Dakota, offering services to anyone who wanted to bundle their finances into a trust and keep it secret in perpetuity.[47]

Even though these perpetual trusts initially met with much derision, Janklow didn't exist in a vacuum; other state governments watched South Dakota's regulatory rollback and tried to get their own piece of the deregulated pie.[48] Following South Dakota's lead, a number of other states by the end of the twentieth century had introduced their own perpetual trust industries.[49] Janklow, though, wouldn't let South Dakota's advantage slip. In 1997, with billions starting to flock to the state to take advantage of the secretive perpetual trust industry, Janklow formed a "Trust Task Force."[50] Comprising legislators and leading figures in the trust industry, the task force proposed tweaks and reforms that made it seem like the trust industry was "writing laws essentially for themselves," said one state legislator.[51] Or as Tom Simmons, an expert on trust law at the University of South Dakota and member of the task force, told me, "It's kind of like sports, you know—you have to keep a few points ahead of the other people."[52]

And what reforms they were. In South Dakota, not only do trusts remain entirely secret from the public—or from journalists or tax authorities or human rights activists trying to track down looted assets—but any court documents pertaining to South Dakota trusts are kept private in perpetuity. No information on South Dakota trusts will ever be shared with other governments. And those looking to hide their funds don't need to move to South Dakota to take advantage of the trusts, or even use any local banks. One trust specialist in the state estimated that nearly all trusts in the state "are what I call shell companies, where you basically have a PO Box or an office and somebody will come here twice a year to have board meetings and meet regulatory requirements. But there's nobody here with feet on the ground."[53] And now, those hiding their money in South Dakota no longer even need beneficiaries like children or grandchildren. Instead, people can set up South Dakota trusts with *themselves* as the listed beneficiaries—using the anonymous perpetual trust industry's secrecy as a shield, keeping their finances hidden from any prying eyes.[54]

To be sure, there are plenty of perfectly legitimate reasons to set up and maintain trusts. Some are aimed at helping spendthrift descendants limit their expenditures. Some are meant to be spent only on education, or to finance the lives of children suffering from disabilities after the parents have died. But what South Dakota introduced was something qualitatively different: something meant to explicitly create new dynasties, which would never have to participate in silly things like taxation or financial transparency. What South Dakota guaranteed was anonymity, from everyone—forever.[55] "South Dakota offers the best privacy and asset protection laws in the country, and possibly in the world, for the wealthy to protect their assets,"[56] one financial adviser told *The Guardian*, with another observer saying that South Dakota "legislators [had turned] the Mount Rushmore State into the Bermuda of the prairie."[57] Or as one South Dakota journalist wrote in 2016, "Forget Switzerland;

South Dakota is actually one of the best places in the world for the wealthy to stash their cash in secret."[58]

Of course, those profiting from South Dakota's sprint to becoming an offshore haven of its own don't see things this way. "We're certainly always worried about the black eye of one nefarious actor, one money laundering or white-collar crime that somehow utilized our trust industry to commit wrongful acts," Simmons, the member of the state's trust task force, claimed. "It's not the Wild West, but rather one of the more regulated industries in our country."[59] But then, the Wild West technically had laws and regulations on its books, too—not that they stopped the railroad barons and white supremacists from bending the laws to their own wills, devastating communities along the way. Which is precisely what South Dakota's trust industry has begun doing, on a global scale.

Starting in the early 2010s, hundreds of billions of dollars in untraceable money began stampeding to the state, with estimates now placing the total worth in these anonymous, unregulated South Dakota trusts at nearly $1 trillion.[60] (Ironically enough, much of it rushed in from Switzerland.) None are subject to any anti–money laundering requirements, or to oversight of any kind. And none are required to ever return any assets to the populations from which they were looted. "The voters [in South Dakota] don't have a clue what this means," Susan Wismer, a local Democratic official, said. "They've never seen a feudal society, they don't have a clue what they're enabling."[61]

We've only just gotten a peek behind South Dakota's offshore curtain in recent years—though not because of South Dakota itself. Instead, it's been filings *elsewhere* that have revealed some of the details of South Dakota's supernova explosion into the world's newest offshore haven. Over the past few years, a number of corporate filings in (of all places) China revealed that a range of Chinese oligarchs have begun smuggling their money into South Dakota. Tens of billions of dollars in suspect Chinese monies have flowed to the state, including billions tied to Chinese real estate developers and billions more tied directly to one of China's wealthiest women. That is, the oligarchs and kleptocrats who've grown wealthy from their ties to the ruling dictatorship in Beijing have effectively partnered with officials in South Dakota to hide their money—to partake in this prairie-based version of American kleptocracy.[62]

* * *

BACK IN MIAMI, Kolomoisky's American helpers wanted to reward themselves for all their hard work in allegedly helping stash the Ukrainian oligarch's funds across the U.S.

Mordechai Korf—a man whose father had slaughtered chickens himself, and who had raised Korf and his siblings on a shoestring budget—bought for himself a nine-bedroom, eight-bathroom mansion in a posh Miami Beach enclave called Sunset Lake, its walls and columns bleached white, a pool shimmering in the back. The tab: $7.7 million. (His compatriot Uri Laber moved a few blocks down, snapping up a similar mansion for $14 million.) Korf also looked elsewhere to display his new wealth. In 2008, a new foundation received tax-exempt status: the Korf Family Foundation. Overseen by Korf, it's unclear what the mission, or even the registered location, of the Korf Family Foundation is. However, the foundation—along with the Laber Foundation, set up by Laber—nonetheless became another prong to move significant sums, funneling tens of millions of dollars toward Jewish nonprofits from 2006 to 2018.[63] "It's the whole concept of wealthy Jews helping the community," Laber claimed at one point. "Let's build something nice."[64]

And people noticed. As *Forward* wrote, Korf and Laber—through their donations, through their status—had come to "represent the pinnacle of generosity to many religious Jews in Florida."[65]

Of course, no one knew exactly where Korf's money came from, nor was anyone quite sure of his connections to Kolomoisky. ("I think [Kolomoisky] is a shareholder," Korf at one point claimed to an inquiring reporter, downplaying a yearslong relationship.[66]) To those on the outside, it all remained a mystery. But no one—not in Cleveland, not in those small Rust Belt steel towns, not in those nonprofits receiving new millions from Korf himself—wanted to look too far, anyway.

A GAPING HOLE

"If I ever saw myself saying I'm excited going to Cleveland, I'd punch myself in the face, because I'm lying."

—Ichiro Suzuki[1]

In the aftermath of Ukraine's 2014 revolution, a new raft of reformers entered power in Kyiv. Investigative journalists joined parliament, spearheading anticorruption inquiries with the levers of state finally in their hands. A new range of pro-transparency bodies burst forth, including the National Anti-Corruption Bureau, tasked specifically with tackling elite-level graft. And the country's banking sector welcomed a new head dedicated to cleaning up networks that had spent years hollowing out Ukraine's financial structures. In the summer of 2014, the government named Valeria Gontareva the new head of the National Bank of Ukraine (NBU)—the first woman appointed to steer the country's banking governing body. Gontareva immediately got to work, cutting bloat, targeting insolvent banks, and earning plaudits from international financiers long wary of the murk and muck surrounding Ukraine's financial sector.[2]

Along the way, though, Gontareva and her colleagues realized there was one primary bank more important to tackle than all the others. PrivatBank had exploded by the mid-2010s into Ukraine's largest banking conglomerate, luring depositors by offering notably higher interest rates than its competitors. The bank, as *bne IntelliNews* wrote, was "present on every high street across Ukraine, with its branches outnumbering those of the state-owned savings bank." Housing one-third of the country's retail deposits, with small-scale Ukrainian depositors entrusting the bank with billions of dollars, PrivatBank was identified by authorities in Kyiv as the only private bank of "systemic importance to the country."[3]

But Gontareva had her suspicions. In Ukraine, it's all "oligarchic banking," she told me, glint-eyed under her blond bob. "These banking licenses are used just for money laundering." And the head of Privat-Bank was hardly some gadfly. Kolomoisky was a well-known quantity in postrevolution Kyiv, and across Ukraine. As such, when it came to PrivatBank, Gontareva sensed something others around her had grown to suspect: money laundering, on a massive scale. "I've been working in this field for thirty years, and could understand that something was wrong," she said. So she began probing the bank's books. And it didn't take long for her to confirm her suspicions. When it came to Ukrainian banks transforming into money laundering machines, "PrivatBank wasn't an exception," Gontareva told me. "The problem was that it was the biggest one."[4]

Soon, Gontareva and her colleagues made a shocking discovery. Rather than the sturdy bastion of the country's private banking industry that PrivatBank claimed to be, it was instead a vacant, cobwebbed cabinet—and billions in deposits were, somehow, missing. In public, the bank presented itself as a staple of financial stability for a country teetering from revolution and invasion. But internal documents told a different story. PrivatBank's loan book was pockmarked with all kinds of offshore entities, all kinds of obscure shells—what the Ukrainian authorities described as "fraud loans."[5] As one analysis detailed, "Hardly any other borrower on the loan book . . . is a recognizable corporate brand, easily identifiable with a real business."[6] The recipients, it appeared, were little more than ghosts. As another analysis described, "99 percent of the loans on the bank's books were fake."[7]

Gontareva and her allies immediately scrambled. Suddenly, Ukrainian authorities and the bank's depositors were staring into the crumbling hole PrivatBank had left behind. The new authorities found only one solution: nationalizing the bank, rescuing it by rerouting billions of dollars in

Ukrainian taxpayer monies in order to cover the missing deposits.[8] They would take care of the missing money now, in the hopes of finding the missing money later. The government swiftly patched a $5.5 billion hole in the bank's finances, if only to save the country's entire banking sector from going belly-up.[9] "Either PrivatBank was going down, and the whole banking system would die with it, or the government had to save it," one Ukrainian journalist who's covered Kolomoisky told me.[10] Or as Daria Kalenyuk, the noted anticorruption activist, added, Kolomoisky "managed to create a bank that was too big to fail."[11]

Instead of acting as a pillar of a new Ukraine, PrivatBank had punched a mile-wide hole into the bleeding Ukrainian budget. And as Gontareva soon discovered, instead of acting as a dependable partner of Ukrainians across the country, those behind PrivatBank had launched the greatest Ponzi scheme the country had ever seen. "No one imagined it was like this," Gontareva told me. "It was all a Ponzi scheme. There were no assets at all. . . . That's why I called this the biggest fraud of the twenty-first century."[12]

*   *   *

AFTER NATIONALIZING PRIVATBANK, authorities in Kyiv had one question: Where had all the money gone? As investigators and forensic accountants later discovered, the PrivatBank Ponzi scheme stood—as with many Ponzi schemes—both confusingly complex and perfectly straightforward. The key to PrivatBank's Ponzi success was what some dubbed a "Shadow Bank"[13] or a "Bank within the Bank."[14]

Here's how the scheme worked, according to both Ukrainian and American authorities. After PrivatBank processed the latest round of deposits from unsuspecting Ukrainians, an internal "credit committee" made up of Kolomoisky's lackeys would meet to discuss what to do with the latest intake. Rather than an independent roster of accountants and financial experts shepherding the bank's best interests, this internal credit committee had one job: turn that money into loans for a wide array of shell companies connected to Kolomoisky (as well as to his oligarchic partner Gennadiy Bogolyubov, whom we met in chapter 4). It didn't matter whether the loans made sense, or if anyone had any reservations. All that mattered was their signature, and that, as a later DOJ filing detailed, they "simply hit 'approve' whenever they received a loan application" from a company connected to Kolomoisky. Not that the employees on the credit committee had much of a choice. "If employees did express dissent, they would lose their bonuses, have work taken away, or simply be fired," the DOJ later said. "Those consequences were particularly harsh in context: PrivatBank offered the highest paying jobs in the region." As one employee said, approving those loans was as expected as "opening the door and walking into the office."[15]

But simply rerouting the loans to Kolomoisky's shell companies would have been a bit too obvious. (The oligarch may have been greedy, but he was hardly stupid.) Instead of keeping the new loans themselves, his companies would then redirect those loans into separate accounts set up at PrivatBank's branch in the Mediterranean nation of Cyprus—which is itself a notorious offshore haven. As one analysis found, these shell companies "had billions of dollars moving in and out of their accounts," even though "the entities had no business, assets, operations, or employees and were shell entities deployed for money laundering purposes."[16] Instead, they "effectively existed only to steal" from the Ukrainian depositors who'd trusted PrivatBank, said the DOJ.[17]

But those Cyprus bank accounts weren't the final step. That Cypriot branch then chopped and bundled the loans themselves, partitioning them among a number of accounts, mixing and mingling and swishing and swirling the incoming money so that, by the time the Cypriot bank was done, there was no telling which monies could be tied to which specific loan. It was as if the money had been atomized, deconstructed, and then built back into something completely different—something completely untraceable, which the oligarch could then use as he saw fit.[18]

Up to this point, the methods were relatively straightforward. A dirty bank bundling loans to insiders, bouncing them among shell companies, obscuring their sourcing: this had been done, time and again, in Mexico and Equatorial Guinea and anywhere oligarchs controlled the levers of financial institutions. But PrivatBank and Kolomoisky had a pair of innovations that made them stand apart.

First, there was the amount of time involved. With a bit of focus, offshoring can be a relatively swift process: some phone calls, some documents signed, some clicks confirming the transfers, and clean money can emerge in the millions in a manner of weeks, or even days if you're lucky. PrivatBank, though, took that speed to another level. It's as if the looted funds were all piled into a blender, a switch was flipped, and voilà: a few minutes later, millions in dirty money had been pureed clean, perfectly available for consumption, indistinguishable from whatever it had been prior. Where previous offshoring schemes took weeks, Kolomoisky's allegedly took minutes.[19]

In just one example, later highlighted by American officials, a loan was "deposited and then withdrawn from the accounts of 13 different shell entities in a total of 17 transactions at PrivatBank's Cyprus branch—all in only 8 minutes."[20] In less time than it takes to bake some cookies, or to watch an inning of baseball, the new mixed-mingled-swished-swirled money emerged, clean and untraceable. It's still unclear exactly how Kolomoisky's system achieved this level of laundering speed and creativity, although suspicions center on some kind of machine-learning or artificial intelligence software that figured out how to best mix and match the funds. "Criminals use technology more efficiently than healthcare professionals," Gontareva told me.[21]

Second, and perhaps more important, the next steps didn't necessarily see Kolomoisky and his cronies park the pureed, clean money in Manhattan high-rises or Malibu beachfronts or Miami condos—the kinds of places that Teodorin, and so many others, had previously turned to in order to transform their dirty money into legitimate assets. Instead, there was something that Ukrainian and American investigators dubbed "loan recycling."[22] The idea behind this, as with the rest of the entire operation, was simple. Kolomoisky's aides would take the mixed-mingled-swished-swirled money from the Cypriot accounts, bundle it and bounce it through a few more banks and a few more accounts across Europe, and then use it to purchase legitimate assets elsewhere. Maybe those assets were commercial buildings in a city like Cleveland. Maybe they were in a steel town like Warren, Ohio. Maybe they were in a factory town like Harvard, Illinois. The details didn't necessarily matter. All that mattered was that the money was then used to pick up physical property, plants and factories and commercial constructs elsewhere.

On paper, the money was still listed as a loan—one that needed to be paid back at some point. However, Kolomoisky and his helpers had a different idea. Instead of using those new physical assets to pay back the initial loans, PrivatBank would simply issue new loans to cover up the initial loans. "The basic idea was simple," a later DOJ filing detailed. Kolomoisky requested money from PrivatBank, which he "always received, and rarely paid it back, except through new loans. . . . PrivatBank was simply recycling the loans and increasing its losses." Everything on paper looked fine. The old loans looked like they'd been taken care of. But while "certain loans were paid when they came due, in reality, they were being paid through the issuance of additional debt." No new money came in to cover those initial loans—only that which had been swiped from the unsuspecting Ukrainian depositors who kept funneling their savings into the bank. All of which meant that Kolomoisky effectively used PrivatBank as his "personal piggybank . . . never expect[ing] to have to pay the money back."[23]

It was an ever-expanding cycle. New PrivatBank loans begat new shell company transfers, which begat new asset purchases, which begat new debts, which begat new loans, which begat new transfers, which begat new purchases, which begat new debts, which begat new loans, on and on and on, all while trusting Ukrainian consumers turned to PrivatBank with their deposits. On paper, all the documentation appeared above-board—old loans appeared to be repaid, and new loans appeared to have perfectly legitimate purposes, listed for things like investments or retail. But the whole thing was, said American officials, a series of "slush funds."[24] As Gontareva said upon discovering the entire process, it appeared to be a scam of momentous proportions. In time, investigators would discover that Kolomoisky and his team had potentially laundered nearly *half a trillion dollars* with this playbook.

"If this is true," said Anders Aslund, an expert on post-Soviet corruption at the Atlantic Council, "this is the biggest case of money laundering in history, and it has been perpetrated by one single group."[25]

*   *   *

BUT AS UKRAINIAN and American authorities discovered, Kolomoisky didn't construct this loan-recycling-cum-Ponzi scheme with just intimidated accountants and unwitting depositors. He also happened to have a group of helpers in the U.S.—a group the DOJ would refer to as the "Optima Family."[26]

By the mid 2010s, Korf and Schochet and the entire Optima network stood atop a sprawling kingdom of commercial real estate, steel towns, and factory plants that cut a swath through the Midwest and Rust Belt. And the Americans had plenty to show for it. Not only was Schochet feted across Cleveland, but Korf and his partner Laber relaxed in Greco-Spanish mansions in Miami, dispensing millions in new money to charities and compatriots. (As American officials later laid out, many of the millions suddenly lining Korf's and Laber's pockets clearly stemmed from Optima-related schemes, including one $13 million transfer from Optima International directly to Korf, Laber, and their families.[27]) And the group's profile in South Florida only kept rising; as the DOJ noted, as "Korf and Laber's resources expanded, they moved [the Optima headquarters in Miami] from the 30th floor to the 36th and finally the 55th floor—the penthouse."[28]

It's unclear when, exactly, they realized the bottom was set to fall out of their empire, and when the spigot of funds from PrivatBank would dry up. Maybe it was after Ukraine heaved into revolution, upending the existing oligarchic networks stripping the country. Maybe it was after the new Ukrainian government grew wary of Kolomoisky's rippling power base, and what he could do with his militias. Or maybe—likely—it wasn't until Gontareva and her colleagues flipped open PrivatBank's playbook, revealing the loan recycling schemes to the world. Because that exposure didn't just reveal Kolomoisky's machinations, or his shell company networks. As Ukrainian and American authorities detailed in a series of staggering findings and investigations, the end stages of the loan recycling networks required Kolomoisky's bagmen to visit a series of overlooked markets across a range of obscure locales, right in the heart of the U.S.

The role of the Optima team was, when boiled down, deceptively straightforward. Korf and Laber "used the Optima Family's funds as one large pool of money," according to Justice Department officials. "They transferred funds back and forth between the different [shell company] entities, both to launder the money and to try to make money."[29] In conversations and interviews, Korf had claimed that he barely knew Kolomoisky, or that the oligarch was simply a "successful businessman" who was "being harassed by the Ukrainian government."[30] But as the DOJ revealed, the American had, in reality, remained in constant communication with the Ukrainian oligarch. "Korf discussed those transfers with Kolomoisky," who "approved the use of the money," wrote American officials.[31]

But it wasn't simply a matter of handling the illicit monies. Korf, along with Laber, "established a complex system of entities in order to facilitate the laundering of the misappropriated funds."[32] That is, according to the investigators, they helped erect a lattice of shell companies to disguise the mixed-mingled-swished-swirled money even further. They especially enjoyed using shell companies located in, naturally, Delaware. One Delaware LLC in particular, Optima Ventures LLC, "was the primary vehicle used to acquire property in the United States with misappropriated funds from PrivatBank."[33] America's favorite financial secrecy haven, used once again to help crooked oligarchs drain a foreign country dry, laundering and injecting ill-gotten gains directly into the U.S., helping the American laundromat churn and swell that much more along the way.

With these Delaware LLCs, these recycled loans, and an ever-expanding pool of Ukrainian depositors to scam, Kolomoisky "spent prolifically" in the U.S. For instance, one $12 million loan from Privat-Bank, according to loan documents, was supposed to be for "funding ongoing operations" for steel production in Ukraine. In reality, it went directly toward the purchase of One Cleveland Center, the chisel-shaped building carving Cleveland's downtown skyline.[34] According to the DOJ, another $13 million loan was scattered across a number of shell company accounts, some of which then redirected the laundered money to fund the Crowne Plaza purchase, landing the Optima group the second-largest hotel in the entire city. The same schemes allowed the Optima Family to pick up the historic Huntington Building, Cleveland's claim to architectural fame. So, too, the Penton Media Building, the half-million-square-foot heavyweight, as well as 55 Public Square, towering over Cleveland's main downtown square.[35] All of those purchases, linked directly to the Ponzi scheme spiraling out of Ukraine.[36] "They were hiding their money in plain sight," said Tom Cardamone, the head of Global Financial Integrity. "No one else is looking at Cleveland."[37]

* * *

NEARLY EVERYONE WILLING to speak about the Optima schemes agrees on one thing: the Optima Family ran their downtown Cleveland investments into the ground, drove tenants away, and showed absolutely no interest in any of their claims of launching Cleveland toward a bright, prosperous future. If Cleveland had already been on a downswing before Schochet arrived, the Optima Family only helped drive a stake through downtown Cleveland's remaining potential. Most of the properties "have fallen into disrepair and suffer from high vacancy rates," the local press reported.[38] "They're pretty much doomed," one journalist covering the purchases said about the entire Optima portfolio. Or as one local familiar with the Optima purchases told me, "They pretty much ruined everything they touched."[39]

Take the Penton Media Building, for instance. At one point an "arrow in [Optima's] quiver," the Optima team found it over 90 percent occupied when they arrived in 2010.[40] Just a few years later, occupancy rates had plummeted by over a third, thanks, as a later lawsuit claimed, to Optima's "mismanagement [that] resulted in high levels of vacancy."[41] Unsurprisingly, the building's assessed value plummeted as well, shaving millions off the building's worth.[42]

Or look at the 55 Public Square investment.[43] At nearly half a million square feet, standing as the former home to a range of white-shoe law firms, the Optima team purchased the building in 2009 in order to cement Optima's downtown dynasty. Before Schochet swooped in, the building was seen, as one outlet called it, as a "moneymaker," with an 85 percent occupancy rate. Fast-forward a decade, and the "once-flourishing" building is "in dire need of a makeover," according to the *Cleveland Plain Dealer*.[44] The alt-weekly *Cleveland Scene* described 55 Public Square as a "situation of disrepair and vacancy," a hollowed-out husk in the middle of downtown. Few businesses, if any, remain. ("The John Q Steakhouse space on the ground floor has been vacant for years," the *Cleveland Scene* noted.[45]) In 2018, the building received an appraised worth at just over half of Optima's purchase price.[46] But even that bottomed-out price wasn't enough for inquiring buyers, with one development firm describing it as "unworkable."[47] As one local familiar with the purchase told me, Optima "just ruined that asset."[48]

Or consider the Huntington Building. That staple of Cleveland's history, its murals and brass and lobby an architectural testament to the city's better times, stood as the keystone of Optima's portfolio in the city. At the time of purchase, the *Plain Dealer* noted, the Huntington was generating significant income, housing accounting firms like Ernst & Young. It was the soaring, gleaming evidence of Optima's arrival in the city. But a half-decade later, the building stood cavernously empty, with little more than sparrows' nests and abandoned desks, and with occupancy rates cratering to lower than 10 percent. According to the *Plain Dealer*, the building—the second-largest office building in the world when it was constructed—is now little more than an aching, bracing emptiness, a "gaping hole" gouging downtown Cleveland.[49]

* * *

AROUND THE SAME time the authorities in Kyiv began probing Privat-Bank's finances, the Optima team began divesting itself of the Cleveland assets, selling some of the properties—the Huntington going for $22 million,[50] the Penton building going for $38 million[51]—to new developers seeking reclamation projects. It's unclear what prompted the sell-off; Korf, Laber, and Schochet all either ignored or declined to answer my questions. But one theory has floated to the fore that would match up with other kleptocratic stories we've seen, time and again, when it comes to American real estate.

For many of the kleptocrats and crooked officials eyeing America, real estate provides a gateway to any opportunity they need. Teodorin, for instance, saw American real estate as a means to his mogul-slash-celebrity lifestyle. Some—such as Iranian officials who secretly used American shell companies to snap up a Manhattan skyscraper—use American real estate to skirt sanctions. Others—such as corrupt Venezuelan officials looting the country's coffers—use it to escape an imploding economy back home.[52] But we've also seen crooked officials and corrupt oligarchs eye American real estate for the same reason the rest of us turn to real estate investments: for a stable, swelling market, generally appreciating, presenting a safe, sturdy investment that can provide a bailout if your financial portfolio goes belly-up. Think of American real estate as a kleptocratic rainy day fund—the greatest rainy day fund in the world, worth trillions and trillions of dollars.[53]

Which is exactly what it appears the Cleveland investments were. For a billionaire like Kolomoisky, it mattered little if the renovations that people like Schochet promised never came to pass, or if millions of dollars ended up knocked off the sale price because he'd let his downtown Cleveland purchases go to rot. The land would always retain its worth, even if the buildings didn't—even if they left "gaping holes" in a dying downtown. And if, as Kolomoisky may have anticipated, his PrivatBank Ponzi scheme ever collapsed, it's always good to have backup assets worth millions dollars, isn't it?

Those hoodwinked by Optima's claims now recognize what American officials have alleged: that the Optima Family, with Kolomoisky as backer, had no designs on rescuing Cleveland, but were more interested in flipping the city into their own personal laundromat, all on behalf of a Ukrainian oligarch-turned warlord. "No one really knew," one local familiar with the purchases said. "It took a few years before people really figured it out. But the writing was on the wall."[54] Still, not everyone involved in hyping the Optima investments wants to discuss them. Mark Vogel, the investment banker who initially described Schochet's presence in the city as a "coup," and who had even attended Schochet's wedding, told me I couldn't quote any of his previous praise for Schochet—even though the quotes were published in *Plain Dealer* articles. "Do not quote me," Vogel told me over the phone. "I mean it. I've been really nice to you. Don't come at me and say you're going to quote me on something a long time ago. Don't fucking do that. . . . I work for Warren Buffett, and I can fucking make your life miserable. Am I going to have to fucking ram up your ass?"[55] (It's unclear what the last sentence meant, and Vogel did not respond to other questions about Schochet.)

But these schemes also pointed to a new chapter in the story of American kleptocracy. No longer were kleptocrats looking to megalopolises like New York or Miami for their laundering needs. Now, America's heartland appeared open for business—and America's overlooked interior was ripe for exploitation. "It's bad enough that the dirty money from abroad has been flooding into Miami and New York, but it intuitively makes sense that criminals and the corrupt would want a Manhattan penthouse," said Clark Gascoigne, one of the U.S.'s leading counterkleptocracy voices (as well as an Ohio native). "But when it infiltrates cities in the heartland of America like Cleveland, it should be a wake-up call to all of us that we have a serious problem—and it can happen anywhere."[56]

And it did. Real estate purchases in Dallas linked directly to Kolomoisky's dirty money, including a local "commercial real estate icon," sit undeveloped and vacant.[57] A major $77 million purchase in downtown Louisville ended up in default, with one American bank arguing that Optima failed to make good on a multimillion-dollar loan that came with the building's purchase.[58] It was the same story Cleveland experienced. How many other cities looked at similar financial spin men as potential financial lifelines? And we've only touched on the commercial side. How many residential buildings faced the same fate? How many units within how many buildings served as little more than sinkholes for the dirty money Kolomoisky and other oligarchs and officials grabbed? What about houses? Or apartment complexes? Or empty lots, entire swaths of acreage, farmland or timberland or grazing land?

How much of the American real estate industry's success rests on modern kleptocracy?[59]

Thanks to rampant anonymity, and the ease with which these kleptocrats and crooked officials can spend their funds in the U.S., we don't know the answer to any of these questions. Nor do we know how many

Americans watched their property taxes jump as these kleptocrats over-paid for these assets. Nor do we know how many areas sagged or emptied out, all because the kleptocrats showed no interest in ever turning their investments into profitable vehicles, desiccating entire neighborhoods, enervating entire chunks of American cities and towns and communities.[60]

We just don't know. But if there's a silver lining, it's that these are just buildings. For the real costs of this new chapter in the story of the American laundromat, you have to visit the steel valleys and the manufacturing plants targeted by the kleptocrats and their American handmaidens.

FUCKING CURSED

"Our society had been a kleptocracy of the highest order, the government doing its best to steal from the Americans, the average man doing his best to steal from the government, the worst of us doing our best to steal from each other."

—Viet Thanh Nguyen[1]

In 2010, a cooling panel at the Warren, Ohio, steel plant began leaking.[2] It wasn't the first time a leak had been spotted nearby. These panels, which were meant to monitor the temperature of the plant's furnace, had become constant sources of dripping, draining water escaping through unpatched holes and faulty tubes. The water leaked directly toward the churning, burning molten steel—a situation that could result in a fiery explosion if the water reached the metal. According to later court documents, workers spotted the leak before it reached the molten mass. They tried to get the attention of the furnace operator, who was then in the process of pouring the metal from the oven. But the furnace operator didn't see, or maybe couldn't hear, his coworkers. He missed the water threading its way toward the lava-like mass, and missed the last few moments before water met metal—before a burst of hot air blasted upward, outward, toward workers and brick walls alike. The explosion tore through the furnace walls, sending bodies sprawling—and sending workers to the hospital, backs bent and bones busted, skin charred and melting off arms and legs. At least one injured worker needed back surgery and years of recovery.[3]

But that wouldn't be the plant's final convulsion. A year later, another blast battered more bricks, shattered more windows, scattered more bodies. "I was like a ping pong ball," one employee, Michael Buckner, later told the International Consortium of Investigative Journalists (ICIJ). "I got thrown down steps. You couldn't see anything." Even those employees who weren't injured nonetheless saw the consequences. "The skin was literally peeling off [Buckner's] forearm," another employee said of the injuries. "It was horrible." Buckner added that reliving that blast, which severely burned a number of his other coworkers, is "a never-ending nightmare—it never goes away."[4]

This second blast prompted a formal investigation from federal regulators tasked with keeping steel plants like the one in Warren safe. Their inspection at Kolomoisky's plant, though, turned up numerous concerning signs. Over a dozen "troubling violations" of basic safety protocols—things like water seeping from cooling panels, meeting molten metal, exploding like a grenade—greeted them. One of the dangers at the plant, one member of the Warren City Council told me, involved the inexplicable decision to replace worker safety glass with cheaper shatter-prone glass that "you could break with a hammer."[5] Not that those still working at the plant were surprised. "They just kept cutting corners," William Norman, who worked testing metal strengths, later said. "They were running a skeleton crew. They would not hire more help. I would tell them they needed to hire more people, but they didn't want to hear it." The new management, ultimately overseen by Kolomoisky, apparently couldn't care less for workplace safety. It "was night and day" compared to previous management, Norman added.[6]

By 2014, the explosions and the bodies and the federal violations seemed to catch up with the plant. Citing "challenging market conditions," management halted operations that March, pledging to reopen by early 2016 and promising to eventually double the workforce when it did.[7] But months went by with no word. The plant continued to idle, as did about 200 steel workers reliant on the plant for their livelihoods.

And then, in January 2016, the United Steelworkers union, which represented the plant operators (or at least those who'd survived the repeated explosions), received a phone call. "We were informed . . . that the company would go from temporary idle to permanent idle," Pat Gallagher, one of the local union directors, said.[8] "Unforeseen business conditions" had forced their hand, management claimed.[9]

Today, the Warren steel plant lies in ruins. Cavernous holes gouge the siding, with peeling yellow and blue paint giving way to swaths of rust and sloshes of mud. Vacant lots and missing windows, crumpled cabinets and offices in disarray—whether trashed by looters or former employees is unclear—round out the place. The mill sits like something out of a dystopic future—or like something out of certain parts of the former Soviet Union, for that matter.

If you visit, you can still get a sense of what the mill once was. "When you climb high up above a factory floor, and stand next to a hook double the size of your entire body, it's something special," Cleveland photographer Johnny Joo, who specializes in photographing abandoned architecture, wrote after visiting the plant in 2017, where he took searing photos of the detritus and the damage remaining. But those hints of what the mill once was pale next to what it now is: a gutted, sickly, abandoned remnant of a time when America's heartland swaggered, before the walls caved in. Before a post-Soviet oligarch, and his team of American helpers, came to town. "I've explored numerous industrial facilities across the country," Joo wrote, "but have never set foot inside something of such immense size and industrial grandeur left to rot."[10]

*   *   *

BUT THERE'S ONE element missing in the story of this Warren plant. The Ohio plant's collapse can't be attributed just to an oligarch-turned-warlord, or just to his American henchmen scurrying across the Midwest, gobbling up forgotten buildings, forgotten plants, forgotten towns. That's certainly what we saw play out in Cleveland, where empty, vacant husks stand as a testament to the Optima Family's interests. The plant in Warren, though, brings another element of this new chapter of kleptocracy to bear: an element that highlights how easily these kleptocratic networks have begun carving Rust Belt carcasses, feasting on what's left behind. Stripping them bare and leaving them—and their towns, and their industries, and their people—to decompose.

Because Kolomoisky wasn't the lone Ukrainian oligarch involved in overseeing the Warren plant. There was Gennadiy Bogolyubov, his long-time partner since the earliest days of Ukrainian independence. And there was a third figure involved: a man named Vadim Shulman, whose path paralleled Kolomoisky's until the relationship between the two broke apart on the back of the American steel industry.[11]

Shulman is a stone-faced oligarch, a bit long in the ears, with a penchant for yachts and tennis.[12] Like Kolomoisky, Shulman joined the procession of those funneling post-Soviet monies into American assets, using similar company networks to invest in American steel plants—including the benighted Warren plant, where he and Kolomoisky became business partners. But according to a series of lawsuits Shulman filed in the U.S., not all went according to plan. As Shulman claims, his relationship with Kolomoisky soon shattered, undercut by a move in Kolomoisky's loan recycling scheme that no one in Warren could have seen coming.[13]

In a number of legal filings, Shulman claimed that Kolomoisky, alongside the Optima Family, secretly oversaw a "long-running, self-dealing, debt-accumulation scheme" to defraud both steel workers and partners like himself.[14] Specifically, in Warren, Kolomoisky oversaw a "series of large-scale and coordinated fraudulent schemes"—all of which swindled Shulman, lined Kolomoisky's pockets, and expedited the destruction of the Warren mill and hundreds of American jobs with it. The schemes, per Shulman's filings, initially appear complex and convoluted, juggling shell companies and financial secrecy jurisdictions and all the wonderful offshoring toys those of the billionaire caste have grown to love. Boiled down, though, they transform the destruction of the Warren plant and the destitution left in its wake from a story of negligence into something far worse.

When the partnership began, Kolomoisky, Shulman, and Bogolyubov all owned equal shares in the plant. But starting in the late 2000s, according to Shulman, Kolomoisky began secretly transferring ownership to a separate offshore entity. (Shulman, whose lawyers didn't respond to interview requests, claims his signatures on the transfer documents were forged.) From there, the Warren mill transformed into a key cog in the broader loan recycling scheme itself. As Shulman's lawsuit lays out, Kolomoisky and his accountants began using the Warren Steel Mill as an entity to specifically provide those "fraudulent loans" that went to pay off the previous loans bouncing around his web of shell companies.[15]

On paper, Kolomoisky's team issued a number of loans that documents claimed would be dedicated to improving the Warren plant—say, improving safety protocols, or preventing future bone-breaking explosions. But then, in the bogus loan carousel Kolomoisky and his team allegedly set up, the loans sped right through the Warren plant itself, reissued as loans the Warren plant was now providing to other Kolomoisky companies. From there, those loans reentered the loan recycling circuit, joining the rest of the mixed-mingled-swished-swirled money, eventually winding their way to destinations elsewhere. (In the legalese Shulman included in one of his lawsuits, "the loan proceeds passed straight through Warren Steel; then through a network of Related Parties before finally being disbursed to other entities and/or individuals, which were owned and/or controlled by Defendants' [sic] Kolomoisky and Bogolyubov."[16])

In effect, Kolomoisky and his crew hustled the loans directly through the Warren plant, making it seem like the Warren plant was the one then issuing the new loans, effectively turning it into their own miniature loan-recycling outpost. Instead of springing for repairs, or new investments, or basic steps to protect employees, Shulman claims that Kolomoisky and his team left the plant itself holding the bag for, on paper, tens of millions of dollars of the recycled loans. All of this, while never intending to actually follow through on any of the claims made to those in Warren, either to the furnace operators and union men reliant on the plant for work or to the city officials reliant on the mill for the town's economic health.[17]

It's unclear why Kolomoisky used this Warren plant specifically, according to Shulman, as opposed to any number of the other American plants he owned. But the implication was clear. It wasn't shifting economic tides that forced Warren's closure, and it wasn't tight-pocketed owners running low on funds. The mill was allegedly a sham purchase from the get-go, meant to obscure a money laundering operation larger than anyone could have realized. "If Shulman's allegations are to be believed," one analysis found, "the official reasons for the closure—a faltering industry and lack of financing—look more like pat excuses, trading on the well-worn economic tropes of the region and obscuring more nefarious causes."[18] As Shulman claimed, "Instead of attempting to operate Warren Steel for a profit, Defendants Kolomoisky and Bogolyubov exploited the business to enrich themselves, all to the detriment of Warren Steel and Plaintiffs."[19]

Yet Warren wasn't the only American steel town obliterated. In West Virginia, a long-standing plant in New Haven, located in a small stitch along the border with Ohio, ran directly into the same issues. The decades-old ferroalloy plant, steered by one of the Kolomoisky-connected companies since 2006, has been battered by a series of lawsuits alleging malpractice when it came to worker safety. Workers interviewed by the *Kyiv Post* revealed "that injuries at the facility were common, due to a lack of maintenance and management's refusal to supply them with equipment, citing cost concerns."[20] One plant worker died in 2009, a 27-year-old employee persuaded to work 90 hours a week, who fell asleep and crashed on his drive home.[21] ("Safety sucks. [U]pper management sucks. . . . Nothing good to say nothing good to say nothing good to say," one mistyped comment on a job review site read.[22])

In Kentucky, another steel plant tucked near the borders with both Ohio and West Virginia went belly-up in 2018, costing another hundred-plus jobs. "This is nothing but bad and sad news," one local official said. As in Warren, the company claimed "current business challenges" forced the plant's closure—nothing about Kolomoisky, or about PrivatBank, or about the schemes and scams allegedly linked to the other American assets and American plants wrapped up in the Ukrainian oligarch's web of illicit money.[23]

It seems none of the American assets went untouched. Some shuttered, as in Ohio and Kentucky and Indiana. Some buckled under piling debts. "At Michigan Seamless Tube and three other steel plants, the bills began to mount," ICIJ found. "[Niagara LaSalle] in Indiana owed a trucker $17,191. Corey Steel in Illinois owed a brass supplier $105,000." Those earlier promises, of job creation and bright futures, collapsed all across the region. "Under Kolomoisky's ownership," ICIJ calculated, "hundreds of steelworkers in Kentucky, New York state and Ohio lost their jobs, and in one case, were left without insurance coverage or the ability to temporarily access their retirement funds, court records state."[24] Jobs lost. Plants destroyed. Neither ever to return.[25]

* * *

THE PLIGHT OF one enormous factory showed just how much of a millstone these assets, caught in the Optima web, could become for an unsuspecting town. After Schochet visited Harvard, Illinois, in 2008 to announce the Optima network's purchase of the former Motorola plant for nearly $17 million, kindling hopes of finally seeing the plant fullfill its potential, he proceeded to ignore the town almost entirely. "Chaim wasn't around much," Charlie Eldredge, the head of the local economic development group, told me. "I would see him once a year, once every other year. . . . I saw him about as often as he came to Harvard. Clearly it wasn't the focus of their interest." As Eldredge added, it quickly became clear that the Optima network "didn't really have any real plans [about] what to do with the facility."[26]

By early 2014, the building not only still stood vacant, but it now stood dark. With a half-million-dollar tab in unpaid electricity bills, the juice was cut off, forcing local officials to visit with flashlights. "It's just heartbreaking to see that beautiful place sitting vacant," one said.[27] Soon thereafter, the heat was also shut off, even though the plumbing hadn't been fully emptied. Unpaid property taxes likewise kept accumulating, starving the strapped local government of hundreds of thousands of dollars.

Along the way, the massive building itself—its factory and fitness center, its childcare rooms and 500-seat auditorium, even its pair of heliports—continued a slow march toward implosion. Weeds began poking through the parking lot. Mold began creeping along the walls, along the roof, into the pipes, into the recesses of the building. The factory's entire fire suppressant system, including over 20,000 sprinkler heads, began falling apart. Their replacement alone, according to one local official, will itself cost upward of $20 million.[28]

On and on and on, one by one by one, the building's issues continue to pile. "The mechanical [equipment] all needs to be replaced," Mayor Michael Kelly told me. "The roof leaks. No one's really taking care of it."[29] Nor, as Kelly and Eldredge point out, is it just that the building's infrastructure continues to degrade. At some point in the none-too-distant future, the issues will cross an accumulated threshold. Like a car on its way to being totaled, the building at some point will have to be condemned rather than recovered. And that point is only a few years away.

"The building won't just be valueless—it will be a catastrophe for the town, because it will have to be demolished," Eldredge told me. "And the net cost for that, after salvage, is probably three to five times the city's annual budget. It will be a financial catastrophe." Eldredge paused, pondering that reality: that this hundred-million-dollar investment, this hundred-million-dollar promise to a small outpost in northern Illinois, ended up with a crooked Ukrainian oligarch interested only in looting and larceny—an oligarch whose involvement now risks dragging the entire town down with it. "I think there's certainly a good many citizens who feel it's better the building had never been built," Eldredge added.[30]

There is a twist to the Harvard story, though. Somehow, Kolomoisky's team found a buyer in 2016 willing to take on the former Motorola plant, infrastructural issues and all. The new buyer, just like the old, was an international syndicate, this one headed by a Chinese-Canadian businessman named Xiao Hua Gong.[31] Gong, who prefers to go by Edward, claimed he wanted to transform the plant into a smartphone manufacturing base. According to Eldredge, Gong was initially "very charming and full of conversation of what wonderful things he was going to do."[32] Not too dissimilar from a certain Ukrainian network that parachuted into Harvard a few years prior, singing much the same tune.

Only a year after the sale, though, officials in Canada dropped a bombshell.[33] Canadian authorities accused Gong of running his own transnational money laundering scheme.[34] Liaising with authorities in China and New Zealand, Canada lobbed multiple charges at Gong, including fraud and money laundering.[35] (Said Eldredge, "By all appearances, he's a con man."[36])

All of which means one thing: the Harvard Motorola plant has apparently entered not one but *two* kleptocratic pipelines. Passed between two kleptocratic networks. Tossed like a volleyball between a pair of foreign oligarchs. Juggled while an American town sinks into oblivion.

Following the charges against Gong, the Motorola plant remains frozen. Local authorities can't touch it, as it's part of ongoing investigations attempting to unwind Gong's network. And those in Harvard watch this factory, this initial promise, sit vacant. Rotting away, along with whatever potential it once held. "It's almost as if these oligarchs, that they have so much money that the rules don't apply to them, they can do whatever they want," Kelly sighed to me. "I think the community sees that the Motorola plant has been a huge albatross for us." He paused, took a breath. "The building is fucking cursed."[37] The reality of this Motorola plant points to yet another new chapter in the unfurling story of American kleptocracy. No longer are these networks out of Ukraine or China or Equatorial Guinea or any other nation, all eyeing the U.S. for their money laundering needs, simply isolated streams of dirty money. Now, assets like the Harvard plant can be traded, can be swapped, can be shared among multiple dirty money networks.

The only reason we know anything about the Harvard plant is because American and Canadian authorities, aided by partners in places like Ukraine and New Zealand, opted to target the specific money laundering networks linked to Kolomoisky and Gong. But given the miles-wide availability of other American money laundering services, there's no reason to think the Harvard plant is the only nine-figure American asset bandied between parallel kleptocratic networks.

If anything, it's the canary in the kleptocratic coal mine.[38]

* * *

THANKFULLY, SOME IN Washington are finally seeing just how wide America's money laundering embrace truly is—and how much it's begun infecting the giant swaths of rural and small-town America that investigators had previously ignored. One of those tracing the contours of this new reality is Karen Greenaway, a former FBI agent who'd previously focused largely on money laundering concerns, especially out of Ukraine. In early 2019, Greenaway sat in a hearing in Washington in front of the U.S. Helsinki Commission, there to discuss the methods of recovering and returning looted funds. Amidst discussions of Manhattan penthouses and anticorruption squads in Southern California, Greenaway turned the hearing's attention to the exact phenomenon Kolomoisky and Gong had highlighted.

"I'm not sure people do understand how damaging taking dirty money really is to the United States," Greenaway started. "I like to use the analogy of—if you've ever lived out in the far West—a dry streambed. Dirty money is like a rainstorm coming into a dry streambed. It comes very quickly, and a lot of it comes very fast, and the stream fills up, and then it gets dry again." The money races in, but there's no constant flow. "So what if you are a company that's purchased by dirty money? That dirty money is not going to be a steady flow into and out of the account so that you can run . . . the business the way it's supposed to."[39]

Just as Warren and Harvard and all those other towns learned, that flash flood of dirty money will wash through—but that streambed will dry up just as quickly, with adverse consequences for everyone outside the oligarch's or the kleptocrat's immediate circle. Greenaway continued:

> Because it's dirty money, and because you sunk $23 million or $48 million of it into the purchase of that property, now you got to go find some other money to pay all of the bills that go with it. And so what does that do if that's now a business that has U.S. workers employed in it? And their operating incomes are constantly being drained so that the oligarch can pay for his next yacht bill, or whatever it might be?
>
> What happens is, of course, is that the safety standard goes down. But people don't want to say anything because they want that job, and they need that job, and they need that business in their community. . . .

And what you're going to find out is that after 2008, when the financial institutions collapsed, essentially, in the United States—was there was a fire sale for a lot of our properties.

And as a result, what we have is people who don't live in the United States, who don't have any intention of really investing in the United States, but they needed a place to put their money. . . . Now the money is drying up. And now those businesses are going into default. And maybe that's the only business in that community that's employing people.[40]

Not just maybe, at least when it comes to the American towns Kolomoisky and his bagmen picked apart. Towns like those in the Steel Valley, reliant on those decades-old steel plants for another generation of jobs that will now never come. Or in those pockets of the Midwest, reliant on the promise of a local factory that will now never function. Or even in places like Cleveland, which watched Kolomoisky and his men roll in and dominate an entire downtown—and leave little more than smoke and detritus in their wake. "I think it's hurting small town America," Greenaway closed. "I just don't think that we've come to that realization yet."[41]

Nor do we know how many other oligarchs, how many other warlords, how many other kleptocrats have sunk their teeth into steel towns, into farming towns, into rural towns, into manufacturing plants and oil hubs and port cities. Thanks to things like anonymous American shell companies and anonymous American real estate purchases and other anonymous American financial secrecy tools, we have no idea how deep these oligarchic tendrils have burrowed into places we'd never expect: in Alaska and New Mexico, in North Dakota and North Carolina, in Kentucky and West Virginia and Ohio. Nor do we have any idea how many towns like Warren and Harvard have suffocated alongside, their livelihoods lost, their budgets strangled, their economic fortunes devastated. All because of this American kleptocracy.

* * *

BY THE MID-2010S, the U.S. had rolled into a new chapter, both in terms of its politics and its antikleptocracy efforts, that few could have seen coming. In the Senate, following nearly four decades of service, Carl Levin finally retired, bringing to a close a career that arguably did more than any other in Washington to highlight the spiraling threats of modern kleptocracy. The PSI continued on, diving into cybersecurity and the opioid crisis and healthcare fraud. But the focus on money laundering and on kleptocracy—despite the U.S.'s passage of legislation like the Magnitsky Act, which specifically sanctioned corrupt Russian officials—waned.

In the White House, the Obama administration watched Russia bulldoze into Crimea, and watched a regime in Syria bulldoze antigovernment protesters. The administration spent its final few years just trying to maintain the post–Cold War order where it could. Dealing with new regimes, the kinds buoyed by kleptocratic dictatorships in places like Moscow and Damascus, sapped the administration's energies and political capital. With everything else happening in the world, the White House's initial focus on kleptocracy dwindled

And in New York, a figure stepped onto a golden escalator, lowering himself into a waiting throng of supporters. A man who claimed he wanted to "drain the swamp"—but who brought with him an addiction, and a connection, to dirty money that few could match.

PART IV

UNITED STATES OF ANONYMITY

"Kleptocratic networks hold sway in military dictatorships and in apparent democracies, under leftist regimes and in countries whose leadership champions ultra-free-market capitalism. Like an invisible odorless gas, the phenomenon has spread, unnoticed, throughout much of the world."

—Sarah Chayes[1]

THE OLIGARCHS ARE JUST FRONTS

"America is the place I know best in the world. It's the only place I know in the world."

—Philip Roth[1]

In 1983, a doughy, muttonchopped 32-year-old named Jean-Claude Duvalier had a problem. A dozen years earlier, Duvalier—known as "Baby Doc" to cronies and detractors alike—had ascended to the presidency of the Caribbean nation of Haiti, following the death of his autocratic father. Almost immediately, Baby Doc smothered any talk of reform or hopes of democratization. As Haitians watched opposition activists go missing and independent media go silent, Baby Doc strangled any hopes that the country's democratic revolution of nearly two centuries prior would finally come to fruition.[2]

But Baby Doc wasn't a staid, stale dictator in his father's mold. He had a kind of malign *joie de vivre*, an almost sociopathic need to make the most of his time crushing his Haitian populace. A multimillion-dollar wedding, perhaps the most lavish the Caribbean has ever seen, included a 101-cannon salute, $100,000 worth of fireworks, and, as the *Washington Post* reported, a setting that "hid [Haiti's] poverty behind a façade of papier-mâché roses."[3] In the years that followed, Duvalier dabbled in crimes against humanity—including housing political prisoners in jails dubbed the "triangle of death,"[4] where many of them suffered unspeakably painful deaths—while regime supporters made sure any critical journalists were tortured or exiled for their reporting.

Looting state coffers, pillaging local populations, pocketing as much national wealth as he could stomach, Duvalier built a personal nest egg worth upward of $800 million—enough to place him alongside genocidaires like Slobodan Milosevic (looted wealth: $1 billion) and crooks like Peru's Alberto Fujimori (looted wealth: $600 million) among the great kleptocrats of the twentieth century.[5] Much of Baby Doc's looted wealth remained in Haiti proper, stashed in gold and banknotes. "If this money had been invested in clean water projects, we would have saved so many thousands of lives," an investigator who tried to track Baby Doc's assets later related to me. "That, to me, is the legacy when I think of Duvalier."[6]

With the help of a few friends, Baby Doc opened an American bank account, and immediately began plowing his dirty millions through the till. The Americans he encountered in those days—before banks had to think twice about servicing dictators, no matter the blood dripping from their regimes—opened their doors easily to Baby Doc. Like another great kleptocratic American client of the era, the Philippines' Ferdinand Marcos (looted wealth: $5–10 billion), those in Washington happily embraced Duvalier in his nominal stand against communism.[7]

Still, Baby Doc didn't want to make his American investments too obvious. He signed up an American lawyer, Kevin MacCarthy, who helped direct a shell company Baby Doc could use to obscure his finances. His American bank account kept growing, with millions in Haitians' missing money congealing for Baby Doc's use. Like Teodorin, Baby Doc scouted South Florida for a yacht, splurging over $6 million in today's money on a schooner he liked.[8] And like so many others, he eyed a place in New York.

Smack in the middle of Manhattan, a new building offered a potential home for Baby Doc's dirty millions. Rising nearly 60 stories, the new tower, looking like a shard of obsidian rising in brick-and-brass Midtown, wanted new tenants. One unit caught Baby Doc's eye: located on the 54th floor, with stunning views of New York City, the pad cost approximately $6 million in today's dollars. This, the dictator decided, was the one he wanted. Baby Doc's lawyer went forward with the purchase, and on April 22, 1983, he inked the deed.[9]

There on the contract was the description of the unit, the signature of the notary present, and the details of the purchase itself. All formal, rote stuff. But there, on the second page of the contract—hovering just above the names of Baby Doc's lawyer and shell company—was a scrawl Americans would become familiar with in the years to come. It belonged to a man who'd come to dominate America's luxury property market, America's reality television circuit, and, in time, America's politics. It belonged to Donald Trump, the man who decided to sell this unit in Trump Tower to one of the most heinous despots the Western Hemisphere had ever seen.[10]

On that day in 1983, decades before Trump entered the White House and upended the entire trajectory of American democracy and American kleptocracy alike, Trump landed his first kleptocrat.

It wouldn't be his last.

*　*　*

WHILE IT WILL take years, and potentially decades, to get a full picture of Trump's financial history, it's clear that Trump's properties in the U.S. alone may have laundered billions of dollars even before he ascended to the White House. According to the most comprehensive analysis available, Trump's American properties sold over 1,300 units—over one-fifth of Trump's total available condos—to buyers matching money laundering profiles: anonymously, to shell companies and cash buyers, often purchased in bulk and without ever revealing the identities of the ultimate beneficiaries. (Even today, thanks to the secrecy regime still in place in the U.S., only a small fraction of the ultimate owners of these Trump units has been disclosed.[11]) The final bill of these suspect purchases ran to a dumbfounding $1.5 billion—and that's before adjusting for inflation.[12]

It seems like every single one of Trump's American properties happily feasted on the diluvial flood of dirty money coming into the U.S. over the past few decades. Take Trump Tower in New York, for instance.

Baby Doc was hardly the only one who viewed the building as a potential personal laundromat. Nearly a quarter of the building's total unit sales went to buyers who, like Baby Doc, fit the money laundering profile. Total value of such sales: $30 million. Or pop over to the west side of Manhattan, where Trump erected the Trump International Hotel and Tower in 1996, one of his keystone properties, dominating Columbus Circle and Central Park's southwest corner. Nearly 30 percent of that building's unit sales went to buyers who fit money laundering profiles. The total value of such sales: $135 million.[13]

Or what about Trump World Tower, one of Trump's newest Manhattan constructs? Hugging the island's eastern border, overlooking the East River, Trump opened the building in 2001. And he made sure to open it to the kinds of buyers who'd long treated him and his buildings so well. Some 10 percent of the building's unit sales went to those same kinds of anonymous buyers, the ones eager to take advantage of the kleptocratic tools the U.S. provides in spades. Total value of such sales: $110 million. Or look at any of the other Trump buildings sprinkled across Manhattan like structural smallpox. Trump Park Avenue took in $80 million from these suspect buyers. Trump Palace Condominiums took in another $43 million. Trump Parc netted another $51 million. Trump SoHo—Trump's newest Manhattan building, and the New York construct most closely affiliated with the entire Trump family—appears to have been built *solely* to service these anonymous clients. After opening in 2010, a staggering 77 percent of unit sales went to buyers who fit money laundering profiles, raking in $110 million.[14] Trump SoHo was, as one lawsuit said about the building, "a monument to spectacularly corrupt money-laundering and tax evasion."[15]

But it's not as if these sales were limited to Trump properties in New York alone. In a nod to the fact that transnational money laundering is a truly American phenomenon, the suspect purchases tied to Trump properties took place across the country. In Florida, Trump Hollywood, tucked along the Atlantic shoreline, opened in 2009, flinging nearly half of its units to anonymous buyers, bringing in $136 million along the way. A bit farther south, Trump Grande 1, which opened in 2008, let one-third of its unit sales go to these suspicious buyers for some $105 million. That same year, a trio of other Trump Florida properties—known a bit blandly as Trump Towers 1, 2, and 3—netted $291 million from buyers that fit traditional money laundering models. Look wherever you want, and the pattern repeats itself. Trump International Hotel Waikiki in Hawaii? Nearly 20 percent of sales went to these buyers, for $161 million. Trump International Hotel and Tower in Chicago? Nearly 15 percent of sales went to these buyers, for $93 million. Trump International Hotel Las Vegas? Over 20 percent of sales went to these buyers, for $56 million.[16] It was American kleptocracy in miniature—American kleptocracy in a single person, who eventually used the proceeds of these suspect sales to help build a war chest that would launch him to the presidency.

Some of these shell companies chomping through Trump properties, like the one funneling Baby Doc's dirty money, were based elsewhere, in places like Panama or the British Virgin Islands. But plenty of suspect buyers took full advantage of using anonymous American shell companies to purchase anonymous American real estate. Delaware, for instance, provided shell companies for some 75 separate Trump-related purchases, good for keeping nearly $130 million perfectly anonymous.[17]

Not that Trump was himself any stranger to Delaware's services. Trump turned to the state time and again for his corporate needs, registering some 378 companies in the state for all sorts of corporate and "tax minimization" schemes.[18] ("It's a lot," Trump would later admit, though how many other anonymous Delaware shell companies Trump himself personally oversaw is anyone's guess.[19]) And of course, Trump's been repeatedly connected to a range of other Delaware shells, even the ones he doesn't nominally oversee. When it emerged in 2018 that Trump had helped steer $130,000 in hush money to former porn actress Stormy Daniels, his since-jailed lawyer, Michael Cohen, knew which state to turn to to suit their anonymous purposes: Delaware.[20] All of it—all this American anonymity, all these shell companies and real estate purchases, all this American kleptocracy wrapped up in a single blustering developer from Queens, New York—for the benefit of the man who would one day be president.

As mentioned above, the identities of hundreds and hundreds of those behind the anonymous purchases of Trump-related properties still remain unclear, shrouded in shell company secrecy. Still, like Baby Doc, a couple of names have slipped from behind the curtain of the secrecy regime in place, largely due either to court cases unveiling their names or Trump's own manic willingness to announce partnerships and new clients, regardless of the other party's background, connections to looted wealth, or clear criminality.

For instance, there was David Bogatin, a former Soviet military veteran best known for working as a Russian organized crime figure who ran scams across Brooklyn, New York.[21] Bogatin also worked as an ally of the morbidly obese Semion Mogilevich, perhaps the leading Russian Mafia figure in the entire world.[22] When Bogatin looked to park some of his ill-gotten money in the U.S., he had a clear outlet: purchasing multiple units in Trump Tower, enriching the future president with no questions asked. Another similar figure, Eduard Nektalov, emerged around the turn of the century as a key figure in a Treasury Department investigation into Colombian money laundering operations.[23] Before being executed at the hands of a hitman in 2004, Nektalov had moved millions directly into a building he knew would keep it safe: Trump World Tower.[24] (Nektalov owned a unit directly beneath Trump's future mealy-mouthpiece, Kellyanne Conway.[25])

There's also Vyacheslav Ivankov, a scruffy, scraggly former Siberian prison camp *exilé*. Another Mogilevich ally, Ivankov arrived in the U.S. in 1992 and proceeded to consolidate the Russian *mafiosi* on American soil. For years, Ivankov dodged FBI investigators, even after they'd fingered him as the man responsible for spreading the Russian mob's influence across the U.S. At last, the FBI discovered Ivankov's headquarters: Trump Tower. This was the building from which Ivankov chose to operate, steering a global criminal conglomerate before being murdered by a sniper on the streets of Moscow.[26]

It's worth noting that not all of Trump's questionable financial connections to suspect Russian figures came via his hotels or towers. In 2008, Trump offloaded a swank Florida mansion to a Russian oligarch named Dmitry Rybolovlev—a deal that netted Trump an incredible $54 million in profit in the most expensive residential sale the U.S. had ever seen at that point.[27]

Trump, however, appeared savvy enough to be able to identify whose money he was really helping to process. As Trump later quipped to his lawyer, "The oligarchs are just fronts for Putin."[28]

* * *

NOT THAT TRUMP'S sordid clients and partners were limited to his American buildings. The soon-to-be president had a penchant for partnering with the most corrupt actors he could find abroad. He also built a habit of exporting his laundering model to other locales, other markets, other countries—to other populations that might require his laundering services.

For instance, there was a planned Trump Tower on the Black Sea coast of the nation of Georgia.[29] That project saw Trump link up with a figure widely viewed as one of the most corrupt actors in the entire post-Soviet space: Timur Kulibayev, a Kazakhstani national whose net worth bulged into the billions after marrying into Kazakhstan's thuggish dictator's family.[30] While the planned Black Sea resort eventually fell through, Trump's connections to flows of suspect money out of Kazakhstan—a country suffering under decades of dictatorship, with few political or civil freedoms to citizens' names—extended back to his American properties, where another Kazakhstani official accused of massive embezzlement picked up a number of Trump SoHo properties.[31] Likewise, ongoing plans for a Trump International Hotel and Tower in Bali have involved a partnership with an Indonesian national named Hary Tanoesoedibjo. Despite governmental allegations of substantial tax fraud—and despite the fact that he was banned from leaving Indonesia after threatening one of Indonesia's most prominent officials—Trump decided to enlist Tanoesoedibjo's services for this supposedly "six-star" project.[32]

The Georgia and Indonesia projects point to the natural extension of Trump's American business model. But it's two projects elsewhere that helped cement Trump's kleptocratic *bona fides*, at least among the international set. Both of these other projects also roped Trump's family into his personal laundering operations, transforming the Trump kleptocratic project into a familial one and ushering in a new generation of Trumps intimately familiar with what it takes to build a paper empire on the back of dirty money.

First, there was Panama. The Trump Ocean Club project in Panama City, completed in 2011, brought the Trump Organization to one of the most notoriously corrupt countries in Central America. (Not only did Baby Doc set up his shell company in Panama, but in 2016 the so-called Panama Papers, which we saw in chapter 3, memorably spilled the secrets of the country's entire offshoring industry.) The 70-foot, sail-shaped complex was the family's "largest project in, actually, all of the Americas," Ivanka Trump, Trump's daughter, once boasted.[33] She would know, too; the building, according to Trump, was destined to be Ivanka's "baby."[34]

Indeed, Ivanka was intimately involved in the creation and associated sales of the Panamanian building. The building's primary broker, Alexandre Henrique Ventura Nogueira, claimed that he met with Ivanka at least 10 times to discuss the Panamanian project, adding that Ivanka was the primary figure responsible for all aspects of the Trump Ocean Club deal.[35] As the anticorruption watchdog Global Witness wrote, the building came with Ivanka's "personal touch."[36] (As Ivanka laughed in a promotional video, "Some people say [the building] resembles a giant D."[37])

One problem, though: the signs of money laundering affiliated with the building were as bright and blinding as anything in the entire Western Hemisphere, and as anything connected to Trump elsewhere. Not only were many units purchased in cash or via anonymous shell companies—including, as with Trump's New York properties, buyers linked to Russian organized crime—but many were likewise purchased in bulk, another traditional sign of money laundering. Some sales were even conducted via so-called bearer shares, tools so closely affiliated with money laundering operations that they've been banned across multiple jurisdictions.[38] ("Bearer shares" allow the holders of certain pieces of paper to be the legal owners of the shell company in question; all one has to do is hand off the paper, and the company's ownership and control has been successfully transferred.[39]) As one of the Global Witness investigators who uncovered the dirty money schemes said, "We found that there were some pretty consistent signs of money laundering."[40]

Or take it from Ventura Nogueira, the man who liaised with Ivanka, time and again; as he later confessed, "When I was in Panama, I was regularly laundering money for more than a dozen companies."[41] The center for all this graft? Ivanka's Panamanian "baby." (Ivanka doesn't talk about the building much these days, not least because the Trump Organization lost its claims to the building in 2018 following a management dispute.[42])

A similar story played out in Azerbaijan, a country already steered by one of the most kleptocratic regimes in the entire world. Trump's efforts at creating a Trump Tower in the capital city of Baku ended up so poorly managed that the deal became, as the *New Yorker* dubbed it, "Trump's worst."[43] It's not hard to see why. Not only did the Trumps work closely with the family of Azeri oligarch Ziya Mammadov—a man dubbed by American diplomats as "notoriously corrupt, even for Azerbaijan"[44]— but as reporter Adam Davidson found, the building's construction may well have been used to launder funds for members of Iran's Revolutionary Guard, breaking American anti-bribery law along the way. "The entire Baku deal is a giant red flag," an assistant dean at George Washington University Law School told Davidson. "Corruption warning signs are rarely more obvious."[45]

The person who oversaw the building's construction? Ivanka, naturally. She publicly claimed that the Trump project in Azerbaijan would "make for an exciting addition to the Trump Organization's expanding portfolio."[46] She "personally approved everything," one Azeri lawyer involved in the project said.[47] Trump's daughter even posted updates from the building directly to her own Instagram, where she described it as "my project."[48] But when word began getting around of all the corruption Ivanka had apparently overlooked on behalf of her father—and when the project itself began falling apart, both physically and figuratively— she tried to scrub her website of any evidence of her involvement.[49]

Of course, the investigators, participants, and buyers looking to move and hide and launder their ill-gotten gains don't forget. When it came to Trump-related properties, the details of these schemes only piled up. And all of them pointed to one, inescapable conclusion: few Americans had profited as much from American kleptocracy, and from the dirty money linked directly to corrupt oligarchs and officials and *mafiosi* abroad, as the Trump family.

In many ways, kleptocracy built Trump's empire. And by the mid-2010s, Trump wanted it to help build something else: a political empire, one that could cement America's transformation—and continue it for generations to come.

* * *

THE U.S.'s 2016 presidential campaign was memorable for any number of reasons, from Trump blathering his way to the GOP nomination to fake Russian Facebook feeds targeting white nationalists and Texas secessionists alike. But there's one other figure who's worth pausing on. Another figure who rode Trump's campaign coattails to a resurgence in relevance, and ultimately to his own doom: Paul Manafort.[50]

The lobbyist had become something of a forgotten entity in Washington by the time Trump tapped him to lead the 2016 campaign. He'd advised George H. W. Bush and Bob Dole[51] on their respective presidential campaigns, but after that he'd kept a low profile—in the U.S., at least. Abroad, Manafort spent his time slithering from one foreign lobbying client to the next, always available to the highest bidder. For instance, he helped whitewash Ferdinand Marcos, one of the greatest kleptocrats of the twentieth century.[52] He helped launder the reputation of Nigerian brute Sani Abacha (looted wealth: $2–5 billion, including money his wife tried to whisk out of the country in 38 different suitcases).[53] He even got to help spin Mobutu Sese Seko, the Zairean despot who joined Baby Doc, Slobodan Milosevic, and others in spending their years looting national coffers and running their millions through Western laundering machines. Indeed, Manafort's roster of clients—the blood-sotted monsters he helped transform into bespoke leaders, feigning interest in things like "human rights" and "democracy"—grew so notorious that it eventually comprised what others called the "Torturers' Lobby."[54]

There was one other client, though, who helped shore up Manafort's kleptocratic résumé in the lead-up to the 2016 election: Ukraine's Viktor Yanukovych, the would-be autocrat we met in chapter 11. Thanks to Manafort's help, Yanukovych proved victorious in the country's 2010 election. Shortly afterward, he promptly began dismantling Ukraine's fragile democracy. He helped launch an immediate investigation into his political rival, Yulia Tymoshenko. When Western nations decried the move, Manafort helped broker an arrangement between Yanukovych's regime and a powerhouse American law firm, Skadden Arps, in order to spin the investigation as something perfectly normal.[55] The man who bankrolled the operation, Ukrainian oligarch Victor Pinchuk,[56] used Manafort's shell company to hide the payment, according to DOJ filings.[57] (Pinchuk denied any financial link to Manafort, despite testimony and filings indicating otherwise.[58])

For a while, the move worked. Yanukovych managed to kneecap his political rival. Manafort kept getting paid for his services, using his shell companies, including a number in Delaware, to disguise his financial flows.[59] Ukraine's coffers slowly bled funds, its budget drying up, with some of the looted funds heading toward Yanukovych's new, palatial estates, and others heading for Manafort's multiple shell companies and multiple secret bank accounts.

Their partnership seemed a match made in kleptocratic heaven. Then, it all fell apart.

The protesters who toppled Yanukovych also sent Manafort scampering back to the U.S. After Ukraine's revolution, Manafort hid out in the U.S., slithering back to his home country. His former clients—Mobutu and Marcos, Abacha and, now, Yanukovych—had all been ousted by successful antiauthoritarian protests, all toppled because of their corruption and bloody criminality. No new clients appeared on the horizon. And despite all the secret payments, Manafort still had bills coming due. He had Russian oligarchs knocking on his door, asking about deals Manafort had reneged on. He had tax authorities beginning to ask questions, wondering about where he'd gotten the money for certain real estate purchases. The walls had begun closing in on him.

But then, in June 2016, Manafort received a phone call. A flagging

Republican candidate for president was looking for help, for someone to shore up his listing campaign. Few gave the candidate much chance. What did the lobbyist think? What would he recommend? Would he perhaps consider becoming the new campaign manager? Manafort didn't hesitate. He agreed to become Trump's campaign manager.[60]

The man who'd spent more of his life than anyone else whitewashing foreign kleptocrats agreed to help a man who'd profited perhaps more than anyone else from America's collapse into money laundering nirvana. Both of them eyed the White House, and everything that comes with it. Both of them knew what could be accomplished with the levers of power in their hands. Both of them knew what could be achieved—and how much they could implode the U.S.'s anticorruption regime, and open the U.S. to all the dirty money they could find—if only Donald Trump could win the presidency.

CORRUPTION IN THE FLESH

"The official, if unspoken, policy was to let the rottenness grow rather than risk the dangers involved in exposure and cleanup."

—Eliot Asinof[1]

In June 2018, back in Equatorial Guinea, strobe lights glanced around a crowd of onlookers, dozens deep as they danced around a catwalk stage. Here in Malabo, Equatorial Guinea's capital, the crust of Obiang's kleptocracy gathered: officials and hangers-on, bartenders in miniskirts and men in white tuxedos, swirling underneath chandeliers and flanked by 20-foot-high holograms bouncing to the music. Hundreds of bottles of alcohol lined the stage, like boozy cattails in a drunken wetland. Creamy leather couches surrounded a cake shaped like a Rolex, while leggy women in feathered *carnaval* headdresses shimmied past glittering, star-spangled walls.[2] The dance floor pooled with swaying visitors, sweat beginning to mist around them, bass shuddering the entire room. It was a party that would have made Jay Gatsby blush. And it was meant to celebrate one thing: Teodorin's fiftieth birthday.[3]

It had been four years since the kleptocrat found himself exiled from his Malibu pad. He was already the "poster child for kleptocracy," as all those around him well knew. And yet, here in Malabo, it felt like nothing had changed. Teodorin's visions of celebrity lived and danced and reveled as they ever had. But if he couldn't enjoy those dreams in the U.S., maybe he could bring a bit of the U.S. with him.[4]

The music paused, drunken attendees tilting as they turned to the stage. There, a man in a white dress shirt and dark tie grabbed a microphone. "Happy birthday," he began in an American accent, addressing Teodorin. "Greatly appreciate the invite. We gonna set this thing on fire!" The camera that captured this moment zoomed in. The man on the stage raised his fist. "As a matter of fact, everybody that's born in Africa—make some noise if you born in Africa." Rising shrieks greet him. "Oh hell yeah," the American responds. He continues, talking about how he's been to Africa plenty of times, but that this is his first time in Malabo. As the camera gets closer, you can see that he's wearing sunglasses and has close-cropped hair, and that there's a hype-man beginning to bounce and wriggle behind him.[5]

It's Chris Bridges—who goes by the stage name Ludacris.[6]

Ludacris, to be fair, was hardly the only celebrity Teodorin convinced to come to Malabo, to come celebrate another trip around the sun for one of the most corrupt figures the world has ever produced. There's Jeezy, another prominent rapper originally from Atlanta, performing on-stage, dodging the towering holograms. There's Akon, American crooner, trying to get the crowd to bop with him.[7] There's Sean Kingston, a thickset one-hit wonder, serenading with "Beautiful Girls," the only song of his anyone remembers. ("It's great to be here in front of my beautiful African people," Kingston yelled from the stage, wearing a Scrooge McDuck shirt. "Now we gonna turn this shit up!"[8]) All of them, there to perform for, and to celebrate, a man Washington accused of being one most obvious kleptocrats to ever visit the U.S.

Nobody knows how much Teodorin paid these men. (None of their representatives responded to my questions.) And they're hardly the first American stars to perform for despots around the world: Beyoncé performed for the horrific Gaddafi family, Hilary Swank attended the birthday party of the Chechen warlord Ramzan Kadyrov, Mariah Carey and Nicki Minaj have both schmoozed with Angola's former despotic family ruling Angola. Britney Spears even once waited, cramped and uncomfortable, inside a giant birthday cake to surprise a Malaysian kleptocrat named Jho Low, who was later targeted in one of the DOJ's biggest antikleptocracy actions to date.

Teodorin's birthday, though, was a measure apart. Never before had such a constellation of star power gathered for one kleptocrat, there dancing and clapping in a plum tuxedo jacket and yellow baseball hat turned sideways. Never before had dirty money, when it comes to wooing American celebrities evidently unconcerned about the source of the funds, gone so far. After all, there were no regulations pertaining to American celebrities or their agents checking the source of the millions they accept—why would they ever do otherwise?

* * *

IT'S NOT THAT Teodorin's 2018 party pointed specifically to the failures of America's antikleptocracy efforts. It's that the event sums up so *much* of those failures, and so many of the struggles of modern counterkleptocracy efforts. To be sure, the U.S.'s efforts against Teodorin, with all the guns of the Kleptocracy Asset Recovery Initiative aimed at him, initially appeared as a success. With Teodorin effectively banned from the U.S. by the Obama administration, and with his mansion and much of his roster of assets seized, the DOJ had done exactly what its Kleptocracy Asset Recovery Initiative was meant to do: identify the stolen assets, seize and freeze them, and return them to the people from whom they were stolen. In this case, Teodorin and the DOJ agreed that tens of millions of dollars that he'd thieved and laundered in the U.S. would be given to a charitable organization in Equatorial Guinea, helping some of the people he and his father and his entire family had pummeled and plundered for decades.

The U.S. settlement sounded a starter gun for other countries to start going after Teodorin's pilfered assets as well. French authorities seized a multimillion-dollar pad in Paris, with a French court even sentencing the kleptocrat to a three-year suspended jail term.[9] Swiss authorities opened their own investigation into Teodorin, and discovered that he'd parked dozens of his high-end cars on Swiss soil, which were promptly seized.[10] Even when trying to travel, Teodorin was suddenly tripped up; during a trip to South America following the U.S. settlement, Brazilian authorities seized 20 diamond-studded watches Teodorin had decided to bring with him, totaling some $15 million in value.[11] (The Equatorial Guinea embassy claimed the watches were for "personal use."[12])

For a bit, it appeared that the gears of a nascent, global counterkleptocracy regime had begun to turn against Teodorin. The poster child of modern kleptocracy had turned into the poster child of what counter-kleptocracy efforts, with the U.S. at the helm, could achieve. Equatorial Guinea still retained some of the world's highest illiteracy and poverty rates, and still suffered under the bootheel of one of the world's longest dictatorships. But at least the U.S. had made an example of Teodorin, both for those in Equatorial Guinea and for those around the world considering using the U.S. as their dirty money playground.

And then, in May 2018, Teodorin suddenly appeared in Times Square. Smiling like a Cheshire cat, bedecked in all black and scoping out women in high heels, Teodorin was back in his favorite playground, freely spending his dirty money once more. Recently promoted by his father to the vice presidency, Teodorin told American officials that he had returned to the U.S. as a simple diplomat, there to attend the United Nations General Assembly—there to do only what diplomatic immunity allowed him.[13] But that was just an excuse. He'd swing by the U.N., claiming Equatorial Guinea was on its way to full democracy. But after that, he'd spend time visiting his old haunts.

Which is exactly what happened. Even after the U.S. tried to make Teodorin the keystone of the global antikleptocracy push, here he was, back in the same country that had tried—and apparently failed—to banish him and his dirty money. It's not as if Teodorin was subtle about it. Guy Christian Agbor, a former legal adviser to Equatorial Guinea's American embassy, said he visited Teodorin at New York's Ritz-Carlton, where he walked in on Teodorin gorging on caviar and champagne. "He threw money on the bed, there in his suite," Agbor remembered. "You open the door to the room, and you see the money on the bed. Two million dollars, just sitting there on the bed."

In Hawaii, he took surfing lessons, stopped by a luau, slow-rode a bike down white sand beaches.[14] In Las Vegas, he continued the party, soaking in the debauchery, swimming amid thousands of others at an outdoor music festival—even, according to those tracking him in the

U.S., throwing his own hotel party that saw one partygoer overdose and die.[15] (This detail remains unconfirmed, though Teodorin did post a photo of a shirtless, shoeless man lying prone in a Las Vegas hotel hallway. "Only in Vegas!" he captioned.[16])

It was as if the past few years—and all the energy the U.S. had expended on its counterkleptocracy efforts—had never happened. "I shouldn't be surprised Obiang is still in the U.S. and spending all that money in Hawaii and Vegas," Laura Stuber, the Senate investigator who tracked down Teodorin and Pinochet and all those others years before, told me. "It's just disgusting."[17] "Teodorin is never ever going to change," Agbor, who has pushed efforts to seize the Obiang family's assets, added. "The only thing that will make him change is if he gets arrested or locked up. Other than that he's never going to change. I know the man. I've talked to the man. Have you ever had a chance to talk to a drug dealer? Just doing what he wants, taking women left and right? That's how Teodorin operates."[18]

And it's not just that Teodorin was back, making a mockery of U.S. efforts to counter him and his corruption and his kind. The other corrupt foreign figures highlighted during the 2010 Senate investigations— those specifically selected alongside Teodorin to illustrate who'd been taking advantage of this American kleptocracy—were still enjoying themselves in the U.S., a decade after they were specifically targeted by American officials. Atiku Abubakar, the wildly corrupt Nigerian official who secretly funneled tens of millions of dollars into the U.S., hired pro-Trump lobbyists and stayed at Trump properties in Washington in order to curry favor with the White House.[19] And the Bongo family, which has pillaged the African country of Gabon for years, has continued to plop down millions to purchase American properties with their dirty money, with nobody batting an eye.[20]

Meanwhile, a decade after the investigation into Teodorin's American assets began, and nearly two decades after the Riggs Bank scandal first broke, Equatoguineans still haven't seen a single cent of Teodorin's stolen funds returned. "We still don't have any disposition of what happened," Ken Hurwitz, the American lawyer who'd helped track Teodorin's assets, told me about the tens of millions of dollars the Americans were supposed to return. Hurwitz pointed out that Teodorin and his father have still refused to sign off on the repatriation. "As a practical matter, Teodorin is saying, 'Fuck you,'" the lawyer said. "He has no incentive for that [money] to be returned to the Equatoguinean people."[21]

Nor would Teodorin's family want to encourage the DOJ in its efforts. After all, even after journalists and investigators exposed the entire ruling regime, American real estate agents remained perfectly happy to continue cycling the Obiangs' money, to continue laundering it into American assets regardless of its source. As of 2020, President Obiang, Teodorin's father, still owns a pair of multimillion-dollar homes in Potomac, Maryland—including one right next door to a mansion owned by former Gambian dictator Yahya Jammeh. These properties are located, in a twist you couldn't make up, next to "Democracy Boulevard."[22]

* * *

BUT MAYBE, AS Stuber said, this shouldn't have been surprising. After all, around the same time, a new figure in Washington had set about annihilating America's entire anticorruption and antikleptocracy *bona fides*.

Trump, to be fair, wasn't technically the first White House tenant who profited from the world of offshoring while in office. Former president Richard Nixon was a customer at the Bahamas' Castle Bank & Trust, perhaps the shadiest bank in the entire Caribbean. When an IRS informant, investigating the largest tax evasion scheme in American history, discovered Nixon's name among the reams of clients at the offshore bank, Nixon's handpicked IRS chief promptly quashed the investigations. (According to one of his mobbed-up buddies, Nixon was "very angry" with the discovery.) A bank source later revealed that the firm had moved millions of dollars into a separate Swiss account on behalf of the one linked to Nixon.[23] But Nixon's offshore dalliances simply set the stage for what we saw blossom under Trump. If Nixon set the example, Trump blasted it into the stratosphere.

Once he was installed in the White House, Trump acted as a battering ram against the entire edifice of the U.S.'s anticorruption architecture.

In only four years, Trump became a detonator that imploded America's reputation as an anticorruption leader, a reputation four decades in the making.

Trump's efforts to dismantle America's anticorruption program began almost as soon as he entered the White House. Take his treatment of the Foreign Corrupt Practices Act (FCPA), for instance. Ushered in during the aftermath of Nixon's Watergate scandal, the FCPA—which bars American companies and figures from bribing foreign officials—remains the linchpin of America's broader anticorruption efforts. Yet Trump entered the presidency having already publicly declared the FCPA a "horrible law."[24] (The only other president to enter office pledging to repeal the FCPA? Ronald Reagan.[25]) Almost immediately, Trump set about attempting to dismantle the entire act. In the spring of 2017, Trump enthused to Secretary of State Rex Tillerson that he wanted the FCPA scrapped entirely. "I need you to get rid of that law," Trump bleated to Tillerson. Trump then ordered one of his advisers to author an executive order to that effect—all but eviscerating America's pro-transparency reputation from the outset of his presidency.[26] Luckily, thanks to the regulatory structure and broad bipartisan support the FCPA still enjoys, Trump's efforts went nowhere. But that didn't stop FCPA-related actions from slowing considerably under Trump; as anticorruption expert Alexandra Wrage said in 2020, "The [FCPA] pipeline is thinning out dramatically."[27] If Trump couldn't decapitate the program, maybe he could slowly strangle it with no one noticing.

Trump's move was a clear shot across the bow of America's anticorruption standing, which only went downhill from there. Around the same time, he announced the U.S. would be pulling back from the Extractive Industries Transparency Initiative (EITI), the leading—and previously American-led—multinational group dedicated to cleaning up the oil, gas, and mining sectors, which comprised the most notoriously corrupt industries on the planet.[28] "We're walking away from something we've been telling other countries to do for years," one anticorruption activist said.[29] Simultaneously, Trump signed a formal repeal of a raft of regulations, including the commitment from U.S. oil and gas companies to disclose payments to foreign officials—officials like, say, the Obiang family, which remains reliant on oil extraction to fuel their rapine kleptocracy.[30] The previous regulations had been "a beacon of U.S. leadership in the global fight against oil and mining corruption," Global Witness wrote.[31] With Trump, though, they were suddenly snuffed out. Trump's move was, Oxfam wrote, "a handout for kleptocrats . . . [which] plays into the hands of corrupt politicians, compromised bureaucrats, and insider lobbyists who thrive on secrecy."[32]

On and on, Trump battered American anticorruption regulations, American anticorruption legacies, American anticorruption precedents.[33] On and on, he spun American anticorruption efforts straight into the ground—all while simultaneously claiming to be leading anticorruption efforts to "drain the swamp."[34]

*   *   *

AND THEN THERE were the hotels, the towers, the Trump-related properties that no previous president had ever brought with them to the White House. Never before had assets—let alone those serving as key nodes in American kleptocracy—presented such a direct highway of financing into an American president's pockets. Trump claimed that he wanted nothing to do with his business as president, that he'd placed his stake in a "blind trust" in order to sever American and Trumpian interests. Such spin was, of course, a farce. Trump continued profiting from his company while he was president, and could continue dropping in to manage the business—and woo more kleptocrats—whenever he wanted.[35]

His buildings presented a throughway for kleptocrats to directly influence the most powerful man in the world. Just keeping up with the foreign governments, the foreign officials, and the foreign figures patronizing and propping up Trump's properties while he was president was an exhausting exercise. There were the formal delegations that hosted events at Trump properties, governments from places like Afghanistan and Kuwait cordoning off entire sections of Trump's buildings for their own use. There were the paid-off lobbyists renting out entire sheaves of Trump properties, like the Saudi lobbyist who paid for 500 rooms at a Trump hotel shortly after Trump's election.[36] There were the foreign Trump properties that continued shoveling money toward the president, places like Trump Towers Istanbul, which fed millions from Turkey directly to Trump while president—millions Americans only learned about in 2020, after Trump's tax returns finally spilled out.[37]

There also were the premiers and presidents and prime ministers who realized that paying for a stay at a Trump hotel was the best way to get into the president's good graces. People like Romanian prime minister Viorica Dăncilă[38] and former Malaysian prime minister Najib Razak[39]—the latter of whom played a key role in looting billions from Malaysia's sovereign wealth fund[40]—who both shacked up at Trump's D.C. hotel. Even those already specifically cited by Congress for their stupefying corruption, like Nigeria's Atiku Abubakar, popped up at Trump properties, helping bankroll a Trump Organization that continued its willingness to house kleptocrats, regardless of previous congressional investigations into their financial malfeasance.[41]

And then, of course, there was the anonymity. As soon as Trump won the GOP nomination in the summer of 2016, the anonymous sales at his businesses erupted. One study from USA Today, published in the summer of 2017, discovered that after Trump took the nomination, "the majority of his companies' real estate sales [went] to secretive shell companies that obscure the buyers' identities."[42] Investigators discovered that a stunning *70 percent* of new Trump tenants hid behind anonymous LLCs, with some purchases running up to $10 million at a time.[43] All sold to new clients whose names and sources of income remained completely unknown. Or put another way: during his pre-presidency days, only one building, Trump SoHo, saw a majority of its sales go to anonymous purchasers. After Trump's path toward the presidency appeared clear, *nearly three-quarters of all new sales* instantly went to anonymous buyers.

Who were these new buyers? The short answer is: we don't know. We have no idea who the vast majority of these purchasers were, or where they came from, or where they got their money, or what they wanted—or how they impacted American policy. It was the American kleptocratic story, spun up by multiple magnitudes, and spun directly into the White House.

We do have an inkling, though, of who stood behind *some* of the anonymous purchases blanketing Trump properties. In 2019, Global Witness, one of the leading pro-transparency organizations extant, revealed that Claudia Sassou-Nguesso, the rotund daughter of Congolese dictator Denis Sassou-Nguesso, secretly controlled a shell company called Sebrit Limited. Sebrit itself acted as a front for a separate LLC, called Asperbras—which just so happened to be on the receiving end of over half a billion dollars thieved from the Congolese treasury.[44]

Sebrit directed the funds to yet another American shell company, itself registered by K&L Gates, an American law firm. (A corrupt ruling central-African family using American shell companies and American law firms to help hide their money in American real estate—sound familiar?) From there, the American shell company finalized a luxury apartment purchase in a behemoth building overlooking a chunk of Central Park: Trump International Hotel and Tower. But that wasn't all. Trump International Realty even brokered the sale—the final step allowing the millions in dirty money looted from languishing Congolese to run through yet another Trump property, washed clean, with a chunk of it finding its way directly into Trump's wallet. "It appears therefore that Claudia Sassou-Nguesso owns the Trump apartment, paid with suspected stolen state funds," Global Witness relayed. "The question now is: did the background checks fail to raise the alarm, or did the Trump companies choose to look the other way?"[45]

Given Trump's business model, the answer appears clear. Not that Trump, or any of his underlings, was under any legal requirements to check Sassou-Nguesso's finances, or run any basic anti–money laundering checks—or that Trump was ever aware that she'd purchased the unit. This is still American real estate, after all. This is still the industry benefiting most spectacularly from America's descent into money laundering heaven.

And that's only one apartment: one multimillion-dollar investment, on one of dozens of floors, in one of dozens of buildings linked directly to Trump. One small building block in an entire portfolio increasingly reliant on anonymous funds. One singular moment of laundering for the benefit of not only a brutal ruling regime elsewhere, but for the man who, as president, helped disembowel American anticorruption policy and build a new, pro-kleptocracy legacy in its stead. The man who had become, as Senator Elizabeth Warren dubbed him, "corruption in the flesh."[46] And the man who would try to bring American kleptocracy to its logical, and tragic, end.

OPEN SEASON

"President Putin and the Russian security services operate like a super PAC."

—Fiona Hill[1]

By the time Trump entered the White House, Ihor Kolomoisky was on the run. Even with his personal militia, even with his power base carved out of central Ukraine, the investigations into Kolomoisky's steering of PrivatBank—and the $5.5 billion hole that authorities discovered, sending them scrambling to nationalize the bank—proved too hot for the oligarch-turned-warlord.[2] He skipped first to Switzerland, holing up in Geneva, and then hopped to Tel Aviv, where he enjoyed Israeli citizenship.[3] Popular revulsion against the oligarch began brewing in Ukraine proper: the one time "patriot" had morphed, in the span of only a few months, into a kind of synecdoche for the entire corrupt roster of oligarchs still running the country.

Kolomoisky the hero had transformed into Kolomoisky the warlord, Kolomoisky the scapegoat, Kolomoisky the enemy.

It was a role the oligarch appeared happy to embrace. Outside Ukraine, Kolomoisky began lobbing public calls for Ukraine to default on much-needed loans from the International Monetary Fund (IMF), claiming Kyiv could stand on its own and that it didn't need any Western financial support, coming as it did with demands for domestic transparency and anticorruption reforms. (The IMF just so happened to be demanding that Kolomoisky never return to a leadership position at PrivatBank, for instance.) The oligarch also abruptly began flipping his rhetoric about Russia. In an interview with the *New York Times*, Kolomoisky sounded like a leopard who'd changed his spots, calling for Kyiv to rebuild ties with the country that had invaded and decimated Ukraine's eastern and southern flanks. "Give it five, 10 years, and the blood will be forgotten," Kolomoisky said. And if the U.S. or the IMF kept pushing anticorruption reforms, or "if they get smart with us, we'll go to Russia." As Kolomoisky added, Moscow was "stronger anyway. . . . Russian tanks will be stationed near [Poland]. Your NATO will be soiling its pants and buying Pampers."[4]

Nor was this all bluster. Back in Kyiv, Valeria Gontareva, who'd led the investigation into PrivatBank, started discovering threatening messages around her home. One day, there was a piece of graffiti on a wall outside her house calling her a "Russian pig." Another tag sprayed the word "killer," with dollar signs scribbled around. Her home itself was vandalized.[5] And then, one morning, she encountered a piece of Kolomoisky's threat portfolio that his rivals had once experienced: an open coffin, containing an effigy of Gontareva clad in black-and-white stripes, a black bouquet placed near her feet, sitting outside the doors of the Ukrainian central bank. Waiting for her to arrive to work.[6]

No one claimed responsibility for the threats, nor for the effigy, nor for the sudden upsurge in pressure to get her to pull back from the investigations into certain oligarchs looting Ukrainian depositors and cycling their dirty money through the U.S. But Gontareva, who outlasted a number of postrevolution finance ministers who couldn't handle the stress, had her suspicions. "I am like the Fenimore Cooper novel, *Last of the Mohicans*," she said. "I was called a killer of oligarchs."[7] Soon, though, the threats metastasized. In London, where Gontareva is now living, a car ran directly into her, sending her to the hospital. Just a few weeks later, her home in Ukraine burned to the ground.[8] Investigations into both proved inconclusive, but it wasn't too much to imagine that a man she'd outed for allegedly running one of the world's greatest Ponzi schemes might be involved.

All the while, an entire buffet of cases regarding Kolomoisky's alleged swindle continued. Lawsuits laying out Kolomoisky and the Optima Family's use of American assets to launder their ill-gotten gains burst forth in the U.S., from former partners and PrivatBank's new owners alike. In Ukraine, lawsuits fingered the laundering operations, with legal filings even popping up in places like the U.K.[9] Kolomoisky denied any allegations of impropriety, and counterpunched by demanding control of the bank once more.[10] These suits and countersuits all took place while the details of the alleged swindle continued to leak out, leaving battered and beleaguered Ukrainians watching from the sidelines.

Kolomoisky, though, spied a potential out. The postrevolution administration of Petro Poroshenko began faltering, growing increasingly unpopular as Ukraine's economic heaves and inability to dislodge Russia became more pronounced. By early 2019, a new challenger rose to unseat him. Volodymyr Zelensky, a cherubic, 40-year-old comedian, had no prior political experience, no previous attachment to any administrations or previous regimes. Instead, he had something Ukrainian politicos had long lacked: charisma. He knew how to work audiences. He knew how to charm voters who'd watched him play a Ukrainian president on television for years.[11] And come April, Zelensky, who'd pledged greater Western engagement, proved that he knew how to do something else: win a presidential election—and do so in a landslide. The comedian routed the oligarch in that year's election, taking nearly 75 percent of the vote over Poroshenko.[12]

Instantly, Ukraine's pro-Western, pro-reform agenda appeared assured. Zelensky promised change, and transparency, and fealty to voters rather than to the oligarchic class that had long gutted the country. Ukraine, nearly three decades after the Soviet collapse, finally appeared on the right footing. But there was one catch. Zelensky himself may not have been an oligarch, and he may not have been involved in any of those previous schemes to loot the country's coffers. But there was one oligarch who appeared in Zelensky's shadow, peeking out from behind the new president. Zelensky's television show, the one where he'd posed as a Ukrainian president, appeared on a Ukrainian television channel that happened to be part of a series of oligarchic holdings. The channel that hosted Zelensky's show—that paid his bills, that reached his audiences, that launched Zelensky directly into the presidency—was owned by none other than Kolomoisky. And maybe it was time for Kolomoisky to capitalize on that relationship with this new, doe-eyed president.[13]

Zelensky never denied the fact that Kolomoisky owned the channel on which the youthful new president had appeared, or that the two had been, by all indications, close. But the new president could read the electorate. "We must do everything we can so that the previous owners [of PrivatBank] do not get a single kopek," Zelensky announced, singling out his former patron.[14] "It's impossible to influence me. Neither Kolomoisky, nor any other oligarch—no one will influence me."[15] Zelensky had put his foot down: Kolomoisky would have no sway over his new administration.

The oligarch quickly put the president's claims to the test. In 2019, shortly after Zelensky's election, Kolomoisky returned to Ukraine. He apparently felt comfortable enough to oversee his legal fight from the belly of Kyiv, showing Ukrainians—and the country's Western financial backers in the IMF and in Washington—that he wouldn't be cowed. Not by investigators. And certainly not by a president he helped launch to power. "If I put on glasses and look at myself like the whole rest of the world, I see myself as a monster, as a puppet master, as the master of Zelensky, someone making apocalyptic plans," Kolomoisky leered. "I can start making this real."[16] He'd become, as one later analyst said, a man in a class of his own—a "super oligarch," dedicated to making his will known to both the new president and the rest of Ukraine alike.[17]

But early indications backed up Zelensky's claims of independence from his former backer. Zelensky held his ground. A year into the new president's administration, Ukraine's parliament pushed through legislation that formally blocked the oligarch from ever regaining control of PrivatBank (known, memorably enough, as the "anti-Kolomoisky law").[18] "Politically, it will mean in the eyes of the general public and political elites that he has lost control over Zelensky, which is a real blow," Tetiana Shevchuk, who works as a lawyer with the country's Anti-Corruption Action Center, said. And Shevchuk was right. Suddenly, Kolomoisky's path back to his assets, and to his power base, appeared stunted, closed on all fronts.[19] Despite his return, his standing in Ukraine had collapsed.

His legal bills piled up, in Ukraine and the U.S. and elsewhere. And the new president hardly appeared to be in his pocket.

For the sinking oligarch, though, Kolomoisky had one card left up his sleeve: a trump card, fittingly enough, still left to play. And by early 2020, Kolomoisky saw his chance.

* * *

WHILE TRUMP DECIMATED America's anticorruption platform, his administration immediately bogged down elsewhere, stalked by claims of Russian collusion and interference during the 2016 campaign. Secret meetings with Kremlin attachés, back-channel promises to lift sanctions, foreknowledge about hacked material and amplification of fake Facebook pages and fake Twitter feeds and fake Instagram accounts— all of it caught up to Trump, almost from the outset of his presidency. When the U.S. Department of Justice tapped Special Counsel Robert Mueller to investigate the Trump campaign's links with Russia and post-Soviet oligarchs, America clung on for a ride into the heart of Russian interference operations, and what the American president knew about it all.[20]

As Americans waited for the results of Mueller's inquiry, information began leaking that illustrated how the tears in America's antikleptocracy fabric had only continued to widen. The leaks and investigative reports pointed to the fact that post-Soviet officials and oligarchs had discovered a pair of new loopholes to exploit and new tools to implement, creating a new pipeline that led them directly into the White House, and directly into the control center of America's anticorruption efforts—and American democracy itself.

The first loophole dealt with an industry that had exploded in importance and net worth over the past decade: hedge funds and private equity. These private investment funds—which target a range of assets, and which bring in investors with far deeper pockets than most—were initially roped into the Patriot Act's anti–money laundering requirements. But because these investment vehicles at the time were relatively small, restricted to things like pension funds and high-net-worth individuals, the Treasury Department decided to do what it did with the real estate industry. They offered the hedge funds and private equity firms a "temporary" exemption from such regulations.

Again, there's no evidence any of this was malign. Treasury's rationale here was the same as with the real estate sector: it wanted to "study" how regulations could affect this growing pillar of the American financial sector. But as with all the other exemptions, by the start of the 2020s that "temporary" exemption was nearly twenty years old—during which time the hedge fund and private equity industry has mushroomed into one of the biggest, and least regulated, financial sectors extant.[21]

The entire industry is now an ocean of anonymous wealth, sucking up trillions of dollars from around the world.[22] And in the U.S., private equity and hedge funds can do so with no obligation to check the sources of client wealth—or even figure out who they're offering their anonymous financial services to. These funds "are doing the same thing as the Swiss banks: anonymizing money on an industrial scale," wrote investigative journalist Tom Burgis.[23] Already we've seen substantial sums from Chinese, Russian, and Saudi sources circling among these private, unregulated investment firms. One *Wall Street Journal* investigation, for instance, found that "the Saudi government has been the largest Silicon Valley startup funder since mid-2016, investing at least $11 billion."[24] But thanks to the Treasury Department's "temporary" exemption, *Bloomberg* wrote, the U.S. knows "shockingly little" about the sources of foreign finance flowing through hedge funds and private equity—or about just how much of those industries is propped up by dirty money.[25]

"With no requirement to disclose even the names of investors or non-voting owners, [private equity] firms are perfect vehicles for money laundering," anticorruption expert Sarah Chayes wrote in 2020. "Private equity funds can shield the identities of all but a very few owners, so they are magnets for questionable money."[26] Added Joshua Kirschenbaum, a former Treasury official who's tried to raise the alarm about the threat these investment vehicles now pose to broader antikleptocracy efforts, these funds are "among the most sophisticated investors and an appealing vehicle for a foreign actor with malign intent, for example one seeking to interfere in an election, cultivate inappropriate political influence, or engage in complex financial crime."[27] In short: hedge funds and private equity are the latest tools for hiding gobs of illicit wealth, available to anyone looking for a safe haven for their dirty money.

The industry's defense, according to those lobbying on its behalf, is that because such funds are largely restricted to deep-pocketed entrepreneurs, and because a multiyear commitment is required before investors can pull their money out, these funds are hardly successful money laundering lures.[28] They essentially ask, "If you're trying to launder money, why would you bury it somewhere you can't access for years on end?" And there's a decent point buried in that spin; if you're looking for a quick laundering turnaround, these funds are the last places you want to look. Yet that completely misunderstands the appeal of hedge funds and private equity in the first place. After all, the crooked oligarchs attracted to such funds aren't looking for quick laundering turnarounds. They're looking to keep their ill-gotten wealth safe, as their kleptocratic nest egg. Billions in dirty money can go in, with no questions asked, and all the oligarchs or officials have to do is wait a few years before they can pull the money out—money that's then perfectly clean. Think of it as someone grabbing the control knob of the American money laundering machine, and turning it to the long cycle.

"If you're human trafficking, or selling drugs, or if it's a business you're running [and] you need to get that money back to get more meth, or to buy more fentanyl, or to pay more coyotes . . . that money's not going into a hedge fund," Alma Angotti, a former Treasury official who tried to implement anti–money laundering procedures for the industry, told me. "But if you're an oligarch stealing oil money, and you don't need all of it, you need to keep it somewhere safe. So you put it in a hedge fund, or real estate. You want to protect it from your own government as much as ours. It's not a good vehicle for narcotraffickers. But it's sure as hell a good vehicle if you're a corrupt public official."[29]

In 2020, a leak of internal FBI documents revealed the bureau's ballooning concerns about the money laundering now swirling the industry. Foreign criminals, foreign oligarchs, and foreign adversaries have begun using hedge funds and private equity firms "to launder money, circumventing traditional [anti–money laundering] programs," the FBI wrote. The bureau pointed directly to the "temporary" exemption that allowed transnational money launderers to take advantage. "The FBI assumes [anti–money laundering] programs are not adequately designed to monitor and detect threat actors' use of private investment funds to launder money," the FBI memo continued. "Criminally complicit investment fund managers likely will expand their money laundering operations as private placement opportunities increase, resulting in continued infiltration of the licit global financial system."[30] The FBI cited a number of examples of recent infiltration into this sector, with the dirty money mixing and churning alongside things like American pension funds. In January 2019, a Mexican cartel opened a number of new accounts with an American hedge fund, laundering at least $1 million every week. In New York, a private equity firm opened its doors to $100 million in wire transfers from a Russian company connected to Russian organized crime.

But it was in Maryland that post-Soviet interference efforts and money laundering via American hedge funds and private equity both came to a head.[31] In 2013, an LLC called ByteGrid sealed a $7.5 million contract with the state in order to manage Maryland's election data, including the oversight of statewide voter registration information and election management systems. At the time, the deal raised no eyebrows; Russian interference in American elections was still a few years off, and few looked at foreign interference, let alone via private equity investments, as a potential concern. But in 2015, ByteGrid was acquired by a private equity company called Altpoint Capital Partners. Again, the move didn't seem to worry anyone; all anyone saw was a private equity firm purchasing a company specializing in computer systems, which just so happened to be overseeing the integrity of Maryland's elections and voter data.[32]

What no one in Maryland realized—what no one knew until Maryland officials received a call from the FBI—was that the principal investor in the private equity company wasn't a distant American investor, or a pension fund looking for solid returns for its constituents. It was, instead, a Russian oligarch, one intimately close with Putin. Vladimir Potanin, a balding, sullen-faced billionaire, had stood as one of Russia's wealthiest oligarchs for years.[33] Potanin gained notoriety as one of the brains behind the much-maligned privatization scandals of the mid-1990s, which funneled much of Russia's natural resources and industrial treasures directly into oligarchs' pockets. As David Hoffman wrote in his seminal 2001 book on Russian oligarchs, Potanin "became a ringleader of all the [oligarchs] in 1995 in their greatest single property grab," helping create a process that "was not open to foreigners, was not transparent, and turned out to be rigged. It also had one profound consequence that they did not foresee: the [privatization process] was the beginning of a merger between the Russian [oligarchs] and the government."[34]

Officials in Maryland had likely never heard of Potanin. But this oligarch was now secretly bankrolling the private equity firm that oversaw the company tasked with maintaining the integrity, the authenticity, and the efficacy of elections in Maryland—including the election in 2016, in which America experienced a shock wave of foreign interference, the kind of which it had never before seen. As State Senate president Thomas V. Miller said when announcing the discovery, "We felt it imperative that our constituents know that a Russian oligarch has purchased our election machinery."[35]

*   *   *

FORTUNATELY, NONE OF Maryland's 2016 votes appeared changed, and there's as yet no indication that Potanin used his anonymous investments to sway American policy. The same can't be said, however, of the financial flows from the roster of post-Soviet oligarchs connected to interference operations into a second, and equally wide open, sector: American nonprofits.

When you think of nonprofits, maybe you think of a local charity, or perhaps a group like Amnesty International, trying to better communities both near and far. But there's another class of American nonprofits that operates on a more elite, highbrow footing. Institutions like high-profile universities, such as Harvard and the University of Southern California. Cultural icons, such as New York's Museum of Modern Art (MOMA) and the Kennedy Center in Washington, D.C. Entities like prestigious think tanks that act as unofficial centers of policymaking, such as the Brookings Institution and the Council on Foreign Relations.

These nonprofits enjoy rarefied status in the U.S., hosting dignitaries, working with legislators to help craft policy, acting as America's font of intellectual and cultural capital, and helping buttress American soft power. In many ways, these institutes and universities and cultural staples are the best of America. But like hedge funds, real estate, or escrow agents before them, they're also not subjected to any anti–money laundering or due diligence procedures.

To be sure, money laundering via nonprofits doesn't seem to make much sense. But these nonprofits serve a different purpose for kleptocrats. Given the lack of any oversight or regulation, American nonprofits have effectively left the door wide open for any kleptocrat who'd like to improve their image: to use their dirty money to launder not their money, but their *reputations*.

The phenomenon is known as "reputation laundering." An oligarch or a crooked official can offer their dirty money as a donation to these nonprofits. The nonprofits don't transform those funds into clean money, as with real estate or hedge funds. Rather, they transform the donor into a "philanthropist," or publish material whitewashing the donor's background, offering them a new, benevolent reputation that helps bury any rumors or suppositions about their corruption and helps dissuade others from looking too closely into their background.[36]

For years, there was little data to back up claims that these American nonprofits had transformed into reputation laundering centers. But as I and a number of anticorruption colleagues, including those with the Anti-Corruption Data Collective, discovered in 2020, these institutes had not only become reputation laundering factories, but they'd become massive magnets for the same questionable foreign monies already worming through American shell companies, American hedge funds, American real estate, and the like.[37] More concerningly, these nonprofits all gladly accepted tainted funds from the entire range of post-Soviet oligarchs directly connected to foreign interference efforts in the U.S.

The numbers we uncovered were staggering. In one of our studies in 2020, we found that donations from the Russian and Ukrainian oligarchs connected to interference investigations totaled anywhere between $372 million and $435 million, all directed to more than 200 of the most prestigious nonprofit institutions in America.[38] Universities like George Washington and Cornell and NYU.[39] Cultural institutes like the Metropolitan Museum of Art and the Guggenheim. Think tanks like the Atlantic Council and the Council on Foreign Relations. All of them recipients of substantial sums from the oligarchs directly connected to foreign interference operations, including some later sanctioned directly by the U.S. for their role in Russia's efforts.[40]

Any number of oligarchs have pursued this tactic. Russian oligarch Viktor Vekselberg, who was sanctioned in 2018 by the U.S. for aiding the Kremlin's efforts and Russia's dictatorship, donated substantial amounts to the Woodrow Wilson International Center for Scholars, a prominent think tank in Washington. (The Wilson Center awarded Vekselberg the "Woodrow Wilson Award for Public Service" for "his outstanding contributions to the rebirth of Russian philanthropy."[41]) Another oligarch, Victor Pinchuk—who had previously bankrolled Paul Manafort's work, according to DOJ filings (though the oligarch later denied it)[42]—used his Ukraine-based foundation to donate significant sums to prestigious think tanks like the Atlantic Council and Brookings Institution. The Ukrainian oligarch even donated a staggering $10–25 million to the Clinton Foundation, including individual gifts of $1–5 million in 2012 and between $5 and $10 million in 2013.[43] All of these donations have helped Pinchuk to be seen as a pro-Western figure, escaping the kinds of criticism some of his other oligarchic compatriots have faced.[44]

But these figures are nothing compared to a post-Soviet oligarch named Len Blavatnik.[45] Despite being worth an estimated tens of billions of dollars, odds are you haven't heard of Blavatnik.[46] However, he's arguably the most successful oligarch to emerge from the entire post-Soviet morass—not least because he managed to obtain American citizenship. Blavatnik made billions in the Russian natural resources industry, working directly alongside a number of now-sanctioned oligarchs like Vekselberg and Oleg Deripaska.[47] After obtaining American citizenship, Blavatnik made his splashiest investment in 2011, when he snapped up Warner Music for $3.3 billion.[48]

Still, Blavatnik's hold in the U.S. remained somewhat precarious; as the *Hollywood Reporter* revealed, the sources of Blavatnik's wealth "aren't entirely clear."[49] As such, Blavatnik turned to a familiar playbook: philanthropy.[50] Donations soon burst forth, either from the oligarch or his company (Access Industries), to dozens of American institutes willing to open their doors for him, willing to transform him from a post-Soviet oligarch with an unclear background into a benefactor *par excellence*. There were the universities, including NYU and USC and Sarah Lawrence, all of which accepted his money. There were the cultural institutions, like New York's Lincoln Center and Carnegie Hall, the latter of which now counts Blavatnik as a trustee.[51] In 2018, Blavatnik outdid himself: his Blavatnik Family Foundation announced a $200 million donation to Harvard Medical School, the largest gift in the school's entire history.[52] "Administrators will rename the school's 10 academic departments located on its main campus the 'Blavatnik Institute at Harvard Medical School,'" the *Harvard Crimson* reported. People forgot all about Blavatnik's background, or about his previous work alongside now-sanctioned Russian oligarchs, and began viewing him simply as a philanthropist.[53]

For a bit, Blavatnik appeared able to toss his money around wherever he liked. But in 2019, news broke that Special Counsel Robert Mueller's office had specifically investigated Blavatnik's massive donations to Trump's inauguration.[54] Vekselberg, one of the Russian oligarchs sanctioned by the U.S., also claimed that he attended Trump's inauguration party at a table Blavatnik paid for.[55] (Blavatnik's spokesperson denied this.) Shortly thereafter, with his reputation taking a significant hit, Blavatnik announced a $13 million donation to the Council on Foreign Relations, heretofore considered one of America's more prestigious think tanks—a move that appeared to directly follow the reputation-laundering playbook mentioned above.[56]

Unlike his previous donations, though, Blavatnik's latest gift was instantly met by a chorus of criticism from the most prominent anticorruption and antikleptocracy voices in the U.S. and elsewhere.[57] In a letter addressed to CFR head Richard Haass, dozens of signatories—including leading experts on post-Soviet kleptocracy and former members of the Treasury Department, State Department, and National Security Council—condemned the CFR's willingness to accept the donation, claiming it was a means of helping "Blavatnik [export] Russian kleptocratic practices to the West." As their letter read:

> We regard [the donation] as another step in the longstanding effort of Mr. Blavatnik—who, as we explain below, has close ties to the Kremlin and its kleptocratic network—to launder his image in the West. . . . It is our considered view that Blavatnik uses his "philanthropy"—funds obtained by and with the consent of the Kremlin, at the expense of the state budget and the Russian people—at leading [Western] academic and cultural institutions to advance his access to political circles. Such "philanthropic" capital enables the infiltration of the U.S. and U.K. political and economic establishments at the highest levels. It is also a means by which Blavatnik exports Russian kleptocratic practices to the West.[58]

Others published similar criticisms. "Blavatnik is entitled to spend his money how he pleases," Ann Marlowe wrote in the *New York Times*. "But institutions . . . which at least in principle stand for the ethical pursuit of knowledge, sully themselves by accepting it."[59] (One of the few groups to return Blavatnik's attempted donation was the Hudson Institute.)

Haass claimed the CFR undertook a "rigorous review" of the funds, as it does with all donations.[60] But Haass stated that the think tank would still be keeping the money nonetheless. Not only that, but Haass proudly announced that the CFR would be renaming their internship program after Blavatnik.[61] (And who, after all, could be against financing underpaid interns?) Blavatnik's successful CFR donation illustrated that "it's frankly open season," Chayes, one of the letter's signatories, told me. "It broadcasts to the Kremlin that if you just disguise your money a little bit, the U.S. system is still fully penetrable."[62]

* * *

IT'S THAT PENETRABILITY that brings us directly back to Trump—and to the final marriage of American kleptocracy, American power, and the potential end of American democracy. In 2014, prompted by a request from the FBI, Austrian authorities arrested a Ukrainian oligarch named

Dmitry Firtash, holding him while he awaited extradition to the U.S. At the time, the arrest sent shudders throughout the oligarchic class, both in Ukraine and beyond. Long viewed as one of the titans of the post-Soviet gas trade—and long associated with the kinds of corrupt, kleptocratic money-moving schemes others like Kolomoisky knew so well—Firtash dodged accusations of high-level corruption by playing the same reputation-laundering games others had long pursued, including wooing former members of the British parliament and donating millions of pounds to Cambridge University in order to bankroll the university's Ukrainian Studies program. (As Cambridge still boasts on its website, "Cambridge Ukrainian Studies, an initiative of the Department of Slavonic Studies, was launched at Cambridge with the support of Mr Firtash in 2008."[63])

But by the mid-2010s, Firtash's schemes caught up with him. After the oligarch revealed his ties to Russian *mafioso* Semion Mogilevich to an American diplomat, the U.S. Department of Justice accused the oligarch of acting as an "upper-echelon [associate] of Russian organized crime."[64] Levying charges of large-scale bribery, the U.S. formally indicted him in 2014. Austrian authorities obliged, and placed the stunned oligarch under house arrest.

For a few years, Firtash wilted in Vienna. One figure seemed to capture the oligarch's ire more than any other: Joe Biden, then serving as vice president and the U.S.'s point man on pushing anticorruption reforms in Ukraine. "I was repulsed" by Biden's presence in Ukraine, the oligarch would later say, blaming Biden for the successful pro-transparency reforms Ukraine instituted following the 2014 revolution. "He was the overlord."[65]

Toward the end of the 2010s, however, Firtash still hadn't flown to the U.S., and still hadn't been forced to face the charges the DOJ had leveled against him. And by then, a new administration was running the show in Washington. A new administration dismantling America's antikleptocracy policies, one decision at a time. A new administration launched into the White House by one of Firtash's old business partners, Paul Manafort, whom Firtash had worked with during Manafort's time in Ukraine.[66] A new administration that, via a network of far-right lawyers and frumpy, cartoonish bagmen, had begun rummaging around for "dirt" on the figure Trump thought posed the greatest threat to his 2020 campaign: Biden.

It was a new administration that, as Firtash saw it, presented an opportunity. In 2019, Firtash dumped his previous legal team, composed of white-collar Washington insiders.[67] He replaced them with a pair of conspiratorial, hard-right lawyers named Victoria Toensing and Joe diGenova.[68] He also hired someone he described as a "translator," a dowdy Ukrainian American named Lev Parnas, who claimed to know both Trump and Trump's befuddled lawyer, Rudy Giuliani. In addition to the money he used to pay Toensing and diGenova, Firtash shelled out hundreds of thousands of dollars directly to Parnas, including funds for private jets and trips to Vienna—transforming Parnas into, as he said, "the best-paid interpreter in the world."[69]

Shortly after Firtash hired the triumvirate, Americans began learning all about how dirty post-Soviet money had upended American politics. They learned about Trump's attempts to shake down the Ukrainian government for "dirt" on Biden: the first time a president had ever strong-armed a foreign government in order to fabricate smears against a political rival. Americans also began learning about all of Giuliani's unregistered work on behalf of shady foreign clients, from Ukraine to Venezuela to Turkey, and his ties to a raft of disgraced Ukrainian officials suddenly spinning lies about Biden's work.[70] Americans further learned that Parnas had secretly funneled suspect post-Soviet monies into the U.S. via an anonymous Delaware shell company—part of the hundreds of millions of dollars Moscow and Beijing have expended to interfere in democratic processes abroad, as the German Marshall Fund's Josh Rudolph and Thomas Morley uncovered in 2020.[71]

At the center of all of these revelations stood one figure: Firtash, the Ukrainian kleptocrat whispering in the ears of the pro-Trump figures he'd surrounded himself with, bankrolling their efforts, serving as the apparent broker between Giuliani's team and those in Ukraine trying to help Trump's shakedown—acting as a black hole of dirty money, around which all the efforts spun. "Giuliani's position on Firtash suddenly changed when the oligarch became useful to Giuliani," Ukrainian journalist Sergii Leshchenko wrote. "And now his friends are working for Firtash as lawyers, and Giuliani himself uses 'evidence' created by Firtash in his plot to defend Trump."[72]

It wasn't difficult to see what Firtash wanted out of the entire affair. As Parnas later revealed, he'd told the oligarch that there were certain ways to get the American extradition request lifted. Perhaps most importantly: helping Trump's broader efforts in Ukraine. Lo and behold, soon after he hired his new legal team, Firtash's pro-Trump lawyers received a sit-down with Attorney General Bill Barr to discuss their client's status—a remarkable development, given that Barr was supposed to be charged with overseeing Firtash's extradition.[73]

Thanks in large part to Trump's rank incompetence, the entire pressure campaign against Ukraine eventually imploded, resulting in Trump's first impeachment. But save for a concerned whistleblower, who revealed Trump's campaign and began the wheels of impeachment spinning, Firtash could have succeeded. Not only in getting the extradition request lifted, but in creating an entirely new mode of how kleptocrats can influence a susceptible, mercenary White House, directly upending American anticorruption and antikleptocracy efforts in the process.[74]

The playbook Firtash created was simple. If you're a kleptocrat who ends up in trouble for money laundering–related crimes, you should hire pro-administration figures and claim to have knowledge of "dirt" on a political opponent, regardless of the accuracy of the information. You should then pledge to trade information and set up meetings in return for the White House lifting American investigations and American charges. And if you succeed, you can promptly return to the world of transnational money laundering these oligarchs know well.

It was something completely unprecedented in American history. And it nearly worked. Some call it "strategic corruption," or the emergence of the strategic usage of corrupt actors to subvert democratic governments and democracy writ large.[75] More colloquially, you can just name it after the kleptocrat who perfected it. Just call it the Firtash Model.

This model is now open and available to any kleptocrats facing American investigations, regardless of the scope of their crimes. Other kleptocrats facing American charges swiftly tried the same playbook, or at least pieces of it. Mykola Zlochevsky, a Ukrainian oligarch connected to the gas trade, allegedly offered Giuliani derogatory information on Trump's political opponents if Giuliani "could help the oligarch curry favor with the Justice Department."[76] Jho Low, the Malaysian kleptocrat who convinced Britney Spears to pretzel herself inside a birthday cake—and who ended up ironically bankrolling the production of *The Wolf of Wall Street*, a film about white-collar criminals, with looted monies—secretly funneled money to GOP fundraiser Elliott Broidy in order to lobby Trump.[77]

But if there's one oligarch who embodied the Firtash Model best, it was Kolomoisky—effectively completing the loop of American kleptocracy writ large, and bringing it all to its final, obvious conclusion.

* * *

HUNKERED IN KYIV in early 2019, Kolomoisky had watched his hopes of wringing concessions out of Zelensky go up in smoke. And he sensed the walls closing in. By 2019, the FBI had learned where he had stashed his ill-gotten gains in the U.S., in places like Cleveland and Illinois and Kentucky. Meanwhile, lawsuits filed against him in the U.S. (and elsewhere) continued to accumulate. The schlubby oligarch-turned-warlord flailed for a response, watching his windows of opportunity quickly closing.

But Kolomoisky knew Firtash, and he watched the latter's maneuvers closely. He saw the fellow oligarch, also subjected to American investigations, hire a pair of lawyers firmly in Trump's camp, and watched them get an extraordinary sit-down with the American attorney general. He watched him toss millions at others in Trump's immediate orbit. He watched a spool of clearly fabricated stories about Biden suddenly spin out, cascading around the White House, with Firtash sitting at the middle of the entire operation, an oligarchic spider at the center of a web of lies and payments.[78] He watched, just like the rest of us, this new Firtash Model play out in real time. And maybe, he thought, he could use it for his own ends.

First, in November 2019, Kolomoisky hired one of Trump's longtime lawyers, Marc Kasowitz, a bulldog attorney who'd worked as part of Trump's team during the Mueller investigation.[79] He also hired a second

American lawyer, Bud Cummins, who'd pushed pro-Trump rhetoric regarding Ukraine before.[80] Alongside these two, he reportedly hired a Ukrainian national named Andrii Telizhenko, who'd joined Firtash's lawyers in helping spread anti-Biden conspiracies among American right-wing propaganda outlets.[81]

Kolomoisky then dove headfirst into the fertile ground of conspiracy theories that the White House and its defenders had gleefully promulgated. When Giuliani visited Ukraine in December, scouring for more "dirt" on Biden, he met with an oafish former Ukrainian official named Kostiantyn Kulyk[82]—a figure who just so happened to work at Kolomoisky's behest as the oligarch's "secret weapon."[83] Kulyk claimed to have damaging information on Biden. Giuliani also had a sit-down meeting with Oleksandr Dubinsky, another malignant official who "head[ed] Kolomoisky's influence group" in Kyiv, according to one Ukrainian journalist.[84]

By late 2019, Kolomoisky spread the word: he had the "dirt" Trump wanted, and he didn't care how it got to the White House. The oligarch began "claiming to have damaging information on the Bidens," *Politico* reported, including on both Joe and his son Hunter.[85] As one attorney familiar with his efforts said, the oligarch used the promise of scandalous intel "to keep himself relevant to the whole [Biden 'dirt'] discussion, and he would also like to ingratiate himself to Trump." The oligarch played coy; he didn't want to trumpet his Biden-related claims to the world—just to the president and his bagmen. "He's been kind of cryptic and cute about it," the lawyer continued. But as one Western diplomat said, Kolomoisky was clearly "trying to become friends with Trump and Giuliani."[86]

The signs, as with Firtash, were unmistakable. As Volodymyr Fesenko, a Kyiv-based political analyst, told Talking Points Memo, "Kolomoisky seems to be trying the same thing as Firtash." He was trying out the Firtash Model, with an American administration more than willing to play along. And the oligarch had one demand: make his issues, all these lawsuits and inquiries, go away. Kill the investigations, in both the U.S. and Ukraine. And let the kleptocratic carousel continue, as it ever had. "Our oligarchs think that if you befriend the main person in a country, then that will solve all your problems," Fesenko continued.[87] With a president like Trump, what oligarch would think otherwise?

By 2020, Kolomoisky had become the logical end point for America's collapse into the global center of modern kleptocracy. He was a man who spent years taking full advantage of American anti–money laundering loopholes, allegedly piling untold millions into American real estate with little more than a desire to obscure his jaw-dropping dirty money operations. And now, as investigators began uncovering his network, he turned to an American president to get his investigations and his charges lifted, with the promise of unfounded "dirt" against a political rival in return. Through Kolomoisky, the marriage of kleptocracy and foreign interference in the era of Trump had been consummated.

But the oligarch misjudged the timing. By the time he'd started using this Firtash Model for his own ends, it was already too late—too many others were already on the hunt for other kleptocrats trying the same strategy. And America, despite Trump's best efforts otherwise, remained a functioning democracy, with pressure from Congress and the broader body politic keeping the heat on the administration. There were too many eyeballs watching what Giuliani and his cronies were doing on the president's behalf. Kolomoisky's efforts, like Firtash's before him, eventually splintered, undone by American democracy.

But he, like Firtash, nearly succeeded. And if he had, that American kleptocratic circle—of using American financial anonymity to hide gargantuan money laundering operations, and then using the proceeds of such operations to convince an American president to end any investigations and lift any charges, allowing the money laundering operations to run on in perpetuity—would have stood complete. The oligarchs, those who'd looked to the U.S. for years for their dirty money needs, would have won.

AMERICAN KLEPTOCRACIES

"There are but two parties now, traitors and patriots, and I want hereafter to be ranked with the latter."

—Ulysses S. Grant[1]

Trump's first impeachment saga in 2019 revealed a great deal, from smear campaigns and physical threats against American diplomats to Trump's use of American power for his own ends. None of it saved him from election loss in 2020, or from becoming the first president to ever be impeached multiple times. And none of it prevented Firtash from facing imminent extradition to the U.S., despite all of his efforts to forestall it.[2]

Nor did Kolomoisky's subterranean efforts to use the Firtash Model for his own ends succeed, either. Once Firtash's efforts crumpled, the heat of the impeachment investigations became too much for the other oligarchs following suit. By mid-2020, with everyone in Washington looking out for foreign oligarchs whispering in the ears of pro-Trump lackeys, Kolomoisky's path to the American president effectively disappeared. And it couldn't have come at a worse time. Because in August 2020, U.S. authorities showed their cards: not only had they begun a formal investigation into Kolomoisky's American assets, but they'd already uncovered enough information to issue formal asset seizures against a number of Kolomoisky's and the Optima Family's American holdings.[3]

With footage of FBI agents ransacking Optima's Cleveland offices,

Kolomoisky was now on the receiving end of a tactic he'd so often employed against his opponents in Ukraine.[4] "Over the course of more than a decade," one of the DOJ complaints against the oligarch read, Kolomoisky (and his partner Bogolyubov) "used . . . PrivatBank to steal billions of dollars of the bank's funds."[5] Backing up investigators in Ukraine, DOJ officials added that the magnitude of Kolomoisky's "fraud and theft was so great that [the National Bank of Ukraine] was forced to bail out the bank by providing $5.5 billion in order to stave off economic crisis for the whole country."[6] All of the details of Kolomoisky, Schochet, and Korf's efforts were there, laid bare in the allegations by American officials. Kolomoisky and his cronies "spent prolifically: they purchased more than five million square feet of commercial real estate in Ohio, steel plants in Kentucky, West Virginia, and Michigan, a cellphone manufacturing plant in Illinois, and commercial real estate in Texas."[7] All that Ukrainian investigators had alleged—all that Gontareva, who'd faced down death threats and arson attacks and hit-and-runs, already knew—was there, in black and white, with the imprimatur of the U.S. Department of Justice. And it came with the full backing of the DOJ's Kleptocracy Asset Recovery Initiative, which celebrated its ten-year anniversary by targeting the man who'd allegedly turned swaths of the American Rust Belt into his personal money laundering fiefdoms.[8]

By the end of Trump's term in office, Kolomoisky stood adrift. The path to Trump's ear had been blocked; the oligarch's American assets were suddenly frozen, his network exposed; legislation in Kyiv specifically forbade him from ever returning to control of PrivatBank. Kolomoisky looked around, and appeared lonelier than ever before. Hemmed in by Ukrainian and American investigations, Kolomoisky had transformed from titan of Ukraine's oligarchy to, instead, a cautionary tale.

And in early 2021, the Americans wielded their hammer. In a public statement, Washington revealed that it was directly sanctioning Kolomoisky and his family. As U.S. secretary of state Antony Blinken said, the sanctions stemmed specifically from Kolomoisky's "involvement in significant corruption," with the oligarch leading "ongoing efforts to undermine Ukraine's democratic processes and institutions."[9] If anyone missed the move, the U.S. embassy in Kyiv tweeted out a photo of Kolomoisky, with a giant red stamp that read, in all caps, "DESIGNATED FOR INVOLVEMENT IN SIGNIFICANT CORRUPTION."[10]

* * *

THE REASON FOR the U.S.'s moves to sanction Kolomoisky was simple enough. A few months earlier, a new administration had taken the reins in Washington—a new presidency pledged to restoring American stewardship and American stability, and to centering anticorruption and antikleptocracy at the heart of a new American chapter. This book is hardly an exaltation of Joe Biden, or a defense of Biden's previous record. (Given Biden's years of working as a senator from Delaware, such a defense would hardly be full-throated.[11]) Rather, Biden's rise to the presidency, unexpected as it was, points to the president's role as a vessel for broader anticorruption and counterkleptocracy reform—and the swelling awareness of a new generation of American policymakers of the intersection of American kleptocracy and national security, electoral legitimacy, and the global tide of authoritarianism.

The new president didn't wait long after the 2020 election to center anticorruption as a primary plank of his administration. As he laid out in a piece in *Foreign Affairs* immediately following his victory, Biden said he would specifically single out corruption as a core policy throughline for his administration, issuing "a presidential policy directive that establishes combating corruption as a core national security interest."[12] To that end, he announced he would specifically target illicit tax havens and expand American efforts to go after stolen and laundered assets. Structurally, Biden pronounced that he'd also usher in a new federal agency, the Commission on Federal Ethics, which would not only ensure "vigorous and unified enforcement" of anticorruption laws but would further be empowered to issue (and enforce) subpoenas and "refer matters for criminal investigation to the DOJ."[13] Internationally, Biden has singled out "weaponized corruption"—the kind that allows kleptocratic regimes to entrench and expand and enhance malign efforts abroad—as a "nontraditional threat," one that NATO member states must focus on combating.[14] "We will take special aim at confronting corruption, which rots democracy from the inside and is increasingly weaponized by authoritarian states to undermine democratic institutions," Biden's White House announced in early 2021.[15]

On their own, the pledges represented the most consequential support for a new anticorruption and counterkleptocracy push that America had ever seen, or at least since the days of Carl Levin and his efforts to get anti–money laundering language into the Patriot Act. But Biden's comments hardly existed in a vacuum. Instead, they rose to the top of a chorus that was already growing louder by the day, building upon a nascent movement to reclaim American anticorruption and counterkleptocracy leadership writ large—a movement that, by early 2021, had seen more energy, more excitement, and more momentum than any moment in American history. Because even before Biden swore his oath and entered the White House, Congress was already taking a momentous step toward ending America's role as the center of global kleptocracy.

On the first day of 2021, the National Defense Authorization Act of 2020 (NDAA) became law. Generally, the passage of the annual bill is a rote affair, shoring up American defense expenditures and offering pork barrel projects to assorted officials. This iteration, though, had one clause that stood out—one piece that made this one of the most consequential counterkleptocracy bills ever passed. At long last, the U.S. would ban anonymous American shell companies. With the bill's passage—which overcame Trump's veto—Congress had finally, formally, forevermore banned the formation of anonymous shells in the U.S.[16]

The anti–shell company language in the NDAA didn't generate many headlines. But it's difficult to overstate the importance of the bill, or of the ban. While journalists and pundits paid attention to everything else in the final weeks of Trump's presidency, from insurrection to impeachment, American legislators, with significant bipartisan backing, had quietly taken a sledgehammer to the edifice of American kleptocracy.[17] "It is certainly the most significant anti–money laundering reform in 20 years," said Clark Gascoigne, who led the push by helping steer the Financial Accountability and Corporate Transparency (FACT) Coalition, bringing support from across the political spectrum. "And probably the most significant anti-corruption reform as well."[18]

To be sure, the ban hardly happened overnight. Previous efforts to eliminate anonymous shells went nowhere, flaming out against lobbying from states like Delaware and Nevada, or from the Chamber of Commerce or the American Bar Association, or from anyone who would see a bit less revenue if they had to stop selling or using anonymous shell companies to hide the dirty money racing through the U.S. Nor was the 2020 bill a panacea; while those setting up companies will now need to identify and report the beneficial owners of the LLCs, such ownership information remains accessible only to American officials, rather than to the public, journalists, or activists.[19]

But those issues can be ironed out in future bills. Because even without a publicly accessible database, the fact that anonymous U.S. shell companies are no more is itself a substantial salvo from Washington against the bedrock of transnational money laundering. For the first time in nearly two decades, the U.S. had passed a remarkable piece of counterkleptocracy legislation. And for the first time in years, perhaps ever, the foundations of America's kleptocratic networks buckled.

* * *

YOU'D BE FORGIVEN for missing the news of America's elimination of shell companies, what with it coming during America's first insurrectionist presidential transition, its first nonpeaceful transfer of power since Abraham Lincoln in 1860. But the fact that Trump's failed power grab overshadowed the landmark passage of anti–shell company legislation points to a broader reality of the American kleptocratic industrial complex. That is, even with the ouster of a would-be authoritarian like Trump, and with the passage of the new anti–shell company legislation, the fight to end the reign of American kleptocracy is hardly tied to a single event, or a single president, or to his removal. If anything, it's just beginning.

There are a few areas of obvious, low-hanging fruit on the counter-kleptocracy front moving forward. (The one benefit of surveying the landscape of loopholes and financial secrecy mechanisms remaining in the U.S.: there's an entire buffet of options for reformers!) And no area merits more attention than the decades-long "temporary" exemptions enjoyed by industries rolling in trillions of dollars, much of it anonymous, much of it coming in dirty and leaving perfectly pristine—leaving those industries now standing as the remaining pillars of the American kleptocratic construct.

The first of these industries is the one that seems to connect all the kleptocrats who race to America for their money laundering needs, including Teodorin and Kolomoisky and all the others mentioned in this book: real estate. "For real estate, the loophole was so huge you could fit a skyline through it," investigative journalist Tom Burgis once wrote. And he's not wrong: thanks to the Patriot Act's "temporary" loophole, entire city skylines have been transformed into key ingredients in the American laundromat—including those in places no one ever expected, like Cleveland. We already know what the solution is: the end of anonymity. The end of anonymous cash purchases, of anonymous shell purchases, of anonymous purchases made via American attorneys who hide the identities of their clients behind attorney-client privilege. Time and again—in skyscrapers and condos, in McMansions and steel mills, in tired factories and entire cities—that anonymity in American real estate has fired the motors of global kleptocracy. For decades, American real estate has provided anonymity for anyone who wants it, for anyone looking to transform their dirty money into legitimate assets. It's a reality that has lined the pockets of the broader real estate industry—and has had devastating effects on sagging downtowns and local communities in the U.S., and on entire nation-states abroad watching their treasuries and banks looted and laundered via American real estate.

Thankfully, prior to Trump's ascension, the U.S. launched a pilot program aimed at fine-tuning the best methods of ending the all-encompassing anonymity in American real estate. Known as Geographic Targeting Orders (GTO), the program, first announced by the Obama administration in 2016, forced title insurers—those providing insurance to the owners of the property in question—to identify the real, beneficial owners of certain properties and purchases. As it was a pilot program, the GTO project only targeted a select few major American cities, including Seattle, New York, Miami, Honolulu, and a handful of others. The program was built on the same theory propounded above: that ending anonymity was the means to ending American kleptocracy, and

ending the real estate industry's role as both a benefactor and propo-
nent, on a scale few could imagine, of transnational money laundering.[20]

Lo and behold, the theory proved true. Revealing the identities of
those behind previously anonymous purchases lifted a veil on the owners, and sent the dirty money searching for anonymity scampering elsewhere. One 2018 study found that anonymous shell company purchases
declined drastically in the areas surveyed—even in places like Miami,
still widely viewed as a city built on little more than money laundering. Even more remarkably, related housing prices dropped alongside,
by nearly 5 percent. It resulted in a bit less money lining luxury realtors'
pockets, yes, but it was also the effective end of residential real estate in
places like Miami as a sink of new dirty money flows. As an added bonus, it provided more affordable housing for the rest of us.[21]

All of which is to say: with anonymous American shell companies
taken care of, the end of anonymity in the American real estate space
must be the next major domino to fall. Whether that comes from the
nationwide expansion of the GTO program or simply from the elimination of the skyline-wide "temporary" exemption for the real estate
industry (or some combination therein) is up for legislators to decide.
But the towers and factories and mills and mansions of anonymity must
reveal their real, beneficial owners, regardless of their connections to
Ukrainian warlords or African oligarchs or *mafiosi* the world over. (It's
also worth looking to solutions proven successful elsewhere, such as the
U.K.'s Unexplained Wealth Orders program, which forces foreign officials to explain the sources of their wealth and face asset seizures if they
can't.[22]) Once those identities are revealed, there should be increased
consideration of things like a vacancy tax, specifically aimed at those
who pocket these properties as little more than laundering vehicles—the
likes of which we've already seen successfully implemented in places like
the Canadian province of British Columbia.[23]

And why stop there? If anonymity remains the kleptocrats' asym-
metric advantage, then transparency remains the best weapon in the
counterkleptocracy movement's arsenal. (Such is the logic behind a
thrust of similar proposals, such as the "global asset registry" proposed
by economist Gabriel Zucman.[24]) In hedge funds and private equity, in

the perpetual trusts of South Dakota and among escrow agents across the country, in all those other areas that dodged the post-9/11 transparency and anti–money laundering requirements, the time for anonymity is over. FBI and Senate investigators, journalists and activists, national security voices and electoral security experts: we have all clamored for years about the need for the end of anonymity in these sectors, these favorite playgrounds of Russian oligarchs and corrupt Chinese kleptocrats and sanctioned Iranian officials. All those sectors that keep the engine of American kleptocracy running at full steam.

As with the shell company legislation, the identities of those pouring billions into trusts and escrow accounts and hedge funds don't need to be made public. (Not initially, at least.) But their identities need to be made accessible to American law enforcement, and to investigators from democratic governments elsewhere—including those struggling to their feet, like investigators in Kyiv who uncover Ponzi schemes rattling entire populations. They should also be made known to other interested parties: the pension fund organizations unwittingly mixing their finances with oligarchs' dirty money, the workers struggling to make a living at a mill secretly owned by a corrupt foreign official, the neighbors wondering why a row of nearby houses is always vacant, despite going for double the market value when they sold.

All of this also goes for those in the art and auction market in the U.S. Despite claims from the industry that the American art and auction market remains untainted by malign actors—they maintain that the industry is just too niche, or just too small, to be of any interest—the kleptocratic examples have only piled higher and higher. There's Teodorin, becoming the world's greatest collector of Michael Jackson memorabilia, courtesy of American anonymity. There's a pair of sanctioned Russian oligarchs, moving and laundering millions, gutting America's sanctions regime, courtesy of anonymity in the art market. There are god-knows-how-many other examples, all turning to the greatest unregulated market in the entire world in order to hide their money.

Given that many of these requirements for transparency are already on the books, applying such transparency is far from the uphill battle it may seem. Nor is that preexisting language in things like the Patriot

Act the only card the U.S. government can quickly play. In 2004, in a little-noticed measure at the height of the Iraq War, Congress granted the Treasury Department the right to create a cross-border payments database. For all the reasons detailed above—internal lethargy, lack of resources, industry-wide pushback—the database never came into existence. But that doesn't mean it can't yet be realized. As Joshua Kirschenbaum and David Murray wrote for the German Marshall Fund, "U.S. banks process trillions of dollars in payments per day, including about half of cross-border funds transfers worldwide."[25] A database highlighting and detailing these payments, which we already have in places like Canada and Australia, would not only help reduce regulatory burdens on banks but would also stymie kleptocrats trying to bounce their funds in and out of American jurisdictions. And as a bonus, Kirschenbaum and Murray add, "technology would make an international payments database straightforward and cost-effective."[26] The only thing better than combating kleptocracy: saving money while you're doing it.

Not all of this requires legislation, per se. For the American non-profits we saw in the previous chapter, sucking up hundreds of millions from questionable sources, new guidelines and best practices must be implemented, with an emphasis on public disclosures of all donor information. And for American lawyers, long able to cloak their work for kleptocrats behind attorney-client privilege, a new slate of legal ethics rules must be implemented. All lawyers creating corporate entities and trusts or helping purchase real estate and luxury yachts should be required to flag suspicious transactions—and face significant punishment if they're found knowingly aiding these kleptocratic networks. Legislation isn't immediately needed on these fronts. But if these industries continue to refuse reform—if, as a *Foreign Policy* headline read, "U.S. lawyers [remain] foreign kleptocrats' best friends"[27]—they're only asking for legislators to take another look.

Of course, even with the end of all this anonymity, this still wouldn't be enough. Asset seizure should continue, and even be expanded. But seizing these assets isn't a viable solution in and of itself, as only a tiny percentage of holdings tied to dirty money is ever frozen, let alone returned to the populations suffering at the hands of the kleptocrats in question. Likewise, legislation and new requirements are only as effective as their enforcement. And if regulatory bodies remain understaffed and underresourced, the new legislation and pro-transparency moves are worth little more than the paper on which they're written.

Few things have illustrated this dynamic more clearly than the so-called FinCEN Files of 2020, which saw a tranche of Treasury Department documents detailing trillions of dollars in bank transactions spill into the open.[28] The leaks raised fresh questions about the efficacy of even the basics of America's counterkleptocracy push, illustrating how overwhelmed the Treasury Department's Financial Crimes Enforcement Network (FinCEN) is when it comes to dealing with suspicious transactions flowing through American banks.[29] As the documents detailed, numerous banks only took pro forma steps toward complying with the U.S.'s stringent anti–money laundering requirements in the banking sector. Some didn't even bother to file required paperwork on certain accounts until years after the suspicious transactions took place—despite increased regulations surrounding things like identifying those behind shell company accounts.[30]

The reason for such lethargy was simple: FinCEN, which was established in 1990 and oversees much of the anti–money laundering apparatus for banks, remained severely understaffed, scrounging for funding and employees. While the rate of banks' Suspicious Activity Report (SAR) filings has doubled in the last decade—more and more bankers at least seem willing to flag potentially kleptocratic customers—total FinCEN staff has shrunk by some 10 percent. FinCEN could barely keep up, let alone try to enforce any infractions. Small wonder that, as one source familiar with the documents said, "most SARs are never even read, let alone acted upon."[31]

Such staffing woes aren't limited to FinCEN, though. The IRS has likewise been effectively gutted, allowing America to bleed tax receipts, and allowing the wealthiest among us to tuck their billions away without any worry about the taxman knocking.[32] Not only has the IRS's overall budget decreased over 20 percent (adjusted for inflation) in recent years, but, at last check, the IRS had fewer auditors at the start of the 2020s than at any point since the 1950s.[33] Small wonder that white-collar criminals, American or not, feel little fear about potential reprisals from the U.S. government.

Staffing up, then, is a must for counterkleptocracy reforms. It's also a relatively easy turnaround for the U.S. For inspiration, all American authorities need to do is look at how the Department of Justice has recently treated the scourge of unreported foreign lobbying. For decades, the DOJ's Foreign Agents Registration Act (FARA) was an effective backwater. Enacted in 1938 as a means of unveiling Nazi lobbyists—sparked in large part by the secret work of Ivy Lee, the so-called father of modern PR, on behalf of Hitler's regime[34]—FARA requires all those lobbying for foreign governments, and their proxies, to reveal their ties, and how much they are making along the way. Yet for years, FARA itself remained little enforced and largely forgotten, with only a scattering of convictions over nearly eight decades It wasn't quite a dead letter, but it was close.[35]

And then, in 2016, the U.S. watched a whole range of foreign forces wheedle their way into Trump's campaign, with corrupt figures out of both Russia and Ukraine linking up with numerous Americans in Trump's orbit. People like disgraced former national security adviser Mike Flynn. People like former deputy campaign manager Rick Gates. And people like the avatar of foreign lobbying itself: Paul Manafort.[36] After the details of Manafort's foreign work began spilling out in 2016, FARA had a new lease on life, and more momentum than at any point since its inception. Suddenly, the DOJ devoted new resources and new personnel toward enforcing FARA registrations and to making sure foreign lobbyists had to reveal the foreign forces lining their pockets. Registrations promptly skyrocketed, a new team at DOJ beefed up compliance, and Americans gained an unprecedented insight into the machinations of foreign lobbying in the U.S.[37] Paradoxically, thanks to Trump and Manafort, FARA ended up funded and enforced to a greater extent than it had ever been during its previous eight decades of existence. Finally, decades after Lee and the Nazis connived to secretly sway unsuspecting Americans, FARA lived up to its promise—which just so happened to jail a number of pro-Trump figures, none of whom had disclosed their foreign work previously.[38]

* * *

ENDING ANONYMITY, REQUIRING greater disclosures, staffing up enforcement and regulatory agencies: these are all relatively disparate, diffuse efforts. But they can be—have to be—part of a broader portfolio of action, of a whole-of-arsenal and whole-of-government approach.[39]

If all this seems daunting, that's understandable. It is. But this call to drive a stake through the heart of American kleptocracy has a historic precedent—one, fittingly enough, found in the period that most closely resembles the American political moment at the end of the Trump era: the Gilded Age, during the end of the nineteenth century. The America of the Gilded Age stood saturated in wealth inequality, in rampaging monopolies, in the kinds of bribes and payoffs and endemic corruption most today would associate with the developing world. The height of the original Gilded Age revealed American capitalism in all its inhumanity, and in all its corruption—much as the Trumpian age has revealed all that is crass, all that is corrupt, about the American political system, and about modern capitalism more broadly. And yet, just a few years after its height, the ravages of the Gilded Age, as well as its attendant corruption, had been largely tamed. Not entirely, of course; corruption never truly dies. But broadly, impressively, and unexpectedly. By the second decade of the twentieth century, most of the excesses—patronage systems, greased palms, officials reliant on pay-for-play schemes across the country—had clearly been tackled. And that process of unwinding endemic American corruption points to the kind of multifaceted approach that will work for those of us now staring down this Second Gilded Age.[40]

Those anticorruption reforms of the late nineteenth and early twentieth centuries didn't happen overnight. They took years, and a combination of factors, including expanded oversight, significant investigations, increased government regulations, and even select high-profile prosecutions. Civil service reform, which prioritized merit over patronage in government hiring, helped stanch corrupt networks at the federal level.

Federal prosecutions of those paying and receiving bribes—creating a "new era of criminal enforcement," as one scholar said[41]—launched new, pro-transparency efforts across the U.S. Combined with new anticorruption legislation, increased election finance transparency, pro-transparency reforms in the lobbying sector, and beefed-up regulatory oversight bodies, the U.S. lurched from the bog of the Gilded Age into a more equitable—and more transparent—time. One that we now know as the Progressive Era.

Toward the end of the 2010s, the calls for a New Progressive Era became impossible to miss. In the U.S., the calls manifested themselves in a revitalized left, fired by the presidential campaigns of Senator Bernie Sanders and a new roster of congressional leaders. While Sanders's campaigns eventually flamed out, his imprint on broader policy will long outlast him. An entire slate of policy proposals, all centered on rising wealth and income inequality, have glommed on to American political discourse, and have proved impossible to dislodge. Things like a wealth tax, which would target substantial holdings of the richest among us. Things like a return to a progressive taxation policy, such as the kind America boasted during the post–World War II period, and which disintegrated amid broader deregulatory reforms. Things like bills specifically targeting the marriage between illicit finance, oligarchy, and the decline of democracy more broadly. "Around the world we have witnessed the rise of demagogues who once in power use their positions to loot the state of its resources,"[42] Sanders said in 2017, adding a year later that we "need to understand that the struggle for democracy is bound up with the struggle against kleptocracy and corruption."[43] If nothing else, Sanders, alongside politicos like Senator Elizabeth Warren, has clarified the relationship between kleptocracy and runaway, unregulated capitalism in a way few have.[44]

Because, at the end of the day, kleptocracy can be understood in many ways as capitalism at its rawest—or as capitalism at its worst. Capitalism unburdened by requirements for transparency or disclosure. Capitalism in which wealth can open any door needed, without any safeguard in place. Capitalism in which brutal ruling classes—as we've seen in Russia and Kazakhstan, in China and Venezuela, in Equatorial Guinea and prerevolution Ukraine—capture the levers of state power, and all the wealth that comes with it, to entrench their regimes forevermore, and to kill off any democratizing efforts along the way. And a capitalism that allows those regimes to turn to the U.S. whenever they need to take advantage of American financial secrecy, keeping their looted wealth safe and secure—and maybe, as Trump illustrated, even using it to help place a man servicing their kleptocratic needs directly in the White House.

* * *

But if we're to enter a New Progressive Era, one to undo the devastation of this American kleptocracy, there's one other lesson to heed, from a more recent point in American history. As Carl Levin and his staff highlighted during the passage of the post-9/11 reforms, none of the success they found would have been possible if the legislation hadn't already been ready. If legislators hadn't already crafted detailed plans to block off American financial institutions from dirty money, the small window of opportunity following the September 11 attacks would have shut, with little to show for it. If legislators hadn't been ready, American banks, those original progenitors of American kleptocracy, would have continued working with whomever they wanted, however they wanted, cycling billions and billions in dirty money. Instead, because Levin and his staff were prepared, America showed how an entire banking sector could be cleaned up, and could shine a path forward for others. All because legislators like Levin were ready. Levin retired in 2015, but a new crop of counterkleptocracy activists has emerged in Washington, working with civil society and legislators to craft bills that can tackle these financial secrecy industries and restore the U.S.'s leadership status in the world of anticorruption efforts.

In the civil society sector, groups like Transparency International, Global Witness, the FACT Coalition, and the Hudson Institute's Kleptocracy Initiative—the latter (where I'm an adjunct fellow) led by new thinkers like Nate Sibley—have collated all these kleptocratic issues into a comprehensive structure and comprehensive story, bundling recommendations to both legislators and experts alike. Helped along by investigative journalists at places like the International Consortium of

Investigative Journalists (ICIJ) and the Organized Crime and Corruption Reporting Project (OCCRP), these groups have all assisted in fleshing out our understanding of modern kleptocracy, as well as how to combat it. And in Congress, the Helsinki Commission—an independent, bipartisan federal commission focused on human rights and pro-democracy policies—has become the unofficial home for the counterkleptocracy brain trust. Led by policy analyst Paul Massaro, himself a font of bottomless pro-democracy energy, the Helsinki Commission has launched bill after bill to begin patching up America's counterkleptocracy regime. Massaro, alongside legislators like Rhode Island senator Sheldon Whitehouse, has picked up the baton from Levin in Washington and has joined with Sibley and others—including luminaries and anticorruption forces like Ben Judah, Elise Bean, Josh Rudolph, Abigail Bellows, Clark Gascoigne, and Jodi Vittori, among plenty more—to usher in a new guard of counterkleptocracy efforts in the U.S., bridging partisan gaps and stitching together policy proposals that have gained widening audiences on both sides of the political aisle.

Indeed, it's that bipartisan nature of the new counterkleptocracy cohort that presents perhaps the greatest reason for hopes of reform. The bill to ban anonymous shell companies, for instance, came with numerous cosponsors, from arch-conservative voices like Senator Tom Cotton to Democratic stalwarts like Senator Bob Menendez, threading liberal and conservative supporters alike.[45] Not that bipartisan support should necessarily be that surprising; after all, Levin enjoyed bipartisan support for his anti–money laundering thrusts at the PSI. And legislators across the political spectrum have all seen how their constituents have suffered as the tentacles of these offshoring networks have reached into communities, crept into industries, and upended and uprooted everything from national security to American elections themselves.

These counterkleptocracy policies can and should be a bipartisan endeavor. Because while progressive, pro-transparency legislation is demanded on this front, the policies detailed above would also present a restoration of American leadership on the global stage, and an extension of historic American leadership in the anticorruption space. From the Foreign Corrupt Practices Act (FCPA) to Levin's banking regulations, from creating FARA to cracking open the Swiss banking sector, the U.S. had claimed the torch of anticorruption leadership for decades. Trump may have tried to snuff it out, but the flame burns still. And it's clear that without American leadership, the efforts to end the broader world of offshoring, or of transnational money laundering, or of rising oligarchies and oligopolies, both foreign and domestic, will ultimately fail.

And without these much-needed efforts, there is little hope for the broader liberal democratic projects around the world. Because the thing that ties all the modern anti-American, antidemocratic regimes and movements together around the globe isn't some illiterate, blinkered ideology like communism, or a moral grotesquery like fascism. It is, instead, greed: rampaging, unrepentant, unalloyed, embodied by the ruling regimes entrenched in the pursuit of power and an ever-expanding pocketbook. It's a kleptocratic greed we've already seen take root in Moscow, with Putin and his cronies clinging to power, posing as Russian nationalists in order to siphon off billions for themselves. It's a kleptocratic greed we've seen spread through Beijing, where the officials and the family members connected to the ruling Chinese Communist Party have transformed themselves into little more than a gluttonous regime dedicated to pillaging the Chinese people, and leading to a genocide against minority ethnicities like Uyghurs along the way.[46] It's a kleptocratic greed we've seen subsume regimes in Caracas and Tehran and Pyongyang. It's a kleptocratic greed we've seen wherever a democracy has tilted into illiberal authoritarianism, or where dictatorships already rule.

It is a kleptocratic greed, unmitigated and unceasing, that now presents the greatest threat to the U.S. and its democratic allies. As journalist Oliver Bullough once wrote, "Kleptocracy is for the 21st century what fascism and communism were for much of the 20th."[47] And he's right. The only difference: this transnational threat isn't emanating from Moscow or Berlin or Beijing or Rome. It is instead reliant on, and sustained by, the kleptocratic services the U.S. provides in droves, which outpace even those provided by the traditional offshore havens of yore. And which offer the keys to this kleptocratic kingdom to whoever comes knocking—even to those who'd prefer to knock down the entire house of liberal democracy itself.

Which is why this fight to end offshoring and financial secrecy and modern kleptocracy begins here, at home. It begins in states like Delaware and Nevada, Wyoming and South Dakota, which have all opened their doors to the torrent of dirty money racing in, helping hide and obscure it for anyone around the world. It begins with legislators pushing policies like those crafted by Massaro and the Helsinki Commission. And it begins in the public square, with Americans pushing back against the lobbyists for the hedge funds and private equity and real estate industries, all of which have gorged themselves at the table of American anonymity, offering their laundering services to kleptocrats destabilizing countries, immiserating populations, devastating ecologies, brutalizing women and children—and threatening democracy on this planet.

Whatever differences once existed between "offshore" and "onshore" have collapsed, disintegrated by those in the U.S. who transformed the country into the biggest financial secrecy haven of them all. What was once "offshore" is now here, beached in the middle of America. Surrounding all of us. Still, for many, too big to see.

Hopefully, though, this book has helped illuminate some of the kleptocracy that is all around us. Because it's here, in the U.S., that it can end. And it has to. For if it doesn't, it's not only the end of liberal democracy but also the imposition of a new, global feudalism—a kind of Hobbesian capitalism in its most disgusting, most uncut form, where all ends justify all means, and where a new caste of the wealthiest detach from the rest of society, disappearing their riches into the offshore-onshore world, bankrolling anything and everything that suits their needs, all while blocking any efforts at transparency, reform, or regulatory oversight. It's a world whose outline—in America, and in so many other places alongside—we can already detect.

But there's still time to prevent that future. Time to implement the policies long overdue, and to restore American leadership in the anticorruption and counterkleptocracy space. Time to bring transparency to worlds, and entire money laundering industries, that thrive on anonymity. Time for us to finally end this American kleptocracy—before this American kleptocracy ends everything else worth saving.

ACKNOWLEDGMENTS

Writing a book on a topic like financial secrecy and offshoring is never an easy feat—which goes double for attempting to do so during a pandemic. Still, while the words (and errors) are mine, this book is only possible because of the counterkleptocracy giants who've come before. My first round of thanks goes to those who've dedicated entire careers to crafting a clear understanding—and slate of responses—to what we've come to understand as modern kleptocracy. This goes for Senator Carl Levin, the godfather of American counterkleptocracy efforts, who was kind enough to walk me through his efforts at unearthing all those involved in transnational crime and corruption. That also goes for Jack Blum, a one-man force against the kleptocrats and financial malefactors sinking their claws into the U.S. And Elise Bean was more than generous in guiding me through the fault lines of the U.S.'s counterkleptocracy efforts, and for making sure I followed the guideposts correctly.

And then there are those who've dedicated their lives to tackling what's here right now—and what's coming next. That includes Paul Massaro, of the U.S.'s Helsinki Commission, an endless source of democratic ingenuity, and a reminder of what can be achieved through bipartisan efforts—as well as how much can be achieved before the age of 30. That also includes Nate Sibley, who has shepherded the Hudson Institute's Kleptocracy Initiative into the foremost body dedicated to tackling kleptocracy. (Few are those with whom you can discuss both birds and transnational corruption.) That likewise includes Charles Davidson, who birthed the Kleptocracy Initiative and first allowed me a foot in the door on the topic, and Ben Judah, whose insights—and ability to navigate the macro- and micro-level impacts of the phenomenon—helped me reframe my own understanding of the stakes. And that includes Robert Manzanares, who lent me hours upon hours in reliving his experiences tracking Obiang, as well as Bobby Rutherford.

There are also the policymakers, civil society activists, and regional experts without whom this book would not be possible. Clark Gascoigne, Gary Kalman, and the entire team affiliated with the work of the FACT Coalition over the past decade are largely responsible for the greatest counterkleptocracy achievement in the U.S. in the past two decades: the banning of anonymous U.S. shell companies in early 2021. Joshua Kirschenbaum, Rick Messick, Ken Hurwitz, Laura Stuber, Anders Aslund, Adam Hofri-Winogradow, Alma Angotti, Mark Hays, Charlie Eldredge, Daria Kalenyuk, Valeria Gontareva, Eric Karl Hontz, Lakshmi Kumar, and Yuri Shevchuk lent me their ears and expertise, as did a range of others who wished to remain behind the scenes. And the indomitable Tutu Alicante, who has dedicated more of his time than anyone else to pulling back the curtain on Teodorin Obiang's crimes against humanity—and all those who've helped Obiang along the way—deserves special thanks for not only his unceasing work but for opening the eyes of an American journalist who knew Obiang only from his penchant for Michael Jackson merch. This would also be a good moment to thank Melissa Aten, Christopher Walker, and the entire team at NED for taking a keen eye to the topic, and for allowing me entrée into a world of voices all trying to catalogue and categorize kleptocracy. Thanks also to my journalistic editors—especially Jason Linkins, Cameron Abadi, Jennifer Williams, Judd Legum, Kiley Kroh, Emily Hazzard, Harry Siegel, and Christian Caryl—who've given me the space to flesh out my ideas and my findings.

This book would also not be possible without the journalists who've come before, and on whose shoulders this book stands, including Oliver Bullough, whose formulations of kleptocracy helped introduce the topic to the world, and Ken Silverstein, whose work I've been reading and citing since graduate school. Likewise, when tracking the Kolomoisky network, few journalists have done more groundbreaking work than Talking Points Memo's Josh Kovensky, RFE/RL's Todd Prince, and Buzz-Feed's Christopher Miller, who will all be receiving free rounds of drinks next time I see them. A number of others likewise provided background advice and feedback, who wish to remain anonymous. As such, I'd like to specifically point readers toward journalistic outfits like the Organized Crime and Corruption Reporting Project and the International Consortium of Investigative Journalists, which you should absolutely support.

There are also those in academia leading the charge to understanding transnational money- and reputation-laundering. They include Columbia University's Alex Cooley, whose unfailing support, advice, and willingness to extend opportunities are among the primary reasons this book exists. Special thanks also to my colleagues at the Global Integrity Anti-Corruption Evidence project: John Heathershaw, Tena Prelec, Jason Sharman, Ricardo Soares de Oliveira, Tom Mayne, and David Lewis.

And then there's the team at St. Martin's Press—including my editor, Pronoy Sarkar, who took a flier on a first-time author trying to pitch a book on a topic that was as convoluted as the name used to describe it. (What the hell is kleptocracy, anyway?) Without Pronoy, there is no *American Kleptocracy*. Thank you, my friend. Hannah O'Grady successfully, and graciously, shepherded this book to its close, as did Alan Bradshaw, Ryan Masteller, Henry Kaufman, and Callum Plews; thanks also to Kathryn Hough, Sara Beth Haring, and Laura Clark. (What a team!) And Samantha Shea of Georges Borchardt remains the best agent an author could ask for.

But again: writing a book during a pandemic is a feat that requires a village. Which is why I'd like to especially thank the friends who kept my sanity during this year unlike any other: Sam Woodard and Justin Young and Nick Farris for long nights of Catan; long discourses on love and baseball with Clement Uduk and Kyle Holmes and Matt Lawyue; Zoom calls with Rice friends who survived Atlantic City, and who helped me relive memories from Brown; evenings at Hibernia with Jillian Ann Rayfield, Talia Benamy, Blair Durst, Eric Doctor (and Vector), and Akshay

Dayal; stoop drinks with Amy Feran and Max Feil (and Ronan and Zoë); and confusion about wombats with Jeremy Blomberg, Crystal Vitagliano, and Matt and Maggie Sermont. I'd like to also specifically thank Joe Dwyer for lending his incomparable voice to the audio version of this book, and for his unceasing faith in the future of the Seattle Mariners. My brother, Norwood Michel, unfailingly answered my phone calls, and humored me whenever the memes I sent him didn't quite land. And my in-laws—Babu Ji and Ama Ji, Jaya and Jacob and Ari—offered their support every step of the way.

This book, however, is dedicated to a trio of figures who I spent more time leaning on than any others. It's for my father, Jules Michel, who sparked whatever initial backbone I've ever shown, who convinced me about the *rightness* of the work, and whose mantra—"focus, and execute"—has served me in whatever successes I've encountered. It's for my mother, Kathy Michel, whose energy, whose wry humor, and whose capacity for love and support cut through whatever doldrums the pandemic may have brought.

And it's for the woman who spent every day—every single day—of a pandemic by my side, as part of this deal of marriage. Versha Sharma is far more successful than I'll ever be—not least because she's the new editor-in-chief of *Teen Vogue*—and will remain out of my league forevermore. She pairs a bottomless well of love with an unceasing ability to navigate right from wrong in a way that awes, day in and day out, and that allows her to plant herself and say, "No, you move." (And not only when I'm in her way in our small apartment.) I'll be working forevermore to be worth the support, and to earn the love, she's shown—even if it just means watching *Schitt's Creek* for the fifth time with her.

Sha: You're simply the best.

NOTES

PROLOGUE: TOO BIG TO SEE

1. **Sources for "Kleptocracy by the Numbers":** James S. Henry, "Taxing Tax Havens," *Foreign Affairs*, 12 April 2016, https://www.foreignaffairs.com/articles/panama/2016-04-12/taxing-tax-havens; UN FACTI Panel Report, February 2021, https://www.factipanel.org/; "New Report on Unrecorded Capital Flight Finds Developing Countries Are Net-Creditors to the Rest of the World," Global Financial Integrity, 5 December 2016, https://gfintegrity.org/press-release/new-report-on-unrecorded-capital-flight-finds-developing-countries-are-net-creditors-to-the-rest-of-the-world/; Claire Provost, "Foreign Aid Reaches Record High," *Guardian*, 8 April 2014, https://www.theguardian.com/global-development/2014/apr/08/foreign-aid-spending-developing-countries; Brett Melson, "Delaware's 2019 Corporate Annual Report Just Released," DelawareInc, 4 August 2020, https://www.delawareinc.com/blog/delaware-releases-annual-report-companies-formed/; Robert Frank, Louise Connelly, and Scott Zamost, "Billionaire Divorce Uncovers Secretive World of Trusts in South Dakota," CNBC, 6 May 2020, www.cnbc.com/2020/05/06/how-marie-and-cd-bosarges-divorce-spotlights-south-dakotas-asset-trusts.html; "FinCEN Reissues Real Estate Geographic Targeting Orders for 12 Metropolitan Areas," 15 May 2019, https://www.fincen.gov/news/news-releases/fincen-reissues-real-estate-geographic-targeting-orders-12-metropolitan-areas; Thomas Frank, "Secret Money: How Trump Made Millions Selling Condos to Unknown Buyers," *Buzzfeed*, 12 January 2018, https://www.buzzfeednews.com/article/thomasfrank/secret-money-how-trump-made-millions-selling-condos-to; While the Cayman Islands are the most secretive financial jurisdiction, just beating out the U.S., the Caymans remain but a single territory—as opposed to an entire country like the U.S. "Financial Secrecy Index 2020 Reports Progress on Global Transparency—but Backsliding from US, Cayman and UK Prompts Call for Sanctions," Tax Justice Network, 18 February 2020, https://www.taxjustice.net/press/financial-secrecy-index

-2020-reports-progress-on-global-transparency-but-backsliding-from-us-cayman -and-uk-prompts-call-for-sanctions/. For the sake of disclosure, I have worked in the past with the Financial Transparency Coalition, of which the Tax Justice Network is a member. Michael Lewis, *The Money Culture* (New York: W. W. Norton, 2011).

2. Interview with author.

3. "Equatorial Guinea's 'God,'" BBC, 26 July 2003, http://news.bbc.co.uk/2/hi/africa /3098007.stm.

4. Jason Sharman, *The Despot's Guide to Wealth Management* (Ithaca, NY: Cornell University Press, 2017).

5. Interview with author.

6. Interview with author.

7. Michelle Jarboe, "The Most Important Guy You've Never Heard of: Chaim Schochet, 25, Builds Downtown Cleveland Empire," *Cleveland Plain Dealer*, 5 February 2012, https://www.cleveland.com/business/2012/02/the_most_important_guy_youve_n .html.

8. "Huntington Building," Encyclopedia of Cleveland History, https://case.edu/ech /articles/h/huntington-building.

9. The details of Schochet's business practices were shared with the author by those familiar with Schochet's operations.

10. Anne Trubek, "How Did Alleged Ukrainian Money Launderers Buy Up Downtown Cleveland?," *Belt Magazine*, 14 January 2020, https://beltmag.com/ukrainian-money -laundering-cleveland/.

11. Jarboe, "The Most Important Guy You've Never Heard of: Chaim Schochet, 25, Builds Downtown Cleveland Empire."

12. Graham Stack, "Oligarchs Weaponized Cyprus Branch of Ukraine's Largest Bank to Send $5.5 Billion Abroad," OCCRP, 19 April 2019, https://www.occrp.org/en/investigations /oligarchs-weaponized-cyprus-eranch-of-ukraines-largest-bank-to-send-5-billion -abroad.

13. Interview with author.

14. Interview with author.

15. Peter Cotorceanu, "Why America Loves Being the World's No. 1 Tax Haven," *Politico*, 8 April 2016, https://www.politico.com/magazine/story/2016/04/panama-papers -america-tax-haven-213800.

16. Global Financial Integrity, "New Report on Unrecorded Capital Flight Finds Developing Countries Are Net-Creditors to the Rest of the World."

17. World Bank GDP calculator, https://data.worldbank.org/indicator/NY.GDP.MKTP .CD.

18. Mark Anderson, "Foreign Aid Close to Record Peak After Donors Spend $135bn in 2014," *Guardian*, 8 April 2015, https://www.theguardian.com/global-development/2015 /apr/08/foreign-aid-spending-2014-least-developed-countries.

19. "Revealed: Global Super-Rich Has at Least $21 Trillion Hidden in Secret Tax Havens,"

Tax Justice Network, 22 July 2012, https://www.taxjustice.net/cms/upload/pdf/The
_Price_of_Offshore_Revisited_Presser_120722.pdf.

20. Libby Nelson, "A Top Expert on Tax Havens Explains Why the Panama Papers Barely
Scratch the Surface," *Vox*, 8 April 2016, https://www.vox.com/2016/4/8/11371712
/panama-papers-tax-haven-zucman.

21. Zack Beauchamp, "How Donald Trump's Kleptocracy Is Undermining American Democracy," *Vox*, 31 July 2017, https://www.vox.com/world/2017/7/31/15959970/donald
-trump-authoritarian-children-corruption.

22. Ann Telnaes, "No to the Trump Kleptocracy," *Washington Post*, 3 July 2019, https://
www.washingtonpost.com/opinions/2019/07/03/no-trump-kleptocracy/.

23. Franklin Foer, "Russian-Style Kleptocracy Is Infiltrating America," *Atlantic*, March 2019,
https://www.theatlantic.com/magazine/archive/2019/03/how-kleptocracy-came-to
-america/580471/.

24. Oliver Bullough, "The Origins of Modern Kleptocracy," National Endowment for Democracy, 9 January 2018, https://www.power3point0.org/2018/01/09/the-origins-of
-modern-kleptocracy/.

PART 1: STATIONARY BANDITS

1. Lil Dicky, "$ave Dat Money," https://genius.com/Lil-dicky-ave-dat-money-lyrics.

CHAPTER 1: THE SOLE MIRACLE

1. "Secret Life of a Shopaholic," Global Witness, 17 November 2009, https://www
.globalwitness.org/en/campaigns/corruption-and-money-laundering/banks/secret
-life-shopaholic/.

2. Interview with author.

3. Peter Maass, "A Touch of Crude," *Mother Jones*, January/February 2005, https://www
.motherjones.com/politics/2005/01/obiang-equatorial-guinea-oil-riggs/.

4. Interview with author.

5. BBC, "Equatorial Guinea's 'God.'"

6. Rafiq Copeland, "Africa's Worst Dictator," ABC, 14 February 2011, https://www.abc
.net.au/news/2011-02-15/dictatorcopeland/44114.

7. Interview with author.

8. "Secret Life of a Shopaholic."

9. Ken Silverstein, "U.S. Government Documents Crime Spree by Dictator's Son: Why
No Action by the Feds?," *Harper's*, 16 November 2009, https://harpers.org/2009/11/us
-government-documents-crime-spree-by-dictators-son-why-no-action-by-the-feds/.

10. "Secret Life of a Shopaholic."

11. Silverstein, "U.S. Government Documents Crime Spree by Dictator's Son: Why No
Action by the Feds?"

12. Ibid.

13. Interview with author.

14. Interview with author.

15. Melissa Mittelman, "The Resource Curse," *Bloomberg*, 19 May 2017, https://www .bloomberg.com/quicktake/resource-curse.

16. Tim McDonnell, "Bribes, Favors, and a Billion-Dollar Yacht: Inside the Crazy World of the Men Who Do Oil Companies' Dirty Work," *Mother Jones*, 14 May 2014, https:// www.motherjones.com/environment/2014/05/exxon-chevron-oil-fixers-silverstein/.

17. "United States of America vs. One Michael Jackson Signed Thriller Jacket and Other Michael Jackson Memorabilia; Real Property Located on Sweetwater Mesa Road in Malibu, California; One 2011 Ferrari 599 GTO," https://www.courtlistener.com/recap /gov.uscourts.cacd.578550.1.0.pdf.

18. Jose Maria Irujo, "The High Price of Doing Business in Equatorial Guinea," *El País*, 3 April 2013, https://english.elpais.com/elpais/2013/04/03/inenglish/1365000844_044894 .html.

19. "United States of America vs. One Michael Jackson Signed Thriller Jacket and Other Michael Jackson Memorabilia; Real Property Located on Sweetwater Mesa Road in Malibu, California; One 2011 Ferrari 599 GTO."

20. Ibid.

21. Irujo, "The High Price of Doing Business in Equatorial Guinea."

22. "United States of America vs. One Michael Jackson Signed Thriller Jacket and Other Michael Jackson Memorabilia; Real Property Located on Sweetwater Mesa Road in Malibu, California; One 2011 Ferrari 599 GTO."

23. Ibid.

24. Interview with author.

25. Angelique Chrisafis, "Son of Equatorial Guinea's President Is Convicted of Corruption in France," *Guardian*, 27 October 2017, https://www.theguardian.com/world/2017 /oct/27/son-of-equatorial-guineas-president-convicted-of-corruption-in-france.

CHAPTER 2: WHY NOT DO AS THE AMERICANS DO?

1. Marcus Walsh-Fuhring, "The Panama Papers: Breaking the Story of How the Rich and Powerful Hide Their Money," *International Affairs*, Oxford University Press, May 2018, https://academic.oup.com/ia/article-abstract/94/3/671/4992408.

2. "Anonymous Companies," Global Financial Integrity, https://gfintegrity.org/issue /anonymous-companies/.

3. L. J. Davis, "Delaware Inc.," *New York Times*, 5 June 1988, https://www.nytimes.com /1988/06/05/magazine/delaware-inc.html.

4. Ibid.

5. Ibid.

6. Ibid.

7. "Beneficial Ownership," Financial Transparency Coalition, https://financialtransparency .org/issues/beneficial-ownership/.

8. Melanie Hicken and Blake Ellis, "These U.S. Companies Hide Drug Dealers, Mobsters

and Terrorists," CNN, 9 December 2015, https://money.cnn.com/2015/12/09/news/shell-companies-crime/index.html.

9. "The Typology of Modern Slavery: Defining Sex and Labor Trafficking in the United States," Polaris, 1 March 2017, https://polarisproject.org/massage-parlor-trafficking/.

10. Max de Haldevang, "How the Family of Vladimir Putin's US-Sanctioned Ally Uses British Companies to Burnish Its Reputation," *Quartz*, 26 July 2017, https://qz.com/1037549/how-the-family-of-vladimir-putins-us-sanctioned-ally-uses-british-companies-to-burnish-its-reputation/.

11. James Kirchick, "Back to Basics," *New Republic*, 27 January 2011, https://newrepublic.com/article/82258/kyrgyzstan-crisis-us.

12. Emily Marie Halter, Robert Mansour Harrison, Ji Won Park, J. C. Sharman, and Emile van der Does de Willebois, "The Puppet Masters: How the Corrupt Use Legal Structures to Hide Stolen Assets and What to Do About It," World Bank, 3 November 2011, https://documents.worldbank.org/en/publication/documents-reports/documentdetail/784961468152973030/the-puppet-masters-how-the-corrupt-use-legal-structures-to-hide-stolen-assets-and-what-to-do-about-it.

13. Michael Findley, Daniel Nielson, and J. C. Sharman, *Global Shell Games* (London: Cambridge University Press, 2014).

14. James Rufus Koren, "How Disney Used Shell Companies to Start Its Magic Kingdom," *Los Angeles Times*, 9 April 2016, https://www.latimes.com/business/la-fi-disney-shell-companies-20160408-story.html.

15. Findley, Nielson, and Sharman, *Global Shell Games*.

16. Tom Burgis, "The Secret Scheme to Skim Millions off Central Asia's Pipeline Megaproject," *Financial Times*, 3 December 2020, https://www.ft.com/content/80f25f82-5f21-4a56-b2bb-7a48e61dd9c6.

17. Luke Harding, "Revealed: The $2bn Offshore Trail That Leads to Vladimir Putin," *Guardian*, 3 April 2016, https://www.theguardian.com/news/2016/apr/03/panama-papers-money-hidden-offshore.

18. Zheping Huang, "China's Elite—Including Xi Jinping—Are Linked to Offshore Deals That Hid Millions of Dollars," *Quartz*, 4 April 2016, https://qz.com/653836/chinas-elite-including-xi-jinping-are-linked-to-offshore-deals-that-hid-millions-of-dollars/.

19. Barbara Demick, "The Times, Bloomberg News, and the Richest Man in China," *New Yorker*, 5 May 2015, https://www.newyorker.com/news/news-desk/how-not-to-get-kicked-out-of-china.

20. Katie Benner, "North Koreans Accused of Laundering $2.5 Billion for Nuclear Program," *New York Times*, 24 June 2020, https://www.nytimes.com/2020/05/28/us/politics/north-korea-money-laundering-nuclear-weapons.html.

21. Pete Schroeder, "U.S. Congress Bans Anonymous Shell Companies," Reuters, 11 December 2020, https://www.reuters.com/article/us-usa-congress-banks/u-s-congress-bans-anonymous-shell-companies-idUSKBN28L2NV.

22. Findley, Nielson, and Sharman, *Global Shell Games*.

23. Ibid.

24. Bizarrely, the World Bank Doing Business Index rewards those who can set up

companies as quickly as possible—regardless of things like due diligence or who the company might actually be for. See: https://www.doingbusiness.org/en/methodology /starting-a-business. Special thanks to Eric Hontz for highlighting this issue.

25. Suzanne Barlyn, "Special Report: How Delaware Kept America Safe for Corporate Secrecy," Reuters, 24 August 2016, https://www.reuters.com/article/us-usa-delaware -bullock-specialreport/special-report-how-delaware-kept-america-safe-for-corporate -secrecy-idUSKCN10Z1OH.

26. Lucy Komisar, "Shells, Shams and Corporate Scams," *American Interest*, 1 January 2011, https://www.the-american-interest.com/2011/01/01/shells-shams-and-corporate -scams/.

27. Casey Michel, "How to Stop Kleptocrats from Stashing Their Cash in America," *New Republic*, 18 September 2019, https://newrepublic.com/article/155100/stop-kleptocrats -stashing-cash-america.

28. Findley, Nielson, and Sharman, *Global Shell Games*.

29. Sharman, *The Despot's Guide to Wealth Management*.

30. Interview with author.

31. Findley, Nielson, and Sharman, *Global Shell Games*.

32. "The Constitution of the United States: A Transcription," National Archives, https:// www.archives.gov/founding-docs/constitution-transcript.

33. Findley, Nielson, and Sharman, *Global Shell Games*.

34. "National Strategy for Combating Terrorist and Other Illicit Financing," U.S. Treasury Department, 2020, https://home.treasury.gov/system/files/136/National-Strategy-to -Counter-Illicit-Financev2.pdf.

35. Max de Haldevang, "The US Defense Department Lost $875 Million to Scams Involv- ing Shell Companies," *Quartz*, 27 November 2019, https://qz.com/1755722/defense -department-has-lost-875-million-to-shell-company-scams/.

36. David Voreacos and Neil Weinberg, "How the Pentagon Gets Duped by Contractors Using Shell Companies," *Los Angeles Times*, 8 January 2020, https://www.latimes.com /business/story/2020-01-08/pentagon-shell-companies.

37. "National Money Laundering Risk Assessment," U.S. Treasury Department, 2015, https:// home.treasury.gov/system/files/246/National-Money-Laundering-Risk-Assessment-06 -12-2015.pdf.

CHAPTER 3: CONTROL EVERYTHING, OWN NOTHING

1. Kelly Carr and Brian Grow, "Special Report: A Little House of Secrets on the Great Plains," Reuters, 28 June 2011, https://www.reuters.com/article/oukwd-uk-usa-shell -companies-idAFTRE75R22L20110628.

2. Davis, "Delaware Inc."

3. Susan Pace Hamill, "The Story of LLCs: Combining the Best Features of a Flawed Business Tax Structure," *Business Tax Stories*, Foundation Press, 2005, https://www.law .ua.edu/misc/hamill/Chapter%2010—Business%20Tax%20Stories%20(Foundation) .pdf.

4. Ibid.
5. Ibid.
6. "Standard Oil," Encyclopedia Brittanica, https://www.britannica.com/topic/Standard-Oil.
7. Davis, "Delaware Inc."
8. *American Law Review* 33 (St. Louis: Review Publishing, 1899), 419.
9. "Tax Competition and the Race to the Bottom," Tax Justice Network, https://www.taxjustice.net/topics/tax-competition-and-the-race-to-the-bottom/.
10. Hamill, "The Story of LLCs: Combining the Best Features of a Flawed Business Tax Structure."
11. *American Law Review* 33, 419.
12. Nicholas Shaxson, *Treasure Islands* (New York: Palgrave Macmillan, 2012).
13. Davis, "Delaware Inc."
14. "Court of Chancery," https://courts.delaware.gov/chancery/.
15. Lacian Arye Bebchuk and Assaf Hamdani, "Vigorous Race or Leisurely Walk: Reconsidering the Competition over Corporate Charters," *Yale Law Journal*, 21 November 2002, https://www.yalelawjournal.org/pdf/383_m98yapvk.pdf.
16. "How the U.S.A. Became a Secrecy Jurisdiction," Tax Justice Network, 27 November 2015, https://www.taxjustice.net/2015/11/27/how-the-u-s-a-became-a-secrecy-jurisdiction-2/.
17. Leslie Wayne, "How Delaware Thrives as a Corporate Tax Haven," *New York Times*, 30 June 2012, https://www.nytimes.com/2012/07/01/business/how-delaware-thrives-as-a-corporate-tax-haven.html.
18. Neil MacFarquhar, "After Centuries of Obscurity, Wilmington Is Having a Moment," *New York Times*, 19 January 2021, https://www.nytimes.com/2020/12/06/us/after-centuries-of-obscurity-wilmington-is-having-a-moment.html.
19. Ibid.
20. Melson, "Delaware's 2019 Corporate Annual Report Just Released."
21. Casey Michel, "The United States of Anonymity," Hudson Institute, 3 November 2017, https://www.hudson.org/research/13981-the-united-states-of-anonymity.
22. "Expedited Serices," Delaware Division of Corporations, https://corp.delaware.gov/expserv/9.
23. Wayne, "How Delaware Thrives as a Corporate Tax Haven."
24. Chuck Collins, *The Wealth Hoarders: How Billionaires Pay Millions to Hide Trillions* (Cambridge: Polity Press, 2021).
25. "Asset Protection for Non-Resident Aliens," DelawareInc.com, https://www.delawareinc.com/asset-protection/non-resident-aliens/.
26. Christopher Bruner, *Re-Imagining Offshore Finance* (London: Oxford University Press, 2016).
27. Bryce Tuttle, "Laboratories of Secrecy: Why Some U.S. States Have Sold Their Sovereignty to Criminals and Kleptocrats," Stanford University, 2020, https://www.academia.edu/43705473/LABORATORIES_OF_SECRECY_Why_Some_U_S_States_Have_Sold_Their_Sovereignty_to_Criminals_and_Kleptocrats.

28. "Viktor Bout, Who Inspired the Movie Lord of War, Has Been Sentenced to 25 Years Prison," AAP, 6 April 2012, https://www.news.com.au/world/viktor-bout-who-inspired-the-movie-lord-of-war-has-been-sentenced-to-25-years-prison/news-story/691a9c826ce4c95d737e579b2a8399ab.

29. "'Merchant of Death' Viktor Bout Sentenced to 25 Years," BBC, 6 April 2012, https://www.bbc.com/news/world-us-canada-17634050.

30. Lynnley Browning, "Delaware Laws, Helpful to Arms Trafficker, to Be Scrutinized," New York Times, 4 November 2009, https://www.nytimes.com/2009/11/05/business/05tax.html.

31. Adam Duvernay and Matthew Albright, "Panama Papers Could Cast Shadow on Delaware," News Journal, 9 April 2016, https://www.delawareonline.com/story/news/local/2016/04/09/panama-papers-could-cast-shadow-delaware/82670000/.

32. Leslie Wayne, "Anti-Shell Corporation Bill Gets Support from Unlikely US State," ICIJ, 3 September 2014, https://www.icij.org/inside-icij/2014/09/anti-shell-corporation-bill-gets-support-unlikely-us-state/.

33. Wayne, "How Delaware Thrives as a Corporate Tax Haven."

34. Mihai Munteanu, "Laszlo Kiss—The Offshore Master," OCCRP, 20 November 2010, https://www.reportingproject.net/offshore/index.php/laszlo-kiss-undercover-with-a-master.

35. Casey Michel, "America Is Importing Corruption. Here's How to Stop It," Washington Post, 9 November 2017, https://www.washingtonpost.com/news/democracy-post/wp/2017/11/09/america-is-importing-corruption-heres-how-to-stop-it//.

36. "Facts and Myths," Delaware Corporate Law, https://corplaw.delaware.gov/facts-and-myths/#:~:text=In%202012%2C%20Delaware's%20Secretary%20of,companies%20or%20anonymity%20and%20secrecy.&text=In%20short%2C%20Delaware%20is%20not,or%20the%20United%20States%20itself.

37. Nick Baumann and Brett Brownell, "Paul Ryan: 'Let's Make This Country a Tax Shelter' (VIDEO)," Mother Jones, 5 October 2012, https://www.motherjones.com/politics/2012/10/paul-ryan-lets-make-country-tax-shelter-video/.

38. J. Weston Phippen, "Nevada, a Tax Haven for Only $174," Atlantic, 6 April 2016, https://www.theatlantic.com/national/archive/2016/04/panama-papers-nevada/476994/.

39. Interview with author.

40. Interview with author.

41. As the state museum in Carson City also explains, Nevada even perfected the art of "divorce mills" for those in the early twentieth century looking to end their marriages at minimal cost, attracting thousands of despondent spouses from across the country before the U.S. liberalized its divorce laws. See the Nevada State Museum website at https://www.carsonnvmuseum.org/.

42. Tim Johnson, "Expecting Rules to Tighten Around Shell Companies After Panama Papers? Not Likely," McClatchy, 1 August 2016, https://www.mcclatchydc.com/news/nation-world/national/article92679482.html.

43. Phippen, "Nevada, a Tax Haven for Only $174."

44. Interview with author.

45. "Despite Connection to Panama Papers Nevada Likely to Remain Tax Haven," *Las Vegas Review-Journal*, 7 August 2016, https://www.reviewjournal.com/local/local-nevada/despite-connection-to-panama-papers-nevada-likely-to-remain-tax-haven/.

46. Interview with author.

47. Interview with author.

48. Steve Reilly, "Dozens of Firms Creating Foreign-Based Shell Companies in Two U.S. States," *USA Today*, 26 May 2016, https://www.usatoday.com/story/news/2016/05/26/dozens-firms-creating-foreign-based-shell-companies-two-us-states/84222480/.

49. Casey Michel, "The U.S. Is a Good Place for Bad People to Stash Their Money," *Atlantic*, 13 July 2017, https://www.theatlantic.com/business/archive/2017/07/us-anonymous-shell-companies/531996/.

50. It's worth noting that the American model of anonymous shell companies, seen most explicitly in Delaware, didn't only serve as inspiration for other states. It also served as inspiration for other non-American territories, and even other *countries*. Among those inspired by the American model to craft their own offshoring services sector were Panama, the British Virgin Islands, Niue, and Nevis. For more, see: Vanessa Ogle, "Archipelago Capitalism: Tax Havens, Offshore Money, and the State, 1950s–1970s," *American Historical Review* 122, no. 5 (December 2017): 1431–58, https://law.unimelb.edu.au/__data/assets/pdf_file/0008/3054536/Vanessa-Ogle-Archipelago-Capitalism-AHR-Dec-2017.pdf.

51. NBI, https://www.nevadaincorporate.com/.

52. Incorporate123, https://incorporate123.co/about-us/.

53. Incorporate123, https://incorporate123.co/asset-protection/offshore-asset-protection/

54. Incorporate123, https://incorporate123.co/about-us/.

55. Reilly, "Dozens of Firms Creating Foreign-Based Shell Companies in Two U.S. States."

56. "Giant Leak of Offshore Financial Records Exposes Global Array of Crime and Corruption," ICIJ, 3 April 2016, https://www.icij.org/investigations/panama-papers/20160403-panama-papers-global-overview/.

57. Tim Johnson, "Anger over Panama Papers Roils Iceland, Pakistan," *McClatchy*, 6 April 2016, https://www.mcclatchydc.com/news/nation-world/national/article70102342.html.

58. "Panama Papers Firm Has Nevada Ties," *Reno Gazette-Journal*, 6 April 2016, https://www.rgj.com/story/news/2016/04/06/panama-papers-firm-has-nevada-ties/82695166/.

59. "Nevada LLCs Feature—English," previously available at https://issuu.com/mossfon/docs/nevada_-_features_-_june_2012.

60. "Panama Papers Triggered Boom in US Tax-Shelter Business, Says Mossack Fonseca Boss," *South China Morning Post*, 21 April 2017, https://www.scmp.com/news/world/united-states-canada/article/2089524/panama-papers-triggered-boom-us-tax-shelter-business.

61. Steve Reilly, "Panama Papers: 1,000 Secret Nevada Firms, 2 Overseas Addresses," *USA*

Today, 7 April 2016, https://www.usatoday.com/story/news/2016/04/07/1000-secret
-nevada-firms-and-most-trace-2-overseas-addresses/82760186/.

62. Ibid.

63. Martha M. Hamilton, "Panamanian Law Firm Is Gatekeeper to Vast Flow of Murky
Offshore Secrets," OCCRP, 3 April 2016, https://www.icij.org/investigations/panama
-papers/20160403-mossack-fonseca-offshore-secrets/#:~:text=Panamanian%20
Law%20Firm%20Is%20Gatekeeper%20To%20Vast%20Flow%20of%20Murky%
20Offshore%20Secrets,-Files%20show%20client&text=Legal%20papers%20filed%20
in%20U.S.,of%20dollars%20from%20government%20contracts.

64. Shane Romig and Santiago Perez, "Hedge Fund Seeks Assets in Nevada in Battle over
Argentine Debt," *Wall Street Journal*, 7 April 2014, https://www.wsj.com/articles/SB1
0001424052702303847804579481762029605186.

65. Jake Bernstein, *Secrecy World* (New York: Picador, 2019).

66. Ibid.

67. Lucy Clarke-Billings, "Panama Papers: The Lowdown on Mossack Fonseca," *Newsweek*, 6 April 2016, https://www.newsweek.com/panama-papers-lowdown-mossack
-fonseca-444689#:~:text=The%20ICIJ%20also%20claims%20to,24%2C%202014%20
email%20allegedly%20read.

68. Hamill, "The Story of LLCs: Combining the Best Features of a Flawed Business Tax
Structure."

69. Interview with author.

70. Interview with author.

71. It's worth noting that the LLC is not Wyoming's only claim to a legacy of corruption.
The state was one of the central players in the Teapot Dome scandal—Teapot Dome
is located in central Wyoming—which, until Trump's arrival, served as the standard-
bearer for presidential-level corruption.

72. Interview with author.

73. Interview with author.

74. "How to Incorporate in Wyoming vs. How to Start a Wyoming LLC," Active Filings,
https://www.activefilings.com/information/state-requirements/wyoming/.

75. Interview with author.

76. Kevin G. Hall and Marisa Taylor, "US Scolds Others About Offshores, but Looks Other
Way at Home," *Miami Herald*, 12 April 2016, https://www.miamiherald.com/news
/nation-world/world/article70008302.html.

77. Interview with author.

78. Leslie Wayne, "A Ukrainian Kleptocrat Wants His Money and U.S. Asylum," *New York
Times*, 6 July 2016, https://www.nytimes.com/2016/07/07/business/international/a
-ukrainian-kleptocrat-wants-his-money-and-us-asylum.html.

79. "Former Ukrainian Prime Minister Sentenced to 97 Months in Prison Fined $9 Mil-
lion for Role in Laundering $30 Million of Extortion Proceeds," U.S. Attorney's Office,
Northern District of California, https://archives.fbi.gov/archives/sanfrancisco/press
-releases/2009/sf111909a.htm.

80. Ibid.

81. "Shell Game: 2,000 Firms Based in One Simple House," NPR, 2 July 2011, https://www.npr.org/2011/07/02/137573513/shell-game-2-000-firms-based-in-one-simple-house.

82. Carr and Grow, "Special Report: A Little House of Secrets on the Great Plains."

83. Casey Michel, "The US 'Offshore' Industry and the Eurasian Connection," *Eurasianet*, 14 April 2017, https://eurasianet.org/the-us-offshore-industry-and-the-eurasian-connection.

84. Jason Sharman, "For Research, We Pretended to Be Crooks and Terrorists and Tried to Buy Shell Companies. The Results Were Disturbing," *Washington Post*, 7 April 2016, https://www.washingtonpost.com/news/monkey-cage/wp/2016/04/07/for-research-we-pretended-to-be-crooks-and-terrorists-and-tried-to-buy-shell-companies-the-results-were-disturbing/.

85. Shaxson, *Treasure Islands*.

86. "Failure to Identify Company Owners Impedes Law Enforcement," Department of Justice, 14 November 2006, https://www.hsgac.senate.gov/imo/media/doc/STMTNashDOJ.pdf.

87. Carr and Grow, "Special Report: A Little House of Secrets on the Great Plains."

88. "Wyoming LLCs Feature—English," https://issuu.com/mossfon/docs/wyo_features_-june_2012.

89. Steve Reilly and Trevor Hughes, "Tiny Wyoming Office at Heart of Panama Papers Empire," *USA Today*, 6 April 2016, https://www.usatoday.com/story/news/2016/04/06/panama-papers-why-wyoming-hub-for-shell-companies/82697186/.

90. When the author visited Cheyenne, it was clear no city he'd visited prior shared a higher concentration of corporate services industries.

91. "24 Companies Identified in 'Panama Papers' Found Registered in Wyoming," *Powell Tribune*, 6 April 2016, https://www.powelltribune.com/stories/24-companies-identified-in-panama-papers-found-registered-in-wyoming,2396.

92. Laura Hancock, "Murray Confirms Wyoming Ties to Panama Papers," *Casper Star-Tribune*, 6 April 2016, https://trib.com/business/murray-confirms-wyoming-ties-to-panama-papers/article_14c6ac1c-5d68-59fb-b671-6fee0d513d25.html.

93. Michel, "The U.S. Is a Good Place for Bad People to Stash Their Money."

CHAPTER 4: NECK-DEEP

1. Misha Glenny, *McMafia* (New York: Vintage Books, 2008).

2. Max Seddon and Roman Olearchyk, "The Bank That Holds the Key to Ukraine's Future," *Financial Times*, 17 July 2019, https://www.ft.com/content/7dd9c784-a3e1-11e9-a282-2df48f366f7d.

3. Interview with author.

4. Interview with author.

5. Anders Aslund, "How Kolomoisky Does Business in the United States," Atlantic Council, 4 June 2019, https://www.atlanticcouncil.org/blogs/ukrainealert/how-kolomoisky-does-business-in-the-united-states.

6. Betsy Swan, "Billionaire Ukrainian Oligarch Ihor Kolomoisky Under Investigation by FBI," *Daily Beast*, 8 April 2019, https://www.thedailybeast.com/billionaire-ukrainian -oligarch-ihor-kolomoisky-under-investigation-by-fbi.

7. "Ihor Kolomoisky," Politically Exposed Persons, https://pep.org.ua/en/person/6790.

8. "Shareholder Profile: Ihor Kolomoisky, Riding Political Victory, Sets Sights on Privat-Bank," Debtwire, 30 May 2019, https://www.mergermarket.com/assets/Shareholder%20 Profile.pdf.

9. Ibid.

10. Ibid.

11. Alessandra Stanley, "Russian Banking Scandal Poses Threat to Future of Privatization," *New York Times*, 28 January 1996, https://www.nytimes.com/1996/01/28/world /russian-banking-scandal-poses-threat-to-future-of-privatization.html.

12. Luke Harding, "Boris Berezovsky: A Tale of Revenge, Betrayal and Feuds with Putin," *Guardian*, 23 March 2013, theguardian.com/world/2013/mar/23/boris-berezovsky -vladimir-putin-feud.

13. Serhiy Verlanov, "Taming Ukraine's Oligarchs," Atlantic Council, 19 November 2020, https://www.atlanticcouncil.org/blogs/ukrainealert/taming-ukraines-oligarchs/.

14. Philip Hanson, "Reiderstvo: Asset-Grabbing in Russia," Chatham House, 1 March 2014, https://www.chathamhouse.org/2014/03/reiderstvo-asset-grabbing-russia.

15. Melik Kaylan, "An Injection of Rule of Law for Ukrainian Business? Oligarch's Lawsuit Could Help Improve the Culture of Business Dealings in the Post Soviet Space," *Forbes*, 15 July 2013, https://www.forbes.com/sites/melikkaylan/2013/07/15/an-injection-of -rule-of-law-for-ukrainian-business-oligarchs-lawsuit-could-help-improve-the-culture -of-business-dealings-in-the-post-soviet-space/?sh=933174c4ebe8.

16. Ken Stier, "The Dangers of Doing Business Abroad," *Miami Herald*, 13 September 2017, https://www.miamiherald.com/news/business/biz-monday/article172421852 .html.

17. "Igor Kolomoisky Buys Studio 1+1 and Kino Channels for $300 Million," *Kyiv Post*, 21 January 2010, https://www.kyivpost.com/article/content/business/igor-kolomoisky -buys-studio-11-and-kino-channels-f-57626.html.

18. Neil Buckley, "Ukraine Takes Needed Steps to Clean Up Its Banks," *Financial Times*, 28 December 2016, https://www.ft.com/content/162c55a6-cc26–11e6–864f-20dcb35cede2.

19. Josh Kovensky and Natalie Vikhrov, "The Spectacular Rise and Fall of Ihor Kolomoisky's Steel Empire," *Kyiv Post*, 2 March 2017, https://www.kyivpost.com/ukraine -politics/spectacular-rise-fall-ihor-kolomoiskys-steel-empire.html.

20. Ibid.

21. "Manganese—It Turns Iron into Steel (and Does So Much More)," U.S. Geological Survey, August 2014, https://pubs.usgs.gov/fs/2014/3087/pdf/fs2014-3087.pdf.

22. "Mordechai Korf," Politically Exposed Persons, https://pep.org.ua/en/person/41354.

23. Molly Boigon, "They Gave $25 Million to Jewish Nonprofits. Was Some of That Money Laundered from Ukraine?," *Forward*, 21 February 2020, https://forward.com/news /longform/440219/florida-chabad-lubavitch-miami-charities-money-laundering-optima -schemes/.

24. Jessica Naiman, "Florida Jews Mark Half a Century of Chabad Activities," *Chabad .org News*, 22 February 2010, https://www.chabad.org/news/article_cdo/aid/1132205 /jewish/Florida-Chabads-Jubilee-Year.htm.

25. Interview with author.

26. Anshel Pfeffer, "Is This Man the Most Powerful Jew in the World?," *Haaretz*, 18 October 2014, https://www.haaretz.com/.premium-the-most-powerful-jew-in-the-world -1.5315512.

27. Interview with author.

28. Boigon, "They Gave $25 Million to Jewish Nonprofits. Was Some of That Money Laundered from Ukraine?"

29. Jarboe, "The Most Important Guy You've Never Heard of: Chaim Schochet, 25, Builds Downtown Cleveland Empire."

30. Interview with author.

31. Interview with author.

32. Johnny Joo, "Warren Steel: The Day the Machines Went Quiet," Architectural Afterlife, 13 November 2017, https://architecturalafterlife.com/2017/11/13/warren-steel/.

33. "Suit Filed over Warren Steel Holdings," *Tribune Chronicle*, 16 June 2015, https://www .tribtoday.com/news/local-news/2015/06/suit-filed-over-warren-steel-holdings/.

34. "Magistrate Says Lawsuit Can't Stop Warren Steel Sale," *Tribune Chronicle*, 19 July 2015, https://www.tribtoday.com/news/local-news/2015/07/magistrate-says-lawsuit -can-t-stop-warren-steel-sale/.

35. Kovensky and Vikhrov, "The Spectacular Rise and Fall of Ihor Kolomoisky's Steel Empire."

36. Lawrence Smith, "Suit Accuses Former Mason County Alloy Plant Owner of Racketeering," *West Virginia Record*, 9 October 2006, https://wvrecord.com/stories/510591065 -suit-accuses-former-mason-county-alloy plant-owner-of-racketeering.

37. Michael Sallah and Tanya Kozyreva, "With Deutsche Bank's Help, an Oligarch's Buying Spree Trails Ruin Across the US Heartland," ICIJ, 22 September 2020, https://www .icij.org/investigations/fincen-files/with-deutsche-banks-help-an-oligarchs-buying -spree-trails-ruin-across-the-us-heartland/?fbclid=IwAR0Y8mtWj6wslh6D1wqlWx fuE4miDSwyy1rUI-cDsFILydfKrzYG60DhVDI.

38. "Optima Specialty Steel Acquires KES Acquisition Co. for $112.5M," *South Florida Business Journal*, 20 November 2012, https://www.bizjournals.com/southflorida/news /2012/11/20/optima-specialty-steel-acquires-kes.html.

39. "Kentucky: 2010," U.S. Census Bureau, https://www.census.gov/prod/cen2010/cph-2 -19.pdf.

40. "CC Metals and Alloys, LLC Is Shutting Down Its Operations on July 1 Due to Poor Market Conditions," *Businesswire*, 24 June 2020, https://www.businesswire.com/news /home/20200624005217/en/CC-Metals-and-Alloys-LLC-is-Shutting-Down-its -Operations-on-July-1-Due-to-Poor-Market-Conditions, and see PrivatBank filing against Kolomoisky here: https://www.atlanticcouncil.org/wp-content/uploads/2019 /06/kolomoisky_case.pdf.

41. "Shareholder Profile: Ihor Kolomoisky, Riding Political Victory, Sets Sights on PrivatBank."

42. Interview with author.

43. Interview with author.

44. Interview with author.

45. Jarboe, "The Most Important Guy You've Never Heard of: Chaim Schochet, 25, Builds Downtown Cleveland Empire."

46. Ibid.

47. Ibid.

48. Interview with author.

49. Interview with author.

50. Jarboe, "The Most Important Guy You've Never Heard of: Chaim Schochet, 25, Builds Downtown Cleveland Empire."

51. Interview with author.

CHAPTER 5: SLAP IN THE FACE

1. Laton McCartney, *The Teapot Dome Scandal* (New York: Random House, 2009).

2. Casey Michel and Ricardo Soares de Oliveira, "The Dictator-Run Bank That Tells the Story of America's Foreign Corruption," *Foreign Policy*, 7 July 2020, https://foreignpolicy .com/2020/07/07/the-dictator-run-bank-that-tells-the-story-of-americas-foreign -corruption/.

3. Peter Truell and Larry Gurwin, *False Profits: The Inside Story of BCCI, the World's Most Corrupt Financial Empire* (New York: Houghton Mifflin, 1992).

4. Ibid.

5. Sharon Walsh, "Altman Trial Starts with a Bang, Winds Down to a Whimper," *Washington Post*, 26 July 1993, https://www.washingtonpost.com/archive/business/1993 /07/26/altman-trial-starts-with-a-bang-winds-down-to-a-whimper/1fd4dc44-3e6e -4672-9eac-fa1d3310def9/.

6. Truell and Gurwin, *False Profits*.

7. "Bank Secrecy Act," IRS, https://www.irs.gov/businesses/small-businesses-self-employed /bank-secrecy-act.

8. Interview with author.

9. "History of Anti-Money Laundering Laws," FinCEN, https://www.fincen.gov/history -anti-money-laundering-laws.

10. "Role of U.S. Correspondent Banking in International Money Laundering," Volume 1, U.S. Senate, 1, 2, and 6 March 2001, https://www.govinfo.gov/content/pkg/CHRG -107shrg71166/html/CHRG-107shrg71166.htm.

11. "Suspicious Activity Reports (SAR)," Office of the Comptroller of the Currency, https://www.occ.treas.gov/topics/supervision-and-examination/bank-operations /financial-crime/suspicious-activity-reports/index-suspicious-activity-reports .html.

12. "Secret Life of a Shopaholic."

13. Zia and BCCI's leadership were so close that it was "almost surprising that [Zia] himself

didn't get a job with the bank," Truell and Gurwin later wrote—though Zia's son did end up getting a job as vice president with Bank of America, which was one of BCCI's American partners. See Truell and Gurwin, *False Profits*.

14. Interview with author.

15. Truell and Gurwin, *False Profits*.

16. Interview with author.

17. "History of the FATF," FATF, https://www.fatf-gafi.org/about/historyofthefatf/.

18. "What Is Money Laundering?," FATF, https://www.fatf-gafi.org/faq/moneylaundering/.

19. Interview with author.

20. Glenny, *McMafia*.

21. Martine Millet-Einbinder, "Writing Off Tax Deductibility," *OECD Observer*, https://web.archive.org/web/20140415154109/https://oecdobserver.org/news/archivestory.php/aid/245/Writing_off_tax_deductibility_.html.

22. The PSI was an outgrowth of broader mid-twentieth-century anticorruption and antiembezzlement investigations, beginning with the Teapot Dome saga, the greatest pre-Trump corruption scandal in American history. As the Supreme Court had found in one of the cases stemming from the Teapot Dome corruption investigations, "the power of inquiry—with process to enforce it—is an essential and appropriate auxiliary to the legislative function." In other words: high-level investigations remained firmly in Congress's writ, regardless of whom the corruption involved logic that eventually launched the PSI some 20 years later. See "Source of the Power to Investigate," Cornell Law School Legal Information Institute, https://www.law.cornell.edu/constitution-conan/article-1/section-1/source-of-the-power-to-investigate.

23. Kelsey Snell, "Corporate World Won't Miss Levin," *Politico*, 11 September 2014, https://www.politico.com/story/2014/09/corporate-america-exhales-carl-levin-110832.

24. "Permanent Subcommittee on Investigations Historical Background," U.S. Senate, 1 December 2000, https://www.hsgac.senate.gov/subcommittees/investigations/media/permanent-subcommittee-on-investigations-historical-background#:~:text=Permanent%20Subcommittee%20on%20Investigations%20Historical%20Background&text=The%20Permanent%20Subcommittee%20on%20Investigations,Expenditures%20in%20the%20Executive%20Departments.

25. David Cay Johnston, "The Legacy of Carl Levin," *American Prospect*, 30 December 2014, https://prospect.org/power/legacy-carl-levin/.

26. Interview with author.

27. Interview with author.

28. Julia Preston, "Mexican Plot: Salinas Family, Swiss Bank and $84 Million," *New York Times*, 25 November 1995, https://www.nytimes.com/1995/11/25/world/mexican-plot-salinas-family-swiss-bank-and-84-million.html.

29. Anne Swardson, "Swiss Call Salinas a Drug Profiteer, Seize Bank Funds," *Washington Post*, 21 October 1998, https://www.washingtonpost.com/archive/politics/1998/10/21/swiss-call-salinas-a-drug-profiteer-seize-bank-funds/18b5a5cb-4b42-482c-a3bc-05ed916ebd27//.

30. Michael Allen, "Citibank Broke Own Laundering Code in Salinas Matter, GAO Report Finds," *Wall Street Journal*, 4 December 1998, https://www.wsj.com/articles /SB91274067751059000.

31. "Private Banking and Money Laundering: A Case Study of Opportunities and Vulnerabilities," U.S. Senate, 9–10 November 1999, https://www.govinfo.gov/content/pkg /CHRG-106shrg61699/html/CHRG-106shrg61699.htm.

32. Laurie Hays, "How Citicorp's Amy Elliott Served Mexico's Raul Salinas," *Wall Street Journal*, 1 November 1996, https://www.wsj.com/articles/SB846798978902024000.

33. Julia Preston and Peter Truell, "Pen in Hand, Raul Salinas Denies Murder and Theft," *New York Times*, 31 October 1997, https://www.nytimes.com/1997/10/31/world/pen -in-hand-raul-salinas-denies-murder-and-theft.html.

34. Elise Bean, *Financial Exposure* (New York: Palgrave, 2018).

35. Ibid.

36. Interview with author.

37. "Opening Statement of Senator Carl Levin Before the U.S. Senate Permanent Subcommittee on Investigations Hearing on the Role of Correspondent Banking in Money Laundering," 2 March 2001, https://www.hsgac.senate.gov/imo/media/doc /levin030201.pdf.

38. Truell and Gurwin, *False Profits*.

39. Raymond Baker, "Transparency First," *American Interest*, 1 July 2010, https://www .the-american-interest.com/2010/07/01/transparency-first/.

40. Bean, *Financial Exposure*.

41. Carl Levin, *Getting to the Heart of the Matter* (Detroit: Wayne State University Press, 2021).

42. Interview with author.

43. Glenny, *McMafia*.

44. "Prepared Testimony of the Honorable Carl Levin (D-MI) United States Senator," 26 September 2001, https://fas.org/irp/congress/2001_hr/092601_levin.html.

45. Interview with author.

46. Interview with author.

47. Glenny, *McMafia*.

48. Baker, "Transparency First."

49. Ibid.

50. Raymond Baker, *Capitalism's Achilles Heel* (New York: Wiley, 2005).

51. Bean, *Financial Exposure*.

52. "USA Patriot Act," FinCEN, https://www.fincen.gov/resources/statutes-regulations /usa-patriot-act.

53. Bean, *Financial Exposure*.

54. Baker, "Transparency First."

55. "Financial Crimes Enforcement Network; Anti-Money Laundering Program Requirements for 'Persons Involved in Real Estate Closings and Settlements,'" U.S. Treasury Department, https://www.treasury.gov/press-center/press-releases/Documents /js1751.pdf.

56. *Federal Register*, Volume 68, No. 69, 10 April 2003, https://www.fincen.gov/sites
/default/files/shared/352_real_estate_04102003.pdf.

57. "Exempted Anti-Money Laundering Programs for Certain Financial Institutions,"
U.S. Treasury Department, https://www.govinfo.gov/content/pkg/CFR-2010-title31
-vol1/pdf/CFR-2010-title31-vol1-sec103-170.pdf.

PART II: LIFESTYLES OF THE RICH AND FAMOUS

1. "One Year After the Panama Papers: Progress on Anonymous Corporate Ownership?,"
Brookings Institution, 30 March 2017, https://www.brookings.edu/wp-content/uploads
/2017/04/20170330_panama_papers_transcript.pdf.

CHAPTER 6: SCOOPING CAVIAR WITH A SHOVEL

1. Interview with author.

2. Glenn R. Simpson, "Riggs Bank Had Longstanding Link to the CIA," *Wall Street Journal*, 31 December 2004, https://www.wsj.com/articles/SB110444413126413199.

3. Emma Brown, "Joe L. Allbritton, Communications Giant Who Led Riggs Bank into Dis-
repute, Dies at 87," *Washington Post*, 12 December 2012, https://www.washingtonpost
.com/local/obituaries/joe-l-allbritton-communications-giant-who-led-riggs-bank into
-disrepute-dies-at-87/2012/12/12/60f8d964-d647-11df-8fa3-6531f2b9c12b_story.html.

4. Interview with author.

5. Terence O'Hara, "HSBC to Open D.C. Branch, Pursue Embassy Clients," *Washington Post*, 5 October 2004, https://www.washingtonpost.com/archive/business/2004
/10/05/hsbc-to-open-dc-branch-pursue-embassy-clients/e8b7f538-c5ca-461f a85b
-17541810e647/.

6. "PNC Agrees to Buy Troubled Riggs Bank," NBC, 16 July 2004, https://www.nbcnews
.com/id/wbna5451203.

7. Andrew Feinstein, "Before the Panama Papers: The Low Point in the History of Offshore
Accounts," *Time*, 15 April 2016, https://time.com/4294170/panama-papers-al-yamamah/.

8. Richard B. Schmitt and Kathleen Hennessey, "Bank, Big Oil Tied to African Payments,"
Los Angeles Times, 15 July 2004, https://www.latimes.com/archives/la-xpm-2004-jul-15
-na-riggs15_-story.html.

9. Richard Messick, "How We Did It: The U.S. Congress' Exposure of the Grand
Scale of Global Corruption," *Global Anticorruption Blog*, 10 October 2018, https://
globalanticorruptionblog.com/2018/10/10/how-we-did-it-the-u-s-congress
-exposure-of-global-corruption-on-a-grand-scale/.

10. Interview with author.

11. "Senate Report: Riggs Bank Helped Pinochet," NBC, 15 July 2004, https://www
.nbcnews.com/id/wbna5442566.

12. "Money Laundering and Foreign Corruption, Enforcement and Effectiveness of the
Patriot Act—Report," U.S. Senate, 15 July 2004, https://www.hsgac.senate.gov/imo
/media/doc/ACF5F8.pdf.

13. Terence O'Hara, "Former Riggs Bank Executive Is Arrested," *Washington Post*, 27 May 2005, https://www.washingtonpost.com/archive/business/2005/05/27/former-riggs-bank-executive-is-arrested/29301e8f-1d16-4830-98b6-698125d34e1c/.

14. Interview with author.

15. Bean, *Financial Exposure*.

16. Ibid.

17. Interview with author.

18. Interview with author.

19. "Money Laundering and Foreign Corruption, Enforcement and Effectiveness of the Patriot Act—Hearing," U.S. Senate, 15 July 2004, https://www.govinfo.gov/content/pkg/CHRG-108shrg95501/html/CHRG-108shrg95501.htm.

20. "Money Laundering and Foreign Corruption, Enforcement and Effectiveness of the Patriot Act—Report."

21. Ibid.

22. Ibid.

23. Timothy L. O'Brien, "At Riggs Bank, a Tangled Path Led to Scandal," *New York Times*, 19 July 2004, https://www.nytimes.com/2004/07/19/us/at-riggs-bank-a-tangled-path-led-to-scandal.html.

24. "Money Laundering and Foreign Corruption, Enforcement and Effectiveness of the Patriot Act—Report."

25. "Money Laundering and Foreign Corruption, Enforcement and Effectiveness of the Patriot Act—Hearing."

26. Ibid.

27. "Money Laundering and Foreign Corruption, Enforcement and Effectiveness of the Patriot Act—Report."

28. Ibid.

29. Ibid.

30. Scott Hempling, "'Regulatory Capture': Sources and Solutions," *Emory Corporate Governance Accountability and Review*, 1, no. 1 (2014), https://law.emory.edu/ecgar/content/volume-1/issue-1/essays/regulatory-capture.html.

31. "Money Laundering and Foreign Corruption, Enforcement and Effectiveness of the Patriot Act—Report."

32. Interview with author.

33. Bean, *Financial Exposure*.

34. "Money Laundering and Foreign Corruption, Enforcement and Effectiveness of the Patriot Act—Report."

35. "Pinochet's Web of Bank Accounts Exposed," *Guardian*, 16 March 2005, https://www.theguardian.com/business/2005/mar/16/chile.pinochet.

36. "Money Laundering and Foreign Corruption, Enforcement and Effectiveness of the Patriot Act—Report."

37. Interview with author.

38. Interview with author.

39. "National Intelligence Reform Act of 2004," *Congressional Record*, 4 October 2004, https://fas.org/irp/congress/2004_cr/s100404.html.

40. Eric Dash, "Riggs Pleads Guilty in Money-Laundering Case," *New York Times*, 28 January 2005, https://www.nytimes.com/2005/01/28/business/riggs-pleads-guilty-in -moneylaundering-case.html.

41. Ken Silverstein, "What Those Glowing Obits Didn't Tell You About Joe Allbritton," *New Republic*, 14 December 2012, https://newrepublic.com/article/111093/joe -allbritton-what-those-glowing-obits-didnt-tell-you.

42. Bean, *Financial Exposure*.

43. Silverstein, "U.S. Government Documents Crime Spree by Dictator's Son: Why No Action by the Feds?"

CHAPTER 7: MENSA-CERTIFIED GENIUS

1. Rick Perlstein, *Reaganland* (New York: Simon & Schuster, 2020).

2. Kate Thomas, "Equatorial Guinea Prepares to Go to Polls," Voice of America, 27 November 2009, https://www.voanews.com/archive/equatorial-guinea-prepares-go -polls.

3. Timothy M. Phelps, "Foreign Official Gives Up Malibu Home in Federal 'Kleptocracy' Probe," *Los Angeles Times*, 10 October 2004, https://www.latimes.com/local/crime/la -me-malibu-kleptocrat-20141011-story.html.

4. Beckie Strum, "Investors Flip Malibu Estate Once Involved in Corruption Scandal for $69.9 Million," *Mansion Global*, 11 April 2017, https://www.mansionglobal.com /articles/investors-flip-malibu-estate-once-involved-in-corruption-scandal-for-69-9 -million-59770.

5. Interview with author.

6. Adrian Glick Kudler, "African Dictator's Son's Malibu House and Michael Jackson Glove Targeted by US Government," *Curbed Los Angeles*, 20 October 2011, https://la .curbed.com/2011/10/20/10432074/african-dictators-sons-malibu-house-michael -jackson-glove-targeted-by.

7. "Gatekeeper Regulations on Attorneys," American Bar Association, https://www .americanbar.org/advocacy/governmental_legislative_work/priorities_policy /independence_of_the_legal_profession/bank_secrecy_act/.

8. "Recommendations," American Bar Association, 9–10 August 2010, https://web .archive.org/web/20110811034854/https://www.americanbar.org/content/dam/aba /migrated/leadership/2010/annual/pdfs/116.authcheckdam.pdf.

9. Alexander Cooley and Casey Michel, "U.S. Lawyers Are Foreign Kleptocrats' Best Friends," *Foreign Policy*, 23 March 2021, https://foreignpolicy.com/2021/03/23/u-s -lawyers-are-foreign-kleptocrats-best-friends/. These lawyers—like accountants and other financial advisory professionals—are part of what author Chuck Collins has described as the "Wealth Defense Industry." Collins, *The Wealth Hoarders*.

10. Arianna Palma Skipper, "The Attorney's Facilitation of Transnational Corruption:

Shortcomings of the United States Anti-Money Laundering Framework," *Georgetown Journal of Legal Ethics* 33, no. 3 (Summer 2020), https://www.law.georgetown.edu /legal-ethics-journal/wp-content/uploads/sites/24/2020/09/GT-GJLE200036.pdf.

11. It's worth noting that plenty of non-American lawyers peddle the same line as U.S. lawyers about anti–money laundering. As Sternford Moyo, the head of the International Bar Association, said in early 2021 about those calling for greater oversight of lawyers helping kleptocrats, "Once you build a system that is based on lawyers being attacked as enablers of crime, you actually undermine confidence in the legal system itself. You undermine confidence in the law itself. Undermining confidence in the law is one of the most dangerous things you can do." See "FACTI Panel Report Launch," FACTI Panel Secretariat, YouTube, https://youtu.be /D2ZHLntvGhs.

12. "Undercover Investigation of American Lawyers Reveals Role of Overseas Territories in Moving Suspect Money into the United States," Global Witness, 12 February 2016, https://www.globalwitness.org/en/press-releases/undercover-investigation -american-lawyers-reveals-role-overseas-territories-moving-suspect-money -united-states/.

13. "Lowering the Bar: How American Lawyers Told Us How to Funnel Suspect Funds into the United States," Global Witness, January 2016, https://humanrightscommission .house.gov/sites/humanrightscommission.house.gov/files/documents/Lowering_the _Bar_0.pdf.

14. Bradley Hope and Tom Wright, *Billion Dollar Whale: The Man Who Fooled Wall Street, Hollywood, and the World* (New York: Hachette, 2018).

15. Theodoric Meyer, "Law Firm That Worked with Manafort in Ukraine Admits to Misleading DOJ," *Politico*, 17 July 2019, https://www.politico.com/story/2019/01/17 /manafort-law-firm-ukraine-justice-department-1110362.

16. Guy Adams, "Teodoro Nguema Obiang: Coming to America (to Launder His Millions?)," *Independent*, 21 June 2012, https://www.independent.co.uk/news/world /americas/teodoro-nguema-obiang-coming-america-launder-his-millions-7855043 .html.

17. Interviews with author.

18. Law Offices of Michael Jay Berger, https://www.bankruptcypower.com/profiles /profile/.

19. Interview with author.

20. "Keeping Foreign Corruption out of the United States: Four Case Histories," U.S. Senate, 4 February 2010, https://www.hsgac.senate.gov/imo/media/doc/FOREIGN CORRUPTIONREPORTFINAL710.pdf.

21. Teodorin actually had another real estate agent, John Kerrigan, already in his employ, scouting for property in Southern California, which may have been how Teodorin first learned of the Malibu property. Teodorin eventually dropped Kerrigan—who reportedly described Teodorin to others as a "minister of a very wealthy country in Africa"—after Baddin allegedly offered to halve the traditional real estate agent

commission. But even after he and Teodorin parted ways, Kerrigan proffered few re-grets; in regard to questions about the legitimacy of Teodorin's wealth, Kerrigan later said, "Who am I to question it?" See ibid.

22. Ibid.
23. Ibid.
24. Ibid.
25. Ibid.
26. Ibid.
27. Ibid.
28. Ibid.
29. Ibid.
30. Ibid.
31. Ibid.
32. "United States of America vs. One Michael Jackson Signed Thriller Jacket and Other Michael Jackson Memorabilia; Real Property Located on Sweetwater Mesa Road in Malibu, California; One 2011 Ferrari 599 GTO."
33. "Keeping Foreign Corruption out of the United States: Four Case Histories."
34. Chris Albin-Lackey, "Lifestyles of the Rich and Infamous," *Forbes*, 19 February 2010, https://www.forbes.com/2010/02/19/patriot-act-dictators-united-states-opinions -contributors-chris-albin-lackey.html?sh=562e46d44489.
35. Interview with author.
36. "Keeping Foreign Corruption out of the United States: Four Case Histories."
37. Ibid.
38. Interview with author.
39. Interview with author.
40. "Keeping Foreign Corruption out of the United States: Four Case Histories."
41. Ibid.
42. Ibid.
43. Ibid.
44. Vivian Wang, "Manhattan Skyscraper Linked to Iran Can Be Seized by U.S., Jury Finds," *New York Times*, 29 January 2017, https://www.nytimes.com/2017/06/29/nyregion/650 -fifth-avenue-iran-terrorism.html.
45. Nicholas Casey, "Jets, Horses and Bribes: How a Venezuelan Official Became a Bil-lionaire as His Country Crumbled," *New York Times*, 23 November 2018, https://www .nytimes.com/2018/11/23/world/americas/venezuela-andrade-corruption-bribes .html.
46. "UK Seeks to Confiscate Convicted Nigerian Politician's Loot," *U.S. News & World Report*, 16 January 2020, https://www.usnews.com/news/world/articles/2020-01-16 /uk-seeks-to-confiscate-convicted-nigerian-politicians-loot.
47. James McClain, "Uzbekistan's Lola Karimova Lists Three Hollywood Hills Villas," *Dirt*, 3 August 2020, https://www.dirt.com/moguls/power-players/lola-karimova-tillyaeva -house-los-angeles-1203331934/.

48. Michael Kunzelman, "US Authorities Move to Seize Ex-Gambia Dictator's Mansion," *Associated Press*, 16, July 2020, https://apnews.com/article/554fa0c0ee8f7a fe43e39e9c6ef9f735.

49. Mengqi Sun, "Prosecutors Seek to Seize Miami Penthouse Allegedly Linked to Republic of Congo President's Son," *Wall Street Journal*, 19 June 2020, https://www .wsj.com/articles/prosecutors-seek-to-seize-miami-penthouse-allegedly-linked-to -republic-of-congo-presidents-son-11592615406.

50. Ken Silverstein, "Teodorin's World," *Foreign Policy*, 21 February 2011, https://foreign policy.com/2011/02/21/teodorins-world/.

CHAPTER 8: FISH PHYSICIAN

1. Michael Jackson, "Smooth Criminal," https://genius.com/Michael-jackson-smooth -criminal-lyrics.

2. "United Nations Convention Against Corruption," United Nations, https://www .unodc.org/unodc/en/treaties/CAC/.

3. George W. Bush, "Proclamation 7750—To Suspend Entry as Immigrants or Nonimmigrants of Persons Engaged in or Benefiting from Corruption," American Presidency Project at the University of California–Santa Barbara, https://www.presidency.ucsb .edu/documents/proclamation-7750-suspend-entry-immigrants-or-nonimmigrants -persons-engaged-or-benefiting.

4. George W. Bush, "President's Statement on Kleptocracy," White House, https:// georgewbush-whitehouse.archives.gov/news/releases/2006/08/20060810 .html#:~:text=High%2Dlevel%20corruption%20by%20senior,interest%20and%20 violates%20our%20values.

5. "Creation of the Department of Homeland Security," Department of Homeland Security, https://www.dhs.gov/creation-department-homeland-security.

6. Elaine Godfrey, "What 'Abolish ICE' Actually Means," *Atlantic*, 11 July 2018, https:// www.theatlantic.com/politics/archive/2018/07/what-abolish-ice-actually-means /564752/.

7. Ian Urbina, "Taint of Corruption Is No Barrier to U.S. Visa," *New York Times*, 16 November 2009, https://www.nytimes.com/interactive/projects/documents/investigating -teodoro-nguema-obiang.

8. Jack Davies, "How Did Cambodia's First Family Afford Their Long Island Home?," Radio Free Asia, 15 November 2019, https://www.rfa.org/english/news/cambodia /hunsen-realestate-11152019165002.html.

9. Tom Wright and Bradley Hope, "The Billion-Dollar Mystery Man and the Wildest Party Vegas Ever Saw," *Wall Street Journal*, 15 September 2018, https://www.wsj .com/articles/the-billion-dollar-mystery-man-and-the-wildest-party-vegas-ever-saw -1536984061.

10. Mark David, "Your Mama Hears . . . ," *Variety*, 2 July 2013, https://variety.com/2013 /dirt/real-estalker/your-mama-hears-21-1201236007/.

11. Interview with author.

12. Interview with author.

13. Interview with author.

14. Ken Silverstein, *The Secret World of Oil* (New York: Verso, 2015).

15. "Keeping Foreign Corruption out of the United States: Four Case Histories."

16. Silverstein, *The Secret World of Oil*.

17. Interview with author.

18. "Keeping Foreign Corruption out of the United States: Four Case Histories."

19. Ibid.

20. Ibid.

21. Silverstein, "Teodorin's World."

22. Interview with author.

23. Matthew Mosco, Megan Chuchmach, and Dana Hughes, "Rapper Eve Has Cameo in New U.S. Senate Investigation on Foreign Corruption," ABC News, 2 February 2010, https://abcnews.go.com/Blotter/rapper-eve-cameo-us-senate-investigation-foreign -corruption/story?id=9727359.

24. Samuel Rubenfeld, "African Leader's Son Planned $380 Million Yacht," *Wall Street Journal*, 1 March 2011, https://www.wsj.com/articles/BL-CCB-4001.

25. Drew Hinshaw, "Did the Son of Equatorial Guinea's Leader Really Try to Buy a $380 Million Yacht Called 'Zen'?," *Christian Science Monitor*, 8 March 2011, https:// www.csmonitor.com/World/Africa/Africa-Monitor/2011/0308/Did-the-son-of -Equatorial-Guinea-s-leader-really-try-to-buy-a-380-million-yacht-called-Zen.

26. Interview with author.

27. Silverstein, *The Secret World of Oil*.

28. The GV wasn't Teodorin's first attempt at landing a luxury jet, which could take him wherever he wanted to go. In 2004, he reached out to U.S.–based Ocean Energy to see if they could purchase him a C-130 Hercules, a bulky transport plane usually associated with military transits. Ocean Energy declined Teodorin's entreaties, after which he apparently dropped the idea—though he never fully explained why he thought he'd need a flying fortress like the C-130. Scott Cohn, "US Increases Pressure on 'Filthy Rich' African Regime," CNBC, 18 June 2012, https://www.cnbc.com/2012/06/18/us -increases-pressure-on-filthy-rich-african-regime.html.

29. "Elise Bean on Financial Fraud, Money Laundering and the Top 3 Policies to Curb Corruption," *KickBack—The Global Anticorruption Podcast*, 22 July 2019, https:// soundcloud.com/kickback-gap/10-elise-bean-on-financial-fraud-money-laundering -and-the-top-3-policies-to-curb-corruption.

30. "Keeping Foreign Corruption out of the United States: Four Case Histories."

31. Ibid.

32. Ibid.

33. Ibid.

34. Ibid.

35. Ibid.

36. Silverstein, "Teodorin's World."

37. Silverstein, *The Secret World of Oil*.

38. Interview with author.
39. Teodorin's lust for the celebrity lifestyle that Jackson inhabited wasn't limited to the high-end toys and bright-bling gaudiness. Court records show that at one point Teodorin launched his own record label, TNO Entertainment—named after Teodorin's initials—whose greatest claim to fame was an album from no-name rapper Won-G, featuring a song called "I Love TNO." The song can still be found here: https://www.allmusic.com/album/explosion-mw0000216311.
40. Silverstein, The Secret World of Oil.
41. "The Art Basel and UBS Global Art Market Report 2019," Art Basel, 8 March 2019, https://www.artbasel.com/news/art-market-report.
42. "The Art Industry and U.S. Policies That Undermine Sanctions," U.S. Senate, 29 July 2020, https://www.hsgac.senate.gov/imo/media/doc/2020-07-29%20PSI%20Staff%20Report%20-%20The%20Art%20Industry%20and%20U.S.%20Policies%20that%20Undermine%20Sanctions.pdf.
43. Interview with author.
44. Interview with author.
45. "United States of America vs. One White Crystal-Covered 'Bad Tour' Glove and Other Michael Jackson Memorabilia; One Gulfstream G-V Jet Airplane Displaying Tail Number VPCES; Real Property Located on Sweetwater Mesa Road in Malibu, California; One 2007 Bentley Azure; One 2008 Bugatti Veyron; One 2008 Lamborghini Murcielago; One 2008 Rolls Royce Drophead Coupe; One 2009 Rolls Royce Drophead Coupe; One 2009 Rolls Royce Phantom Coupe; One 2011 Ferrari 599 GTO," https://www.courtlistener.com/recap/gov.uscourts.cacd.500873.1.0.pdf.
46. Lauren Pfeifer, "9 Insane Things Teodorin Obiang Spent His Allegedly Embezzled Money On," One, 29 January 2020, https://www.one.org/international/blog/9-insane-things-teodorin-obiang-spent-his-allegedly-embezzled-money-on/.
47. "United States of America vs. One White Crystal-Covered 'Bad Tour' Glove and Other Michael Jackson Memorabilia; One Gulfstream G-V Jet Airplane Displaying Tail Number VPCES; Real Property Located on Sweetwater Mesa Road in Malibu, California; One 2007 Bentley Azure; One 2008 Bugatti Veyron; One 2008 Lamborghini Murcielago; One 2008 Rolls Royce Drophead Coupe; One 2009 Rolls Royce Drophead Coupe; One 2009 Rolls Royce Phantom Coupe; One 2011 Ferrari 599 GTO."
48. "One of Michael Jackson's gloves SOLD!," YouTube, https://www.youtube.com/watch?v=kE9XoNkgmBc.
49. With the buyer's premium, an additional charge the winner is required to pay, the final total for Jackson's glove came to an astonishing $275,000—some ten times the estimate of the glove's projected price, and the most Teodorin shelled out on a single Michael Jackson item. For more, see James V. Grimaldi, "U.S. Trying to Seize More Than $70M from Dictator's Son over Alleged Corruption," Washington Post, 26 October 2011, https://www.washingtonpost.com/politics/us-trying-to-seize-more-than-70m-from-dictators-son-over-alleged-corruption/2011/10/25/gIQAYknmIM_story.html.

50. "Jacko Auction a Thriller; Fetches $1 Million," CNBC, 26 June 2010, https://www
.cnbc.com/2010/06/26/jacko-auction-a-thriller-fetches-1-million.html.

51. "United States of America vs. One White Crystal-Covered 'Bad Tour' Glove and
Other Michael Jackson Memorabilia; One Gulfstream G-V Jet Airplane Displaying
Tail Number VPCES; Real Property Located on Sweetwater Mesa Road in Malibu,
California; One 2007 Bentley Azure; One 2008 Bugatti Veyron; One 2008 Lamborgh-
ini Murcielago; One 2008 Rolls Royce Drophead Coupe; One 2009 Rolls Royce Drop-
head Coupe; One 2009 Rolls Royce Phantom Coupe; One 2011 Ferrari 599 GTO."

52. Interview with author.

53. Interview with author.

54. Interview with author.

55. Interview with author.

56. Interview with author.

CHAPTER 9: UNITED STATES VS. THRILLER JACKET

1. Sarah Chayes, *On Corruption in America* (New York: Knopf, 2020).

2. Interview with author.

3. Interview with author.

4. "Attorney General Holder at the African Union Summit," U.S. Department of Justice,
25 July 2010, https://www.justice.gov/opa/speech/attorney-general-holder-african
-union-summit.

5. Ibid

6. "Assistant Attorney General Lanny A. Breuer Delivers Keynote Address at Money
Laundering Enforcement Conference," U.S. Department of Justice, 19 October 2010,
https://www.justice.gov/opa/speech/assistant-attorney-general-lanny-breuer-delivers
-keynote-address-money-laundering.

7. Ibid.

8. Interview with author.

9. Interview with author.

10. Interview with author.

11. Interview with author.

12. Interview with author.

13. Interview with author.

14. Interview with author.

15. Nick Mathiason, "HSBC Accused of Aiding 'Unusual' Angolan $50m Money Trans-
fer," *Guardian*, 4 February 2010, https://www.theguardian.com/business/2010/feb/04
/hsbc-angola-us-senate.

16. Stephanie Kirchgaessner, "Lawmakers Push to Close 'Dirty Money' Loopholes," *Financial Times*, 3 February 2010, https://www.ft.com/content/b1bf8dfe-110b-11df-9a9e
-00144feab49a.

17. As investigators discovered, Abubakar was also set to receive a bribe from William
Jefferson, a Louisiana representative in Congress. As *Politico* reported, Jefferson "was

planning to bribe [Abubakar] with $100,000 provided to him by an FBI informant," who secretly filmed the handoff. When federal agents finally moved on Jefferson, they discovered $90,000 sitting in his freezer. For more, see John Bresnahan, "Report Revisits Jefferson Scandal," *Politico*, 5 February 2010, https://www.politico.com/story /2010/02/report-revisits-jefferson-scandal-032593.

18. "Keeping Foreign Corruption out of the United States: Four Case Histories."

19. Ibid.

20. Interview with author.

21. Interview with author.

22. Nashira Davids, "South Africa: How African President's Son Blew Millions," *AllAfrica*, 20 August 2006, https://allafrica.com/stories/200608210487.html.

23. "Department of Justice Seeks to Recover More Than $70.8 Million in Proceeds of Corruption from Government Minister of Equatorial Guinea," U.S. Department of Justice, 25 October 2011, https://www.justice.gov/opa/pr/department-justice-seeks -recover-more-708-million-proceeds-corruption-government-minister.

24. Scott Cohn, "African Nation Leader Forced to Give Up Assets in DOJ Settlement," CNBC, 10 October 2014, https://www.cnbc.com/2014/10/10/african-nation-leader -forced-to-give-up-assets-in-doj-settlement.html.

25. Leslie Wayne, "Shielding Seized Assets from Corruption's Clutches," *New York Times*, 30 December 2016, https://www.nytimes.com/2016/12/30/business/justice-department -tries-to-shield-repatriations-from-kleptocrats.html.

26. Interview with author.

27. "United States of America v. One Michael Jackson Signed Thriller Jacket and Other Michael Jackson Memorabilia; Real Property Located on Sweetwater Mesa Road in Malibu, California; One 2011 Ferrari 599 GTO," https://www.justice.gov /sites/default/files/press-releases/attachments/2014/10/10/obiang_settlement _agreement.pdf.

28. "Second Vice President of Equatorial Guinea Agrees to Relinquish More Than $30 Million of Assets Purchased with Corruption Proceeds," U.S. Department of Justice, 10 October 2014, https://www.justice.gov/opa/pr/second-vice-president-equatorial -guinea-agrees-relinquish-more-30-million-assets-purchased.

29. For more on the difficulties of returning stolen assets, see: "Justice Department Settlement Successfully Releases More Than $115 Million in Alleged Corruption Proceeds to People in Kazakhstan," U.S. Department of Justice, 9 December 2015, https://www .justice.gov/opa/pr/justice-department-settlement-successfully-releases-more-115 -million-alleged-corruption.

30. Interview with author.

31. Interview with author.

32. Interview with author.

33. Interview with author.

34. Interview with author.

PART III: AMERICAN WARLORDS

1. David Shimer, *Rigged* (New York: Knopf, 2020).

CHAPTER 10: NOT A GAMBINO

1. Tom Burgis, *Kleptopia* (New York: Harper, 2020).
2. "HASTILY MADE CLEVELAND TOURISM VIDEO," YouTube, https://www.youtube.com/watch?v=ysmLA5TqbIY.
3. "Hastily Made Cleveland Tourism Video: 2nd Attempt," YouTube, https://www.youtube.com/watch?v=oZzgAjjuqZM.
4. "Population History of Cleveland from 1840–1990," http://physics.bu.edu/~redner/projects/population/cities/clcvcland.html.
5. Sam Allard, "Ukrainian Oligarchs Left Trail of Devastation as They Bought, Then Abandoned, Heartland Real Estate," *Cleveland Scene*, 23 September 2020, https://www.clevescene.com/scene-and-heard/archives/2020/09/23/ukrainian-oligarchs-left-trail-of-devastation-as-they-bought-then-abandoned-heartland-real-estate.
6. Phyllis Flowers, "Booming Business in Mason County: Felman Production Inc.," *West Virginia Executive*, 24 October 2019, http://www.wvexecutive.com/booming-business-in-mason-county-felman-production-inc/.
7. Jarboe, "The Most Important Guy You've Never Heard of: Chaim Schochet, 25, Builds Downtown Cleveland Empire."
8. Ibid.
9. Ibid.
10. When contacted, Hurtuk told me that I "do not have permission to use this quote since it's from several years ago." See Jarboe, "The Most Important Guy You've Never Heard of: Chaim Schochet, 25, Builds Downtown Empire."
11. Interview with author.
12. Interview with author.
13. "One Cleveland Center," *Crain's Cleveland*, 1 August 2005, https://www.crainscleveland.com/article/20050801/LANDMARK/51121001/one-cleveland-center.
14. Michelle Jarboe, "One Cleveland Center Sold for $86 Million," *Cleveland Plain Dealer*, 16 March 2008, https://www.cleveland.com/business/2008/05/one_cleveland_center_sold_for.html.
15. Interview with author.
16. Jarboe, "The Most Important Guy You've Never Heard of: Chaim Schochet, 25, Builds Downtown Cleveland Empire."
17. "55 Public Square," Optima Management Group, http://www.optimamanagementgroup.com/property/55-public-square/.
18. Michelle Jarboe, "Optima Pays $46.5 Million for Penton Media Building in Downtown Cleveland," *Cleveland Plain Dealer*, 17 August 2010, https://www.cleveland.com/business/2010/08/optima_pays_465_million_for_pe.html.

19. Interview with author.
20. Michelle Jarboe, "Miami Investor Buys Cleveland's Huntington Building for Bargain Price," *Cleveland Plain Dealer*, 23 June 2010, https://www.cleveland.com/business /2010/06/miami_investor_buys_clevelands.html.
21. Jarboe, "Optima Pays $46.5 Million for Penton Media Building in Downtown Cleveland."
22. Ibid.
23. Ibid.
24. Nate Sibley, "Exposing Kleptocrats to Defend America's Borders," Hudson Institute, 2 October 2019, https://www.hudson.org/research/15357-exposing-kleptocrats-to -defend-america-s-borders.
25. Kevin Sun, "EB-5 from the Other Side," *Real Deal*, 1 February 2020, https://therealdeal .com/issues_articles/eb-5-from-the-other-side/.
26. Belinda Li, "The Other Immigration Crisis," Hudson Institute, 17 January 2017, https://www.hudson.org/research/13247-the-other-immigration-crisis.
27. Scott Suttell, "A Federal Grand Jury in Cleveland Is Looking at a Ukrainian Oligarch's U.S. Real Estate Activities," *Crain's Cleveland*, 20 May 2020, https://www .crainscleveland.com/scott-suttell-blog/federal-grand-jury-cleveland-looking -ukrainian-oligarchs-us-real-estate.
28. It's unclear who made Schochet's Wikipedia page, or why one—nominally about a midlevel employee at a real estate firm—should exist. It does have a few gems, though, including the claim that "Schochet describes himself as: 'a long-term investor interested in any property that produces a healthy income.'" See "Chaim Schochet," Wikipedia, https://en.wikipedia.org/wiki/Chaim_Schochet.
29. Jarboe, "The Most Important Guy You've Never Heard of: Chaim Schochet, 25, Builds Downtown Cleveland Empire."
30. A breakdown of the alleged pricing structures can be found in one of the myriad lawsuits facing the Optima group, located here: https://www.atlanticcouncil.org/wp -content/uploads/2019/06/kolomoisky_case.pdf. Further breakdowns of the ownership structures used to purchase certain of these plants can be found here: Nadiya Burdey, "Who Controls Oligarch Ihor Kolomoisky's Offshore Assets?," *Kyiv Post*, 16 May 2019, https://www.kyivpost.com/ukraine-politics/who-controls-oligarch-ihor -kolomoiskys-offshore-assets.html.
31. The Louisville property sold for $77,050,000, while the Dallas property sold for $47,400,000. "Justice Department Seeks Forfeiture of Two Commercial Properties Purchased with Funds Misappropriated from PrivatBank in Ukraine," U.S. Department of Justice, 6 August 2020, https://www.justice.gov/opa/pr/justice -department-seeks-forfeiture-two-commercial-properties-purchased-funds -misappropriated.
32. Carolyn Starks and Jeff Long, "Motorola Plant Has a Taker," *Chicago Tribune*, 15 August 2008, https://www.chicagotribune.com/news/ct-xpm-2008-08-15-0808141200 -story.html.
33. Interview with author.

34. Nicole Franz, "Timeline of Motorola Campus in Harvard," *Northwest Herald*, 22 March 2017, https://www.shawlocal.com/2017/03/22/timeline-of-motorola-campus-in-harvard/a701fm3/.

35. Starks and Long, "Motorola Plant Has a Taker."

36. Ibid.

CHAPTER 11: THE WILD WEST

1. Tony Judt, "On Intellectuals and Democracy," *New York Review of Books*, 22 March 2012, https://www.nybooks.com/articles/2012/03/22/intellectuals-and-democracy/.

2. Luke Harding, "Former Trump Aide Approved 'Black Ops' to Help Ukraine President," *Guardian*, 5 April 2018, https://www.theguardian.com/us-news/2018/apr/05/ex-trump-aide-paul-manafort-approved-black-ops-to-help-ukraine-president.

3. Christopher Miller and Mike Eckel, "On the Eve of His Trial, a Deeper Look into How Paul Manafort Elected Ukraine's President," RFE/RL, 27 July 2018, https://www.rferl.org/a/on-eve-of-trial-a-deeper-glimpse-into-how-paul-manafort-elected-ukraine-s-president/29394601.html.

4. Emily Lodish, "26 Things Found in Yanukovych's Compound That Made Him Look Even Worse," PRI, 22 February 2014, https://www.pri.org/stories/2014-02-22/26-things-found-yanukovychs-compound-made-him-look-even-worse.

5. Andrew E. Kramer, Mik McIntire, and Barry Meier, "Secret Ledger in Ukraine Lists Cash for Donald Trump's Campaign Chief," *New York Times*, 14 August 2016, https://www.nytimes.com/2016/08/15/us/politics/what-is-the-black-ledger.html.

6. "Poroshenko Blames Yanukovych for Ukrainian Army's Weak State When Russia Seized Crimea," RFE/RL, 15 June 2020, https://www.rferl.org/a/poroshenko-blames-yanukovych-ukrainian-army-weak-state-russia-seized-crimea/30671818.html.

7. Ironically enough, following Russia's forced annexation, Russian officials began floating the idea of transforming Crimea into a "tax haven" specifically modeled on Delaware. There's little evidence Moscow has succeeded. Katie Marie Davies, "Russia Unveils New Bill to Transform Crimea into Tax Haven," *Moscow Times*, 28 April 2017, https://www.themoscowtimes.com/2017/04/28/russia-unveils-new-bill-to-transform-crimea-into-tax-haven-a57855.

8. Gabriela Baczynska, "Kiev Pins Hopes on Oligarch in Battle Against Eastern Separatists," Reuters, 23 May 2014, https://www.reuters.com/article/us-ukraine-crisis-oligarch/kiev-pins-hopes-on-oligarch-in-battle-against-eastern-separatists-idUKBREA4M0OU20140523?edition-redirect=uk.

9. Andrew E. Kramer, "Residents in Eastern Ukraine City Rally Against Separatism," *New York Times*, 28 March 2015, https://www.nytimes.com/2015/03/29/world/europe/residents-in-eastern-ukraine-city-rally-against-separatism.html.

10. "Global Banks Defy U.S. Crackdowns by Serving Oligarchs, Criminals and Terrorists," ICIJ, 20 September 2020, https://www.icij.org/investigations/fincen-files/global-banks-defy-u-s-crackdowns-by-serving-oligarchs-criminals-and-terrorists.

11. Roman Olearchyk, "Ukraine Oligarch: Putin Is a "Schizophrenic of Short Stature,"

Financial Times, 3 March 2014, https://www.ft.com/content/d2609f36-f8ce-3dd9-9c8b
-8682710bfc13.

12. Alec Luhn, "Ukrainian Oligarch Offers Bounty for Capture of Russian 'Saboteurs,'"
Guardian, 17 April 2014, https://www.theguardian.com/world/2014/apr/17/ukrainian
-oligarch-offers-financial-rewards-russians-igor-kolomoisky.

13. Alan Cullison, "Ukraine's Secret Weapon: Feisty Oligarch Ihor Kolomoisky," *Wall
Street Journal*, 27 June 2014, https://www.wsj.com/articles/ukraines-secret-weapon
-feisty-oligarch-ihor-kolomoisky-1403886665.

14. Interview with author.

15. Cullison, "Ukraine's Secret Weapon: Feisty Oligarch Ihor Kolomoisky."

16. Sophie Pinkham, "Watching the Ukrainian Oligarchs," *New Yorker*, 2 April 2015,
https://www.newyorker.com/news/news-desk/watching-the-ukrainian-oligarchs.

17. "Ukraine Governor Kolomoisky Sacked After Oil Firm Row," BBC, 25 March 2015,
https://www.bbc.com/news/world-europe-32045990.

18. Richard Balmforth, "Ukrainian Oligarch Under Fire After Night Raid on State Oil
Firm," Reuters, 20 March 2015, https://www.reuters.com/article/us-ukraine-crisis
-kolomoisky/ukrainian-oligarch-under-fire-after-night-raid-on-state-oil-firm-idUSKBN
0MG2A320150320.

19. Pinkham, "Watching the Ukrainian Oligarchs."

20. Interview with author.

21. Swan, "Billionaire Ukrainian Oligarch Ihor Kolomoisky Under Investigation by FBI."

22. Eamon Javers, "Why Did the US Pay This Former Swiss Banker $104M?," CNBC,
30 April 2015, https://www.cnbc.com/2015/04/30/why-did-the-us-pay-this-former
-swiss-banker-104m.html.

23. Evan Thomas, "UBS: A Swiss Bank's Shadowy Operations," *Newsweek*, 13 March
2009, https://www.newsweek.com/ubs-swiss-banks-shadowy-operations-76447.

24. Bean, *Financial Exposure*.

25. "Banker Pleads Guilty to Helping American Real Estate Developer Evade Income Tax
on $200 Million," U.S. Department of Justice, 19 June 2008, https://www.justice.gov
/archive/tax/txdv08550.htm.

26. Haig Simonian, "Diamonds in Toothpaste as Bankers Sought to Help," *Financial Times*, 22
February 2009, https://www.ft.com/content/a1897486-0108-11de-8f6e-000077b07658.

27. Katherine Rushton, "Credit Suisse Helped Americans Hide $10bn from Taxman,
Government Claims," *Telegraph*, 25 February 2014, https://www.telegraph.co.uk
/finance/newsbysector/banksandfinance/10661725/Credit-Suisse-helped-Americans
-hide-10bn-from-taxman-government-claims.html.

28. Bean, *Financial Exposure*.

29. "UBS Admits to US Tax Fraud, Agrees to $780 Million in Fines," France24, 19 Febru-
ary 2009, https://www.france24.com/en/20090219-ubs-admits-us-tax-fraud-agrees
-780-million-fines-.

30. Bean, *Financial Exposure*.

31. "Credit Suisse Pleads Guilty to Conspiracy to Aid and Assist U.S. Taxpayers in Filing False Returns," U.S. Department of Justsice, 19 May 2014, https://www.justice.gov

/opa/pr/credit-suisse-pleads-guilty-conspiracy-aid-and-assist-us-taxpayers-filing -false-returns.

32. Cotorceanu, "Why America Loves Being the World's No. 1 Tax Haven."

33. "Summary of Key FATCA Provisions," Internal Revenue Service, https://www.irs.gov /businesses/corporations/summary-of-key-fatca-provisions.

34. "What Is the CRS?," Organisation for Economic Co-operation and Development, https://www.oecd.org/tax/automatic-exchange/common-reporting-standard/.

35. It's worth noting that FATCA has since come under considerable, and reasonable, criticism—largely because the U.S. has failed to offer reciprocal transparency about non-Americans holding assets in U.S. accounts. Whereas FATCA forced foreign governments to reveal American accounts abroad, the U.S. was under no compunction, legal or otherwise, to share information on non-Americans opening up accounts in the U.S. proper. That is, while the U.S. gained detailed information on where Americans were opening bank accounts abroad—and helped spark a revolution in tax transparency more broadly—Washington was not going to reciprocate for governments elsewhere. Casey Michel, "How the US Became the Center of Global Kleptocracy," Vox, 3 February 2020, https://www.vox.com/policy-and-politics/2020/2/3/21100092 /us-trump-kleptocracy-corruption-tax-havens.

36. "America's Notorious Tax-Compliance Law Faces Another Challenge," Economist, 5 October 2019, https://www.economist.com/finance-and-economics/2019/10/03/americas -notorious-tax-compliance-law-faces-another-challenge.

37. Zachary R. Mider, "Moguls Rent South Dakota Addresses to Dodge Taxes Forever," Bloomberg, 27 December 2013, https://www.bloomberg.com/news/articles/2013-12 -27/moguls-rent-south-dakota-addresses-to-dodge-taxes-forever.

38. Casey Michel, "Trusting the Process," Hudson Institute, 1 March 2017, https://web .archive.org/web/20170325053418/http://kleptocracyinitiative.org/2017/03/trusting -the-process/.

39. "Secret History of the Credit Card," PBS, 23 November 2004, https://www.pbs.org/ wgbh/pages/frontline/shows/credit/interviews/janklow.html#:~:text=Bill%20Jank- low%20was%20governor%20of,take%20off%20in%20the%201980s.&text=%22It's%20 unbelievable%2C%20the%20lack%20of,consumer%20credit%2C%22%20he%20says.

40. Oliver Bullough, "The Great American Tax Haven: Why the Super-Rich Love South Dakota," Guardian, 14 November 2019, https://www.theguardian.com/world/2019 /nov/14/the-great-american-tax-haven-why-the-super-rich-love-south-dakota-trust -laws.

41. "Secret History of the Credit Card."

42. Bullough, "The Great American Tax Haven: Why the Super-Rich Love South Dakota."

43. Michel, "Trusting the Process."

44. Andres Knobel, "Trusts: Weapons of Mass Injustice?," Tax Justice Network, 13 February 2017, https://www.taxjustice.net/wp-content/uploads/2017/02/Trusts-Weapons -of-Mass-Injustice-Final-12-FEB-2017.pdf.

45. Shaxson, Treasure Islands.

46. Kara Scannell and Vanessa Houlder, "US Tax Havens: The New Switzerland," *Financial Times*, 8 May 2016, https://www.ft.com/content/cc46c644-12dd-11e6-839f-29229 47098f0.

47. Paul Sullivan, "The Ins and Outs of Trusts That Last Forever," *New York Times*, 5 December 2014, https://www.nytimes.com/2014/12/06/your-money/estate-planning/the -ins-and-outs-of-perpetual-trusts.html.

48. One academic—who described "perpetual trusts" as "loony"—crunched the numbers on these new trusts, finding that "350 years after the settlor's death, a perpetual trust could have, on average, 114,688 living beneficiaries (16,384 great-great-great-great-great-great-great-great-great-great-great-great-great-grandchildren, 32,768 great-great-great-great-great-great-great-great-great-great-great-great-great-great-grandchildren, and 65,536 great-great-great-great-great-great-great-great-great-great-great-great-great-great-great-grandchildren). The settlor's genetic relationship to the great-great-great-great-great-great-great-great-great-great-grandchildren would be 0.0061035%, to the great-great-great-great-great-great-great-great-great-great-great-grandchildren would be 0.0030517%, and to the great-great-great-great-great-great-great-great-great-great-great-great-grandchildren would be 0.0015258%." Lawrence W. Waggoner, "From Here to Eternity: The Folly of Perpetual Trusts," University of Michigan Public Law Working Paper No. 259, 9 July 2016, https://papers .ssrn.com/sol3/papers.cfm?abstract_id=1975117.

49. Wyoming, for some reason, decided to keep its cap on the number of years trusts can exist—but extended it to 1,000 years, leaving it to accountants and lawyers in the thirty-first century to distribute any remaining assets. Robert H. Sitkoff and Max M. Schanzenbach, "Jurisdictional Competition for Trust Funds: An Empirical Analysis of Perpetuities and Taxes," *Yale Law Journal* 115, no. 2 (November 2005), https://www .yalelawjournal.org/pdf/396_e4p5nu1m.pdf.

50. "Governor's Task Force on Trust Administration Review and Reform," South Dakota Department of Labor and Regulation, https://dlr.sd.gov/banking/trusts/trust_task _force.aspx.

51. Michel, "Trusting the Process."

52. Interview with author.

53. Scannell and Houlder, "US Tax Havens: The New Switzerland."

54. One of those who took full advantage of the loosening of American trust law: Jeffrey Epstein. As the *New York Times* discovered in 2021, "Epstein's specialty was suggesting ways for wealthy clients to use sophisticated trusts and other investment vehicles." For more details on Epstein's use of trusts, see Matthew Goldstein and Steve Elder, "What Jeffrey Epstein Did to Earn $158 Million from Leon Black," *New York Times*, 26 January 2021, https://www.nytimes.com/2021/01/26/business/jeffrey-epstein-leon -black-apollo.html.

55. Mider, "Moguls Rent South Dakota Addresses to Dodge Taxes Forever."

56. Bullough, "The Great American Tax Haven: Why the Super-Rich Love South Dakota."

57. Mider, "Moguls Rent South Dakota Addresses to Dodge Taxes Forever."

58. Drew Matthews, "Why South Dakota Is a Tax Haven for the Rich," *Rapid City Journal*,

10 April 2016, https://rapidcityjournal.com/news/local/why-south-dakota-is-a-tax
-haven-for-the-rich/article_bfe0d2ee-56c4-58fe-a7d0-32354c0b28f8.html.

59. Interview with author.

60. Robert Frank, Louise Connelly, and Scott Zamost, "Billionaire Divorce Uncovers Secretive World of Trusts in South Dakota," CNBC, 6 May 2020, https://www.cnbc.com
/2020/05/06/how-marie-and-ed-bosarges-divorce-spotlights-south-dakotas-asset
-trusts.html.

61. Bullough, "The Great American Tax Haven: Why the Super-Rich Love South Dakota."

62. Eli Binder and Katrina Northrop, "China's Global Treasure Map," *Wire China*, 20 September 2020, https://www.thewirechina.com/2020/09/20/chinas-global-treasure-map/.

63. Boigon, "They Gave $25 Million to Jewish Nonprofits. Was Some of That Money
Laundered from Ukraine?"

64. Larry Tye, *Home Lands: Portraits of the New Jewish Diaspora* (New York: Henry Holt,
2001).

65. Boigon, "They Gave $25 Million to Jewish Nonprofits. Was Some of That Money Laun-
dered from Ukraine?"

66. Stier, "The Dangers of Doing Business Abroad."

CHAPTER 12: A GAPING HOLE

1. Joe Noga, "Ichiro Once Said He'd 'Punch Himself in the Face' If He Ever Lied About
Wanting to Go to Cleveland," *Cleveland Plain Dealer*, 21 March 2019, https://www
.cleveland.com/tribe/2019/03/ichiro-once-said-hed-punch himself-in-the-face-if-he
-ever lied about-wanting-to-go-to-cleveland.html.

2. Jack Laurenson, "UK Police Investigate After Ex-Head of NBU Gontareva Struck by
Car in Central London," *Kyiv Post*, 30 August 2019, https://www.kyivpost.com/world
/uk-police-investigate-after-ex-head-of-nbu-gontareva-struck-by-car-in-central
-london.html.

3. Graham Stack, "Privat Investigations: PrivatBank Lending Practices Threaten Ukraine's
Financial Stability," *bne IntelliNews*, 1 November 2016, https://www.intellinews.com
/privat investigations-privatbank lending-practices-threaten-ukraine-s-financial
-stability-108734/.

4. Interview with author.

5. Ben Aris, "Ukraine's Talks with the International Monetary Fund Have 'Stalled' Says
NBU," *bne IntelliNews*, 14 October 2019, https://www.intellinews.com/ukraine-s
-talks-with-the-international-monetary-fund-have-stalled-says-nbu-169622/.

6. "Ukrainian Authorities Take Over Biggest Private Lender PrivatBank," *bne IntelliNews*, 19 December 2016, https://www.intellinews.com/ukrainian-authorities-take
-over-biggest-private-lender-privatbank-112466/?source=bne-banker.

7. Ben Aris, "Ukraine's PrivatBank Wins London Case Blocking Oligarch Kolomoisky from
Unfreezing $2bn in Assets," *bne IntelliNews*, 15 October 2019, https://www.intellinews
.com/ukraine-s-privatbank-wins-london-case-blocking-oligarch-kolomoisky-from
-unfreezing-2bn-in-assets-169755/.

8. "Ukraine's Biggest Lender PrivatBank Nationalised," BBC, 19 December 2016, https://www.bbc.com/news/business-38365579.

9. Stack, "Oligarchs Weaponized Cyprus Branch of Ukraine's Largest Bank to Send $5.5 Billion Abroad."

10. Interview with author.

11. Interview with author.

12. Interview with author.

13. "Kroll Confirms: Before Nationalisation PrivatBank Was Subjected to a Large Scale and Coordinated Fraud, Which Resulted in a Loss of at Least USD 5.5 Billion," National Bank of Ukraine, 16 January 2018, https://bank.gov.ua/en/news/all/kroll-pidtverdili-do-natsionalizatsiyi-pat-privatbank-bulo-obyektom-masshtabnih-ta-skoordinovanih-shahrayskih-diy-scho-prizvelo-do-zbitkiv.

14. Stack, "Oligarchs Weaponized Cyprus Branch of Ukraine's Largest Bank to Send $5.5 Billion Abroad."

15. "Justice Department Seeks Forfeiture of Two Commercial Properties Purchased with Funds Misappropriated from PrivatBank in Ukraine," U.S. Department of Justice, 6 August 2020, https://www.justice.gov/opa/pr/justice-department-seeks-forfeiture-two-commercial-properties-purchased-funds-misappropriated.

16. Lauren Caryer, "Steal Country: The Case of Ukrainian Money Laundering in Northeast Ohio," Kreller Group, 1 November 2019, https://www.kreller.com/post/steal-country.

17. "United States of America vs. Real Property Located at 7505 and 7171 Forest Lane, Dallas, Texas 75230, with All Appurtenances, Improvements, and Attachments Thereon, and Any Right to Collect and Receive Any Profit, Rent, Income, and Proceeds Therefrom," https://www.justice.gov/opa/press-release/file/1302006/download.

18. "Justice Department Seeks Forfeiture of Two Commercial Properties Purchased with Funds Misappropriated from PrivatBank in Ukraine."

19. Ibid.

20. "United States of America vs. All Right to and Interest in PNC Corporate Plaza Holdings LLC Held, Controlled, or Acquired, Directly or Indirectly, by Optima CBD Investments LLC and/or CBD 500 LLC, Including Any Interest Held in or Secured by the Real Property and Appurtenances Located at 500 West Jefferson Street, Louisville, KY 40202; Any Right to Collect and Receive Any Profit, Rent, Income, and Proceeds Therefrom; and Any Interest Derived from the Proceeds Invested in PNC Corporate Plaza Holdings LLC by Optima CBD Investments LLC and/or CBD 500 LLC," https://www.justice.gov/opa/press-release/file/1302001/download.

21. Interview with author.

22. Seddon and Olearchyk, "The Bank That Holds the Key to Ukraine's Future."

23. "United States of America vs. All Right to and Interest in PNC Corporate Plaza Holdings LLC Held, Controlled, or Acquired, Directly or Indirectly, by Optima CBD Investments LLC and/or CBD 500 LLC, Including Any Interest Held in or Secured by the Real Property and Appurtenances Located at 500 West Jefferson Street,

Louisville, KY 40202; Any Right to Collect and Receive Any Profit, Rent, Income, and Proceeds Therefrom; and Any Interest Derived from the Proceeds Invested in PNC Corporate Plaza Holdings LLC by Optima CBD Investments LLC and/or CBD 500 LLC."

24. Ibid.

25. Aslund, "How Kolomoisky Does Business in the United States."

26. "Justice Department Seeks Forfeiture of Two Commercial Properties Purchased with Funds Misappropriated from PrivatBank in Ukraine."

27. "United States of America vs. Real Property Located at 55 Public Square, Cleveland, Ohio, with All Appurtenances, Improvements, and Attachments Thereon, and Any Right to Collect and Receive Any Profit, Rent, Income, and Proceeds Therefrom," https://www.justice.gov/opa/press-release/file/1349786/download.

28. Ibid.

29. "United States of America vs. All Right to and Interest in PNC Corporate Plaza Holdings LLC Held, Controlled, or Acquired, Directly or Indirectly, by Optima CBD Investments LLC and/or CBD 500 LLC, Including Any Interest Held in or Secured by the Real Property and Appurtenances Located at 500 West Jefferson Street, Louisville, KY 40202; Any Right to Collect and Receive Any Profit, Rent, Income, and Proceeds Therefrom; and Any Interest Derived from the Proceeds Invested in PNC Corporate Plaza Holdings LLC by Optima CBD Investments LLC and/or CBD 500 LLC."

30. David Smile, Alex Daugherty, and Nicholas Nehamas, "Congress Candidate's Husband Has Financial Ties to Scandal-Plagued Ukrainian Oligarch," *Miami Herald*, 16 July 2018, https://www.miamiherald.com/news/politics government/article214974800.html.

31. "United States of America vs. All Right to and Interest in PNC Corporate Plaza Holdings LLC Held, Controlled, or Acquired, Directly or Indirectly, by Optima CBD Investments LLC and/or CBD 500 LLC, Including Any Interest Held in or Secured by the Real Property and Appurtenances Located at 500 West Jefferson Street, Louisville, KY 40202; Any Right to Collect and Receive Any Profit, Rent, Income, and Proceeds Therefrom; and Any Interest Derived from the Proceeds Invested in PNC Corporate Plaza Holdings LLC by Optima CBD Investments LLC and/or CBD 500 LLC."

32. The DOJ didn't mince words about Korf and Laber's role, alleging at one point, "Korf and Laber took many steps to hide the identity and ownership of their 'partners,' and the fact that the money they spent under the Optima name had initially come from PrivatBank loans. Among other things, they (1) made quick transfers of funds among entities, which served no business purpose; (2) used misleadingly similar names of entities and changed those names with no legitimate business purpose; (3) used a convoluted ownership structure of their many entities to hide the true beneficial ownership of assets; and (4) changed the ownership structure of the Optima Family of companies as Kolomoisky and [Bogolyubov's] crimes in Ukraine were made public." "Justice Department Seeks Forfeiture of Third Commercial Property Purchased with Funds Misappropriated from PrivatBank in Ukraine," U.S. Department of Justice, 30 December 2020, https://www.justice.gov/opa/pr/justice-department-seeks-forfeiture

-third-commercial-property-purchased-funds-misappropriated. Curiously, the DOJ made no mention of Schochet's role.

33. "United States of America vs. All Right to and Interest in PNC Corporate Plaza Holdings LLC Held, Controlled, or Acquired, Directly or Indirectly, by Optima CBD Investments LLC and/or CBD 500 LLC, Including Any Interest Held in or Secured by the Real Property and Appurtenances Located at 500 West Jefferson Street, Louisville, KY 40202; Any Right to Collect and Receive Any Profit, Rent, Income, and Proceeds Therefrom; and Any Interest Derived from the Proceeds Invested in PNC Corporate Plaza Holdings LLC by Optima CBD Investments LLC and/or CBD 500 LLC."

34. Ibid.

35. Even after the purchases, the "Optima Family" wasn't done. New Delaware LLCs linked to Optima kept popping up, trading ownership of the Cleveland buildings, disguising the real ownership, and obscuring the network that much further. Not that the schemes were necessarily the most creative: one LLC, Optima 925, transferred ownership of the hulking Huntington Building to . . . Optima 925 II. The move was supposed to "obscure Kolomoisky's . . . ownership interest in the building," American officials later said. "United States of America vs. Real Property Located at 7505 and 7171 Forest Lane, Dallas, Texas 75230, with All Appurtenances, Improvements, and Attachments Thereon, and Any Right to Collect and Receive Any Profit, Rent, Income, and Proceeds Therefrom."

36. The DOJ's detailed allegations on the financing of 55 Public Square reveal a bit of the convoluted, confusing nature of the ownership, and the links between shell companies, Kolomoisky, and Korf and Laber. As the DOJ wrote about 55 Public Square, "To acquire the property, Korf and Laber incorporated Optima 55 Public Square in Delaware on April 29, 2008 and registered it in Ohio on May 5, 2008. The mailing address was 200 South Biscayne Boulevard, Miami, Florida. Optima 55 Public Square was a wholly owned subsidiary of Optima Ventures, which also operates from 200 South Biscayne Boulevard, Miami, Florida. Optima International, which is located at the same Miami office, entered into a purchase and sale agreement with 55 Public Square LLC on March 6, 2008. Optima 55 Public Square was then substituted as the purchaser. On July 10, 2008, Optima 55 Public Square completed the purchase of the Defendant Asset for $34,000,000. Korf signed the paperwork associated with the purchase. The purchase included Optima 55 Public Square's assumption of the outstanding mortgage of $21,844,014.41 from 55 Public Square LLC, Loan Number 03–0250448. It also included a payment of $12,832,838.76 in cash, which covered various closing fees. That payment, as explained below, included funds misappropriated from PrivatBank." "United States of America vs. Real Property Located at 55 Public Square, Cleveland, Ohio, with All Appurtenances, Improvements, and Attachments Thereon, and Any Right to Collect and Receive Any Profit, Rent, Income, and Proceeds Therefrom."

37. Sallah and Kozyreva, "With Deutsche Bank's Help, an Oligarch's Buying Spree Trails Ruin Across the US Heartland."

38. Sam Allard, "How Ukrainian Oligarchs Secretly Became the Largest Real Estate Own-

ers in Downtown Cleveland," *Cleveland Scene*, 11 June 2019, https://www.clevescene
.com/scene-and-heard/archives/2019/06/11/how-ukrainian-oligarchs-secretly
-became-the-largest-real-estate-owners-in-downtown-cleveland.

39. Interview with author.

40. Jarboe, "Optima Pays $46.5 Million for Penton Media Building in Downtown Cleveland."

41. Allard, "How Ukrainian Oligarchs Secretly Became the Largest Real Estate Owners in Downtown Cleveland."

42. Michelle Jarboe, "AECOM Centre in Downtown Cleveland Sells to New Jersey Buyer with Renovation Plans," *Cleveland Plain Dealer*, 30 January 2019, https://www
.cleveland.com/realestate-news/2018/06/aecom_centre_in_downtown_cleve.html.

43. "Justice Department Seeks Forfeiture of Third Commercial Property Purchased with Funds Misappropriated from PrivatBank in Ukraine."

44. Michelle Jarboe, "K&D Strikes Deal to Buy 55 Public Square Office Tower, with Mixed-Use Renovation Plans," *Cleveland Plain Dealer*, 30 May 2018, https://www
.cleveland.com/realestate-news/2018/05/kd_strikes_deal_to_buy_55_publ.html.

45. Allard, "How Ukrainian Oligarchs Secretly Became the Largest Real Estate Owners in Downtown Cleveland."

46. Jarboe, "K&D Strikes Deal to Buy 55 Public Square Office Tower, with Mixed-Use Renovation Plans."

47. Allard, "How Ukrainian Oligarchs Secretly Became the Largest Real Estate Owners in Downtown Cleveland."

48. Interview with author.

49. Michelle Jarboe, "Millennia Buys Downtown Cleveland's Near-Vacant 925 Building in $40 Million Deal," *Cleveland Plain Dealer*, 30 January 2019, https://www.cleveland
.com/realestate-news/2018/05/millennia_buys_downtown_clevel.html.

50. "Newmark Grubb Knight Frank Sells Huntington Building in Cleveland for $22 Million," *REjournals*, 4 April 2017, https://rejournals.com/newmark-grubb-knight-frank
-sells-huntington-building-in-cleveland-for-22-million/.

51. Stan Bullard, "N.J. Firm Set to Acquire AECOM Centre for $38M," *Crain's Cleveland*, 10 June 2018, https://www.crainscleveland.com/article/20180610/news/164531/nj-firm
-set-acquire-aecom-centre-38m.

52. Zach Despart, "Corrupt Businessmen Looted Venezuela, and Now Many Live Quietly in Houston and Miami," *Houston Press*, 18 April 2017, https://www.houstonpress.com
/news/many-corrupt-venezuelans-hide-in-houston-and-miami-9335232.

53. Amy Mackinnon, "Biden Expected to Put the World's Kleptocrats on Notice," *Foreign Policy*, 3 December 2020, https://foreignpolicy.com/2020/12/03/biden-kleptocrats-dirty
-money-illicit-finance-crackdown/.

54. Interview with author.

55. Interview with author.

56. Interview with author.

57. Sabra Ayres, "Dallas Real Estate Entangled in International Money Laundering Probe," Spectrum News 1, 1 October 2020, https://spectrumlocalnews.com/tx/san-antonio

/news/2020/09/24/dallas-real-estate-entangled-in-international-money-laundering
-probe.

58. Marty Finley, "EXCLUSIVE: Downtown Louisville Office Tower Facing Foreclosure," *Louisville Business First*, 7 February 2018, https://www.bizjournals.com/louisville/news
/2018/02/07/exclusdowntown-louisville-office-tower-facing.html.

59. "Doors Wide Open: Corruption and Real Estate in Four Key Markets," Transparency International, 2017, https://www.transparency.org/en/publications/doors-wide-open
-corruption-and-real-estate-in-four-key-markets.

60. Louise Story and Stephanie Saul, "Stream of Foreign Wealth Flows to Elite New York Real Estate," *New York Times*, 7 February 2015, https://www.nytimes.com/news-event
/shell-company-towers-of-secrecy-real-estate.

CHAPTER 13: FUCKING CURSED

1. Viet Thanh Nguyen, *The Sympathizer* (New York: Grove, 2016).

2. Kovensky and Vikhrov, "The Spectacular Rise and Fall of Ihor Kolomoisky's Steel Empire."

3. Sallah and Kozyreva, "With Deutsche Bank's Help, an Oligarch's Buying Spree Trails Ruin Across the US Heartland."

4. Ibid.

5. Interview with author.

6. Sallah and Kozyreva, "With Deutsche Bank's Help, an Oligarch's Buying Spree Trails Ruin Across the US Heartland."

7. Dan O'Brien, "Unforeseen Conditions Closes Warren Steel Holdings," *Business Journal*, 12 January 2016, https://businessjournaldaily.com/utilities-cut-to-warren-steel-holdings/.

8. Ibid.

9. Ibid.

10. Joo, "Warren Steel: The Day the Machines Went Quiet."

11. "Ukrainian Oligarchs Sued over $100M Loan 'Sham,'" *Law360*, 26 August 2019, https://www.law360.com/articles/1192470.

12. "Vadim Shulman," OCCRP, https://www.occrp.org/en/paradisepapers/profiles/vadim
-shulman.

13. "As Biden-Trump, Ukraine Debate Rages, Related Court Cases Land in Delaware," *Delaware Online*, 2 October 2019, https://www.delawareonline.com/story/money
/business/2019/10/02/biden-trump-ukraine-debate-rages-related-court-cases-land
-delaware/2374838001/.

14. Caryer, "Steal Country: The Case of Ukrainian Money Laundering in Northeast Ohio."

15. "Vadim M. Shulman; Bracha Foundation v. Igor Valeryevich Kolomoisky; Gennadiy Borisovich Bogolyubov; Mordechai Korf; Panikos Symeou; Joint Stock Company Commercial Bank PrivatBank; Warren Steel Holdings, LLC; Optima Acquisitions, LLC; Optima Group, LLC; Optima International; CC Metals and Alloys, LLC; Felman Trading, Inc.; Optima Fixed Income, LLC; Optima Ventures, LLC; Querella Holdings, Ltd.; Optima International of Miami, Inc.; 5251 36th Street, LLC; Georgian American

Alloys, Inc.; Halliwel Assets, Inc.," https://www.scribd.com/document/456427613 /Vadim-Shulman-August-2019-Delaware-Lawsuit-Against-Ihor-Kolomoisky.

16. Ibid.

17. Ibid.

18. Caryer, "Steal Country: The Case of Ukrainian Money Laundering in Northeast Ohio."

19. "Vadim M. Shulman; Bracha Foundation v. Igor Valeryevich Kolomoisky; Gennadiy Borisovich Bogolyubov; Mordechai Korf; Panikos Symeou; Joint Stock Company Commercial Bank PrivatBank; Warren Steel Holdings, LLC; Optima Acquisitions, LLC; Optima Group, LLC; Optima International; CC Metals and Alloys, LLC; Felman Trading, Inc.; Optima Fixed Income, LLC; Optima Ventures, LLC; Querella Holdings, Ltd.; Optima International of Miami, Inc.; 5251 36th Street, LLC; Georgian American Alloys, Inc.; Halliwel Assets, Inc."

20. Kovensky and Vikhrov, "The Spectacular Rise and Fall of Ihor Kolomoisky's Steel Empire."

21. Ibid.

22. "Felman Production Employee Reviews in New Haven, WV," Indeed, https:// www.indeed.com/cmp/Felman-Production/reviews?fcountry=US&floc =New+Haven%2C+WV.

23. Mike James, "KES to Shut Down Permanently," Independent, 9 January 2018, https:// www.dailyindependent.com/news/kes-to-shut-down-permanently/article_e299d072 -f589-11e7-8a3e-ab5b224c8b8d.html.

24. Sallah and Kozyreva, "With Deutsche Bank's Help, an Oligarch's Buying Spree Trails Ruin Across the US Heartland."

25. Hundreds of American steelworkers have fallen prey to Kolomoisky's designs, but as journalist Todd Prince reported in 2020, Kolomoisky may no longer need them. One of the remaining plants, located in western Kentucky, reportedly laid off the entirety of its workforce—and proceeded to turn into a "Bitcoin-mining operation," with "a warehouse full of computers that are churning out cryptocurrency," while the plant itself remains idle. Todd Prince, "Layoffs, Cryptocurrency, and Uncertainty at a Ukrainian Tycoon's Kentucky Factory," RFE/RL, 10 December 2020, https://www.rferl.org/a/layoffs-cryptocurrency and uncertainty-at-a-ukrainian-tycoons-kentucky-factory/30993969.html.

26. Interview with author.

27. Gregory Harutunian, "Harvard Motorola Site in Forfeit by Justice Department," McHenry Chronicle, 7 November 2018, https://chronicleillinois.com/news/mchenry -county-news/harvard-motorola-site-forfeited-by-justice-department/.

28. Interview with author.

29. Interview with author.

30. Interview with author.

31. Brittany Keeperman, "Owner of Former Motorola Campus in Harvard Faces Fraud Charges in Canada," Northwest Herald, 5 January 2018, https://www.shawlocal.com /2018/01/03/owner-of-former-motorola-campus-in-harvard-faces-fraud-charges-in -canada/aixf2dr/.

32. Alby Gallun, "Why One Far-Flung Suburb Is Fed Up with This Rogue Developer," *Crain's Chicago Business*, 2 August 2019, https://www.chicagobusiness.com/commercial -real-estate/why-one-far-flung-suburb-fed-rogue-developer.

33. Sherri Welch, "Former Hyatt Regency Hotel in Dearborn Shut Down by City," *Crain's Detroit*, 14 December 2018, https://www.crainsdetroit.com/hospitality/former-hyatt -regency-hotel-dearborn-shut-down-city.

34. Craig Offman, Steven Chase, and Xiao Xu, "Chinese Evidence, Canadian Charges: Accused Businessman Says Fraud Case Built with Coercion," *Globe and Mail*, 8 November 2018, https://www.theglobeandmail.com/politics/article-chinese-evidence-canadian -charges-accused-businessman-edward-gong/.

35. Sam Hurley, "How to Hide $53m: Mogul Used Mother and Son's Finance Firm," *New Zealand Herald*, 25 November 2019, https://www.newstalkzb.co.nz/news/business /chinese-canadian-mogul-edward-gong-used-auckland-mother-and-sons-finance-firm -to-hide-53m/.

36. Interview with author.

37. Interview with author.

38. Burgis, *Kleptopia*.

39. "Asset Recovery in Eurasia: Repatriation or Repay the Patron?," U.S. Helsinki Commission, 13 February 2019, https://www.csce.gov/sites/helsinkicommission.house .gov/files/unofficial-transcript/0213%20Asset%20Recovery%20in%20Eurasia%20 -%20Repatriation%20or%20Repay%20the%20Patron_Scrubbed.pdf.

40. Ibid.

41. Ibid.

PART IV: UNITED STATES OF ANONYMITY

1. Chayes, *On Corruption in America*.

CHAPTER 14: THE OLIGARCHS ARE JUST FRONTS

1. Philip Roth, *Reading Myself and Others* (New York: Vintage, 2007).

2. Randal C. Archibold, "Jean-Claude Duvalier Dies at 63; Ruled Haiti in Father's Brutal Fashion," *New York Times*, 4 October 2014, https://www.nytimes.com/2014/10/05 /world/americas/jean-claude-duvalier-haitis-baby-doc-dies-at-63.html.

3. "Duvalier Weds in Style," *Washington Post*, 28 May 1980, https://www.washingtonpost .com/archive/politics/1980/05/28/duvalier-weds-in-style/52843118-8bf3-485d-8909 -f95ce6e4dd13//.

4. "Haiti: Justice Denied by Duvalier's Death," Human Rights Watch, 4 October 2014, https://www.hrw.org/news/2014/10/04/haiti-justice-denied-duvaliers-death.

5. Sharman, *The Despot's Guide to Wealth Management*.

6. Interview with author.

7. Sharman, *The Despot's Guide to Wealth Management*.

8. Elaine Sciolino, "Reagan Orders Assets of the Duvaliers Frozen," *New York Times*, 20 March 1987, https://www.nytimes.com/1987/03/20/world/reagan-orders-assets-of-the -duvaliers-frozen.html.

9. Frank, "Secret Money: How Trump Made Millions Selling Condos to Unknown Buyers."

10. Betsy Swan and Tim Mak, "Trump Tower: Dictators' Home Away from Home," *Daily Beast*, 14 April 2017, https://www.thedailybeast.com/trump-tower-dictators-home -away-from-home.

11. The only reason we know of Baby Doc's investment in Trump properties—and of Trump personally signing the deed over to Baby Doc's lawyer, pocketing the proceeds—is the former Haitian dictator's ignominious end. In the mid-1980s, Haitians finally rose en masse against the despot, successfully ousting him from his perch. The succeeding government opened an investigation into Baby Doc's laundering operations. One investigator managed to track Baby Doc's financial streams directly to Trump Tower—though, as he tells it, it wasn't especially difficult. Baby Doc was "not the sharpest nail in the box," said the investigator; on one of the myriad checks Baby Doc used to loot the treasury, he'd written, "Apartment in Trump Tower." As the investigator said, "Even we could figure that one out." William Finnegan, "The Secret Keeper," *New Yorker*, 12 October 2009, https://www.newyorker.com/magazine/2009/10/19/the-secret-keeper

12. Frank, "Secret Money: How Trump Made Millions Selling Condos to Unknown Buyers."

13. Ibid.

14. Ibid.

15. Jim Zarroli and Alina Selyukh, "Trump SoHo: A Shiny Hotel Wrapped in Glass, but Hiding Mysteries," NPR, 7 November 2017, https://www.npr.org/2017/11/07 /560849787/trump-soho-a-shiny-hotel-wrapped-in-glass-but-hiding-mysteries.

16. Frank, "Secret Money: How Trump Made Millions Selling Condos to Unknown Buyers."

17. Ibid.

18. Rupert Neate, "Trump and Clinton Share Delaware Tax 'Loophole' Address with 285,000 Firms," *Guardian*, 25 April 2016, https://www.theguardian.com/business/2016 /apr/25/delaware-tax-loophole-1209-north-orange-trump-clinton.

19. Harper Neidig, "Trump Has 378 Businesses Registered in Delaware," *Hill*, 22 April 2016, https://thehill.com/blogs/ballot-box/presidential-races/277326-trump-has-378 -businesses-registered-in-delaware.

20. Karl Baker, "Delaware Dissolves Shell Companies Created to Pay Off Women by Trump-Fixer Michael Cohen," *Delaware News Journal*, 5 October 2020, https://www .delawareonline.com/story/news/2020/10/05/delaware-dissolves-llcs-created-pay-off -women-trump-fixer-michael-cohen/3623443001/.

21. Craig Unger, *House of Trump, House of Putin* (New York: Dutton, 2018).

22. "Semion Mogilevich," FBI Most Wanted, https://www.fbi.gov/wanted/topten/topten -history/hires_images/FBI-494-SemionMogilevich.jpg/view.

23. Craig Horowitz, "Iced," *New York*, 19 November 2004, https://nymag.com/nymetro /news/people/features/10490/.

24. Michael Weiss and Casey Michel, "The Alleged Russian Mobsters in Trump World's Orbit: A Dirty Dozen," *Daily Beast*, 6 December 2019, https://www.thedailybeast.com /the-alleged-russian-mobsters-in-trump-worlds-orbit-a-dirty-dozen.

25. Craig Unger, "Trump's Russian Laundromat," *New Republic*, 13 July 2017, https:// newrepublic.com/article/143586/trumps-russian-laundromat-trump-tower-luxury -high-rises-dirty-money-international-crime-syndicate.

26. Craig Unger, "Trump's Businesses Are Full of Dirty Russian Money. The Scandal Is That It's Legal," *Washington Post*, 29 March 2019, https://www.washingtonpost.com /outlook/trumps-businesses-are-full-of-dirty-russian-money-the-scandal-is-thats -legal/2019/03/29/11b812da-5171-11e9-88a1-ed346f0ec94f_story.html.

27. Alexandra Clough, "Trump in Palm Beach: Did Russian Mansion Buyer Make Money?," *Palm Beach Post*, 17 February 2019, https://www.palmbeachpost.com/news/20190217 /trump-in-palm-beach-did-russian-mansion-buyer-make-money.

28. Frank Cerabino, "Cerabino: A New Twist in the Old Saga of That Palm Beach Mansion Trump Made a Killing off Of," *Palm Beach Post*, 11 September 2020, https://www .palmbeachpost.com/story/news/columns/2020/09/11/michael-cohens-take-trumps -sale-palm-beach-estate-russian/3468953001/.

29. Kevin G. Hall and Ben Wieder, "Trump Dreamed of His Name on Towers Across Former Soviet Union," *Miami Herald*, 30 June 2017, https://www.miamiherald.com /news/politics-government/article158519159.html.

30. Burgis, "The Secret Scheme to Skim Millions off Central Asia's Pipeline Megaproject."

31. Aubrey Belford, Sander Rietveld, and Gabrielle Paluch, "The Winding Money Trail from Kazakhstan to Trump SoHo," *McClatchy*, 26 June 2018, https://www.mcclatchydc .com/news/nation-world/article213846794.html.

32. Richard C. Paddock and Eric Lipton, "Trump's Indonesia Projects, Still Moving Ahead, Create Potential Conflicts," *New York Times*, 31 December 2016, https:// www.nytimes.com/2016/12/31/world/asia/indonesia-donald-trump-resort.html? _r=1.

33. "Ivanka Trump Exclusive at Trump Ocean Club Panama," YouTube, https://www .youtube.com/watch?v=Z1ixnO2_x9Y.

34. Ned Parker, Stephen Grey, Stefanie Eschenbacher, Roman Anin, Brad Brooks, and Christine Murray, "Ivanka and the Fugitive from Panama," Reuters, 17 November 2017, https://www.reuters.com/investigates/special-report/usa-trump-panama/.

35. "Narco-a-Lago: Money Laundering at the Trump Ocean Club Panama," November 2017, Global Witness, https://www.globalwitness.org/en/campaigns/corruption-and -money-laundering/narco-a-lago-panama/.

36. "Lifestyles of the Rich and Shameless: Trump Edition 2006–2011," Global Witness, 17 November 2007, https://www.globalwitness.org/en/campaigns/corruption-and -money-laundering/lifestyles-rich-and-shameless-trump-edition-2006-2011/.

37. "Trump Ocean Club Panama," YouTube, https://www.youtube.com/watch?v =BMSlAb4RD7M.

38. Casey Michel, "Ivanka Trump's Starring Role in Her Father's Financial Troubles," *New Republic*, 30 September 2020, https://newrepublic.com/article/159546/ivanka-trump -tax-evasion-foreign-corruption.

39. Hogan Lovells, "Bearer Shares Abolished from 26 May 2015," Lexology, 2 June 2015, https://www.lexology.com/library/detail.aspx?g=a8e97ede-6a00-4191-b844-2bc f5ae90e9d.

40. Casey Michel, "Why Has Congress Stalled on Investigating Money Laundering Allegations at Trump Properties?," *ThinkProgress*, 11 April 2019, https://archive.thinkprogress .org/where-are-the-investigations-into-the-trump-properties-linked-to-foreign -money-laundering-705464010f8a/.

41. Parker et al., "Ivanka and the Fugitive from Panama."

42. David A. Fahrenthold, "Owners of Former Trump Hotel in Panama Say President's Company Evaded Taxes," *Washington Post*, 3 June 2019, https://www.washingtonpost .com/politics/owners-of-former-trump-hotel-in-panama-say-presidents-firm-evaded -taxes/2019/06/03/fe70d344-866b-11e9-a870-b9c411dc4312_story.html.

43. Adam Davidson, "Donald Trump's Worst Deal," *New Yorker*, 5 March 2017, https:// www.newyorker.com/magazine/2017/03/13/donald-trumps-worst-deal.

44. Robbie Gramer, "Trump Hotel in Baku Partnered with 'Notoriously Corrupt' Oligarch Family with Ties to Iranian Revolutionary Guard Corps," *Foreign Policy*, 6 March 2017, https://foreignpolicy.com/2017/03/06/trump-hotel-in-baku-partnered -with-notoriously-corrupt-oligarch-with-ties-to-iranian-revolutionary-guard-corps -new-yorker-report-azerbaijan-iran-corruption-conflict-of-interest-mammadov/.

45. Davidson, "Donald Trump's Worst Deal."

46. Michel, "Ivanka Trump's Starring Role in Her Father's Financial Troubles."

47. Martha Ross, "Ivanka Trump Played Key Role in Her Father's Failed—and Potentially Corrupt—Azerbaijan Hotel Deal, Report Says," *Mercury News*, 10 March 2017, https://www.mercurynews.com/2017/03/10/ivanka-trump-played-key-role-in-her -fathers-failed-and-potentially-corrupt-azerbaijan-hotel-deal-report-says/.

48. Ivanka Trump, Instagram, https://www.instagram.com/p/vys5QXikA2/.

49. Despite Ivanka's best efforts, her alleged involvement with the Azeri project still remains available via Internet Archive: "From Ivanka's Desk: Trump Hotel Baku," 11 November 2014, https://web.archive.org/web/20150502122726/https://www.ivankatrump .com/ivankas-office-trump-tower-baku/.

50. Meghan Keneally, "Timeline of Paul Manafort's Role in the Trump Campaign," ABC News, 30 October 2017, https://abcnews.go.com/Politics/timeline-paul-manaforts -role-trump-campaign/story?id=50808957.

51. While he's not often associated with America's kleptocratic transformation, it's worth noting that no former presidential candidate has made anywhere near the money that Bob Dole, the former Kansas senator and 1996 GOP candidate, has from lobbying on behalf of sleazy, corrupt foreign clients. Not only did Dole specifically help whitewash Russian oligarch Oleg Deripaska, now sanctioned by the U.S. for his role in Russia's 2016 interference efforts, but he sat on the board of Kyrgyzstan's Asia Universal Bank, one of the most crooked banks the former Soviet region has ever produced.

As one former Kyrgyz official told me about Dole, "I remember being disgusted by how cheap U.S. politicians [were] on sale." Casey Michel, "We Finally Know Why a Former GOP Presidential Nominee Joined the Most Crooked Bank in Central Asia," *ThinkProgress*, 28 August 2018, https://archive.thinkprogress.org/paul-manafort-bob-dole-board-of-crooked-bank-central-asia-413f55b4ce82/.

52. Sharman, *The Despot's Guide to Wealth Management*.

53. Ibid.

54. Nesima Aberra, "On Paul Manafort and Foreign Lobbying: A Q&A with the Author of 'The Torturers' Lobby,'" Center for Public Integrity, 8 August 2018, https://publicintegrity.org/politics/on-paul-manafort-and-foreign-lobbying-a-qa-with-the-author-of-the-torturers-lobby/.

55. Meyer, "Law Firm That Worked with Manafort in Ukraine Admits to Misleading DOJ."

56. See Skadden Arps registration statement with the U.S. Department of Justice at https://efile.fara.gov/docs/6617-Registration-Statement-20190118-1.pdf; and Maximilian Hess, "Wooing the West: Who Is Ukraine's Viktor Pinchuk?," *Eurasianet*, 26 February 2020, https://eurasianet.org/wooing-the-west-who-is-ukraines-viktor-pinchuk.

57. "Prominent Global Law Firm Agrees to Register as an Agent of a Foreign Principal," U.S. Department of Justice, 17 January 2019, https://www.justice.gov/opa/pr/prominent-global-law-firm-agrees-register-agent-foreign-principal.

58. Bermet Talant, "Pinchuk Denies He Paid US Law Firm for Report About Tymoshenko," *Kyiv Post*, 21 January 2019, https://www.kyivpost.com/ukraine-politics/us-law-firm-behind-report-whitewashing-tymoshenko-prosecution-thought-pinchuk-paid-for-it.html; Josh Gerstein, "Democratic Pollster Divulges Details to Jurors About Greg Craig's Ukraine Work," *Politico*, 16 August 2019, https://www.politico.com/story/2019/08/16/greg-craig-trial-ukraine-1466669; and "Gregory Craig statement-4–11–19," YouTube, https://www.youtube.com/watch?v=HDT3Xsc87sA.

59. One of the members of the Trump campaign's infamous 2016 meeting at Trump Tower with a number of Kremlin-linked figures was a gentleman named Ike Kaveladze, who had previously been outed for setting up approximately 2,000 shell companies in Delaware for myriad Russian nationals. These companies moved over $1.4 billion, though the sources of these funds were unknown. Kaveladze, as Levin later said, was the "poster child" for shell companies and money laundering. Raymond Bonner, "Laundering of Money Seen as 'Easy,'" *New York Times*, 29 November 2009, nytimes.com/2000/11/29/business/laundering-of-money-seen-as-easy.html%20and%20https://www.nbcnews.com/news/us-news/ike-kaveladze-named-eighth-person-trump-meeting-n784216.

60. Philip Elliott, "How Donald Trump Hired and Fired Paul Manafort," *Time*, 30 October 2017, https://time.com/5003298/paul-manafort-indictment-donald-trump/.

CHAPTER 15: CORRUPTION IN THE FLESH

1. Eliot Asinof, *Eight Men Out* (New York: Henry Holt, 1963).

2. https://www.instagram.com/p/BknayFBgcC2/?taken-by=boorossinicte.

3. https://www.instagram.com/p/BkghoSxgpZa/?igshid=10mliilqisrim.

4. https://www.instagram.com/p/Bkp3v8QAmZH/.

5. https://www.instagram.com/p/BkggHjlg_ld/.

6. https://www.instagram.com/p/BkfVFnlD_N-/?igshid=1wt83207hjnt4.

7. https://www.instagram.com/p/Bkgg6-wAZZm/.

8. https://www.instagram.com/p/Bkp3v8QAmZH/.

9. "Equatorial Guinea VP Teodorin Obiang Sentenced in France," BBC, 27 October 2017, https://www.bbc.com/news/world-europe-41775070.

10. "Swiss to Auction 25 Supercars Seized from Son of Equatorial Guinea Dictator," *Guardian*, 28 September 2019, https://www.theguardian.com/world/2019/sep/29/swiss-to -auction-25-supercars-seized-from-son-of-equatorial-guinea-dictator.

11. Maria Clara Pestre and Gram Slattery, "Brazil Probes Money Laundering After Seizing Diamond-Studded Watches," Reuters, 10 October 2018, https://www.reuters .com/article/us-brazil-equatorial/brazil-probes-money-laundering-after-seizing -diamond-studded-watches-idUSKCN1MK22G.

12. "Teodorin Obiang: '$16m Seized' from E. Guinea Leader's Son," BBC, 17 September 2018, https://www.bbc.com/news/world-africa-45546655.

13. It's worth noting that Teodorin's ascension to the presidency of Equatorial Guinea has one hurdle remaining in the form of his half brother, Gabriel Obiang Lima, who is no stranger to transnational money laundering himself. Currently Equatorial Guinea's minister of hydrocarbons, Gabriel—despite the fact that he was a central player in the Riggs Bank scandal—is widely viewed as far more financially and politically savvy than Teodorin, with a far keener ability to maintain a low profile. Given that children of ruling despotic kleptocrats elsewhere (including Kazakhstan's Dariga Nazarbayeva and Uzbekistan's Gulnara Karimova) fell from grace after investigators discovered their laundered assets in the West, Teodorin might not want to imagine himself on Equatorial Guinea's throne just yet. Delfin Mocache Massoko (*Diario Rombe*), Antonio Baquero (OCCRP), Micael Pereira (*Expresso*), Flora Alexandrou, Linda van der Pol, Mark Anderson (OCCRP), and Stelios Orphanides (OCCRP), "Equatorial Guinea's Oil Minister Allegedly Siphoned Off Millions from Public Construction Project," OCCRP, 8 January 2021, https://www.occrp.org/en/investigations/equatorial-guineas -oil-minister-allegedly siphoned off-millions-from-public-construction-project.

14. https://www.instagram.com/p/BjdS2regh_L/.

15. https://www.instagram.com/p/BjD13WbjaEZ/.

16. https://www.instagram.com/p/BjDt5UEAJEB/.

17. Interview with author.

18. Interview with author.

19. Katherine Sullivan, "How a Nigerian Presidential Candidate Hired a Trump Lobbyist and Ended Up in Trump's Lobby—'Trump, Inc.' Podcast," *ProPublica*, 27 February 2019, https://www.propublica.org/article/trump-inc-podcast-nigerian-presidential -candidate-atiku-abubakar.

20. Pierre Dupont, Roshanak Taghavi, and Kira Zalan, "Gabon's First Family Stashed Cash in DC Property," OCCRP, 23 November 2020, https://www.occrp.org/en/investigations /gabons-first-family-stashed-cash-in-dc-property.

21. Teodorin's also back in the legal game in the U.S., having retained a California lawyer named Kevin Fisher to try to claim he lost out on money from the sale of his seized Malibu mansion.

22. Max Bearak, "The Real Dictators of Potomac, Maryland," *Washington Post*, 3 February 2017, https://www.washingtonpost.com/news/worldviews/wp/2017/02/03/the -real-dictators-of-potomac-maryland/.

23. Anthony Summers, *The Arrogance of Power* (New York: Penguin, 2001).

24. Jim Zarroli, "Trump Used to Disparage an Anti-Bribery Law; Will He Enforce It Now?," NPR, 8 November 2017, https://www.npr.org/2017/11/08/561059555/trump -used-to-disparage-an-anti-bribery-law-will-he-enforce-it-now.

25. Perlstein, *Reaganland*.

26. Jeanna Smialek, "Trump Tried to Kill Anti-Bribery Rule He Deemed 'Unfair,' New Book Alleges," *New York Times*, 15 January 2020, https://www.nytimes.com/2020/01 /15/business/economy/trump-bribery-law.html.

27. "The 2020 Election: An Anti-Corruption and Compliance Perspective," *Bribe, Swindle, or Steal*, 28 October 2020, https://podcasts.apple.com/us/podcast/2020-election -anti-corruption-compliance-perspective/id1231612850?i=1000496320745.

28. Casey Michel, "Trump Administration Deals a Blow to International Anti-Corruption Efforts," *ThinkProgress*, 15 November 2017, https://archive.thinkprogress.org/trump -anti-corruption-measures/.

29. Casey Michel, "Donald Trump's Quiet Christmas Gift to the Kleptocrats," *New Republic*, 6 January 2020, https://newrepublic.com/article/156130/donald-trumps-quiet -christmas-gift-kleptocrats.

30. Cataloguing all of the Trump administration's pro-corruption moves—including gutting anticorruption efforts in Guatemala, pardoning individuals like Manafort, etc.—would take up an entire book, so we'll let these examples suffice for a far broader trend. See, for instance: Mary Beth Sheridan, "How U.S. Apathy Helped Kill a Pioneering Anti-Corruption Campaign in Guatemala," *Washington Post*, 14 June 2019, https://www.washingtonpost.com/world/the_americas/how-us-apathy-helped-kill-a -pioneering-anticorruption-campaign-in-guatemala/2019/06/14/cc4f464a-1e5e-11e9 -a759-2b8541bbbe20_story.html.

31. "Proposed US Oil Anti-Corruption Rule Would Fail to Deter Corruption," Global Witness, 19 December 2019, https://www.globalwitness.org/en/press-releases/proposed-us -oil-anti-corruption-rule-would-fail-deter-corruption/.

32. "Draft SEC Oil and Mining Rule Would Facilitate Corruption," Oxfam, 18 December 2019, https://www.oxfamamerica.org/press/draft-sec-oil-and-mining-rule-would -facilitate-corruption/.

33. "A Look At President Trump's Anti-Corruption Record," NPR, 8 October 2019, https:// www.npr.org/2019/10/08/768373873/a-look-at-president-trumps-anti-corruption -record."

34. Justin Sink, "Trump Revokes Lobbying Ban After Promising to 'Drain the Swamp,'" *Bloomberg*, 20 January 2021, https://www.bloomberg.com/news/articles/2021-01-20 /trump-revokes-lobbying-ban-after-promising-to-drain-the-swamp.

35. Gemma Acton, "US Ethics Chief Slams Trump 'Halfway Blind' Trust as Failing to Meet Acceptable Standard," CNBC, 12 January 2017, https://www.cnbc.com/2017/01/12/us-ethics-chief-slams-trump-halfway-blind-trust-as-failing-to-meet-acceptable-standard.html.

36. David Fahrenthold and Jonathan O'Connell, "Saudi-Funded Lobbyist Paid for 500 Rooms at Trump's Hotel After 2016 Election," *Washington Post*, 5 December 2018, https://www.washingtonpost.com/politics/saudi-funded-lobbyist-paid-for-500-rooms-at-trumps-hotel-after-2016-election/2018/12/05/29603a64-f417-11e8-bc79-68604ed88993_story.html.

37. Russ Buettner, Susanne Craig, and Mike McIntire, "Long-Concealed Records Show Trump's Chronic Losses and Years of Tax Avoidance," *New York Times*, 27 September 2020, https://www.nytimes.com/interactive/2020/09/27/us/donald-trump-taxes.html.

38. Ilya Marritz, Justin Elliott, and Zach Everson, "Romanian Prime Minister Is Staying at Trump's D.C. Hotel," *ProPublica*, 25 March 2019, https://www.propublica.org/article/trump-inc-podcast-viorica-dancila-trump-hotel.

39. Jonathan O'Connell, "From Trump Hotel Lobby to White House, Malaysian Prime Minister Gets VIP Treatment," *Washington Post*, 12 September 2017, https://www.washingtonpost.com/politics/from-trump-hotel-lobby-to-white-house-malaysian-prime-minister-gets-vip-treatment/2017/09/12/1b296f54-97d1-11e7-87fc-c3f7ee4035c9_story.html.

40. Bill Chappell, "Malaysia's Former PM Najib Razak Begins Trial on 1MDB Slush-Fund Charges," NPR, 3 April 2019, https://www.npr.org/2019/04/03/709388200/malaysias-former-pm-najib-razak-begins-trial-on-1mdb-slush-fund-charges.

41. Raymond Arke, "Failed Nigerian Presidential Candidate Lobbying US to Recognize Him as 'Authentic President,'" *OpenSecrets*, 8 April 2019, https://www.opensecrets.org/news/2019/04/failed-nigerian-presidential-candidate-lobbying-u-s-to-recognize-him-as-authentic-president/.

42. Nick Penzenstadler, Steve Reilly, and John Kelly, "Most Trump Real Estate Now Sold to Secretive Buyers," *USA Today*, 13 June 2017, https://www.usatoday.com/story/news/2017/06/13/trump-property-buyers-make-clear-shift-secretive-llcs/102399558/.

43. Nick Penzenstadler, Steve Reilly, and John Kelly, "Here's Who Is Behind LLCs Buying Trump Real Estate," *USA Today*, 21 June 2017, https://www.usatoday.com/story/news/2017/06/13/heres-who-behind-llcs-buying-trump-real-estate/102382726/.

44. Jesse Drucker, "$7 Million Trump Building Condo Tied to Scandal-Scarred Foreign Leader," *New York Times*, 10 April 2019, https://www.nytimes.com/2019/04/10/business/trump-congo.html.

45. "Trump's Luxury Condo: A Congolese State Affair," Global Witness, 10 April 2019, https://www.globalwitness.org/en/campaigns/corruption-and-money-laundering/trumps-luxury-condo-a-congolese-state-affair/.

46. Steve Peoples and Will Weissert, "At Rally, Warren Decries Trump as 'Corruption in the Flesh,'" Associated Press, 17 September 2019, https://apnews.com/article/6539d6cff0c047f9862e72bd01a4f0af.

CHAPTER 16: OPEN SEASON

1. John Cassidy, "The Extraordinary Impeachment Testimony of Fiona Hill," *New Yorker*, 21 November 2019, https://www.newyorker.com/news/our-columnists/the-extraordinary-impeachment-testimony-of-fiona-hill.

2. Aisha Kehoe Down, "President's Oligarch Friend Suspected of Theft Returns to Ukraine," OCCRP, 20 May 2019, https://www.occrp.org/en/daily/9757-president-s-oligarch-friend-suspected-of-theft-returns-to-ukraine.

3. Taras Kuzio, "Two Ways the West Enables Corruption in Ukraine," Atlantic Council, 3 April 2018, https://www.atlanticcouncil.org/blogs/ukrainealert/two-ways-the-west-enables-corruption-in-ukraine/.

4. Anton Trojanovski, "A Ukrainian Billionaire Fought Russia. Now He's Ready to Embrace It," *New York Times*, 13 November 2019, https://www.nytimes.com/2019/11/13/world/europe/ukraine-ihor-kolomoisky-russia.html.

5. Steven Mufson, "She Fixed Ukraine's Economy—and Was Run Out of Her Job by Death Threats," *Washington Post*, 6 May 2017, https://www.washingtonpost.com/business/economy/she-fixed-ukraines-economy-and-was-run-out-of-her-job-by-death-threats/2017/05/05/2f556f40-2f90-11e7-8674-437ddb6e813e_story.html.

6. Natalia Zinets, "Ukrainian Reformers Under Fire as Battle over PrivatBank Heats Up," Reuters, 27 June 2019, https://www.reuters.com/article/uk-ukraine-cenbank-reformers-insight/ukrainian-reformers-under-fire-as-battle-over-privatbank-heats-up-idUKKCN1TS0OL?edition-redirect=uk.

7. Mufson, "She Fixed Ukraine's Economy—and Was Run Out of Her Job by Death Threats."

8. Shaun Walker and Andrew Roth, "'It's Revenge': Ukraine's Ex-Central Banker Blames Oligarch for Attacks," *Guardian*, 12 November 2019, https://www.theguardian.com/world/2019/nov/12/revenge-ukraine-ex-central-banker-oligarch-attacks.

9. Tom Arnold and Natalia Zinets, "PrivatBank Wins London Appeal in Lawsuit Against Ex-Owners," Reuters, 15 October 2019, https://www.reuters.com/article/us-ukraine-privatbank/privatbank-wins-london-appeal-in-lawsuit-against-ex-owners-idUSKBN1WU1JE.

10. Michael Sallah, Tanya Kozyreva, and Christopher Miller, "This Billionaire Oligarch Is Being Investigated by a US Federal Grand Jury for Alleged Money Laundering," *BuzzFeed*, 19 May 2020, https://www.buzzfeednews.com/article/mikesallah/ukraine-billionaire-oligarch-money-laundering-investigation.

11. Patrick Reevell, "What to Know About Volodymyr Zelensky, the Comedian-Turned President of Ukraine," ABC News, 25 September 2019, https://abcnews.go.com/International/comedian-volodymyr-zelensky-played-president-tv-now-favorite/story?id=62038641.

12. "Ukraine Election: Comedian Zelensky Wins Presidency by Landslide," BBC, 22 April 2019, https://www.bbc.com/news/world-europe-48007487.

13. Fabrice Deprez, "How an Embattled Ukrainian Oligarch Has Kept His Grip on an Eco-

nomic Empire," *Eurasianet*, 10 April 2020, https://eurasianet.org/how-an-embattled
-ukrainian-oligarch-has-kept-his-grip-on-an-economic-empire.

14. "Zelensky Holds All-Day Press Conference (LIVE)," *Kyiv Post*, 10 October 2019,
https://www.kyivpost.com/ukraine-politics/zelensky-holds-6-hour-press-conference
-live.html.

15. Matthias Williams and Natalia Zinets, "Comedian Faces Scrutiny over Oligarch Ties
in Ukraine Presidential Race," Reuters, 1 April 2019, https://www.reuters.com/article
/us-ukraine-election-zelenskiy-oligarch/comedian-faces-scrutiny-over-oligarch-ties
-in-ukraine-presidential-race-idUSKCN1RD30L.

16. "Ukrainian Tycoon Kolomoisky's Change of Heart over Russia, in Quotes," *Moscow
Times*, 13 November 2019, https://www.themoscowtimes.com/2019/11/13/ukrainian
-tycoon-kolomoiskys-change-of-heart-over-russia-in-quotes-a68157.

17. Brian Whitmore, "Ukraine's Third Revolution," *The Power Vertical*, 18 December 2020,
https://podcasts.apple.com/us/podcast/the-power-vertical-podcast-by-brian-whitmore
/id1538016458?i=1000502860468.

18. "What Ukraine's 'Anti-Kolomoisky' Law Is and What It Does," *Hromadske*, 14 May 2020,
https://en.hromadske.ua/posts/what-the-anti-kolomoisky-law-changes-and-whether
-its-necessary.

19. David L. Stern and Robyn Dixon, "Ukraine Blocks Oligarch's Bid to Regain Bank
and Clears Way for International Funds," *Washington Post*, 13 May 2020, https://www
.washingtonpost.com/world/europe/ukraine-zelensky-kolomoisky-bank-imf/2020
/05/13/3fbd2802-8571-11ea-81a3-9690c9881111_story.html.

20. Trump didn't do much to dispel questions and concerns about his relationship with
Moscow. He offered hints about potentially recognizing Russian control of Crimea,
and held one-on-one meetings with Russian president Vladimir Putin with no note
takers present. He displayed an odd, treacly fealty toward the Russian dictator, time
and again. He also treated the fledgling Ukrainian government, which had previously
looked to the U.S. for support, with clear disdain—despite the fact that the country
was on the front lines of the fight between democracy and kleptocratic autocracy. In
private, Trump wondered aloud if Ukraine was even a "real country." All the while,
as the *Washington Post* reported, Trump and his administration "sought repeatedly to
cut foreign aid programs tasked with combating corruption in Ukraine"—including
funds allocated for the National Anti-Corruption Bureau, Kyiv's foremost anticorruption body. Erica Werner, "Trump Administration Sought Billions of Dollars in
Cuts to Programs Aimed at Fighting Corruption in Ukraine and Elsewhere," *Washington Post*, 23 October 2019, https://www.washingtonpost.com/us-policy/2019/10
/23/trump-administration-sought-billions-dollars-cuts-programs-aimed-fighting
-corruption-ukraine-abroad/.

21. Heather Vogell, "Why Aren't Hedge Funds Required to Fight Money Laundering?,"
ProPublica, 23 January 2019, https://www.propublica.org/article/why-arent-hedge
-funds-required-to-fight-money-laundering.

22. Bei Ju, "Hedge Fund Assets Dip Below $3 Trillion to Least in Six Years," *Bloomberg*,

23 April 2020, https://www.bloomberg.com/news/articles/2020-04-24/hedge-fund-assets-dip-below-3-trillion-to-least-in-six-years.

23. Burgis, *Kleptopia*.

24. Joshua Kirschenbaum and David Murray, "An Effective American Regime to Counter Illicit Finance," German Marshall Fund, 18 December 2018, https://securingdemocracy.gmfus.org/an-effective-american-regime-to-counter-illicit-finance/.

25. Joshua Kirschenbaum and David Murray, "Do You Know Which Nations Own Your Data? The U.S. Government Doesn't," *Bloomberg*, 23 May 2019, https://www.bloomberg.com/opinion/articles/2019-05-23/private-equity-hides-foreign-capital-from-u-s-scrutiny.

26. Chayes, *On Corruption in America*.

27. Kirschenbaum and Murray, "An Effective American Regime to Counter Illicit Finance."

28. Timothy Lloyd, "FBI Concerned over Laundering Risks in Private Equity, Hedge Funds—Leaked Document," Reuters, 14 July 2020, https://www.reuters.com/article/bc-finreg-fbi-laundering-private-equity/fbi-concerned-over-laundering-risks-in-private-equity-hedge-funds-leaked-document-idUSKCN24F1TP.

29. Interview with author.

30. Lloyd, "FBI Concerned over Laundering Risks in Private Equity, Hedge Funds—Leaked Document."

31. Ibid.

32. Ovetta Wiggins, "Election System Firm with Maryland Contract Has Ties to Russian Oligarch, FBI Tells State," *Washington Post*, 13 July 2018, https://www.washingtonpost.com/local/md-politics/marylands-election-system-tied-to-russian-oligarch-fbi-tells-state/2018/07/13/89b8ce56-86fa-11e8-8f6c-46cb43e3f306_story.html.

33. "Maryland Elections Company Bought by Russian Oligarch Close to Putin," *Guardian*, 14 July 2018, https://www.theguardian.com/us-news/2018/jul/14/maryland-elections-company-russian-oligarch-putin.

34. David Hoffman, *The Oligarchs* (New York: PublicAffairs, 2011).

35. Luke Broadwater and Jean Marbella, "State Investigates Russian Investor's Ties to Maryland Elections Software," *Baltimore Sun*, 13 July 2018, https://www.baltimoresun.com/politics/bs-md-election-russia-20180713-story.html.

36. "At Your Service," Transparency International, October 2019, https://www.transparency.org.uk/tags/reputation-laundering.

37. Anti-Corruption Data Collective, https://www.acdatacollective.org/.

38. The donation information we accessed often only captured the monetary range in which each donation fell, rather than its specific value—i.e., "donated between $1 million and $5 million"—which is why the numbers cited are based on these ranges. Casey Michel and David Szakonyi, "America's Cultural Institutions Are Quietly Fueled by Russian Corruption," *Foreign Policy*, 30 October 2020, https://foreignpolicy.com/2020/10/30/americas-cultural-institutions-are-quietly-fueled-by-russian-corruption/.

39. It's worth noting that American universities don't always need donations to help kleptocrats launder their images in the West. For instance, in 2009 at Rice University

(where I was then studying as an undergraduate), the school's Baker Institute for Public Policy hosted none other than President Obiang. According to the program, Obiang—again, the longest-tenured dictator in the world—was a leader whose "government has made significant investments in increasing transparency in its financial practices and diversifying its economy, modernizing its infrastructure, strengthening its public health system, and promoting education to build a strong foundation for the future of the country. Under Obiang's leadership, Equatorial Guinea has reopened schools, expanded primary education, and restored public utilities and roads." There was nothing in the release regarding Obiang's history of torture, or his regime's disappearance of opposition figures and journalists. "Equatorial Guinea: A Vision of the Future," James A. Baker III Institute for Public Policy, Rice University, https://www.bakerinstitute.org/media/files/event/cbca3620/EF-event-ObiangProgram-091809.pdf.

40. Michel and Szakonyi, "America's Cultural Institutions Are Quietly Fueled by Russian Corruption."

41. "Wilson Center Honors Vekselberg and Cloherty at First Kathryn and Shelby Cullom Davis Awards Dinner," Wilson Center, 15 November 2007, https://www.wilsoncenter.org/article/wilson-center-honors-vekselberg-and-cloherty-first-kathryn-and-shelby-cullom-davis-awards.

42. Skadden Arps registration statement.

43. "Recognizing Our Generous Supporters," Clinton Foundation, https://www.clintonfoundation.org/contributors?category=%2410%2C000%2C001+to+%2425%2C000%2C000.

44. Hess, "Wooing the West: Who Is Ukraine's Viktor Pinchuk?"

45. Casey Michel, "Kill the Messenger: How Russian and Post-Soviet Oligarchs Undermine the First Amendment," Free Russia Foundation, 16 April 2020, https://www.4freerussia.org/kill-the-messenger-how-russian-and-post-soviet-oligarchs-undermine-the-first-amendment/.

46. At last check, Blavatnik was worth just north of $30 billion, making him the 46th-richest person in the world—and now the wealthiest person in the United Kingdom. "Len Blavatnik," Forbes, https://www.forbes.com/profile/len-blavatnik/?sh=188db4a456f3.

47. Henry Foy and Max Seddon, "From Russian Oil to Rock'n'roll: The Rise of Len Blavatnik," Financial Times, 6 June 2019, https://www.ft.com/content/c1889f48-871a-11e9-a028-86cea8523dc2.

48. Zack O'Malley Greenburg, "Billionaire Len Blavatnik Buys Warner Music Group For $3.3 Billion," Forbes, 6 May 2011, https://www.forbes.com/sites/zackomalleygreenburg/2011/05/06/billionaire-len-blavatnik-buys-warner-music-group-for-3-3-billion/?sh=5a0e557e7eea.

49. Kim Masters, "Music's Mystery Mogul: Len Blavatnik, Trump and Their Russian Friends," Hollywood Reporter, 10 October 2018, https://www.hollywoodreporter.com/features/why-is-warner-music-group-owner-len-blavatnik-russia-probe-1150550.

50. Devon Pendleton, "The Meteoric Rise of Billionaire Len Blavatnik," Bloomberg, 26 April 2019, https://www.bloomberg.com/news/features/2019-04-26/the-meteoric-rise-of-billionaire-len-blavatnik.

51. "Board of Trustees," Carnegie Hall, https://www.carnegiehall.org/About/Leadership -and-Staff/Board-of-Trustees.

52. Alvin Powell, "A Gift to Turn Medical Discoveries into Treatments," *Harvard Gazette*, 8 November 2018, https://news.harvard.edu/gazette/story/2018/11/a-gift-to-harvard -to-turn-medical-discoveries-into-treatments/#:~:text=A%20foundation%20 headed%20by%20philanthropist,medical%20discoveries%20into%20patient%20 treatments.

53. Dan Friedman, "A Soviet-Born Billionaire Is Buying Influence at US Institutions. Anti-Corruption Activists Are Worried," *Mother Jones*, 8 October 2019, https://www .motherjones.com/politics/2019/10/council-on-foreign-relations-leonard-blavatnik -russia/.

54. John Santucci, Matthew Mosk, Katherine Faulders, and Soo Rin Kim, "EXCLU-SIVE: Special Counsel Probing Donations with Foreign Connections to Trump In-auguration," ABC News, 11 May 2018, https://abcnews.go.com/beta-story-container /Politics/exclusive-special-counsel-probing-donations-foreign-connections-trump /story?id=55054482.

55. Foy and Seddon, "From Russian Oil to Rock'n'roll: The Rise of Len Blavatnik."

56. Jennifer Gould, "Council on Foreign Relations Faces Backlash over $12M Len Blavat-nik Donation," *New York Post*, 7 October 2019, https://nypost.com/2019/10/07 /council-on-foreign-relations-faces-backlash-over-12m-len-blavatnik-donation/.

57. Max de Haldevang, "Top US Think Tank Criticized for Taking $12 Million from a Russia-Tied Oligarch," *Quartz*, 16 October 2019, https://qz.com/1721240/council-of -foreign-relations-criticized-for-russia-tied-donation/.

58. Casey Michel, "Money Talks: Len Blavatnik and the Council on Foreign Relations," *Bellingcat*, 10 October 2019, https://www.bellingcat.com/news/2019/10/10/money -talks-len-blavatnik-and-the-council-on-foreign-relations/.

59. Ann Marlowe, "Is Harvard Whitewashing a Russian Oligarch's Fortune?," *New York Times*, 5 December 2018, https://www.nytimes.com/2018/12/05/opinion/harvard -russian-oligarch-whitewash.html.

60. De Haldevang, "Top US Think Tank Criticized for Taking $12 Million from a Russia-Tied Oligarch."

61. Richard Haass, Twitter, https://twitter.com/richardhaass/status/1171519768077029376 ?lang=en.

62. Interview with author.

63. "Cambridge Becomes a Home for Ukrainian Studies," Cambridge University, 28 Sep-tember 2010, https://www.cam.ac.uk/research/news/cambridge-becomes-a-home-for -ukrainian-studies.

64. Kylie Mackie, "US: Ukrainian Oligarch and His Associate Are Tied to Russian Orga-nized Crime," OCCRP, 27 July 2017, https://www.occrp.org/en/daily/6775-us-ukrainian -oligarch-and-his-associate-are-tied-to-russian-organized-crime.

65. Betsy Swan and Adam Rawnsley, "Ukrainian Oligarch Seethed About 'Overlord' Biden for Years," *Daily Beast*, 28 October 2019, https://www.thedailybeast.com /ukrainian-oligarch-dmytro-firtash-seethed-about-overlord-joe-biden-for-years.

66. Tom Winter, "DOJ: Ex-Manafort Associate Firtash Is Top-Tier Comrade of Russian Mobsters," NBC News, 26 July 2017, https://www.nbcnews.com/news/us-news/doj-ex-manafort-associate-firtash-top-tier-comrade-russian-mobsters-n786806.

67. One of the lawyers Firtash dumped: Lanny Davis, who also happened to be on retainer to none other than President Obiang of Equatorial Guinea. The world of servicing kleptocratic figures can be a small one in Washington. Isaac Chotiner, "One Washington Lobbyist's 'Secret' Mission: To Empower a Dictator," New Republic, 22 October 2013, https://newrepublic.com/article/115296/lanny-daviss-career-empowering-dictators. In early 2021, Firtash rehired Davis; see Mikayla Easley, "Ukrainian Oligarch Rehires Political Consultant Lanny Davis in Bribery Case," ForeignLobby.com, 20 April 2021, https://www.foreignlobby.com/2021/04/20/ukrainian-oligarch-rehires-political-consultant-lanny-davis-in-bribery-case/. Another former lawyer who worked directly for Firtash: Michael Chertoff, now the trustee board chair of Freedom House.

68. Jo Becker, Walt Bogdanich, Maggie Haberman, and Ben Protess, "Why Giuliani Singled Out 2 Ukrainian Oligarchs to Help Look for Dirt," New York Times, 25 November 2019, https://www.nytimes.com/2019/11/25/us/giuliani-ukraine-oligarchs.html.

69. Vicky Ward and Marshall Cohen, "'I'm the Best-Paid Interpreter in the World': Indicted Giuliani Associate Lev Parnas Touted Windfall from Ukrainian Oligarch," CNN, 1 November 2019, https://www.cnn.com/2019/11/01/politics/parnas-firtash-giuliani-ties/index.html.

70. Casey Michel, "The Law That Could Take Down Rudy Giuliani," New Republic, 15 October 2019, https://newrepublic.com/article/155387/law-take-rudy-giuliani.

71. Josh Rudolph and Thomas Morley, "Covert Foreign Money: Financial Loopholes Exploited by Authoritarians to Fund Political Interference in Democracies," German Marshall Fund, 18 August 2020, https://www.gmfus.org/publications/covert-foreign-money-financial-loopholes-exploited-authoritarians-fund-political.

72. Sergii Leshchenko, "By Helping Giuliani, Ukrainian Politicians Help Russia," Ukraine Today, 25 December 2019, https://ukrainetoday.org/2019/12/25/8461/.

73. Matt Zapotosky, Rosalind S. Helderman, Tom Hamburger, and Josh Dawsey, "Prosecutors Flagged Possible Ties Between Ukrainian Gas Tycoon and Giuliani Associates," Washington Post, 22 October 2019, https://www.washingtonpost.com/politics/prosecutors-flagged-possible-ties-between-ukrainian-gas-tycoon-and-giuliani-associates/2019/10/22/4ee22e7c-f020-11e9-b648-76bcf86eb67e_story.html.

74. For a sense of just how successful Firtash was, compare his campaign to that of Kazakhstan's decades-long dictator, Nursultan Nazarbayev, a frumpy ogre dedicated to pillaging the country's national treasury, who demanded bribes from Western officials along the way. After the U.S. DOJ accused Nazarbayev of gobsmacking bribery—snowmobiles and speedboats for him and his family, and financial flows involving a series of secret Swiss bank accounts—Nazarbayev tried to lean on the Bush administration for help. The dictator sicced his underlings on Vice President Dick Cheney, who dodged Nazarbayev's efforts. (According to the Financial Times, Cheney "rebuffed" the Kazakhs, "recommending in essence that they hire a good lawyer.")

Nazarbayev then turned directly to Bush himself—but, as the *New York Times* reported, the dictator's henchmen were "told there was nothing the administration could do about the investigation." Jeff Gerth, "Bribery Inquiry Involves Kazakh Chief, and He's Unhappy," *New York Times*, 11 December 2002, https://www.nytimes.com/2002/12/11/world/bribery-inquiry-involves-kazakh-chief-and-he-s-unhappy.html, and Michel, "Donald Trump's Quiet Christmas Gift to the Kleptocrats."

75. Philip Zelikow, Eric Edelman, Kristofer Harrison, and Celeste Ward Gventer, "The Rise of Strategic Corruption," *Foreign Affairs*, July/August 2020, https://www.foreignaffairs.com/articles/united-states/2020-06-09/rise-strategic-corruption.

76. Natasha Bertrand, "Former Giuliani Associate Raises Questions About Hunter Biden's 'Hard Drive from Hell,'" *Politico*, 24 October 2020, https://www.politico.com/news/2020/10/24/hunter-biden-hard-drive-lev-parnas-432108.

77. It's worth noting that this wasn't Low's first alleged play for influence in Washington. As Bradley Hope and Tom Wright wrote, the Malaysian kleptocrat befriended Pras Michel (no relation to the author), a former member of the Fugees. In 2012, Low was said to have transferred some $20 million to a pair of companies linked to Michel, who then allegedly funneled some of the funds to a pro-Obama super PAC, with Low effectively using the former hip-hop star as a cutout on his way to the White House. See Hope and Wright, *Billion Dollar Whale*.

78. Viola Gienger and Ryan Goodman, "Timeline: Trump, Giuliani, Biden, and Ukrainegate," *Just Security*, 31 January 2020, https://www.justsecurity.org/66271/timeline-trump-giuliani-bidens-and-ukrainegate/.

79. Greg Farrell, "Trump Lawyer Kasowitz Bolsters Defense of Wealthy Ukrainian," *Bloomberg*, 14 November 2019, https://www.bloomberg.com/news/articles/2019-11-14/trump-lawyer-kasowitz-takes-on-ukrainian-billionaire-as-client.

80. Josh Kovensky, "EXCLUSIVE: Oligarch Kolomoisky Linked to Giuliani Campaign for Dirt," *Talking Points Memo*, 9 December 2019, https://talkingpointsmemo.com/muckraker/kolomoisky-giuliani-cummins-ukraine-biden-dirt.

81. Kenneth P. Vogel and Nicholas Fandos, "Senate Panel Delays Subpoena Vote over Concerns About Ukraine Witness," *New York Times*, 11 March 2020, https://www.nytimes.com/2020/03/11/us/politics/senate-subpoena-ron-johnson-ukraine.html.

82. Kenneth P. Vogel and Benjamin Novak, "Giuliani, Facing Scrutiny, Travels to Europe to Interview Ukrainians," *New York Times*, 4 December 2019, https://www.nytimes.com/2019/12/04/us/politics/giuliani-europe-impeachment.html.

83. Sergii Leshchenko, "How Kolomoisky's Prosecutor Fueled Giuliani's Conspiracies," *Kyiv Post*, 4 December 2019, https://www.kyivpost.com/article/opinion/op-ed/sergii-leshchenko-how-kolomoiskys-prosecutor-fueled-giulianis-conspiracies.html.

84. Ibid.

85. Ben Shreckinger, "Ukraine Scandal Ropes In Clinton-Era GOP Operatives," *Politico*, 3 October 2019, https://www.politico.com/news/2019/10/03/ukraine-scandal-digenova-toensing-022049.

86. Kovensky, "EXCLUSIVE: Oligarch Kolomoisky Linked to Giuliani Campaign for Dirt."

87. Ibid.

CHAPTER 17: AMERICAN KLEPTOCRACIES

1. Louisa Woodville, "Common Bonds: The Duty and Honor of Lee and Grant," *Humanities*, July/August 2007, https://www.neh.gov/humanities/2007/julyaugust/feature/common-bonds-the-duty-and-honor-lee-and-grant.

2. Tom Winter, Ken Dilanian, and Dan De Luce, "Who Is Dmytro Firtash? The Man Linked to $1 Million Loan to Giuliani Ally Has a Shadowy Past," NBC News, 25 January 2020, https://www.nbcnews.com/politics/politics-news/who-dmytro-firtash-man-linked-1-million-loan-giuliani-ally-n1121561.

3. Betsy Swan, "DOJ Moves to Seize Property from Ukrainian Oligarch Linked to Rudy Giuliani," *Politico*, 6 August 2020, https://www.politico.com/news/2020/08/06/doj-ukrainian-oligarch-392405.

4. John Caniglia and Eric Heisig, "FBI Raids Offices at Downtown One Cleveland Center Building Tied to Ukrainian Oligarch," *Cleveland Plain Dealer*, 5 August 2020, https://www.cleveland.com/court-justice/2020/08/fbi-raids-offices-at-downtown-one-cleveland-center building tied-to-ukrainian-oligarch.html.

5. "United States of America vs. Real Property Located at 55 Public Square, Cleveland, Ohio, With All Appurtenances, Improvements, and Attachments Thereon, and Any Right to Collect and Receive Any Profit, Rent, Income, and Proceeds Therefrom."

6. Ibid.

7. "United States of America vs. Real Property Located at 7505 and 7171 Forest Lane, Dallas, Texas 75230, with All Appurtenances, Improvements, and Attachments Thereon, and Any Right to Collect and Receive Any Profit, Rent, Income, and Proceeds Therefrom."

8. "Justice Department Seeks Forfeiture of Two Commercial Properties Purchased with Funds Misappropriated from PrivatBank in Ukraine."

9. "Public Designation of Oligarch and Former Ukrainian Public Official Ihor Kolomoyskyy Due to Involvement in Significant Corruption," U.S. Embassy in Ukraine, 5 March 2021, https://ua.usembassy.gov/public-designation-of-oligarch-and-former-ukrainian-public-official-ihor-kolomoyskyy-due-to-involvement-in-significant-corruption/.

10. U.S. Embassy Kyiv Twitter account, https://twitter.com/USEmbassyKyiv/status/1367825782182121474.

11. Christopher Maag, "President-Elect Joe Biden's Hometown of Wilmington, Delaware Is a Hub for Secrets," *NorthJersey.com*, 13 November 2020, https://www.northjersey.com/story/news/columnists/christopher-maag/2020/11/13/joe-biden-wilmington-delaware-hub-secrets/6225673002/.

12. Joe Biden, "Why America Must Lead Again," *Foreign Affairs*, March/April 2020, https://www.foreignaffairs.com/articles/united-states/2020-01-23/why-america-must-lead-again.

13. "The Biden Plan to Guarantee Government Works for the People," https://joebiden.com/governmentreform/.

14. Biden, "Why America Must Lead Again."

15. "Interim National Security Strategic Guidance," White House, March 2021, https://www.whitehouse.gov/wp-content/uploads/2021/03/NSC-1v2.pdf.

16. Jen Kirby, "The US Has Made Its Biggest Anti-Money-Laundering Changes in Years," *Vox*, 4 January 2021, https://www.vox.com/22188223/congress-anti-money-laundering-anonymous-shell-companies-ban-defense-bill.

17. Jack Hagel, "Defense-Bill Override Paves Way for Overhaul of Anti-Money-Laundering Rules," *Wall Street Journal*, 1 January 2021, https://www.wsj.com/articles/defense-bill-override-paves-way-for-overhaul-of-anti-money-laundering-rules-11609542221.

18. Zachary Warmbrodt, "Lawmakers Clinch Deal on Decadelong Fight Against Shell Companies," *Politico*, 25 November 2020, https://www.politico.com/news/2020/11/25/lawmakers-fight-shell-companies-440618. Full disclosure: I've written for the FACT Coalition in the past.

19. Kirby, "The US Has Made Its Biggest Anti-Money-Laundering Changes in Years."

20. "Georgaphic Targeting Orders," U.S. Treasury Department, 4 November 2020, https://www.fincen.gov/sites/default/files/shared/508_Real%20Estate%20GTO%20Order%20FINAL%20GENERIC%2011.4.2020.pdf.

21. Sean Hundtofte and Ville Rantala, "Anonymous Capital Flows and U.S. Housing Markets," University of Miami Business School Research Paper No. 18-3, 28 May 2018, https://papers.ssrn.com/sol3/papers.cfm?abstract_id=3186634.

22. Iliana Magra, "Britain Is Targeting 'Dirty Money' with Unexplained Wealth Orders," *New York Times*, 30 May 2019, https://www.nytimes.com/2019/05/30/world/europe/harrods-unexplained-wealth-order.html.

23. "Speculation and Vacancy Tax," British Columbia Government, https://www2.gov.bc.ca/gov/content/taxes/speculation-vacancy-tax.

24. Ben Steverman, "The Wealth Detective Who Finds the Hidden Money of the Super Rich," *Bloomberg*, 23 May 2019, https://www.bloomberg.com/news/features/2019-05-23/the-wealth-detective-who-finds-the-hidden-money-of-the-super-rich.

25. Kirschenbaum and Murray, "An Effective American Regime to Counter Illicit Finance."

26. Ibid.

27. Cooley and Michel, "U.S. Lawyers Are Foreign Kleptocrats' Best Friends."

28. Matthew Collin, "What the Fincen Leaks Reveal About the Ongoing War on Dirty Money," Brookings Institution, 25 September 2020, https://www.brookings.edu/blog/up-front/2020/09/25/what-the-fincen-leaks-reveal-about-the-ongoing-war-on-dirty-money/.

29. "FinCEN Files," ICIJ, https://www.icij.org/investigations/fincen-files/.

30. "FinCEN Files," *BuzzFeed*, https://www.buzzfeednews.com/fincen-files.

31. Jason Leopold, Anthony Cormier, John Templon, Tom Warren, Jeremy Singer-Vine, Scott Pham, Richard Holmes, Azeen Ghorayshi, Michael Sallah, Tanya Kozyreva, and Emma Loop, "The FinCEN Files," *BuzzFeed*, 20 September 2020, https://www.buzzfeednews.com/article/jasonleopold/fincen-files-financial-scandal-criminal-networks.

32. Paul Kiel and Jesse Eisinger, "How the IRS Was Gutted," *ProPublica*, 11 December 2018, https://www.propublica.org/article/how-the-irs-was-gutted.

33. Emmanuel Saez and Gabriel Zucman, *The Triumph of Injustice* (New York: W. W. Norton, 2019).

34. Ray Eldon Hiebert, "Ivy Lee: 'Father of Modern Public Relations,'" *Princeton University Library Chronicle* 27, no. 2 (Winter 1966), https://www.jstor.org/stable /26409644#metadata_info_tab_contents.

35. Jahad Atieh, "Foreign Agents: Updating FARA to Protect American Democracy," *University of Pennsylvania Journal of International Law* 31 (2010), https://scholarship.law .upenn.edu/jil/vol31/iss4/4/.

36. "Recent FARA Cases," U.S. Department of Justice, https://www.justice.gov/nsd-fara /recent-cases.

37. Katie Benner, "Justice Dept. to Step Up Enforcement of Foreign Influence Laws," *New York Times*, 6 March 2019, https://www.nytimes.com/2019/03/06/us/politics/fara-task -force-justice-department.html.

38. I'd like to specifically thank my wife at this juncture for agreeing to allow one of our wedding hashtags to be #reformFARA.

39. At the beginning of the Biden administration, a range of policy recommendations burst forth, all pointing in the same direction and worth implementing in full. These write-ups include. Nate Sibley and Ben Judah, "Countering Global Kleptocracy: A New US Strategy for Fighting Authoritarian Corruption," Hudson Institute, January 2021, https://www.hudson.org/research/16608-countering-global-kleptocracy-a-new-us -strategy-for-fighting-authoritarian-corruption; Josh Rudolph, "Treasury's War on Corruption," German Marshall Fund, 22 December 2020, https://securingdemocracy .gmfus.org/treasurys-war-on-corruption/; Trevor Sutton and Simon Clark, "The Treasury Department Should Lead the Fight Against Corruption and Kleptocracy," Center for American Progress, 10 December 2020, https://www.americanprogress .org/issues/security/reports/2020/12/10/493519/treasury-department-lead-fight -corruption-kleptocracy/; Jessica Brandt and Josh Rudolph, "Spies and Money: Legal Defenses Against Foreign Interference in Political Campaigns," German Marshall Fund, 25 January 2021, https://securingdemocracy.gmfus.org/spies-and-money -legal-defenses-against-foreign-interference-in-political-campaigns/; Trevor Sutton and Ben Judah, "Turning the Tide on Dirty Money," Center for American Progress, 26 February 2021, https://www.americanprogress.org/issues/security/reports /2021/02/26/495402/turning-tide-dirty-money/; and Alexandra Wrage and Michelle D. Gavin, "Why Biden Needs to Confront Corruption," *Foreign Policy*, 22 December 2020, https://foreignpolicy.com/2020/12/22/why-biden-needs-to-confront -corruption/.

40. Mariano-Florentino Cuéllar and Matthew Stephenson, "Taming Systemic Corruption: The American Experience and Its Implications for Contemporary Debates," Harvard Public Law Working Paper No. 20-29, 23 October 2020, https://papers.ssrn .com/sol3/papers.cfm?abstract_id=3686821.

41. Zephyr Teachout, *Corruption in America* (Cambridge, MA: Harvard University Press, 2016).

42. Alex Ward, "Read: Bernie Sanders's Big Foreign Policy Speech," *Vox*, 21 September 2017, https://www.vox.com/world/2017/9/21/16345600/bernie-sanders-full-text-transcript -foreign-policy-speech-westminster.

43. Bernie Sanders, "Sanders Speech at SAIS: Building a Global Democratic Movement to Counter Authoritarianism," 9 October 2018, https://www.sanders.senate.gov/newsroom /press-releases/sanders-speech-at-sais-building-a-global-democratic-movement-to -counter-authoritarianism.

44. Elizabeth Warren, "My Plan to Fight Global Financial Corruption," 17 December 2019, https://elizabethwarren.com/plans/international-corruption?source=soc-WB-ew-fb -rollout-20191216&fbclid=IwAR3br1q9rBwByc5hlrRDZpKQR7EP_bgfz1S5sfEKJFcL5j -dxcC8s-a_4Ys.

45. ILLICIT CASH Act Cosponsors, https://www.congress.gov/bill/116th-congress/senate -bill/2563/cosponsors?q={%22search%22:[%22The+Improving+Laundering+Laws+a nd+Increasing+Comprehensive+Information+Tracking+of+Criminal+Activity+in+S hell+Holdings%22]}&r=1&s=6&searchResultViewType=expanded.

46. Nate Sibley, "Failure to Confront China's Corruption Will Exacerbate Coronavirus Crisis," Hudson Institute, 20 March 2020, https://www.hudson.org/research/15846-failure -to-confront-china-s-corruption-will-exacerbate-coronavirus-crisis.

47. Oliver Bullough, "Oligarchy Newsletter," *Coda Story*, 2 December 2020, https://mailchi .mp/codastory/oligarchy-december-2.

INDEX